CARDINALISM

THEORY AND DECISION LIBRARY

General Editors: W. Leinfellner (*Vienna*) and G. Eberlein (*Munich*)

Series A: Philosophy and Methodology of the Social Sciences

Series B: Mathematical and Statistical Methods

Series C: Game Theory, Mathematical Programming and Operations Research

Series D: System Theory, Knowledge Engineering and Problem Solving

SERIES A: PHILOSOPHY AND METHODOLOGY OF THE SOCIAL SCIENCES

VOLUME 19

Scope: This series deals with the foundations, the general methodology and the criteria, goals and purpose of the social sciences. The emphasis in the new Series A will be on well-argued, thoroughly analytical rather than advanced mathematical treatments. In this context, particular attention will be paid to game and decision theory and general philosophical topics from mathematics, psychology and economics, such as game theory, voting and welfare theory, with applications to political science, sociology, law and ethics.

The titles published in this series are listed at the end of this volume.

CARDINALISM

A Fundamental Approach

Edited by

MAURICE ALLAIS
Ecole Nationale Supérieure des Mines de Paris

and

OLE HAGEN
Norwegian School of Management, Oslo

SPRINGER SCIENCE+BUSINESS MEDIA, B.V.

Library of Congress Cataloging-in-Publication Data

Cardinalism : a fundamental approach / edited by Maurice Allais and Ole Hagen.
p. cm. -- (Theory and decision library. Series A, Philosophy and methodology of the social sciences ; v. 19)
Includes bibliographical references.
ISBN 978-94-010-4384-7 ISBN 978-94-011-0888-1 (eBook)
DOI 10.1007/978-94-011-0888-1
1. Utility theory. 2. Value. 3. Decision-making. 4. Consumers' preferences. I. Allais, Maurice. II. Hagen, Ole, 1921- III. Series.
HB201.C336 1994
658.4'03--dc20 93-8838

ISBN 978-94-010-4384-7

Printed on acid-free paper

TABLE OF CONTENTS

FOREWORD

THE CONCEPTION OF THIS VOLUME

This volume, *Cardinalism*, has been initiated by Ole Hagen, and is now published due to his perseverance and to Kluwer Academic Publishers.

Because of various activities and duties, my contribution to the general conception of this volume has only been formal, and all the credit for it is due to Ole Hagen. I should also emphasize that the responsibility for the year's delay in the publishing of this volume is entirely mine, for two reasons. First of all, I have been involved in many works in very different fields. Second, the English translation of my 1943 contribution to the concept of cardinal utility took some time.

The points of view the reader will find in this volume are often different and sometimes contradictory, but this can only increase the interest of its reading. In any case, this is not the editors' part to side with or against. Thus contributions to this volume are presented as they have been submitted to the editors. Of course, this does not mean that they entirely agree with the analyses presented.

MAURICE ALLAIS

INTRODUCTION

Everyone's conscious choices are assumed to reflect their preferences in different situations. For some purposes it serves the theorist's preference for simplicity to assume that a person's life style can be described by the values of some concrete variables, such as quantities of goods available.

We must make allowance for the philosophical possibility that as well as preference there is also indifference, but we do not believe that a human or even an ass would, like that of Johannes Buridan, die from hunger between two equally attractive haystacks. We further assume transition between the preferences.

Now if we attach numbers to each situation in inverse order of preferences, we have what in the literature is generally named an ordinal utility function. If we subject all the numbers to the same strictly positive transformation, we still have an ordinal utility function. But why is it numbered in inverse order, and why is it called utility? Like pure paper money, this can only be explained historically. We shall return to this problem.

The order of the set of all preferences can be divided into subsets defined in such a way that any element within a subset has numbers that are positive linear transformations of those of any other element in that subset.

If a person claims a particular validity or relevance or usefulness for one of these sets, he or she is a cardinalist and has defined (the observed person's) alleged cardinal utility up to a positive linear transformation. Of course a cardinal utility is also an ordinal utility. So what is an ordinalist? It is a person who believes that no cardinal utility can exist, or if it does the fact is totally irrelevant and of no consequence.

We know that cardinalism is older than ordinalism, but we do not know how old cardinalism is. It is of no use to search for its beginnings among the classics of economics. As an example: About 1900 years ago a story was written about an offering in a temple. People donated gifts of various magnitudes. Up came a poor widow who gave (in free translation) two pennies. A lay preacher, son of a carpenter, who was in the habit of making surprising statements, said that she gave more than the others, because they gave from their abundance, while she gave her means of subsistence. She "gave more". More of what? Though the term was not coined, what was meant could only be a piece of cardinal utility.

The originator of this story was not only a cardinalist, he also foreshadowed the theory of the diminishing utility of money, and took sides in the discussion on interpersonal comparison, in which there are today cardinalists on both sides.

M. Allais and O. Hagen (eds.), Cardinalism, ix–xiv.

When economic theorists began to focus their interest on the demand side of the market and specifically consumer's choices, the notion of utility (later called cardinal –) evolved quite naturally like that of the ancient storyteller (who probably was not the first). It was just a short step then to Gossen's law; of course if the amount of utility could be increased by shifting a penny from buying one good to buying another, this would be done, so marginal utility/price must be the same for all goods in the point of optimal budget allocation.

Pareto stated (1911) that the map of a consumer's (one period) preferences was invariant under a strictly positive transformation, following from Gossen's law.

It was not till the 1930s that significant conclusions were made that marked the beginning of the ordinalistic revolution. Cardinal utility became taboo. The non-belief in the existence of cardinal utility became a firm, devout belief in its non-existence.

At this stage let it be admitted that any preferences ordering can of course be *described* by ordinalistic theory, but can it be *explained*? And can from the base of ordinalism hypotheses be formed without, maybe subconciously drawing on the deductions that follow from the cardinalistic notions? The chart of indifference curves, convex to the origin, which is acceptable to cardinalists and ordinalists alike – has it ever really been constructed by asking people about their preferences? Is it not really deduced from the notion of declining marginal utility ('meaningless' to the ordinalist) and then confirmed by its testable implications? And why do they name their preference function 'utility', if not because it is a cardinalistic legacy, which they have afterwards stripped of 'unnecessary' characteristics?

Is not ordinalistic theory a special case of the self-evident truth that people do what they do because they would rather do what they do than anything else they could have done. To this writer ordinalistic theory gives a feeling of *déjà vu*. What is relived is a text giving sex information to children. In both cases the reader may wonder: "Now I know what they do, but why do they do it?" What is left out in both cases are the forces that motivate actions. A force can be strong or weak. So a preference can have more or less strength behind it. In which case you have cardinality.

During half a century of ordinalistic dominance, there was a moment of embarrassment: the appearance of the von Neuman/Morgenstern utility index, which was defined up to a linear positive transformation, just as the classical cardinal utility. The problem of coexistence was "solved" by subtle and sophisticated interpretations: The index does not show the outcome, but was only a mathematical device for indirectly expressing a person's attitude to risk. Also, the index only showed the preferences between games, not the comparative strength of the preference, disregarding fact that if three games has three different values of the vN–M index, the ratio between the two intervals can not be changed.

To the question (Does it exist?) concerning the vN–M index and cardinal utility in the classical sense respectively, there are four pairs of answers actually given: YY, YN, NY and NN. In the case of YY there are two answers to the question if they are identical.

Most of the problems mentioned above and some others are discussed by the contributors to this book. It is not necessarily a balanced picture. The contributors are selected mainly in order to show what the cardinalist side has to offer. But once a contributor is invited, there has been no censorship. Unfortunately not all invitations have resulted in a contribution, for various reasons. Before proceeding any further, an introductory survey may be in order.

Maurice Allais is Professor of Economics (emeritus) at Ecole National Superier des Mines de Paris. Originally educated as an engineer, he started his academic career in 1943 by publishing *A la Recherche d'une Discipline Economique*. This book set in train a development in basic economic theory that resulted in several Nobel Prizes, the latest (1988) awarded to himself.

At that time he was in fact better known as a critic of the expected utility model for decisions under risk. His work in this field was considered very controversial and the sad truth for the academic community was that it was not taken quite seriously. The "Allais Paradox" was frequently referred to, but the comments often showed that the commentator had not bothered to study the original, with the foundations of an alternative model, even after his first publication in English in this field (1979).

Allais has from the beginning in 1982 been a pillar of strength in the series of FUR conferences (International conferences on the Foundations of Utility and Risk theory).

One chapter from Allais's book in 1943, *Satisfactions Absolues*, now appears for the first time in English, *Absolute Satisfaction*. Here he establishes cardinalism not on introspection alone, but on systematic use of experimental results and analogies from psychology and physics. In some cases he discovers old treasures, but I suspect that young scholars may have some pleasant surprises, like finding among "old hats" stored as outmoded some that are now again quite *en vogue*.

Allais's other contributions, *Cardinal Utility: History, Empirical Findings, and Applications – An Overview* and *Determination of Cardinal Utility According to an Intrinsic Invariant Model*, give an overview of the history of cardinal utility, and presents the development of his intrinsic invariant model for determining the cardinal utility of changes in wealth. It includes extensive experimental evidence. Allais's method is to ask respondents directly about utility intervals. The validity of these is tested through comparison over time. The essence of his conclusion is that each person has a cardinal utility function, formed by a common generating function and an individual parameter. The utility functions have common characteristics that they are mostly logarithmic, but flatten out at high levels, near satiation. Individual differences are essentially caused by differences in the respondent's actual wealth.

This is the first time in the history of utility that exact measurements of utility have been carried out. The consistency over time and persons give them scientific validity.

The historical overview contains a concise presentation of Allais's whole philosophy of utility in five points.

Tore Ellingsen is in the final stage of his Ph.D at the London School of Economics and Political Science.*

In *Cardinal Utility – A History of Hedonimetry* he gives an informative and thought provoking, survey of the development of theory and also empirical work in the field. He makes no secret of his own views, and his points are mostly well taken. His presentation of the different scales is very concise, informative and clarifying, including a few scales that are often left out in short surveys.

Erik Grønn is an Associate Professor at the Norwegian School of Management. He studied and for some time worked at Frisch and Haavelmoes Institute of Economics at the University of Oslo.

In *Cardinalism and Dynamic Analysis in Economic Theory* he discusses the possible difference in the relevance of cardinality in static and dynamic analysis. Though he does not reach a final conclusion to this, he does note that ordinal utility is incapable of treating calender time dependent preference and Boehm–Bawerk's rate of pure time preference.

Ole Hagen is Professor of Managerial Economics at the Norwegian School of Management (Oslo region), which he joined after leaving The Norwegian School of Economics and Business Administration (Bergen), after he started critical analysis of the EU theory in 1969. He has produced several articles in this field and edited books, previously jointly with Allais, and has been active in organizing the FUR conferences.

His special angle on the question of cardinality is the relevance and operationality of indirect second order derivatives. In *The Short Step from Ordinal to Cardinal Utility* he shows that second derivatives keep their interval ratios in all ordinal utility functions. What is needed for identifying the relevant cardinal subset is the distinction between positive/negative. Examples are given to support the operationality.

Manfred Kraft is Assistant Professor of Statistics, Econometrics and Decision Theory at the University of Paderborn. He has published works on statistics, applied econometrics and business cycle theory. Peter Weise is Professor of Economics at the University of Kassel. He has published works on microeconomics, labour economics and law in relation to economics.

They give an example of application of cardinal utility in macroeconomics in their study of the alterations in strength and direction in the effect of the business climate on individual decisions in *A Cardinal Utility Approach to the Theory of the Business Cycle.*

Roman Krzystofowicz is a Professor in the Department of Systems Engineering, University of Virginia. For many years he has worked with the problems of decisions under uncertainty. He has made a large scientific contribution, both in basic and applied fields, and has been the head of several large prospects. He has received three distinguished awards.

In his contributions to this book he deals with the role of cardinal utility in the context of decisions under risk.

In *Generic Utility: Explanatory Model, Behavioral Hypotheses, Empirical evidence* he gives a thorough general analysis of the matter and presents a model which decomposes the utility of a game into two factors: a value function and a risk function. He is aiming at crystallizing empirical foundations for "nonlinear" (not EU) models and filtering probability induced biases in measuring utility for EU models.

It is by now well known that attempts to determine the vN–M utility index give conflicting results depending on, for example, the probability distributions used. In *Filtering Risk Effect in Standard-gamble Utility Measurement* Krzystofowicz proposes a method characterised by using certainty equivalents of sequential 50–50 games and a simple parameter for risk attitude. There is no final conclusion. Further research is in progress.

I cannot finish this introduction without apologizing to all concerned for unforeseen delays, due in part to health reasons, which also prevented me from attending the fourth International Conference on the Foundation and Application of Utility and Risk Theory, FUR, in Budapest, 1988.

The contributors to this book have expressed various and in part conflicting views. Speaking as one of them, I think we all hope that many readers will find them provocative.**

P.T. University of Bonn in May 1990 OLE HAGEN

NOTES

* Finished 1991. He is now at the Stockholm School of Economics.

** A forum for comment could be FUR VII in Sandvika, 30 June to 3 July, 1994.

POSTSCRIPT

At the final stage of my editing part of Allais' foreword a new, original contribution by Maurice Allais was developed and included as 'The Fundamental Cardinalist Approach and Its Prospects'. It is put at the end of the volume as Chapter X.

This rounds off his own contribution as well as the structure of this book and I think it gives significant pointers for future research in the fields where cardinal utility is highly relevant.

Norwegian School of Management O.H.
January 1994

MAURICE ALLAIS

ABSOLUTE SATISFACTION*

> Mathematics have no symbols for confused ideas. – HENRI POINCARÉ

I. ABSOLUTE MEASURE OF SATISFACTION

1. The Law of Psychologically Equivalent Increments

Psychological introspection shows that in a more or less conscious manner each individual proceeds mentally through *equivalences* between successive increases in its consumption. Thus one admits generally that drinking the fourth glass of wine gives a pleasure of less magnitude than the first.

In assuming that the realization of such equivalences is actually possible and that one has chosen an arbitrary scale of measurement S of satisfaction,[1] one could determine the increase ΔS_2 of satisfaction from a value S_2 deemed psychologically equivalent to an increase ΔS_1 from a value S_1. Thus one would have

$$\Delta S_2 = f(\Delta S_1, S_1, S_2)$$

which would, assuming ΔS_1 is small enough, be

$$\Delta S_2 = g(S_1, S_2)\,\Delta S_1 \tag{1}$$

It is easy to see that the function $g(S_1, S_2)$ is of the form $h(S_1)/h(S_2)$, $h(S)$ being a given function of S. Let ΔS_3 be the increase of satisfaction from the value S_3 which is deemed equivalent to the increase ΔS_1. This latter increase being deemed equivalent to the increase ΔS_2, the increase ΔS_2 would likewise be equivalent to it and one would have

$$\Delta S_3 = g(S_1, S_3)\,\Delta S_1$$
$$\Delta S_3 = g(S_2, S_3)\,\Delta S_2$$

and consequently

$$g(S_1, S_3)\,\Delta S_1 = g(S_2, S_3)\,\Delta S_2$$

But in this relation nothing prevents regarding S_3 as a constant; thus putting

$$g(S, S_3) = h(S)$$

one would then have

$$h(S_1)\,\Delta S_1 = h(S_2)\,\Delta S_2$$

M. Allais and O. Hagen (eds.), Cardinalism, 1–29.

and consequently

$$(2) \qquad h(S)\,\Delta S = \text{constant}$$

This relation represents analytically the psychological equivalences made by the individual considered between his different increments of satisfaction. We shall call it *The law of psychologically equivalent increments.*

2. *Absolute Scales of Measurement of Satisfaction*

One can now choose a particular scale of measurement $\bar{S}$ of satisfaction which can give the simplest possible analytic expression of this law. One sees immediately that any scale $\bar{S}$ answering to this condition will satisfy the relation

$$(3) \qquad \Delta\bar{S} = \lambda h(S)\,\Delta S$$

where λ is a constant. With such a scale, the law of psychologically equivalent increments is expressed by the condition

$$(4) \qquad \Delta\bar{S} = \text{constant}$$

Or, in other words, two equivalent increments correspond to two equal increases in the function $\bar{S}$.

The condition found gives

$$(5) \qquad \bar{S}_1 = \bar{S}_0 + \lambda \int_0^1 h(S)\,\Delta S$$

where the indices 0 and 1 correspond to two states (M_0) and (M_1) of consumption. As S is a given function $\Phi(A, B, \ldots, C)$ of the consumption $A, B, \ldots, C$ one sees that the most general function $\bar{S}$ satisfying this relation is of the form

$$(6) \qquad \bar{S} = K\Psi(A, B, \ldots, C) + K'$$

where K and K' are arbitrary constants and Ψ a well defined function of the consumptions $A, B, \ldots, C$. Accordingly there exist an infinity of scales $\bar{S}$ depending on two arbitrary constants.[2]

Any scale of satisfaction $\bar{S}$ so defined is such that equivalent increases in pleasure will be represented by equal increases of this index of satisfaction. It is the simplest type of scale that one can conceive for representing the psychological equivalences made by a given individual and it corresponds to our *a priori* intuition about a measure of satisfaction. For this reason we shall name such a scale the *absolute scale of satisfaction.*[3]

Naturally the existence of psychologically equivalent increments of satisfaction results only from a simple psychological intuition. In fact, if a man or woman can know that the third glass of wine will give him or her less satisfaction than the second, that does not mean that he or she can determine in a precise manner how much wine he or she should drink after the second glass to achieve the same increase in his of her satisfaction that the second glass of wine gave him or her. It follows that the possibility of an absolute measure of satisfaction can only be considered as a hypothesis.

Thus, whereas the *practical* existence of indifference surfaces should be considered a certainty,[4] that of an absolute scale of satisfaction remains problematic, at least in the present state of our knowledge.[5]

In any case the use of such a scale corresponding to the psychological intuition which we have *a priori* of the measure of satisfaction and not being in any way contradictory to experience, we shall henceforth consider that the index $\bar{S}$ represents *effectively* an absolute measure of satisfaction.

3. The Law of Minimum Perceptible Increments

Experimental physiological psychology shows that when a given stimulus (E) increases by ΔE this increase is not perceived unless it is greater than a value ΔE_p of E that one can name *minimum perceptible increment.*[6]

It seems likely that this notion could be generalized, at least theoretically,[7] to economic psychology. Our introspection shows us indeed that very small variations ΔA in a consumption good (A) are certainly not perceptible, while strong variations certainly are. Thus we see without any difficulty that there exist minima perceptible increments.

Given any function of satisfaction like S, the minimum perceptible step ΔS_p would be a well-defined function of S and one would have

$$(7) \qquad \Delta S_p = f(S)$$

This relation represents what one could call the *law of minima perceptible increments*.

Naturally, one should consider the minima perceptible increments as psychologically equivalent. Thus, the law of minima perceptible increments can be expressed by the relation

$$(8) \qquad \Delta \bar{S}_p = e$$

where e is a constant representing the minimum perceptible increment, and $\bar{S}$ one of the absolute measures of satisfaction.[8] One can of course choose for e any arbitrary value.

We shall name *jevon* the unit of absolute satisfaction such that:

$$e = 1$$

The jevon thus represents the change in absolute satisfaction corresponding to a minimum perceptible increment.

Putting

$$\bar{S} = \varphi(S)$$

one will then have

$$\Delta\bar{S}_p = (\bar{S} + \Delta\bar{S}_p) - \bar{S} = \varphi(S + \Delta S_p) - \varphi(S)$$

and finally the equation of finite differences

$$\varphi[S + f(S)] - \varphi[S] = e \tag{9}$$

which determines the function $\varphi(S)$ up to one constant.

If the value of $f(S)$ is small compared to that of S, one can write

$$\varphi'_S\, f(S) = e \tag{10}$$

and consequently

$$\bar{S} = \varphi(S) = e \int \frac{\mathrm{d}S}{f(S)} \tag{11}$$

If the value of e is given, the function $\bar{S}$ is then determined up to a constant.[9]

4. *Convention*

As we have seen above, any scale of absolute measure of satisfaction is of the form (6)

$$\bar{S} = K\Psi(A, B, \ldots, C) + K'$$

where K and K' are two arbitrary constants.

By convention, we shall determine the constant K in putting $e = 1$, i.e. in measuring absolute satisfaction in jevons.

As for the constant K' we observe that the determination of the function Ψ should be considered as resulting from subjective valuations made at the initial moment under consideration.[10] These valuations are made while taking into account acquired experience; they consist essentially in the choices made from all the possible variations in the consumption goods from the last combination actually made.[11] It appears then natural to choose this last combination as the origin. The absolute satisfaction should then be of the form

$$\bar{S} = \Psi(A, B, \ldots, C) - \Psi(A_0, B_0, \ldots, C_0) \tag{12}$$

$A_0, B_0, \ldots, C_0$ representing the last actually realized combination and thus it will be fully determined.[12]

As the reader can convince himself, such conventions do not modify in any way the rigour of the deductions which follow; they only serve to determine the absolute satisfaction in a non ambiguous manner.

5. Properties of Absolute Satisfaction

Continuity

As for the satisfactions in general,[13] we assume that the absolute satisfactions are continuous functions, i.e. that they cannot pass from one value to another without taking all the values between, or that like all the consumed quantities they increase or decrease by infinitely small changes.[14]

Heterogenity

At a given moment the absolute satisfactions of the different individuals are not comparable to one another without an arbitrary convention. The same goes for the absolute satisfaction for the same individual over time.[15, 15′]

6. Remark. The So-Called Arbitrary Character of the Absolute Satisfactions

It has been stated that the definition of absolute satisfaction should be strict by maintaining "that a physicist would certainly be in error if defining the unity of force as corresponding to the minimum perceptible muscular sensation".[16]

This objection does not stand up to analysis. In the case of force there exists a great number of objective laws that come into play and these laws have a practical importance much greater than the law of perceptible minimum relative to force. Then it is normal that one makes the chosen scale of measurement of force in such a way that the corresponding physical laws be the most simple.

In the case of satisfaction, on the contrary, *the only laws* whose expression depends on its arbitrary character[17] are the laws of equal increments and of minimum perceptible increments. It is therefore natural to try to render the expression of these laws as simple as possible in adopting an appropriate scale of measurement of satisfaction.

In fact, the consideration of absolute satisfaction illustrates in a striking manner the relative character of the scales of measurement we use for measuring the magnitudes that intervene in the laws we observe.[18]

II. PROPERTIES OF ABSOLUTE DESIRABILITIES

If we assume that the function $\bar{S}$ effectively represents an absolute measure of satisfaction experienced by the individual, one may enunciate, from elementary psychological introspection, a certain number of properties which seem plausible.

1. Sign of Absolute desirabilities

The first property of absolute desirabilities, $\bar{\delta}_B$, is that it is always positive.[1] This property follows essentially from the fact that the satisfaction cannot decrease when the quantities consumed increase. This is obvious because it is about economic and not material consumptions.[2] Thus, if we use the simplified notation, we have:

$$(1) \qquad \frac{\partial \bar{S}}{\partial B} > 0 \text{ or } \bar{\delta}_B > 0$$

$\bar{S}$ being the absolute satisfaction and B one of the consumed goods.

2. Internal first partial derivatives[3]

Psychological introspection shows that in general *the desirability decreases as the quantity consumed increased*, in other words if the quantity consumed is supposed to increase by constant quantities, each successive increment produces less satisfaction than the preceding one.[4] So one has

$$(2) \qquad \frac{\delta}{\delta B}\,\bar{\delta}_B \leq 0 \text{ or } \frac{\delta^2 \bar{S}}{\delta B^2} \leq 0$$

This is actually a general fact that the more we have of a good the less precious each of the units of that good is to us. The first glass of water produces more pleasure than the second to him or her who is thirsty; the first portion of food produces more pleasure than the second to him or her who is hungry.[5]

Variation of Total Desirability

Experimental psychology[6] shows that if one represents the ratio $\Delta E_p/E$ of the minimum perceptible increment ΔE_p of a stimulus (E) to the value E of the intensity of this stimulus as a function of the logarithm of E, the representative curve has the form shown in Figure 1; in other words one has

$$(3) \qquad \frac{\Delta E_p}{E} = g(LE)$$

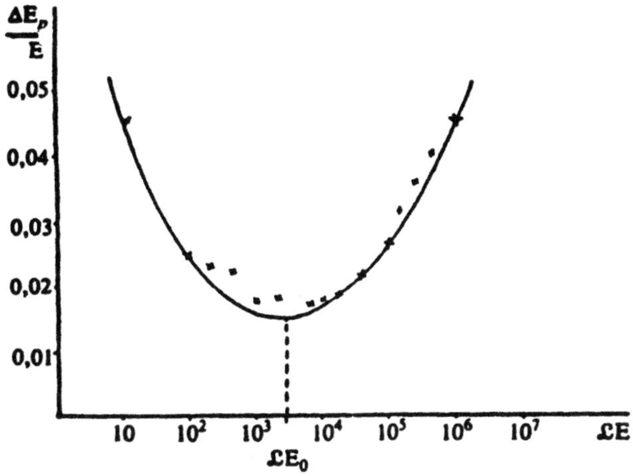

Fig. 1.

where $g(x)$ is a function which passes a minimum for an intermediary value x_0 of x.[7, 8]

The corresponding psycho-physiological sensation $\bar{S}$ is given by the relation[9]

$$(4) \qquad \bar{S} = e \int \frac{\mathrm{d}E}{f(E)}$$

and consequently

$$\Delta \bar{S}_p = e \, \frac{\Delta E_p}{f(E)}$$

and, since $\Delta \bar{S}_p = e$, we have $\Delta E_p = f(E)$, and consequently according to equation (3)

$$(5) \qquad f(E) = E\, g(LE)$$

and finally, from equation (4)

$$(6) \qquad \bar{S} = e \int \frac{\mathrm{d}E}{E\, g(LE)} = h(LE)$$

It is easy to see that for the medium value LE_0 of LE the curve representing the function $\bar{S} = h(LE)$ has a point of inflexion to the left of which the increase in the sensation increases faster that the logarithm of the stimulus and to the right of which it is the inverse.[10] In other words, for $E > E_0$, one has

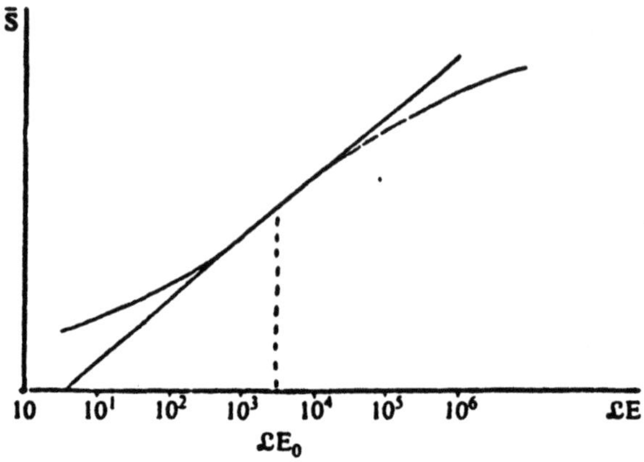

Fig. 2.

$$(7) \qquad \frac{d^2\bar{S}}{(dLE)^2} < 0$$

and

$$(8) \qquad \frac{d}{dE}\left(E\,\frac{d\bar{S}}{dE}\right) < 0$$

If one observes that the inflexion takes place in the medium interval of the logarithms, one sees that the product of the marginal sensation by the intensity of the stimulus is a decreasing function of that intensity *in the greater part of its domain of variation.*[11, 12]

If one applies these results to the psychological phenomenom of economic consumption, one sees that the curve representing the satisfaction, as a function of the logarithm of the quantity consumed should have a shape like the curve C in Figure 4. This curve has a horizontal tangent at the point M_m that corresponds to satiety.[13]

One sees thus that, to the extent that the properties of the physiological psychology can be extrapolated, the product of the desirability of a good by the quantity consumed of this good, that we have named total desirability, is represented, throughout the greater part of the domain of variation of this quantity, by a decreasing function.[14]

3. Internal Second Order Partial Derivatives

Not only does the second glass of wine produce less satisfaction that the first, and the third less than the second, but the difference between the

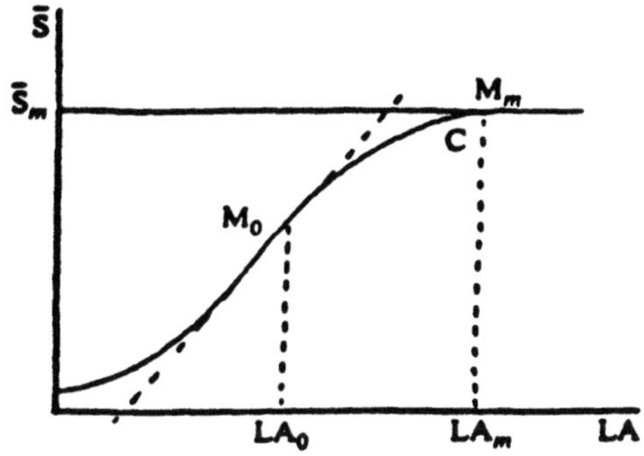

Fig. 4.

satisfaction that the second produces and that produced by the third is in general less than the difference between the satisfaction produced by the first and that produced by the second. One then has in general:

$$[\bar{S}(B+2\Delta B)-\bar{S}(B+\Delta B)]- [\bar{S}(B+3\Delta B)-\bar{S}(B+2\Delta B)] < [\bar{S}(B+\Delta B)-\bar{S}(B)]- [\bar{S}(B+2\Delta B)-\bar{S}(B+\Delta B)]$$

an inequality which reduces to the condition

$$(9) \qquad \frac{\partial^3 \bar{S}}{\partial B^3} \geq 0 \text{ or } \frac{\partial^2}{\partial B^2}\,\bar{\delta}_B \geq 0$$

This condition means that the curve representing the desirability of a good as a function of the quantity consumed of that good is convex to the origin (Figure 5). One can also say that at each point the desirability increases more than linearly as the consumption decreases.[15, 16]

Moreover, if we remark that the total desirability $B\bar{S}'_B$ begins to increase, attains a maximum $(B\bar{S}'_B)_m$, then decreases, when B increases, we see that the curve representing the desirability as a function of B (Figure 5) is tangent externally to the equilateral hyperbola H:[17]

$$xy = (B\bar{S}'_B)_m$$

4. *External First Partial Derivatives*

In general, the desirability of a good depends on the quantities consumed of other goods, in other words the external first derivatives of the desirability of a good in respect to other goods

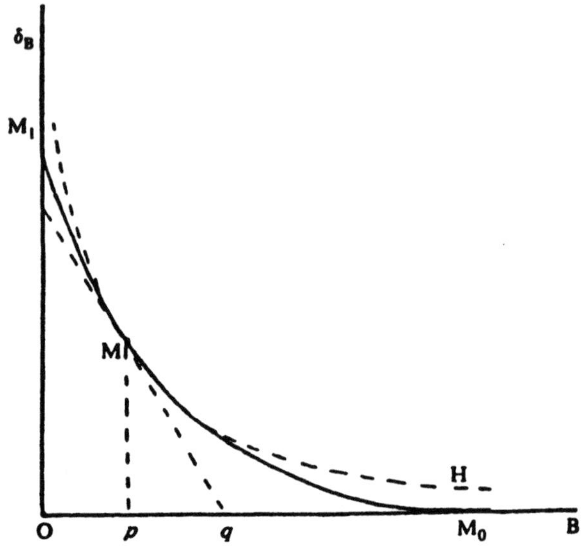

Fig. 5.

$$(10) \qquad \frac{\partial}{\partial B}\,\bar{\delta}_A = \bar{S}''_{AB}$$

are not zero.

It is fairly obvious indeed, for example, that the pleasure $\Delta\bar{S}$ that a given quantity ΔA of rabbit meat gives an individual (Y_i) does not depend solely on this quantity, but also on the quantity of other goods that the individual consumes, like salt to season the rabbit meat, the combustible for roasting, the meat of chicken, of veal, etc. that he or she might prefer to rabbit etc. Consequently the ratio $\Delta\bar{S}/\Delta A$ depends on the other consumptions B. In fact the desire one may have for a given good depends essentially on the quantities of other goods that one has already at disposal; this is the case of oil, bedlinen, carpets, libraries, which combine together respectively with the number of lamps, beds, books, that one already possesses.

It is rather rare that such dependence does not exist and it is difficult to be able to speak of independent consumptions[18] if it is not a pure abstraction, as did, consciously or not, the first economists who have studied the phenomena of desirability and who could not immediately confront the problem in its complexity.

Thus, and in general, the function of satisfaction and its derivatives depend on all the parameters characterizing the consumption.

Dependence

One can characterize the dependence existing between two consumed goods A and B by the value $\bar{S}''_{AB}$ relatively to those of $\bar{S}''_{A^2}$ and $\bar{S}''_{B^2}$. However, it is clear that the ratios

$$\frac{\bar{S}''_{AB}}{\bar{S}''_{A^2}} \quad \text{and} \quad \frac{\bar{S}''_{AB}}{\bar{S}''_{B^2}}$$

depend essentially on the measuring units of the goods A and B and that they have no intrinsic meaning.[19] This inconvenience disappears if one considers the parameters[20]

$$(\overline{ab}) = \frac{\bar{S}''_{AB}}{\bar{S}'_A \bar{S}'_B} \qquad (\overline{aa}) = \frac{\bar{S}''_{A^2}}{\bar{S}'^2_A} \qquad (\overline{bb}) = \frac{\bar{S}''_{B^2}}{\bar{S}'^2_B}$$

We shall say then that two consumptions A and B have little dependence if the parameters $(\overline{ab})$ are negligible compared to the parameters $(\overline{aa})$ and $(\overline{bb})$. One sees immediately that, in this case, for a given change ΔA of one of the consumption the relative change in the desirability $\bar{S}'_B$ of the other consumption (B) is negligible compared to the relative change in the desirability $\bar{S}'_A$ of the consumption A.

In the opposite case the goods (A) and (B) will be said to be dependent. *Independence of the two goods will be characterized by a zero value of* $\bar{S}''_{AB}$.[21]

Weak Statistical Dependence Between Different Goods

While the dependence between desirabilities cannot be neglected, when one considers important variations of the consumptions, it seems admissible that, when variations are small, one can consider, at least as a first approximation, most of the consumptions as mutually independent; in other words, it seems possible that *in the neighbourhood of a given point* the function $\bar{S}$ is of the form

$$(11) \qquad \bar{S} = \Psi_A(A) + \Psi_B(B) + \ldots + \Psi_C(C)$$

the functions Ψ depending on the point under consideration.

It is certain that one who suffers horribly from frost has little appreciation of a dainty drink; he who is starving does not experience great pleasure from regarding a picture, to listen to a well delivered speech, and if he is given food it is of little importance to him if he is served with crude pottery or fine procelain.[22]

However it seems that for small variations in quantity, the main part of the variations of the desirability results from the variation of the quantity of the consumed good under consideration. Thus:

It is preferable to eat a chicken from a nice plate, but on the whole, if the plate is more or less beautiful, the pleasure is not very much different. Inversely, the pleasure that one experiences by using a beautiful plate depends mainly on that plate and does not vary much with whether the chicken is more or less big, or of more or less fine quality.[22]

This approximation seems only to be at fault when we consider goods which are close substitutes or strongly complementary.[23] Thus if one considers the quantities of fish and meat eaten in the same meal, it seems that the desirability of fish is of the same order of magnitude as that of meat when the quantity of meat varies, but then one may remark that the desirability of fish decreases less rapidly, for an individual filled up with meat might still want a good plate of fish.

Of course the variations to be considered are the relative variations of the desirabilities and the preceding indications mean that the parameters $(\overline{ab})$ are generally small compared to the parameters $(\overline{aa})$.

Complementarities and Substitutes

We say that two goods A and B are complementary if the absolute desirability of one increases when the quantity consumed of the other increases, in other words if

$$\bar{S}''_{AB} > 0$$

and that they are substitutes, or competing goods, in the opposite case.[24]

If the cases of strong complementarity appears to be more frequent than the cases of close substitutability, it seems rather that among the pairs of little dependence the cases of complementarity are not more frequent than those of substitutability. As the cases of great dependence can be considered as statistically exceptional, one can assume that the median $(\overline{mn})$ of the parameters $(\overline{ab})$ is extremely close to zero and can be considered as practically nil.[25]

Independent Goods

When the different goods are independent, one has rigorously at every point

$$\bar{S} = \Psi_A(A) + \Psi_B(B) + \ldots + \Psi_C(C)$$

As we have already indicated,[25'] it is on functions of that type that Walras has built his theory.

In fact the hypothesis of Walras constitutes a first approximation to the study of an extremely complex question, but as we have seen, it can not be maintained in its whole generality.

Fig. 6.

Indeed, when one reasons solely about very small variations, i.e. when one studies psychological characteristics only in the neighbourhood of a given situation, it is possible to consider the different desirabilities as dependent only on the corresponding consumptions.[26] But, when one is concerned with very large variations, one must consider that the desirability of one factor is dependent not only of the size of that consumption but also of that of the other consumptions.

5. *The Case of Work*

Naturally if, instead of consumptions, the factor (B) represents a piece of work (Y), the signs of the derivatives *of even order* of desirabilities should be changed,[27] so that

$$(12) \qquad \frac{\partial \bar{S}}{\partial Y} < 0 \quad \frac{\partial^2 \bar{S}}{\partial Y^2} < 0 \quad \frac{\partial^3 \bar{S}}{\partial Y^3} < 0$$

or

$$(13) \qquad \bar{\delta}_Y < 0 \quad \frac{\partial}{\partial Y}\,|\bar{\delta}_Y| > 0 \quad \frac{\partial^2}{\partial Y^2}\,|\bar{\delta}_Y| > 0$$

Thus the desirability of work is negative. We shall design its absolute value by the expression *painfulness of work.* One sees that the painfulness of work increases when the quantity of work Y increases and that it increases so much more the greater Y is.[28]

6. *Psychological Yield*

Let $A, B, \ldots, C$ be a consumption basked and let $\Delta A, \Delta B, \ldots, \Delta C$ be finite increases of these consumptions such that one has

$$(14) \qquad \Delta A = \lambda\alpha \quad \Delta B = \lambda\beta \quad \ldots \quad \Delta C = \lambda\gamma$$

$\alpha, \beta, \ldots, \gamma$ being constants and λ one variable.

Our psychological introspection leads us to consider that when λ increases the increase of satisfaction

$$\Delta\bar{S} = \bar{S}(A + \Delta A, B + \Delta B \ldots C + \Delta C) - \bar{S}(A, B \ldots C)$$

increases more slowly than λ, in other words that the ratio

$$r = \frac{\Delta\bar{S}}{\lambda} \tag{15}$$

which one could call *psychological yield* is a decreasing function of λ.[29] We shall name this property *the law of decreasing psychological yields*.

Since one has

$$\frac{dr}{d\lambda} = -\frac{\Delta\bar{S} - \sum_B \Delta B \bar{S}'_B(A + \Delta A, B + \Delta B \ldots C + \Delta C)}{\lambda^2} \tag{16}$$

we have

$$\bar{S}(A + \Delta A \ldots C + \Delta C) - \bar{S}(A\,B \ldots C) - \sum_B \Delta B \bar{S}'_B(A + \Delta A \ldots C + \Delta C) > 0 \tag{17}$$

This condition gives immediately the conditions.[30]

$$\bar{S}(A\,B \ldots C) - \bar{S}(0, 0, \ldots, 0) - \sum_B B\bar{S}'_B(A\,B \ldots C) > 0 \tag{18}$$

$$\bar{S}(A\,B \ldots C) - \bar{S}(0\,B \ldots C) - A\bar{S}'_A(A\,B \ldots C) > 0 \tag{19}$$

$$\bar{S}(A + \Delta A \ldots C + \Delta C) - \bar{S}(A\,B \ldots C) - \sum \Delta B \bar{S}'_B(A\,B \ldots C) < 0 \tag{20}$$

When the increases $\Delta A, \Delta B, \ldots, \Delta C$ are infinitely small, this last condition can be written as

$$d^2\bar{S} = \sum \bar{S}''_{\lambda^2} \frac{dA^2}{2} + \sum \bar{S}'_{AB} dA\, dB < 0 \tag{21}$$

and it must be verified whatever the variations $dA, dB, \ldots, dC$.

According to the theory of quadratic forms this condition implies, as a necessary and sufficient condition that the n determinants

$$\bar{S}''_{\lambda^2}, \quad \begin{vmatrix} \bar{S}''_{A^2} & \bar{S}''_{AB} \\ \bar{S}''_{AB} & \bar{S}''_{B^2} \end{vmatrix} \ldots \delta \begin{vmatrix} \bar{S}''_{A^2} & \bar{S}''_{AB} & \cdots & \bar{S}''_{AC} \\ \bar{S}''_{AB} & \bar{S}''_{B^2} & \cdots & \bar{S}''_{BC} \\ \vdots & \vdots & & \vdots \\ \bar{S}''_{AC} & \bar{S}''_{BC} & \cdots & \bar{S}''_{C^2} \end{vmatrix} \tag{22}$$

be alternatively negative and positive.[30′] If we consider the characteristic parameters $(\overline{ab})$, these conditions mean that the determinants

$$(23) \qquad (\overline{aa}), \quad \begin{vmatrix} (\overline{aa}) & (\overline{ab}) \\ (\overline{ab}) & (\overline{bb}) \end{vmatrix} \ldots \delta \begin{vmatrix} (\overline{aa}) & (\overline{ab}) & \cdots & (\overline{ac}) \\ (\overline{ab}) & (\overline{bb}) & \cdots & (\overline{bc}) \\ \vdots & \vdots & & \vdots \\ (\overline{ac}) & (\overline{bc}) & \cdots & (\overline{cc}) \end{vmatrix}$$

be alternatively negative and positive.[31] These conditions imply

$$(24) \qquad C_n^1 + \ldots + C_n^n = 2^n - 1$$

equivalent conditions obtained by all possible permutations of the letters $a\, b \ldots c$.[32]

The first of these conditions writes as

$$S''_{A^2} < 0$$

We thus meet again the law of decreasing desirabilities, obviously implied in the law of decreasing psychological yields. It means that *on the average* the $|(\overline{ab})|$ are small compared to the $(\overline{aa})|$.[33] Thus one meets again the results found from direct introspection.

Inversely, it is easy to see that if the $(\overline{aa})$ are negative and if the $(\overline{ab})$ are small compared to the $(\overline{aa})$, the conditions for decreasing psychological yields are verified.[34]

Equivalence of the Relative Characteristics[35] of the Absolute Desirabilities and of the Intrinsic Characteristics of the Relative Desirabilities

We have seen[36] that, in accordance with the data of our introspection, the parameters $(\overline{ab})$ should be considered on the average as small compared to the parameters $(\overline{a})$. If this hypothesis is valid, we must admit that the median $(\overline{mn})$ of the parameters $(\overline{ab})$ has an extremely low value which can be regarded as practically nil.[37] As one has[38]

$$[ab] = [(\overline{ab}) - (\overline{mn})] \sum_B B\bar{S}'_B$$

one sees that one has

$$(26) \qquad [ab] = (\overline{ab}) \sum B\bar{S}'_B$$

with at least a very strong approximation.

Finally one verifies that if the parameters $(\overline{ab})$ are small compared to $(\overline{aa})$ it is likewise for the parameters $[ab]$ and $[aa]$ and reciprocally; in other words the definition of dependence with respect to the consideration

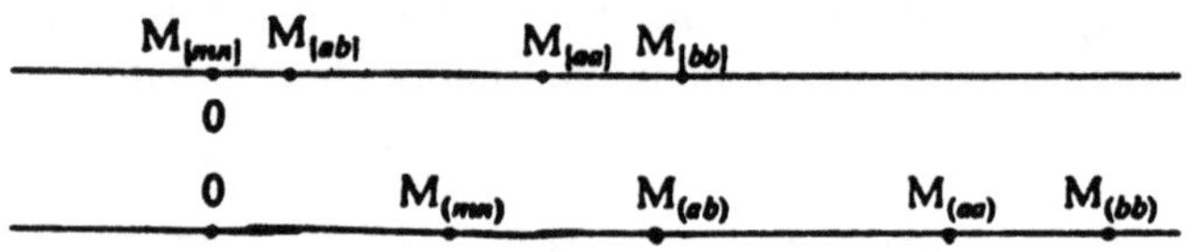

Fig. 7.

of absolute desirabilities does coincide with that deduced directly from the study of the indifference curves.

One verifies also that the parameters $(\overline{ab})$ and $[ab]$ are of the same sign. It follows that the definitions of complementarity and substituability given for absolute satisfactions coincide rigorously[39] with those following from the indifference curves alone.

In a general way any relation that is valid for the parameters $(\overline{ab})$ is equally so for the parameters $[ab]$ and inversely.[40]

It is easy to realize the profound reasons for this correspondence. To the properties of the absolute satisfactions $\bar{S}$ one can make to correspond the properties of the relative desirabilities $\bar{S}'_A/\bar{S}'_B$ and consequently of the relative desirabilities S'_A/S'_B which are equal to them. One sees thus how from the properties of the absolute desirabilities one can deduce the intrinsic properties of the relative desirabilities.

Inversely, the obtained properties of the relative desirabilities show that in any point one can define a transformation $\bar{S} = \varphi(S)$ such that one has[41]

$$(\overline{ab}) \sum B\bar{S}'_B = [ab]$$

Thus the intrinsic properties of $[ab]$ deduced from the intrinsic properties of the relative desirabilities correspond well to the determined properties of the absolute desirabilities corresponding to the absolute satisfaction $\bar{S}$.

Geometrically if one marks to the right of an origin 0 the values of the parameters $[ab]$ and (ab), it follows from the correspondence existing between these parameters.[41']

$$[ab] = [(ab) - (mn)] \sum_B BS'_B$$

that the most general figure formed by the points $M(ab)$ follows from that which is formed by the points $M[ab]$ homothetically in reference to 0 and translation

Since the properties of the indifference surfaces only depend on the relative positions of the points $M_{(ab)}$, one can see that they can equally well be deduced from considering the absolute desirabilities $((\overline{mn}) = 0)$ or fro that of the relative desirabilities $((mn) \# 0)$.

In fact, as the reader has been able to see, the general properties of the indifference surfaces[42] can be deduced far more easily from the consideration of absolute satisfactions rather than that of relative desirabilities.

If nevertheless we have thought that we should first consider only the indifference curves, it is because in this way we have underlined that these properties are absolutely independent of the consideration of the absolute satisfactions[42'] and that the whole economic theory can be built without referring to them. This justification being given, *we shall thereafter be able* to limit ourselves[43] to consider the absolute satisfactions which allow simpler developments[44] and also a quicker and more elegant exposition.[45, 46]

III. ANALOGY WITH THE PHYSICAL SCIENCES

It follows from the above that the concept of absolute satisfaction is useful for the exposition of the theory of economic equilibrium, but is not necessary for its construction.

The hypothesis of the effective existence of an absolute measure of satisfaction is in no way necessary for the validity of the general economic results that could be obtained from it. In fact, as already indicated, only the ratios two to two of the first derivatives of the functions of satisfaction intervene in the general economic theory of equilibrium. These ratios being fully determined by the indifference surfaces, *the results obtained can in no way depend on the hypothesis of the practical possibility* of an absolute measure of satisfaction.

As it corresponds to an intuitive notion, and as it is commodious in application, and since it does not influence in any way the results obtained, the consideration of an absolute measure of satisfaction is therefore fully justified.

This circumstance is absolutely comparable to that which one meets in the physical sciences, and the notion of absolute satisfaction which occurs in pure economics a role analogous to that which applies by the notion of force and others similar concepts in rational mechanics.

Thus, for example, the principles of dynamics can be well presented without making reference to the notion of force; it is for purposes of convenience only that one defines force as product of the acceleration vector by the mass; force appears thus as a notion derived and defined with the aid of other quantities.[1]

Indeed it is a general principle in science that arbitrary but commodious conventions are found to be fully justified when the results whose deduction they permit are fully independent of them.

Likewise the theory of economic equilibrium can be established and presented without making use of the concept of absolute satisfaction. The theory of equilibrium is based uniquely and directly *on the experience* which shows the existence of preferences and indifferences between different consumption sets. Not only is it not necessary to compare satisfactions between different individuals, nor between those of a same individual over time, but for a given individual considered at a given moment nothing is necessarily intervening, but the indifference surfaces in a small space around the point representing the situation which is studied. Thus it is independent of any arbitrary consideration and it supposes nothing but knowledge of objective phenomena, i.e. susceptible to concrete manifestations.[2]

It is only to facilitate and abbreviate the exposition of the theory that one can start from the empirical fact of preferential choice to arrive at the derived and abstract notion of absolute satisfactions and to the functions representing them.[3]

NOTES[1]

Notes to Part I

* Extracts from Chapter II of Maurice Allais, *A la Recherche d'une Discipline Economique* (To the Search for an Economic Discipline, Paris, 1943); republished as *Traité d'Economie Pure* (Treatise on Pure Economics) 1952; third edition, as *Traité d'Economie Pure*, Editions Clément Juglar, Paris, 1992.
Parts I, II, and III correspond without any modification to §§ 68, 69 and 70 of Chapter II.

1 As indicated in Nos 53 and 54 (of the preceding developments of the book).

2 The reasoning we have carried out to determine the functions $\bar{S}$ rests on the possibility of discerning very small differences ΔS. This hypothesis is indeed not essential and the demonstrations carried out could be generalized without difficulty to the case where the ΔS are not very small, but finite. The differential relation (3) will then simply be replaced by an equation of finite differences and the solution of this equation would still be of type (6).

3 We shall see below (No 92–96 of the book) that following the denominations currently used, the absolute measure of a magnitude can be defined as the measure of this magnitude when the measuring scale used is, or in conformity with, our direct intuition, or such that form of the physical laws be the the simplest.

4 The economic behaviour of individuals is in fact nothing but the manifestation of choice. From that it follows that the general properaties of the indifference surfaces show themselves in objective phenomena and are indeed observable.

5 In fact, in general and in the actual state of affairs, this scale does not appear in any concrete external manifestation. Thus it remains a pure subjective datum of our introspection.

However, it is necessary to underline that it would be at least unwise to conclude from this the impossibility of the practical determination of an absolute scale of satisfaction.

Thus, in physiological psychology one has for a long time held that the sensation was a magnitude escaping any absolute measurement. Nevertheless, recently, one has been able

---

[1] In the following text some references are given to some sections in Allais, 1943, *A la Recherche d'une Discipline Economique* (To the Search of an Economic Discipline).

to realize precise experiments giving in evidence the value of psychologically equivalent increments. (Measure of discernable increments – see Pieron, *Psychologie Experimentale*, Colin, 1927, pp. 93 ff.).

Moreover, there exists a case where the subjective notion of equivalent increments can be deduced from the objective notion of equivalent choice alternatives, in other words where the absolute scales of satisfaction can be determined from the sole indifference surfaces.

As a matter of fact suppose that the absolute satisfaction $\bar{S}$ be of the form

$$\text{(1)} \qquad \bar{S} = \Psi_A(A) + \Psi_B(B) + \ldots + \Psi_C(C)$$

but that one does not know the functions Ψ and that we know only the indifference curves.

Putting

$$\Psi'_A(A_0) = K$$

we have

$$\bar{S}(A, B, \ldots, C) - \bar{S}(A_0, B_0, \ldots, C_0) = \sum_B \int_{B_0}^{B} \psi'_B(B)\, \mathrm{d}B$$

$$= K \left(\frac{\Psi'_{B_0}}{\Psi_{A_0}}\right) \int_{A_0}^{A} \left(\frac{\Psi'_A}{\Psi_{B_0}}\right) \mathrm{d}A + K \sum_{B}^{B \neq A} \int_{B_0}^{B} \left(\frac{\Psi'_B}{\Psi_{A_0}}\right) \mathrm{d}A$$

$$= K[\theta_A(A) + \theta_B(B) + \ldots + \theta_C(C)]$$

the functions θ being well defined because the ratios (Ψ'_B/Ψ'_A) are well defined in all points of the space as given by the indifference surfaces. If we note that one can give to K any value, one sees finally that $\bar{S}$ is well defined, up to a coefficient and a constant $\bar{S}_0$, by the properties of the indifference curves.

6 Naturally this only concerns statistical means. In fact, one usually takes as a measure of ΔE_p the value of ΔE which is perceived in 75% of the cases.

7 This reservation is only valid in the present state of the science and it is not impossible that in the future of economic psychology one will realize experiments similar to those of physiological psychology.

8 Naturally one could define directly a scale of absolute measurement for satisfaction as a measurement scale such that the law of minimum perceptible increments be expressed by equation (8).

9 Thus one verifies that in the most general case, any function $\bar{S}$ depends on two arbitrary constants.

10 See note 2 of No 58 (in preceding developments of the book).

11 This corresponds to combinations actually realized and not to combinations actually consumed. By combination actually realized we understand it to be the last choice actually made. As this choice implies future consumptions, it can evidently not be a question of actual consumption. As one passes from the moment t_0 to the moment $t_1 = t_0 + T_1$, only the choices of the moment t_0 concerning the perio T_1 can be translated to an actual consumption.

[12] Some authors have considered they could fix arbitrarily the value of $\bar{S}$ for a consumption $A, B, \ldots, C$ nil. A convention like that seems to us not acceptable. It is practically impossible to figure mentally the sum of perceptible increments that would take us to a consumption nil. In any case everything leads us to think that this sum is very large and one should in all likelihood consider it as practically infinite. If it is actually so, fixing as infinity the origin of $\bar{S}$ in no way defines the function $\bar{S}$.

Other authors have believed they could fix arbitrarily the maximum value of the function $\bar{S}$. A convention like that would be acceptable if one could consider the existence of this maximum as certain. In fact this is not true, and if there exists in fact for each good a value of satiety, the number of goods to consider should be regarded as very great so that the maximum of the function $\bar{S}$ should be considered as practically infinite, and in any case inaccessible.

[13] No 59 (in the book).

[14] This is naturally only an approximation of reality because the existence of minimum perceptible increments just introduce discontinuities.

[15] However, we shall see that the comparison of absolute satisfactions such as we have defined them can be seen as natural and that in any case it is the only one of all the possible conventions that can be justified. We shall then arrive at interesting deductions.

Nevertheless, as the study of pure economics is absolutely independent of particular conventions on the definition of absolute satisfaction and that in particular it necessitates neither the comparison between them of satisfactions of different individuals nor of different scales of satisfaction used successively by an individual over time, we have preferred to reject the corresponding developments in the passages of Parts II and III in the book to which they would fit more closely.

[15'] Naturally this observation has the same validity for the intrinsic parameters $[ab]$

$$[ab] = (\sum_B BS'_B)\ [(ab) - mn)]$$

$$(ab) = S''_{AB}/S'_A S'_B \quad (mn) \;=\; \text{median of the } (ab)$$

(No 65 of the book) that are intrinsic only relatively to transformations $S_1 = \varphi(S)$ and to the units of measurement of the goods A and B.

[16] Irving Fisher, 1892, *Mathematical Investigations in the Theory of Value and Price* (French translation, *Recherches sur la Théorie de la Valeur et des Prix*, Giard, p. 6).

[17] In fact, as already indicated, the economic laws using the concept of ordinal satisfaction are absolutely independent of the arbitrary character of its scale of measurement.

[18] See No 92–96 in the book.

Notes to Part II

[1] Naturally this property is not particular to absolute desirabilities (Note 1 to No 62, in the book).

[2] No 52 in the book.

[3] We define the *internal derivatives* of the relative desirability δ_{BA} as the partial derivatives relatively to A or B, and the *external derivatives* as the partial derivatives taken relatively to the other factors C (Note 14 to No 65, in the book).

[4] It is in order to underline "that when we here use the term 'successive' it is not to be taken as indicating time. The succession we have in view is not a succession in time

but a succession in thought. We consider the consumption of the good B in a series of different hypotheses that we examine successively" (Irving Fisher, *The Nature of Capital and Income*. French translation, *De la Nature du Capital et du Revenu*, Giard, 1911, p. 57).

[5] Moreover, taking notation analogous to that of § 3, Part I, above, one can observe that according to our psychological introspection the minimum perceptible increment

$$(1) \qquad \Delta B_p = f(B)$$

corresponding to a good (B) is an increasing function of the quantity consumed B for given values of the other consumed goods.

Since B corresponds to S, it follows from relations (7) and (11) of § 3 of Part I that we have

$$(2) \qquad \bar{S} = e \int \frac{\mathrm{d}B}{f(B)}$$

Thus we verify that $\delta_B = \bar{S}'_B$ is indeed a decreasing function of B.

[6] Pieron, *Psychologie experimentale* (Experimental Psychology), Armand Colin, 1927, p. 96.

[7] Figure 1 corresponds to experiments realized in the study of luminous sensations.

[8] The law

$$g(x) = \text{constant}$$

represents the approximate psycho-physiological law, called "Weber's law" (note 8 above).

[9] Relation (11) of Part I.

[10] In the middle region, one has

$$\bar{S} = KL\,\frac{E}{E_0}$$

which is the approximate law of Fechner which corresponds to the law of Weber.

[11] i.e. in Figure (2) from $E = 3,000$ to $E = 10$ millions.

[12] It seems that as a first approximation one could take for $g(x)$ a function of the form

$$(1) \qquad g(x) = \mu^2[\lambda^2(x - x_0)^2 + 1]$$

where λ is a constant less than unity, of the order of 1/3.

If so and making $\bar{S} = 0$ for $E = 0$ one finds

$$(2) \qquad \bar{S} = \frac{e}{\lambda\mu^2}\left[\frac{\pi}{2} + \operatorname{arct} g\lambda(LE - LE_0)\right]$$

The curve representative of the function $\bar{S}$ has then the form shown in the Figure 3 below. The point M_0 is a point of symmetry and the straight lines Δ and Δ_1 are asymptotes.

Moreover one has

$$(3) \qquad \bar{S}''_{E^2} = -e\,\frac{g + g'}{E^2 g^2}$$

and then

$$(4) \qquad g + g' = \mu^2\lambda^2\left[(x - x_0)^2 + 2(x - x_0) + \frac{1}{\lambda^2}\right]$$

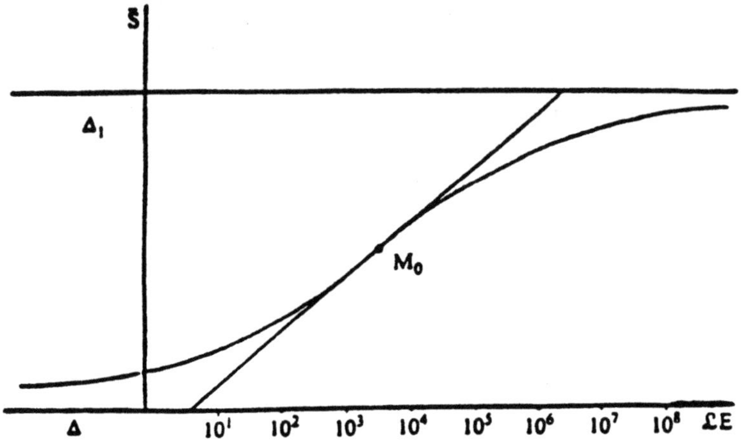

Fig. 3.

and one sees that the polynom in brackets is constantly positive if $\lambda \leq 1$, a condition which is effectively satisfied. Thus one verifies that the found function $\bar{S}$ satisfies the condition

$$\bar{S}''_{E^2} < 0$$

for all values of E.

[13] See No 53 in the book. Naturally this satiety point corresponds to a relative maximum, the other quantities being assumed to be constant. In fact, this maximum always exists, for the satisfaction procured by the consumption of one given good cannot increase indefinitely. It results, in particular, that from a certain value of the consumption, its desirability is necessarily decreasing.

[14] On can even say that the desirability decreases more rapidly than the consumption increases, in other words if the consumption increases by $n\%$, the desirability decreases by more than $n\%$.

[15] It is interesting to note that the functions found in note (12) as representative of the sensation resulting from luminous sensations verify this condition throughout its domain of variation when the parameter λ is less than unity, a condition which is in fact fulfilled.

[16] It seems indeed to result from our psychological introspection that the tangents in M_0 and M_1 do not coincide with the axes and that they have different directions. Thus in the neighbourhood of satiety we realize that a small decrease in the consumption involves a reduction of satisfaction which is comparatively neither very small nor very large.

[17] According to the properties of the square hyperbola the tangent in the point M (Figure 5) is characterized by the condition

$$op = pq$$

[18] Which means that the desirability of a good be independent of the quantities consumed of other goods.

[19] Relatively to these units of measurement and not to the absolute satisfaction which is well determined.

[20] The definition of the parameters $(\overline{ab})$ is thus analogous to that of the parameters

$$(ab) = S''_{AB}/S'_A S'_B$$

of note 15' of Part I (No 65 in the book). The bar above indicates simply that it corresponds to the absolute satisfaction $\bar{S}$. We shall generalize this convention to desirabilities δ and to the parameters $[ab]$, $(\alpha\beta)$ and $[\alpha\beta]$ of No 65 in the book defined as follows:

$$[ab] = (\sum_B BS'_B)\ [(ab) - (mn)]$$
$$(ab) = (ab) - \tfrac{1}{2}[(aa) + (bb)]$$
$$[\alpha\beta] = [ab] - \tfrac{1}{2}[(aa) + (bb)]$$

where (mn) represents the median of the parameters (ab).

These coefficients are invariant in any transformation $\phi(S)$ of S and in any change of the units of measurement of the consumptions $A, B, \ldots, C$.

The coefficients $[\alpha\beta]$ are called *distances*. They are equal to zero for perfect substitutes.

[21] These definitions are naturally distinct from those given in No 65, § 4 in the book. However, they are identical with them when $(mn) = 0$.

As a matter of fact independence is defined in No 65–4 by the condition

$$[ab] = \left(\sum_B BS'_B\right) [(ab) - (mn)] = 0$$

Since $[ab]$ is invariant we have

$$[ab] = [ab] = \left(\sum_B BS'_B\right) [(ab) - (mn)]$$

If $(mn) = 0$ the conditions

$$[ab] = 0 \qquad S''_{AB} = 0$$

are equivalent.

[22] Pareto, *Manuel d'Economie Politique*, Giard, 1927, p. 252.

[23] In the sense of our definition in No 64 in the book.

[24] A couple of goods being given, it seems indeed to result from our psychological introspection that the marginal desirability S''_{AB} has a constant sign whatever the considered consumption set $A, B, \ldots, C$.

[25] If one assumed that the cases of substitutability are as frequent as those of complementarity, we realize that from this point of view the study of an economy of independent goods should allow the general *shape* of the real phenomena to be represented.

[25'] In No 65 in the book.

[26] If we neglect as a first approximation the exceptional cases of strong substitutability and complementarity.

[27] As we have already indicated in No 62 in the book, one can put $B = Y = 1 - X$, X representing the good corresponding to the available time.

More directly it results from our introspection that the satisfaction decreases and that painfulness (or disutility) of work increases when Y increases. This painfulness increases even more the greater Y is.

[28] If the different goods are independent, one can write

$$\bar{S} = \Psi_A(A) + \Psi_B(B) + \ldots \Psi_C(C) - \Psi_Y(Y)$$

and then

$$\frac{d}{dY}\Psi_Y > 0 \quad \frac{d^2}{dY^2}\Psi_Y > 0 \quad \frac{d^3}{dY^3}\Psi_Y > 0$$

29 We define the psychological yield by relation (15) and not by the relation

$$r = \frac{\bar{S}(\lambda\alpha, \ldots, \lambda\gamma)}{\lambda}$$

for our psychological introspection gives us no information about the total satisfaction $\bar{S}$; and in fact it enlightens us only on its differential variations (see the indications already given in Part I, note 12 above).

30 It suffices to make for the first

$$A = B = \ldots = C = 0$$
$$\Delta A = A_1 \ldots \Delta C = C_1$$

for the second

$$A = 0 \quad \Delta B = \ldots = \Delta C = 0$$
$$\Delta A = A_1$$

and for the third

$$A + \Delta A = A_1 \ldots C + \Delta C = C_1$$
$$\Delta A = -\Delta A_1 \ldots \Delta C = -\Delta C - 1$$

30′ See Mathematical Appendix I M in the book.

31 The Condition (21) can therefore be written

$$\Sigma(ab)\, dA\, dB < 0$$

for any system of values $dA, dB, \ldots dC$.

32 Commissaire, *Cours de Mathématiques Spéciales*, Vol. I, no 11, Masson, 1941.

33 Unfortunately we have not been able to find a general proof of this property that we have determined by induction from the investigation of particular cases.

Thus in the particular case of two goods we should have according to (23)

(1) $$(\overline{ab})^2 < (\overline{aa})(\overline{bb})$$

Likewise in the particular case where one has

(2) $$(\overline{aa}) = \ldots = (\overline{cc}) = x \quad (\overline{ab}) = (\overline{bc}) = \ldots = y$$

one finds the condition

(3) $$(y - x)^{p-1}\, [x + (p-1)^y] < 0$$

which should be verified for any p less than n, n being the number of goods (A) considered.

This condition gives immediately the condition

(4) $$x < y < -\frac{x}{n-1}$$

and

$$(5) \qquad (\overline{aa}) < (\overline{ab}) < -\frac{(\overline{aa})}{n-1}$$

These examples show that on the average the $|(\overline{ab})|$ should be less than the $|(\overline{aa})|$ without excluding that certain $|(\overline{ab})|$ could be greater than certain $|(\overline{aa})|$. Naturally the $(\overline{ab})/(\overline{aa})$ should be the smaller the more rapidly the psychological yield decreases.

Remark I. One should take care not to conclude from this last example that the $(\overline{ab})$ are in general negative. If it is so that is only as a result of the particular hypothesis which we have made and according to which all the coefficients $(\overline{ab})$ are equal.

If for example one had assumed a table of the $(\overline{aa})$, $(\overline{ab})$ like the following table

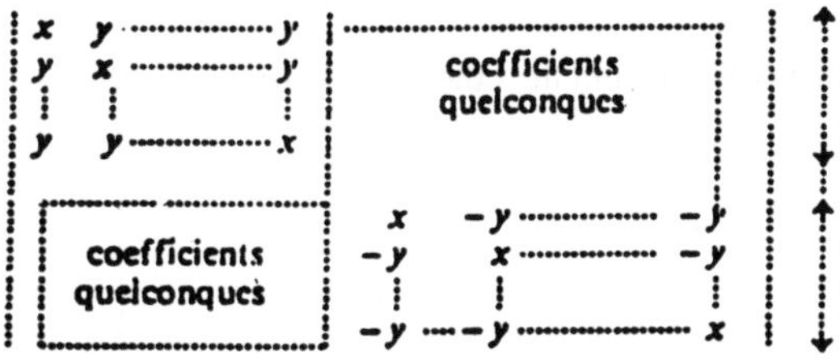

a hypothesis which maybe is more close to reality since the introspection shows the existence of coefficients $(\overline{ab})$ both positive and negative, one should find the double condition

$$x < y < -\frac{x}{\frac{n}{2}+1} \qquad\qquad x < -y < -\frac{x}{\frac{n}{2}+1}$$

which would give

$$|y| < |x| / \left(\frac{n}{2}+1\right) \quad \text{that is} \quad |(\overline{ab})| < |(\overline{aa})| / \left(\frac{n}{2}+1\right)$$

Remark II. We do not believe it to be useless to give the principles of the calculation of th determinant δ when conditions (2) above are fulfilled. It is sufficient to consider the calculation of a determinant of the type

$$(6) \qquad \alpha = \begin{vmatrix} 1+a_1 & 1 & 1 & \cdots & 1 \\ 1 & 1+a_2 & 1 & \cdots & 1 \\ \vdots & \vdots & \vdots & & \vdots \\ 1 & 1 & 1 & \cdots & 1+a_n \end{vmatrix} =$$

$$a_1 a_2 \ldots a_n \begin{vmatrix} 1+\frac{1}{a_1} & \frac{1}{a_2} & \cdots & \frac{1}{a_n} \\ \frac{1}{a_1} & 1+\frac{1}{a_2} & \cdots & \frac{1}{a_n} \\ \vdots & \vdots & & \vdots \\ \frac{1}{a_1} & \frac{1}{a_2} & \cdots & 1+\frac{1}{a_n} \end{vmatrix}$$

Adding the different columns to the first, one has

$$\alpha = a_1 a_2 \ldots a_n \left(1 + \frac{1}{a_1} + \ldots + \frac{1}{a_n}\right) \begin{vmatrix} 1 & \frac{1}{a_2} & \cdots & \frac{1}{a_n} \\ 1 & 1+\frac{1}{a_2} & \cdots & \frac{1}{a_n} \\ \vdots & \vdots & & \vdots \\ 1 & \frac{1}{a_2} & \cdots & 1+\frac{1}{a_n} \end{vmatrix}$$

and

$$\alpha = a_1 \left(1 + \frac{1}{a_1} + \ldots + \frac{1}{a_n}\right) \begin{vmatrix} 1 & 1 & \cdots & 1 \\ 1 & 1+a_2 & \cdots & 1 \\ \vdots & \vdots & & \vdots \\ 1 & 1 & \cdots & 1+a_n \end{vmatrix}$$

By subtracting the first column from the others, we have

$$\text{(7)} \qquad \beta = \begin{vmatrix} 1 & 1 & \cdots & 1 \\ 1 & 1+a_2 & \cdots & 1 \\ \vdots & \vdots & & \vdots \\ 1 & 1 & \cdots & 1+a_n \end{vmatrix} = \begin{vmatrix} 1 & 0 & \cdots & 0 \\ 1 & a_2 & \cdots & 0 \\ 1 & 0 & \cdots & 0 \\ \vdots & \vdots & & \vdots \\ 1 & 0 & \cdots & a_n \end{vmatrix} = a_2 \ldots a_n$$

and finally

$$\text{(8)} \qquad \alpha = a_1 a_2 \ldots a_n \left(1 + \frac{1}{a_1} + \quad + \frac{1}{a_n}\right)$$

[34] One can show that if the parameter $(\overline{ab})$ are small compared to the quantities

$$\frac{[(\overline{aa})(\overline{bb})\ldots(\overline{cc})]^{\frac{1}{p}}}{p}$$

where $(A), (B), \ldots, (C)$ represent p of the n goods considered, the different determinants (23) are equivalent to the products

$$(\overline{aa}), (\overline{aa})(\overline{bb}), \ldots, (\overline{aa})(\overline{bb})\ldots(\overline{cc})$$

which are in fact alternatively negative and positive if one supposes all the parameters $(\overline{aa})$ negative.

[35] Which means that they are not invariant in a transformation

$$\Sigma = \varphi(\bar{S})$$

[36] § 4 above of this Part II.

[37] This hypothesis is so much more plausible as *a priori*, and as we have seen, one can approximately consider that there are as many positive parameters $(\overline{ab})$ as negative parameters $(\overline{ab})$.

Anyway, one can observe that if it were not so, it would suffice for finding the results enunciated to take as a couple (MN) the couple (AB) such that

$$\bar{S}''_{AB} = 0$$

a couple which certainly exists, since our introspection shows us the existence of goods that are psychologically independent, at least in a small domain.

Thus the hypothesis of the median $(\overline{mn})$ being nil or at least a very small value is only an useful hypothesis which nothing seems to contradict and which, in any case, has no influence on the classification obtained of couples of goods. One can therefore consider it as *scientifically true.*

38 Because the parameter $[ab]$ is an invariant (No 65, in the book), we have $[ab] = \overline{[ab]}$ (notes 20 and 221 above).

39 With the reserve of the indications of note 37 above.

40 Thus the relation

$$\Sigma(\overline{ab})\,\mathrm{d}A\,\mathrm{d}B < 0$$

(note 31 above) gives the condition

$$(1) \qquad \Sigma[ab]\,\mathrm{d}A\,\mathrm{d}B < 0$$

for any system of the value of the parameters.

The determinants (23) written with the replacing of all $(\overline{ab})$ by the $[ab]$ should therefore be alternatively negative and positive.

In particular one has then

$$(2) \qquad [ab]^2 < [aa]\,[bb]$$

Now one knows that for $xy = k^2$ the minimum of $x + y$ is equal to $2K$, x and y being two positive parameters. One deduces that from condition (2) follows the condition

$$(3) \qquad |[aa]| + |[bb]| > 2|[ab]|$$

the equality not being possible unless if $|[aa]| = |[bb]|$. Since $[aa]$ and $[bb]$ have the same sign, one sees thus that the condition

$$[\alpha\beta] = [ab] - \tfrac{1}{2}([aa] + [bb]) = 0$$

(note 20 above) implies the equalities

$$[aa] = [bb] = [ab]$$

and one obtains thus a confirmation of the condition (21) in No 65 in the book corresponding to perfect substitutes.

In No 65 in the book it is shown (relation (25)) that

$$-1 < K_{AB} < 1$$

with

$$K^2_{AB} = \frac{[ab]^2}{[aa]\,[bb]}$$

$K_{AB} = -1$ for perfect substitutability, 0 for independence, and $+1$ for perfect complementarity.

41 This transformation $S'' = \varphi(S)$ will be defined by the condition

$$(\overline{mn}) = 0$$

(note 21 above) which can be written

$$\frac{\varphi''}{\varphi'^2} + \frac{mn}{\varphi'} = 0$$

and which gives the value of φ''/φ', (mn) being the median of the (ab) (note 20 above).

[41'] No 65 in the book, and note 20 above.

[42] i.e. the properties characterizing the relative situations of the points $M(ab)$ on Figure 7.

[42'] Except however the inequality $K^2_{AB} < 1$ which could not be established (relation 24 of No 65 in the book) without referring to the properties of absolute satisfaction, note 40, relation (2) above, but, as the reader can easily assure himself, this property does not intervene in the development of the economic theory.

[43] When we shall deem it necessary at least. In principle, we shall introduce the functions $\bar{S}$ only when it results in an appreciable simplification of the exposition.

[44] Because notably of the smallness of the $\bar{S}''_{AB}$.

[45] One can affirm that if our introspection would not give us the notion of an absolute satisfaction of which the derivatives $\bar{S}''_{AB}$ are generally small, it would be mathematically useful to substitute to the consideration of the most general function S the particular function $\bar{S}$ which makes the median $(\overline{mn})$ zero. See note 41 above.

[46] Some developments of the theory which precedes may to the non-specialist reader have appeared as tedious. *They are nonetheless necessary to establish the economic theory on rigorous and incontestable foundations.*

In the later years researchers have forced themselves to disengage economic theory from the consideration of absolute satisfaction (notably Hicks, J.R., *Théorie Mathématique de la Valeur en Régime de Concurrence*, Hermann, 1937), but in making a *tabula rasa* of properties, such as decreasing desirabilities, which until then were universally admitted, their works did not fail to spread some confusion. Moreover such approach necessitated complicated calculations.

As the reader shall be able to convince himself in the following, the theory we have presented removes all uncertainty and it builds a solid bridge between old theories and the more modern theories in showing not only that they are compatible, but that they enlighten each other mutually.

Notes to Part III

[1] P. Appel, *Traité de Mécanique rationelle*, second edition, Vol. I, Paris, 1902, pp. 84–85.

[2] See Part I, note 15, above.

[3] The role, in economics, of the absolute satisfaction cannot be fully understood if we do not know the fundamental nature of a true scientific theory. In a given state of science, a theory, to be acceptable, must lead to deductions verified by experience and it must be as simple as possible. If these two conditions are met, the considered theory may be deemed as scientifically true.

REFERENCES

Allais, Maurice (1943) *A la Recherche d'une Discipline Economique* (To the Search for an Economic Discipline), Paris, 1943; republished as *Traité d'Economie Pure* (Treatise on Pure Economics), 1952; third edition as *Traité d'Economie Pure*. Editions Clément Juglar, Paris, 1992.

Appel, P. *Traité de Mécanique Rationnelle*, Vol. I, second edition, Gauthier-Villars, Paris.
Commissaire (1941) *Cours de Mathématique Spéciale*, Vol. I. Masson, Paris.
Fisher, Irving (1892) *Mathematical Investigations in the Theory of Value and Price*. Yale University Press, 1965, p. 126. French translation, *Recherches sur la Théorie de la Valeur et des Prix*. Giard, Paris, 1917, p. 205.
Fisher, Irving (1911) *The Nature of Capital and Income*. New York and London, MacMillan. French translation, *De la Nature du Capital et du Revenu*, Giard, Paris, 1926.
Hicks, J.R. (1937) *Théorie Mathématique de la Valeur en Régime de Concurrence*. Hermann, Paris.
Pareto, Vilfredo (1927) *Manuel d'Economie Politique*. Giard, Paris.
Pieron (1927) *Psychologie Expérimentale*. Armand Colin, Paris.

MAURICE ALLAIS

DETERMINATION OF CARDINAL UTILITY ACCORDING TO AN INTRINSIC INVARIANT MODEL

ABSTRACT. The purpose of this paper is to show that it is possible to represent all the empirical data of the 1952 Experiment (19 subjects) and of the 1975 Experiment (8 subjects) by only one model, the same whatever the subjects considered.

An invariant formulation is presented of the generating function $X = f(A)$ corresponding to the condition $s(U_0 + X) = 2s(U_0 + A)$ where $s(U_0 + X)$ represents cardinal utility of a given subject, and U_0 his psychological assets, that is his psychological estimate of his assets.

The function of cardinal utility of any one subject can be deduced from the knowledge of his generating function. The function of cardinal utility is invariant from one subject to the next once one considers the ratio X/μ, in which μ represents the index of a subject with respect to a reference subject.

All the empirical data can be validly represented by the same generating function and a single function of cardinal utility which together constitute the intrinsic invariant model. This agreement is the more remarkable in that the intrinsic invariant model was deduced from the analysis of the empirical data of the 1952 experiment alone, and it applies equally as well to the empirical data of the 1975 experiment.

Not only the preceding analysis gave undeniable evidence of the existence of cardinal utility, but its expression appears effectively to be invariant from one subject to the next both at a given moment and over time, at least as a first approximation.

This conclusion is the more significant in that the expression of cardinal utility as a function of variable X shows a very striking similarity to the expression for psycho-physiological sensation as a function of luminous stimulus determined by Weber's and Fechner's successors.

INTRODUCTION

The purpose of this paper is to show that it is possible to represent all the empirical data of the 1952 experiment (19 subjects) and of the 1975 experiment (8 subjects) by only one model, the same whatever the subjects considered: *The Intrinsic Invariant Model.*

The 1952 experiment was organized after the May 1952 Paris International Colloquium. The limited 1975 experiment was organized to check the main results of the 1974–1975 analysis of the data of the 1952 experiment.[1]

The present paper is only a very abridged version of my 1984 Memoir *The Cardinal Utility and its Determination – Hypotheses, Methods and Empirical Results*[2] in which the reader will find all necessary justifications and appropriate comments.

For sake of brevity the main mathematical formulas and numerical results of the model considered are presented below in Tables I to XIII, the

M. Allais and O. Hagen (eds.), Cardinalism, 31–64.

following text being limited to the statement of fundamental properties. All the results obtained are illustrated by Charts.

In my 1977 Memoir only the log-linear approximation of the cardinal utility function was used (T II).

1. THE INTRINSIC INVARIANT CARDINAL UTILITY MODEL[3]

1.1. Fundamental Hypotheses of the Invariant Cardinal Utility Model

The general properties of the invariant cardinal utility model are derived from very simple hypotheses on the cardinal utility function (T I and T III).

1.2. Generating Function of the Invariant Cardinal Utility Model

The generating function $X = f(A)$ of the cardinal utility model corresponds to the condition $s(U_0 + X) = 2s(U_0 + A)$ considered by the 1952 and 1975 experiments with $A \geq 0$. For a given subject $s(U)$ represents the cardinal utility function for $U = U_0 + X$ where U_0 represents his *psychological assets*, that is his *psychological estimate of his assets*, and X a virtual increase of U_0 (T I).

For a given subject, his answers X are represented as functions of A by charts like Chart I.

The general properties of the generating function are derived from the general properties of the cardinal utility function. It has two components, f_1 and f_2. The component f_1, valid for small values of X, is log-linear. The component f_2 can be determined only by the analysis of the empirical data (T IV).

From the invariance of the function of cardinal utility and of the generating function for all subjects it results that it is possible to deduce the cardinal utility function and the generating function of any subject from the knowledge of the cardinal utility function and the generating function of a particular subjects taken as reference. This *reference subject* can be defined by the abscissa $K = K_R$ of the vertical asymptote of the generating function of the reference subject. Any subject is characterized relatively to the reference subject by the coefficient $\mu = U_0/U_{0R}$, U_{0R} being the value of U_0 for the reference subject (T V).

The particular mathematical form of the component f_2 of the generating function has been deduced from the *general properties* of the generating function and from the *empirical analysis* of the data of the 1952 experiment. As a matter of fact its sole justification is its capacity to represent correctly these data. The generating function so deduced depends on three parameters, α, a and μ (T VI):

- α and a are specific parameters common to all the subjects; they characterize the general cardinal utility model.

CHART I (§1.42)

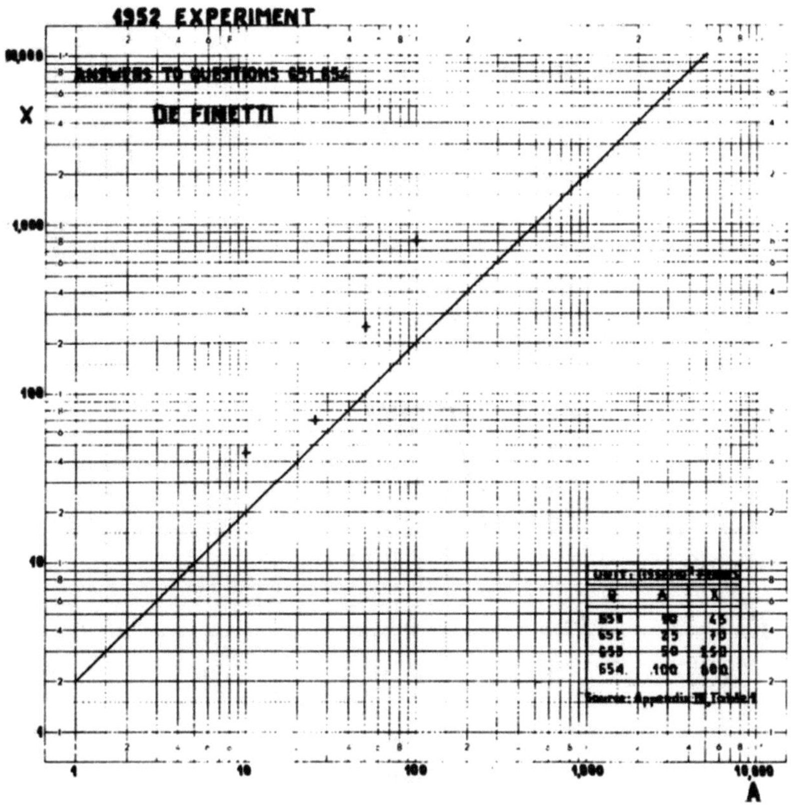

Chart I.

- the parameter μ characterizes the subject considered in relation to the reference subject.

The curves representing the generating functions of the different subjects are identical within a displacement along the straight line $X = 2A$. *They depend only on the coefficients α, a and μ, and their structure is invariant for the different subjects* (T VI,5).

For a given series of observations the parameters α, a and μ of the generating function can be determined by very simple processes (T VII).

CHART II (§1.5)

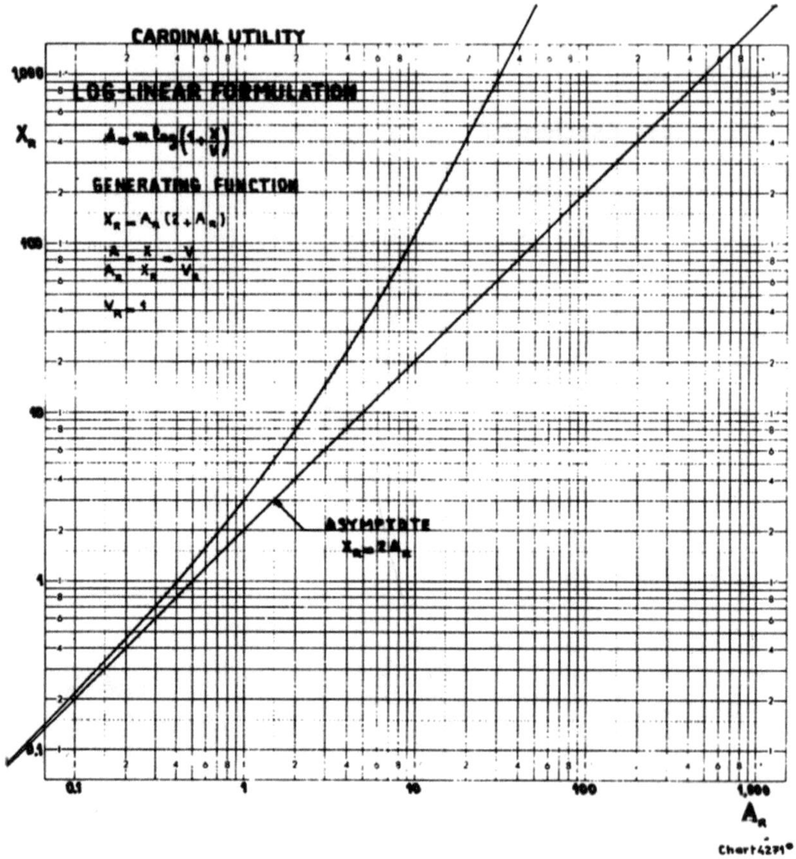

Chart II.

1.3. Cardinal Utility Function of the General Model

The function of cardinal utility $s = s(1 + X/U_0)$ of any one subject can be deduced point by point from the knowledge of his generating function (T VIII).

The function of cardinal utility is invariant from one subject to the next once one considers the ratio $X/\mu = X_R$, in which μ represents the index of the subject considered with respect to the reference subject. It is remarkable that the invariant cardinal utility function is *approximately log-linear over a very large domain* (T IX).

1.4. Intrinsic Invariant Model of Cardinal Utility

The intrinsic invariant model is defined by two specific values α^* and a^*, of the coefficients α and a of the invariant cardinal utility model. The coefficients α^* and a^* are deduced from the sole consideration of the mathematical properties of the generating function and the corresponding cardinal utility function of the invariant cardinal utility model (T X and T XI).

The generating function and the cardinal utility function of the intrinsic invariant cardinal utility model are represented in Charts VIII and IX. Chart IX shows that the cardinal utility function is *approximately log-linear over a very wide range* (T XI,3).

As regards applications, the intrinsic invariant model only comprises *a single arbitrary parameter* μ, the ratio of the psychological assets of the subjects considered to that of the reference subject (T XI,5).

In last analysis the justification of the particular choice of the values α^* and a^* for the coefficients α and a *rests essentially* on the capacity of the *intrinsic invariant model* to represent correctly not only the empirical data of the 1952 experiment but also those of the 1975 experiment.

2. EMPIRICAL VERIFICATION OF THE INTRINSIC INVARIANT MODEL[4]

2.1. 1952 Experiment

The agreement of the intrinsic invariant model with the empirical data of the 1952 experiment is all the more remarkable as the specific values α^* and a^* of the coefficients α and a are determined only *from pure mathematical considerations* and consequently are independent of the empirical data (for illustration see T XII,2, and Charts XII, XIII, XIV and XV).

2.2. 1975 Experiment

The agreement of the intrinsic invariant model with the empirical data of the 1975 experiment appears *all the more significant* in that it relates to a small number of subjects, and to a wide range of questions between 1 and 1,000, whereas the fitting of the model depends only on one parameter μ (for illustration see T XII,3 and Charts XVII and XVIII).

This agreement is all the more remarkable in that the intrinsic invariant model has been deduced *from the sole analysis* of the empirical data of the 1952 experiment. Indeed *the invariance of the intrinsic invariant model* for very different subjects at very distant epochs is very striking (for illustration see T XII,4 and Charts XXI and XXII).

CHART VIII (§5.2, Tables I and II, and §5.4)

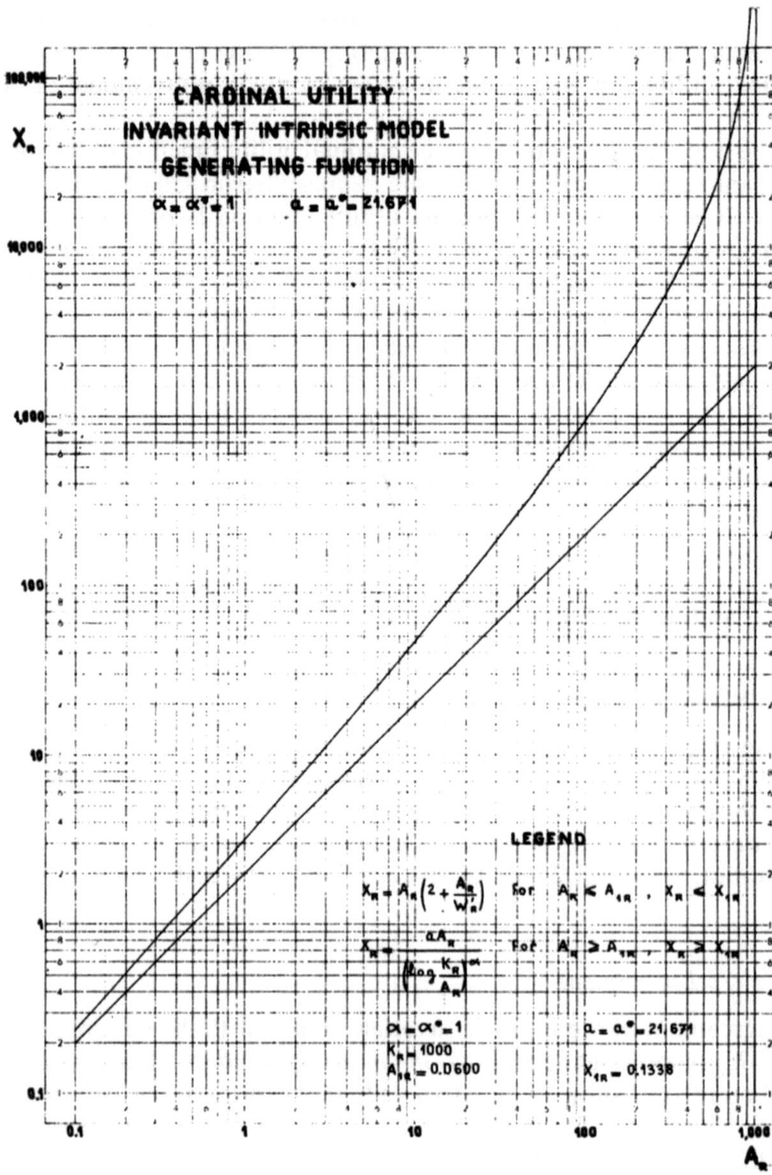

Chart VIII.

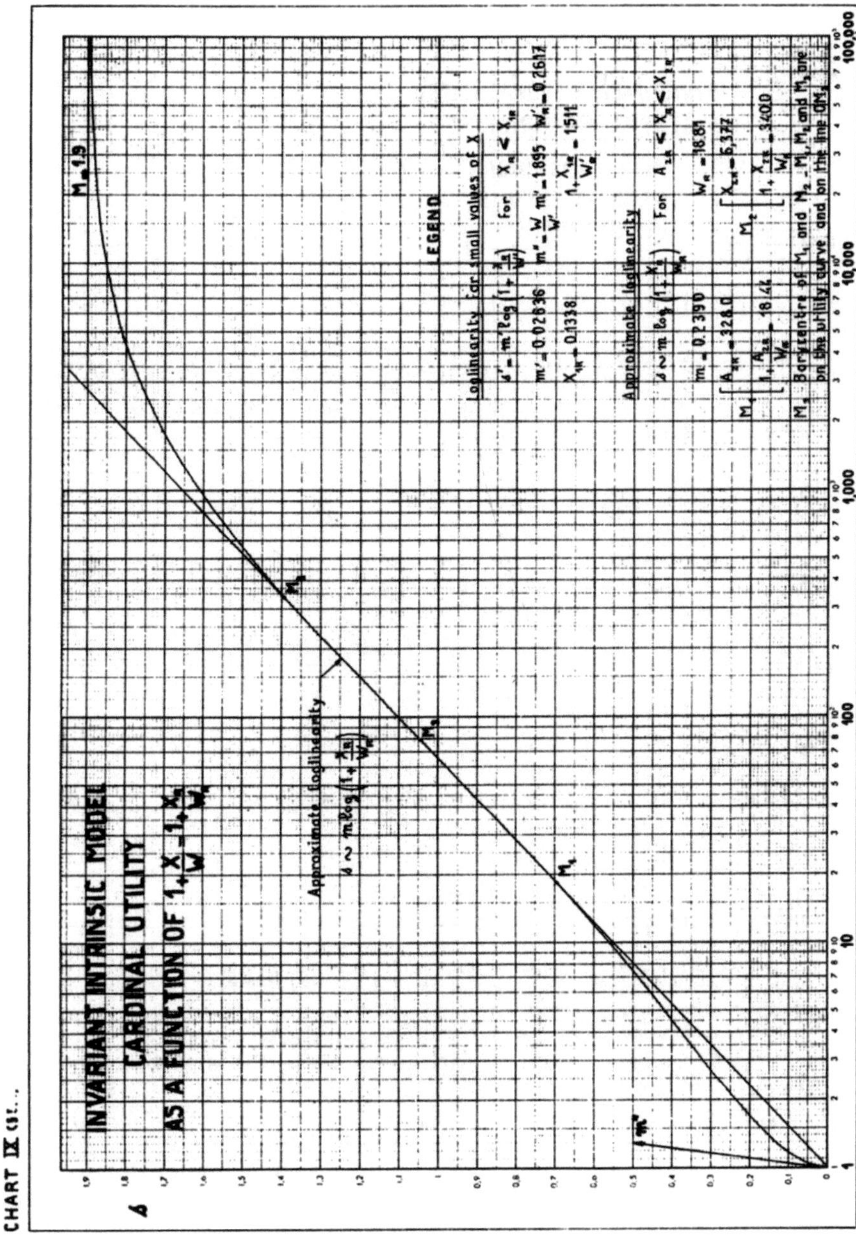
CHART IX (ct...
INVARIANT INTRINSIC MODEL
CARDINAL UTILITY
AS A FUNCTION OF
Approximate loglinearity
LEGEND
Loglinearity for small values of X
Approximate loglinearity
m = 0.2390
m' = 0.02836
m' = 1.895
W'R = 0.2617
X1R = 0.1338
WR = 18.81
A1R = 328.0
X2R = 5.377
M1
M2
M3
M = 1.9
Barycentre of M1 and M2 – M1, M2 and M3 are on the utility curve and on the line OM3
10
100
1,000
10,000
100,000

Chart IX.

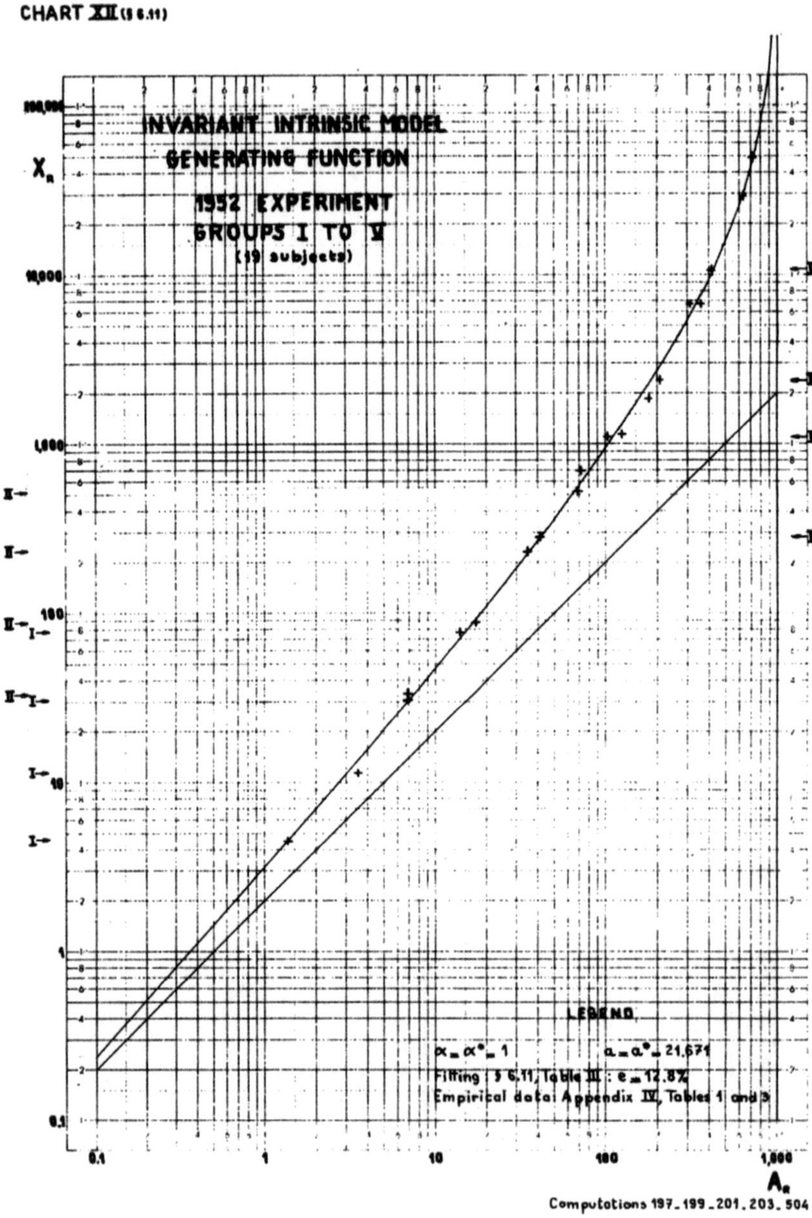
CHART XII (§ 6.11)
INVARIANT INTRINSIC MODEL
GENERATING FUNCTION
1952 EXPERIMENT
GROUPS I TO V
(19 subjects)
LEGEND
Computations 197-199-201-203-504

Chart XII.

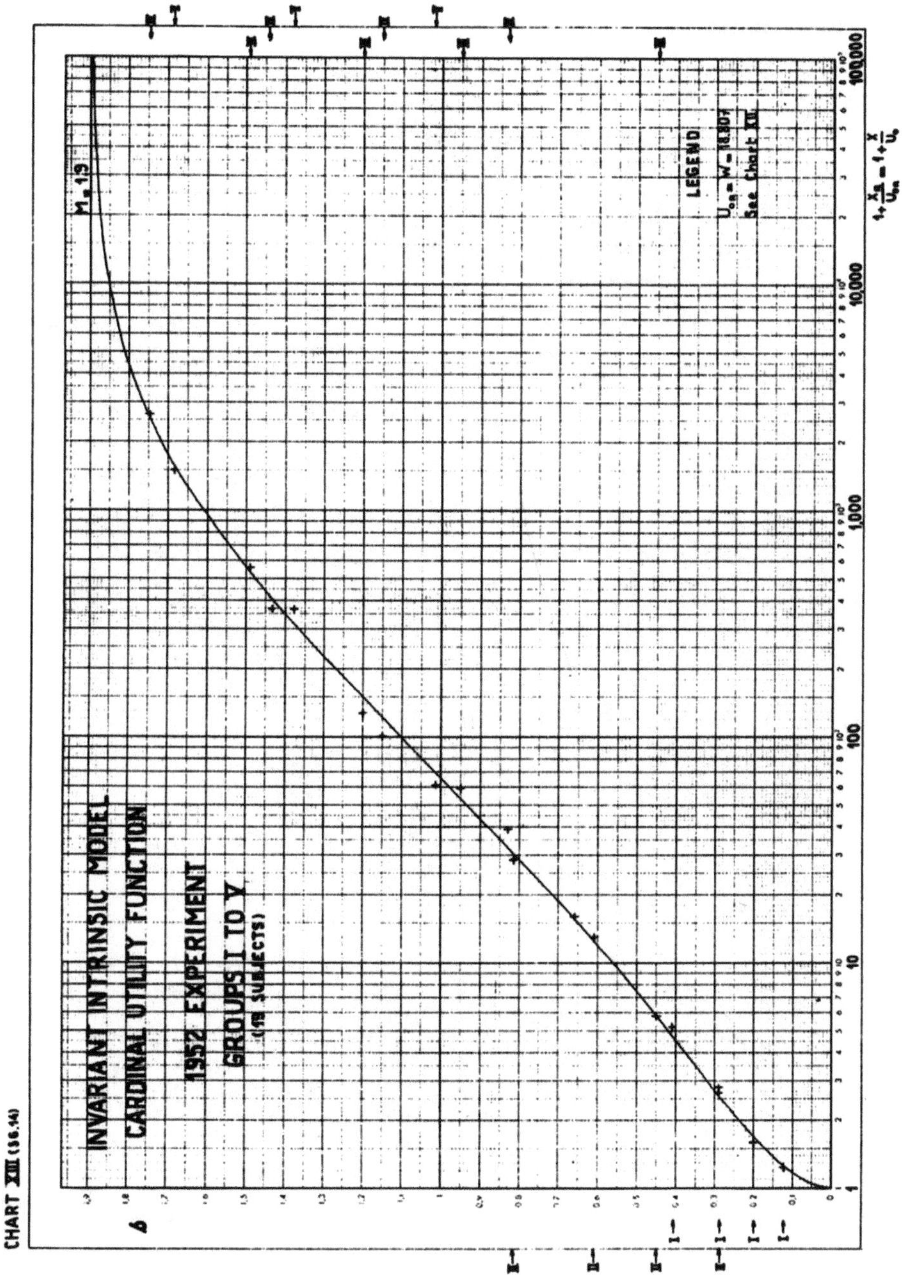
CHART XIII
INVARIANT INTRINSIC MODEL
CARDINAL UTILITY FUNCTION
1952 EXPERIMENT
GROUPS I TO V
LEGEND

Chart XIII.

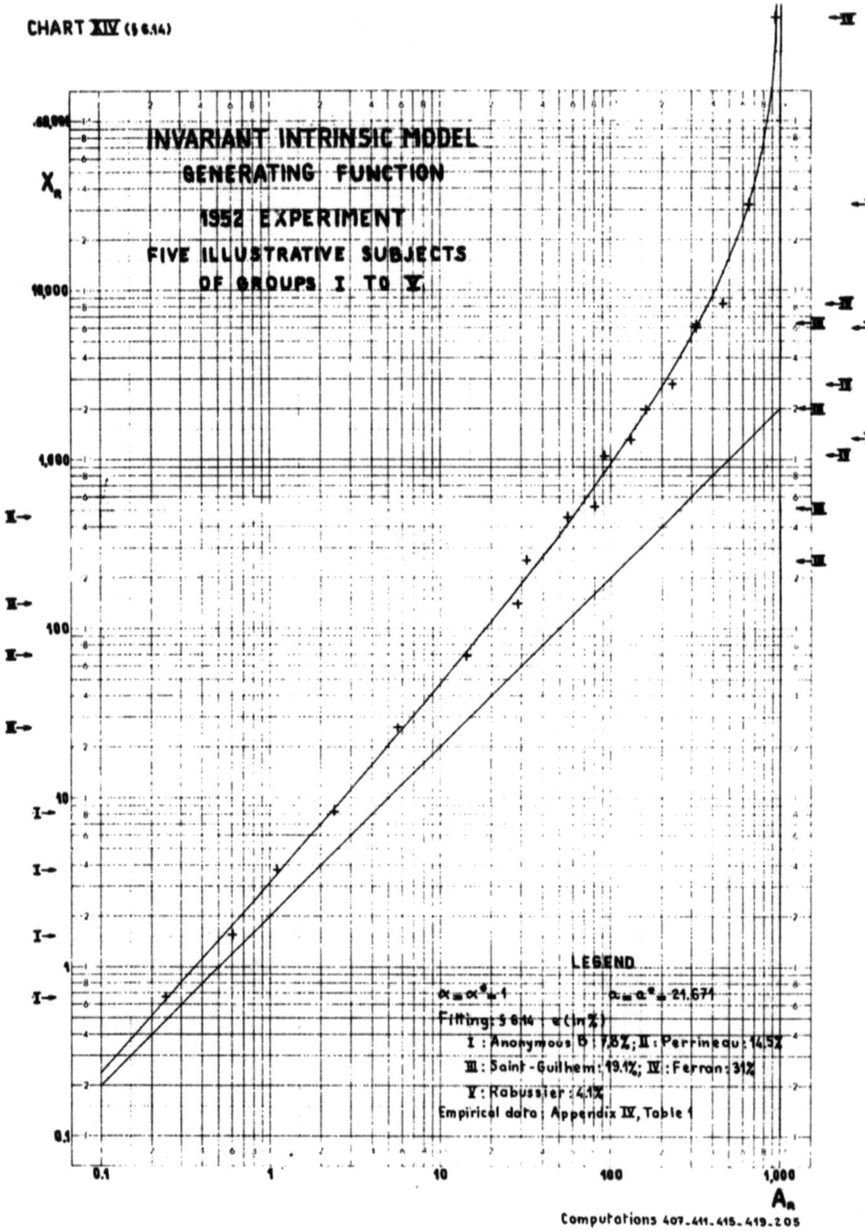
CHART XIV (§ 6.14)
INVARIANT INTRINSIC MODEL
GENERATING FUNCTION
1952 EXPERIMENT
FIVE ILLUSTRATIVE SUBJECTS
OF GROUPS I TO V
X_R
10,000
1,000
100
10
1
0.1
0.1
1
10
100
1,000
A_R
LEGEND
α = α* = 1
α = α* = 21.671
Fitting: § 6.14 ; e (in %)
I : Anonymous B : 7.8%; II : Perrineau : 14.5%
III : Saint-Guilhem : 19.1%; IV : Ferran : 31%
V : Robussier : 4.1%
Empirical data : Appendix IV, Table 1
Computations 407-411-415-419-205

Chart XIV.

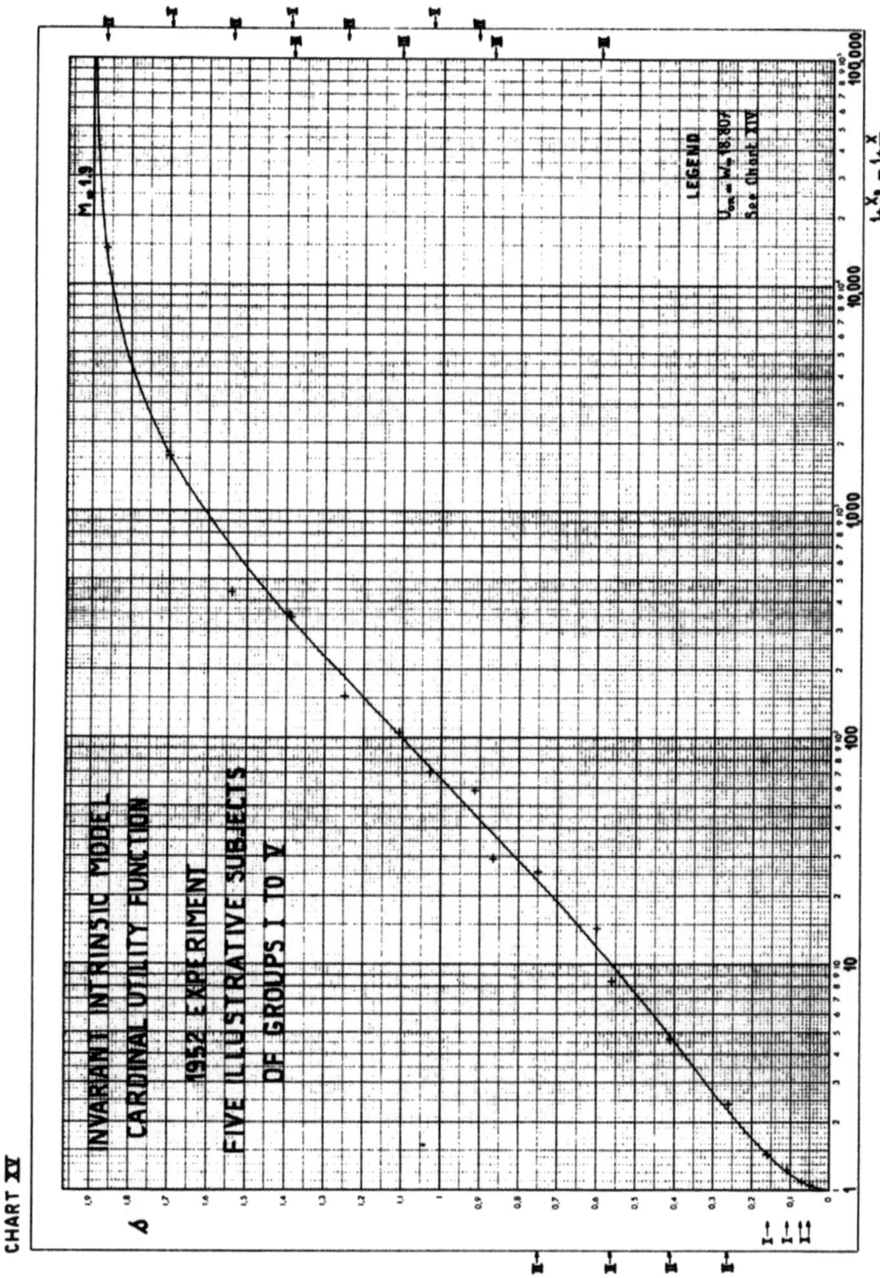
CHART XV
INVARIANT INTRINSIC MODEL
CARDINAL UTILITY FUNCTION
1952 EXPERIMENT
FIVE ILLUSTRATIVE SUBJECTS
OF GROUPS I TO V
LEGEND
See Chart XIV

Chart XV.

CHART XVII (§ 6.2)

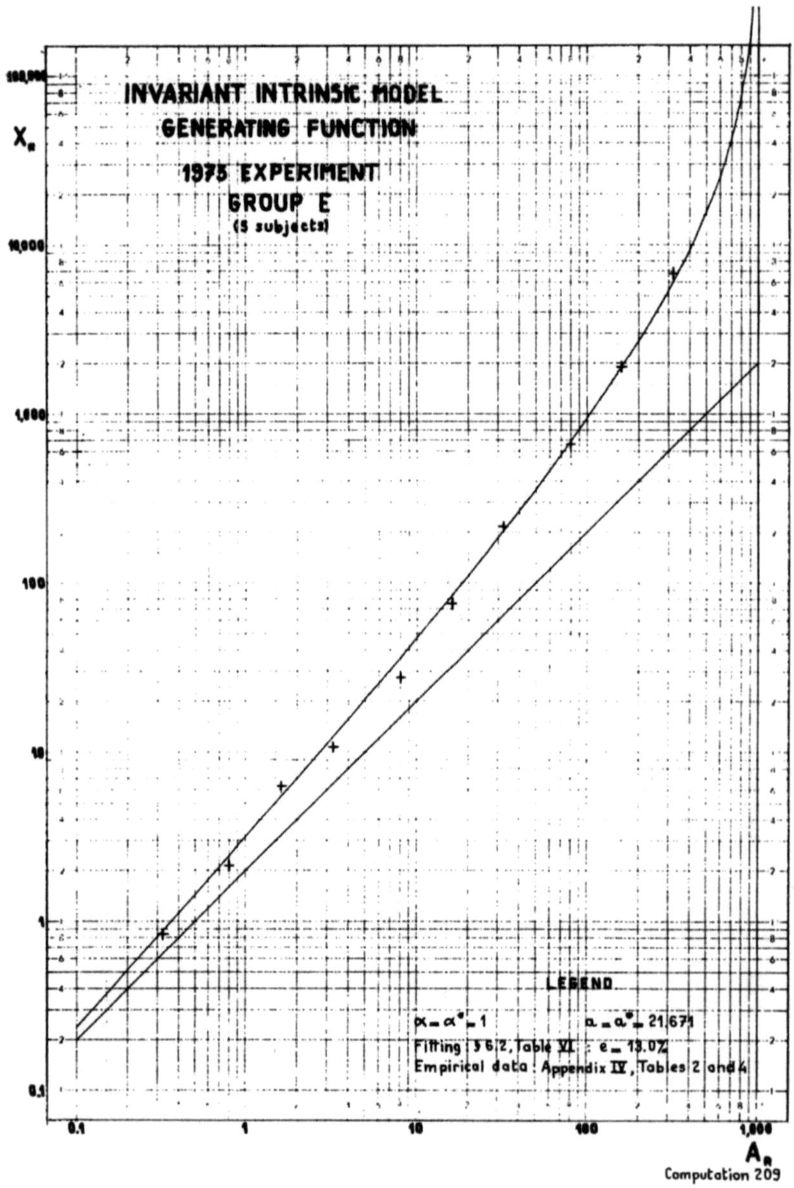

Chart XVII.

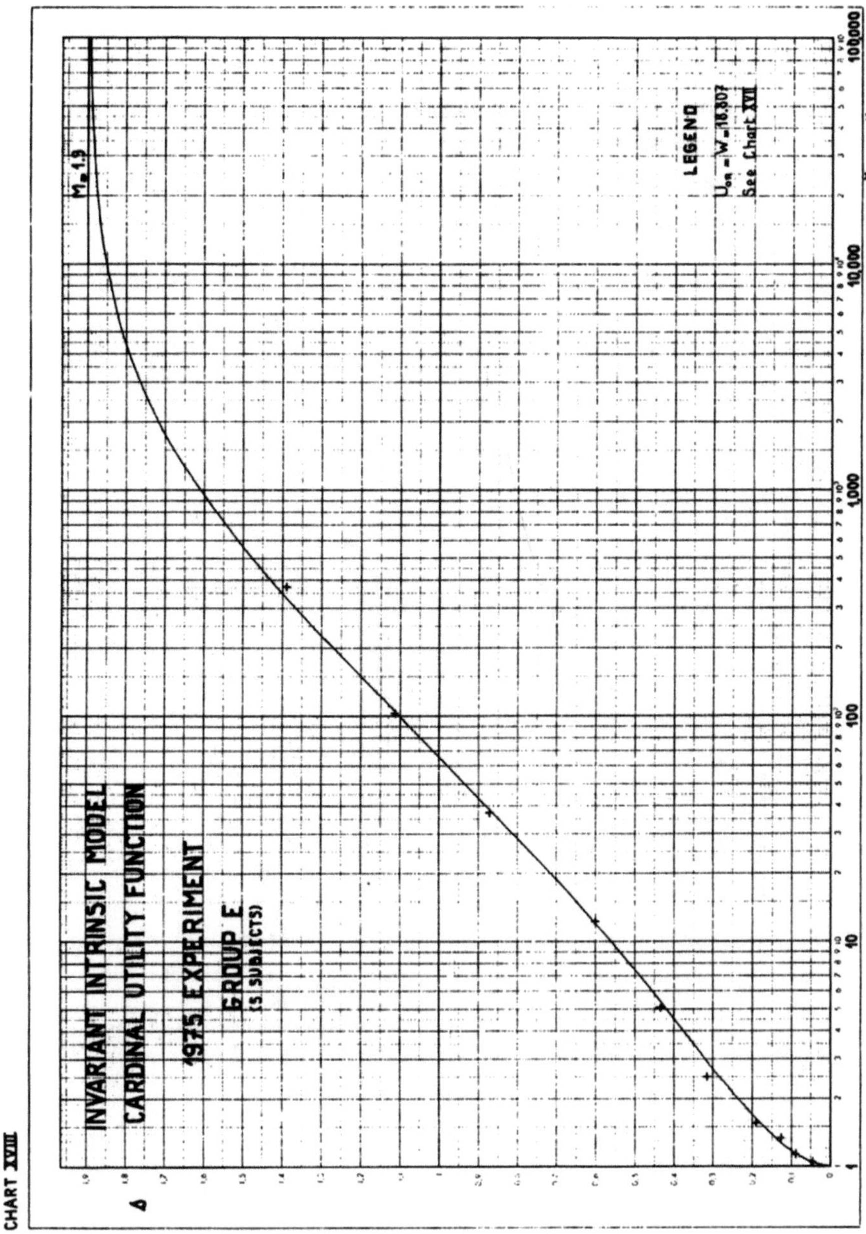
CHART XVIII
INVARIANT INTRINSIC MODEL
CARDINAL UTILITY FUNCTION
1975 EXPERIMENT
GROUP E
(5 SUBJECTS)
LEGEND
See Chart XVII
1
10
100
1,000
10,000
100000

Chart XVIII.

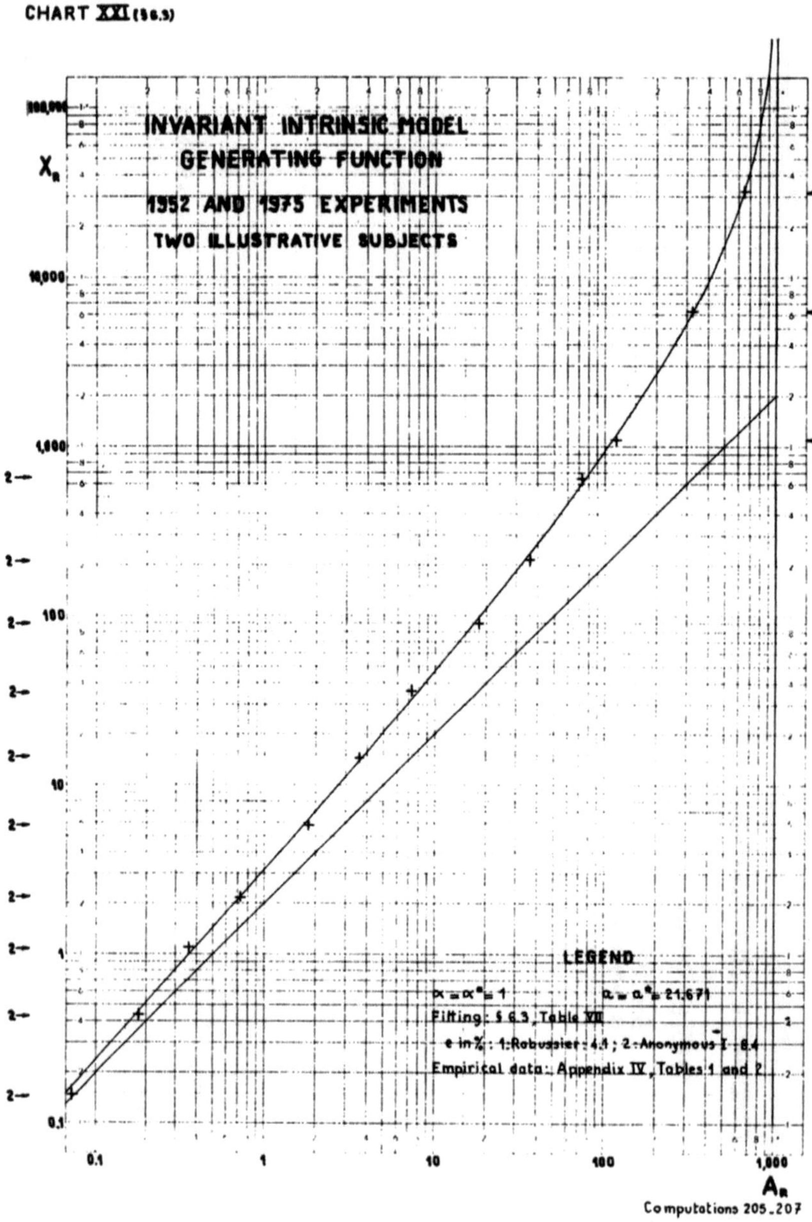
CHART XXI (§6.3)
INVARIANT INTRINSIC MODEL
GENERATING FUNCTION
1952 AND 1975 EXPERIMENTS
TWO ILLUSTRATIVE SUBJECTS
X_n
100,000
10,000
1,000
100
10
1
0.1
0.1
1
10
100
1,000
A_n
LEGEND
α = α* = 1
a = a* = 21,671
Fitting: § 6.3, Table VII
e in % : 1: Robussier : 4.1 ; 2: Anonymous I : 8.4
Empirical data: Appendix IV, Tables 1 and 2
Computations 205_207

Chart XXI.

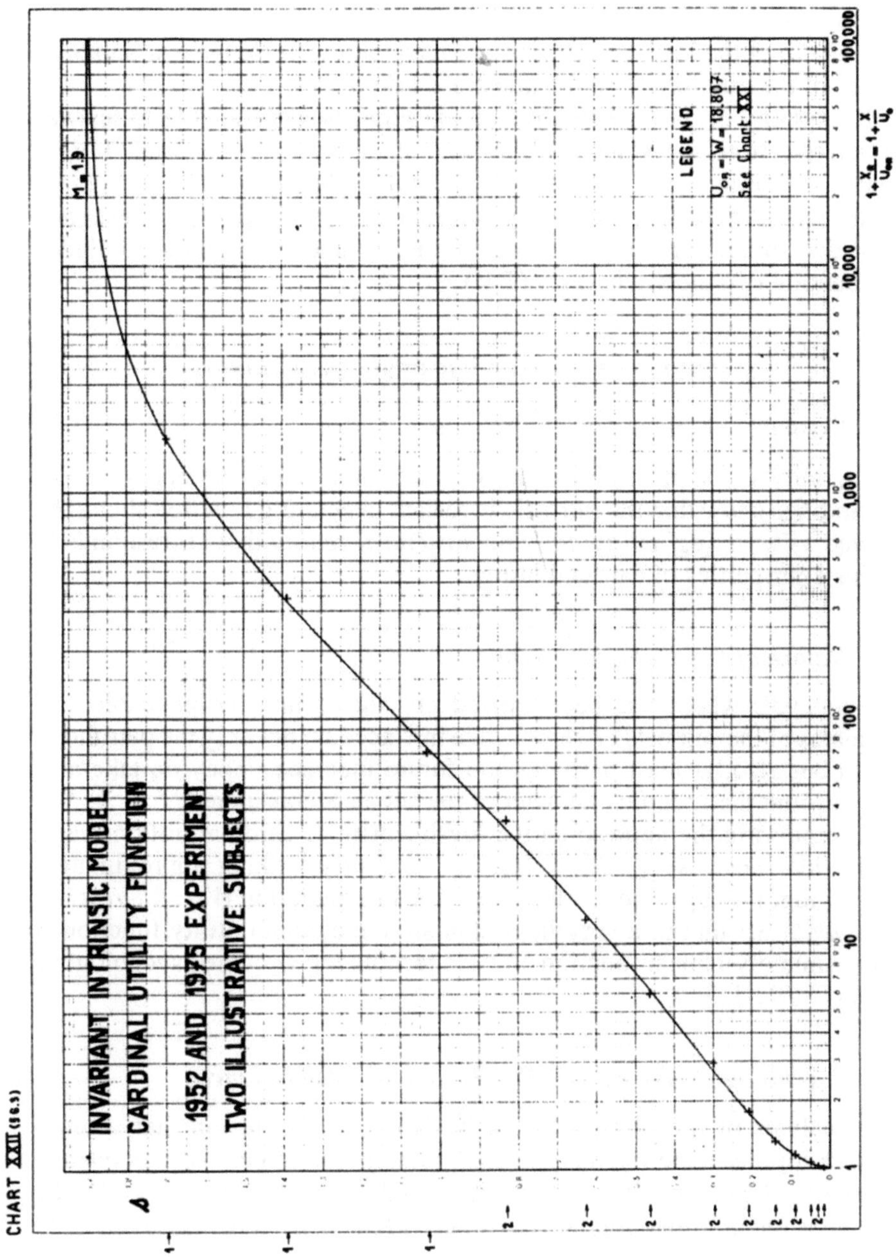
CHART XXII
INVARIANT INTRINSIC MODEL
CARDINAL UTILITY FUNCTION
1952 AND 1975 EXPERIMENT
TWO ILLUSTRATIVE SUBJECTS
M = 1.9
LEGEND
See Chart XXI
1
10
100
1,000
10,000
100,000

Chart XXII.

2.3. Explanation of all the Previously Observed Difficulties

The intrinsic invariant model explains the deviations observed in the fit of data relating t the log-linear formulation equally well for the low and high values of the answers X to the questions asked.

It explains in particular why certain subjects were unable to answer certain questions for which the threshold of satiety is overcrossed (T V,5).

By admitting a horizontal asymptote corresponding to satiety (Chart IX), the curve representing cardinal utility effectively corresponds to the data of our introspection, whereas the log-linear formulation includes no situation of satiety whatever (T II).

3. INTERPRETATION OF THE RESULTS OBTAINED[5]

3.1. Existence of an Underlying Structural Coherence

The quality of fit of the intrinsic invariant model and the coherence of the findings show that the intrinsic invariant generating function should be viewed as covering and *underlying structural reality* that corresponds to intrinsic properties of cardinal utility.

3.2. Nature of Psychological Assets

The analysis which has been carried out shows that the psychological estimates of the sujbects' assets do take into account not only the patrimony assets but also, at least partially, the future incomes. They do take also into account the specific character of the subjects considered.

Considering the approximative log-linearity of cardinal utility over a very wide range $A_2 \leq X \leq X_2$, i.e. the very striking approximation $s \sim m \log(1 + X/W)$ over this range, the interpretation $W = U_0$ *rests on the hypothesis* that in a very large domain the cardinal utility function is approximately a linear function of the logarithm log U of the psychological assets U (T XI, 3–4).

3.3. Psychological Assets and Psychological Cash Balances

The analysis of the observed data leads to the conclusion that when a subject appraises the intensity of his preferences, he behaves *completely differently* depending on whether the virtual changes in his assets that he can envisage are relatively small or very high. This conclusion emerged as *incontrovertible*.

Whereas in the latter case the subject considers his total psychological assets U_0, in the form he refers to a much smaller amount the order of magnitude of which corresponds to his psychological cash balances U_0', i.e. his psychological estimate of his cash balances.

As for the psychological cash balances U_0', the justification of the estimate $U_0' = W'$ *relies on the hypothesis* that the cardinal utility function is approximately a linear function of the logarithm log U' of $U' = U_0' + X$ for the small values of X (T IX,2 and T XI,4).

3.4. Indexes of Psychological Indetermination

On the whole the answers to the different questions are *remarkably* consistent. The deviations from the formulation of the intrinsic invariant model correspond to *psychological errors* relating to the intensity of preferences. These errors are comparable in nature to the errors made by any measuring device in other domains, whatever the domain considered.

The deviations observed correspond to the subjects' hesitation in determining the values of their answers X; and the *indexes of psychological indetermination* which can be deduced from the analysis of their answers to the questions asked allow the order of magnitude of the errors made by the subjects in estimating their intensity of preference to be measured (T XIII, 1–3).

The deviations observed suggest that the psychological estimates of cardinal utility are subject to a margin of error of approximately 7% when they are compared with the total variation M of the function or cardinal utility considered for positive values of X.

It is particularly significant to observe that the *indexes of psychological indetermination* which can be deduced from the answers of the subjects are all of the same order of magnitude, regardless of the age, profession, social back-ground, . . ., of the subjects considered in the 1952 experiment.

As a matter of fact this analysis allows the determination of the standard psychological error on X corresponding to the psychological indetermination.

This standard psychologica error σ_p is of the order of 36.5% for the considered subjects of the 1952 experiment when the standard deviation of (log X − log X^*) of the corresponding individual fittings is approximately 36.8%. It should be underlined that the calculus of σ_p is *totally independent* of any hypothesis on the expression of the cardinal utility function (T XIII,4).

4. OVERALL VIEW[6]

4.1. The Intrinsic Invariant Model and Empirical Data

All the empirical data of the 1952 and 1975 experiments can be validly representd, at least as a first approximation, by the same generating function and a single function of cardinal utility which together constitute the intrinsic invariant model.

This agreement is the more remarkable *in that the intrinsic invariant model was deduced from the analysis of the empirical data of the 1952 experiment alone, and it applies itself as well to the empirical data of the 1975 experiment*, whose twelve questions however covered a far wider range between 1 and 1,000 than the four questions asked in 1952 covering only a range of variation of 10 to 100 of A.

4.2. Existence of a Cardinal Utility

The results obtained confirm in a striking and indisputable way the effective existence for each subject considered of a cardinal utility which indeed is real, and not at all meta-physical, as Savage contended in defending his neo-Bernoullian theory and as is still contended by very numerous neo-Bernoullians.

However, the proof of the existence of cardinal utility goes far beyond the debate on neo-Bernoullian theories. In fact this proof fully reinstates in economic theory *a psychological concept* which has been banished from its after Pareto's time as a result of erroneous analyses and interpretation.

In fact, although this concept *does not need to be considered* in working out the theory of general economic equilibrium and the theory of economic efficiency, or, in a general frame, the general theory of surpluses, it is *indispensable* for establishing any effective theory relating to conflicts opposing economic agents in sharing the obtained surpluses, conflicts whose final settlement depend not only on their preferences, *but basically on the intensity of their preferences*. The consideration of the cardinal utility concept is also indispensable for any comprehensive theory of governmental choices and decisions, in particular regarding their effects on income distribution. The same is also true of the specification of any theory of choice within a family, based on the consideration of the relative intensity of the preferences of its members and on interpersonal comparisons.

4.3. The Cardinal Utility Function, a Psychological Invariant

As regards my previous works, relating to invariants in economic behaviour, especially to invariants in monetary psychology, the intrinsic invariant model of cardinal utility provides a new and striking example of invariance in space and over time. Not only the preceding analysis gave undeniable evidence of the existence of cardinal utility, but its expression appears to be *invariant from one subject to the next both at a given moment and over time, at least as a first approximation.*

This conclusion is the more significant in that the expression of cardinal utility as a function of the variable X shows *a very striking similarity* to the expression for psycho-physiological sensation as a function of luminous stimulus, determined by Weber's and Fechner's successors (Charts XXV

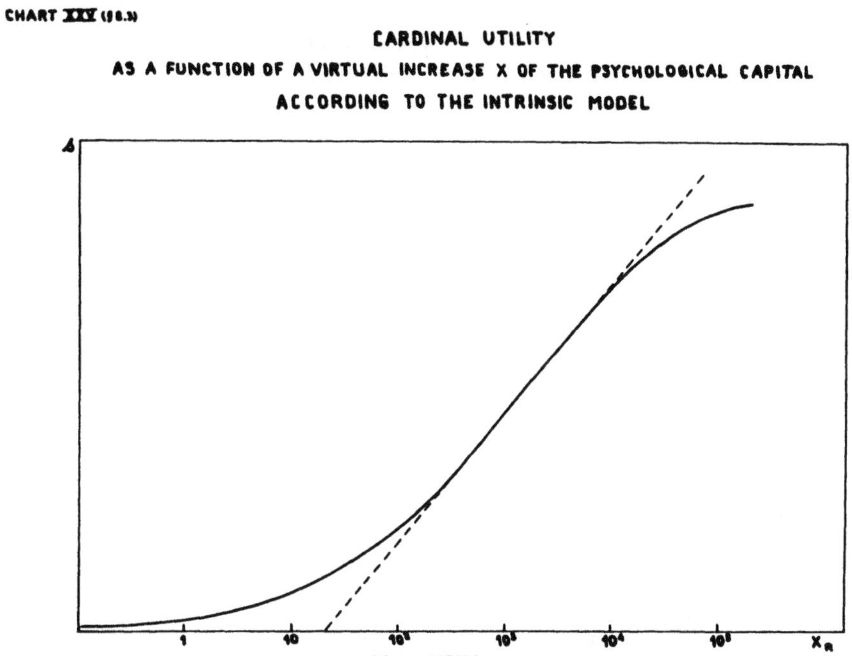

Chart XXV.

and III).

As a result it appears that basic principles of the laws of psycho-physiology remain valid in the field of economic psychology.

4.4. The Future of the Intrinsic Invariant Formulation

The present paper is not presented as the elaboration of a definitive model of cardinal utility, but simply as a stage defining an empirical approach, methods of analysis, guiding principles and hypotheses, and a basis of reflection for the study of human economic psychology following the path opened up over a century ago by Weber and Fechner in their psycho-physiological analysis of sensations and in the 18 century by Daniel Bernoulli in his analysis of the Saint Petersburg Paradox.

As a matter of fact the intrinsic invariant generating function which I have derived from the empirical analysis of the results of the 1952 experiment has incontestably a *contingent character*. It is thus possible, if not probable, that this function will be replaced by another sooner or later. However, if it is, it will be replaced by a *neighbouring* function which can represent observed data at least as well, and the same will be true of the corresponding function of cardinal utility.

In any case, three significant conclusions seem to be established, namely that:

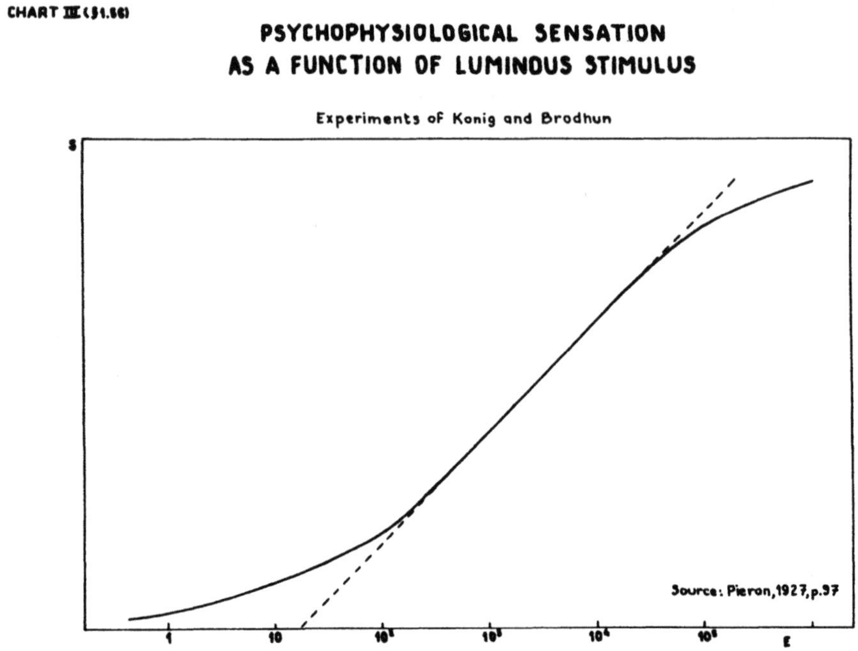

Chart III.

1. *the cardinal utility function of any subject has an upper limit corresponding to satiety*;
2. *the function of cardinal utility of any subject can be represented, at least as a first approximation, by one and only one function, invariant in space and over time*;
3. *the subjects' behaviour vis-à-vis the intensity of their preferences differs entirely depending on whether the virtual changes of their psychological assets are likely to change their living conditions radically or not.*

NOTES (TEXT, TABLES AND BIBLIOGRAPHY)

[1] On these experiments see Allais, 1952c, and Allais, 1977; § 3, pp. 447–449; § 6, pp. 451–454; and Appendix C, § C.5–C.9, pp. 614–620; and Charts I to VI, pp. 640–645. See also Allais, 1984, Appendices II, III and IV.

[2] This Memoir, the French version of which has been distributed in the Venice Conference, will be published shortly in the Review *Theory and Decision*.

[3] Allais, 1984, Parts II, III, IV and V.

[4] Id., Part VI.

[5] Id., Part VII.

[6] Id., Part VIII.

[7] Id., § 1.4.

[8] Id., § 1.5.
[9] Id., § 2.2.
[10] Id., § 2.4.
[11] Id., § 2.5.
[12] Id., § 3.5–3.6.
[13] Id., § 3.7.
[14] Id., § 4.2.
[15] Id., § 4.6.
[16] Id., § 5.1–5.3.
[17] Id., § 5.1–5.3.
[18] Id., § 6.1–6.4.
[19] Id., § 7.6.
[20] The reader will find an extensive bibliography in Allais (1984).

Requests for reprints should be sent to: Allais, Centre d'Analyse Economique, 62 Bld St. Michel, 75006, Paris, France.

I. CARDINAL UTILITY ANALYSIS DEFINITIONS AND NOTATIONS[7]

1. General Notation

s : cardinal utility
U_0 : psychological assets
U'_0 : psychological cash balances
X : virtual increase of psychological assets
(1) $U = U_0 + X$: virtual psychological assets
(2) $s(U_0 = 0$
Unit of value: one million (1952) francs (approximately equivalent to US$ 10,000, 1983).

2. Psychological Equivalent Intervals

Psychological intervals $(U_0, U_0 + A)$ and $(U_0 + A, U_0 + X)$ are equivalent if

$$s(U_0 + A) - s(U_0) = s(U_0 + X) - s(U_0 + A) \quad (3)$$

i.e.

$$s(U_0 + X) = 2s(U_0 + A) \quad (4)$$

3. Generating Function and Determination of the Cardinal Utility Function

$$\text{(5)} \qquad \boxed{\frac{X}{U_0} = f\left(\frac{A}{U_0}\right) \quad \text{for} \quad s\left(\frac{X}{U_0}\right) = 2s\left(\frac{A}{U_0}\right)}$$

$$\text{(6)} \qquad \boxed{s\left[f\left(\frac{A}{U_0}\right)\right] = 2s\left(\frac{A}{U_0}\right)}$$

The knowledge of the generating function f determines the cardinal utility function s by condition (6).

4. Empirical Data

1952 and 1975 Experiments: $A > 0, \; X > 0$
1952 Experiment : 4 Questions : $A_i, \; X_i$; 19 subjects j
1975 Experiment : 12 Questions : $A_i, \; X_i$; 8 subjects j

5. Average subject of a group of subjects

(7) Geometric averages : $A_i = \bar{A}_{ij} \quad X_i = \bar{X}_{ij}$

II. LOG-LINEAR MODEL OF CARDINAL UTILITY[8]

1. Hypothesis

(1) $s = m \; \log (1 + X/V)$

2. Generating Function

(2) $X = A(2 + A/V) \qquad A \geq 0$

Logarithmic graphic representation:

(3) Asymptote: $\log X = \log A + \log 2 \qquad (X = 2A)$

3. Interpretation of V (Estimate of the Psychological Assets)

(4) $V = U_0$

4. Reference Subject

$$(5) \qquad V = V_R = 1$$

5. Invariance Conditions

$$(6) \qquad \frac{X}{X_R} = \frac{A}{A_R} = \frac{V}{V_R} = \frac{U_0}{U_{0R}} = \lambda$$

6. Fitting

$$(7) \qquad X = A(2 + A/\lambda) \qquad V = \lambda$$

7. Analysis of the 1952 and 1975 Experiments

The log-linear formulation has been used, as a first approximation, in the analysis of the results of the 1952 and 1975 experiments in Allais (1977): Appendix C, § C5–C9, pp. 614–620; § C21–C22, pp. 632–634; and Charts I to VI, pp. 640–645.

8. Limited Validity of the Log-linear Formulation

The log-linear model is not valid: for the small values of X; for the very large values of X (satiety).

III. INVARIANT CARDINAL UTILITY MODEL POSTULATES ON THE CARDINAL UTILITY FUNCTION[9]

Postulate I: Invariance

The cardinal utility of a given subject is an invariant function of X/U_0.

Postulate II: Continuity

s and $\mathrm{d}s/\mathrm{d}X$ are continuous functions for every value of X.

Postulate III: Satiety

$$(1) \qquad s(X/U_0) = \infty) = M$$

Postulate IV: Log-linearity for Small Values of X

(2) $s = m'u'$ for $X/U_0 \leq X_1/U_0'$

(3) $u' = \log(1 + X/W') \qquad X \geq 0$

(4) W' = estimate of the psychological cash balances U_0'

Postulate V: Approximate Log-linearity Over a Wide Range of X

(5) $s \sim \log(1 + X/W)$ for $A_2 \leq X \leq X_2$

(6) W = estimate of the psychological assets U_0

IV. INVARIANT CARDINAL UTILITY MODEL GENERATING FUNCTION[10]

1. Fundamental Properties

1.1. Invariance (Consequence of Postulate I)

The function

(1) $X/U_0 = f(A/U_0)$

is the same for all subjects.

1.2. Satiety – Vertical Asymptote X = K (Consequence of Postulate III)

(2) $X/U_0 = f(K/U_0) = \infty \qquad (K/U_0) = M/2$

Representative curve of the generating function : vertical asymptote of abscissa K.

1.3. Small values of X/U_0 (Consequence of Postulate IV)

(3) $$\frac{X}{U_0} = f_1\left(\frac{A}{U_0}\right) = \frac{A}{U_0}\left(2 + \frac{A/U_0}{W'/U_0}\right) \text{ for } \frac{A}{U_0} \leq \frac{A_1}{U_0}$$

Asymptote: $X = 2A$

2. Components of the Generating Function

(5) $f_1 : X/U_0 = f(A/U_0) = f_1(A/U_0)$ for $A/U_0 \leq A_1/U_0$

(6) $f_2 : X/U_0 = f(A/U_0) = f_2(A/U_0)$ for $A/U_0 \geq A_1/U_0$

Component f_1 : corresponds to Postulate IV.
Component f_2 : to be deduced from the analysis of the empirical data of the *1952 experiment* (T VI below).

3. Continuity Conditions of the Two Components f_1 and f_2 (Consequences of Postulate II)

(7) $$X/U_0 = f_1(A/U_0) = f_2(A/U_0) \text{ for } X = X_1 \;\; A = A_1$$

(8) $$df_1/dA = df_2/dA \text{ for } X = X_1 \;\; A = A_1$$

V. INVARIANT CARDINAL UTILITY MODEL REFERENCE SUBJECT[11]

1. Definition

The subject of reference is defined by the condition

(1) $$\boxed{K = K_R}$$

2. Generating Function of the Reference Subject

(2) $$f_1 : X_R = A_R(2 + A_R/W'_R) \text{ for } A_R \leq A_{1A} \;\; X_R \leq X_{1R}$$

(3) $$f_2 : X_R/U_{0R} = f_2(A_R/U_{0R}) \text{ for } A_R \geq A_{1R} \;\; X_R \geq X_{1R}$$

3. Cardinal Utility Function of the Reference Subject

$$s = s(X_R/U_{0R})$$

4. Invariance Conditions for a Given Subject

(4) $$\left(\begin{array}{lll} K = \mu K_R & W' = \mu W'_R & U_0 = \mu U_{0R} \\ A = \mu A_R & X = \mu X_R & \\ A_1 = \mu A_{1R} & X_1 = \mu X_{1R} & \end{array} \right.$$

μ = coefficient characterizing the considered subject relatively to the reference subject

5. *Satiety*

When $A \geq K$ the subject is unable to answer, the corresponding value X being infinite.

VI. INVARIANT CARDINAL UTILITY MODEL CHARACTERISTIC PARAMETERS OF THE GENERATING FUNCTION OF THE REFERENCE SUBJECT[12]

1. *Definition of the Reference Subject*

$$(1) \qquad \boxed{K_R = 1000}$$

2. *Generating Function of the Reference Subject*

$$(2) \qquad f_1 : X_R = A_R(2 + A_R/W'_R) \text{ for } A_R \leq A_{1A} \quad X_R \leq X_{1R}$$

$$(3) \qquad f_2 : X_R/\alpha A_R/\left(\log \frac{K_R}{A_R}\right)^{\alpha} \text{ for } A_R \geq A_{1R} \quad X_R \geq X_{1R}$$

The component f_2 is deduced *from the empirical analysis of the 1952 data.*

3. *Implications of the Continuity Conditions (T IV)*

$$(4) \qquad W'_R = \frac{\zeta'(1+\alpha)}{\alpha a e^{\zeta'}} K_R \quad A_{1R} = \frac{K_R}{e^{\zeta'}} \quad X_{1R} = \frac{aK_R}{\zeta'^{\alpha} e^{\zeta'}}$$

(5) ζ' = the greatest root of equation (6)

$$(6) \qquad 2\zeta'^{(1+\alpha)} - a\zeta' + a\alpha = 0$$

4. *Values of W, A and X corresponding to the smallest root of equation (6)*

$$(7) \qquad W_R = \frac{\zeta^{(1+\alpha)}}{\alpha a e^{\zeta}} K_R \quad A_{2R} = \frac{K_R}{e^{\zeta}} \quad X_{2R} = \frac{aK_R}{\zeta^{\alpha} e^{\zeta}}$$

ζ = the smallest root of equation (6)

5. Generating Function of a Given Subject (Invariance Condition)

(9) $f_1 : X = A(2 + A/W') \text{ for } A \leq A_1 \;\; X \leq X_1$

(10) $f_2 : X/\alpha A/(\log K/A)^\alpha \text{ for } A \geq A_1 \;\; X \geq X_1$

(11) $$\frac{A}{A_R} = \frac{X}{X_R} = \frac{K}{K_R} = \frac{A_1}{A_{1R}} = \frac{X_1}{X_{1R}} = \frac{A_2}{A_{2R}} = \frac{X_2}{X_{2R}} = \mu$$

The invariant cardinal model depends only of two specific parameters α and a, *the same for all subjects.*

VII. INVARIANT CARDINAL UTILITY MODEL FITTING METHODS[13]

1. Structural Relation

(1) $$X = aA/\left(\log \frac{\mu K_R}{A}\right)^\alpha$$

2. Determination of α, a and μ for a Given Series of N Observations (A_i, X_i)

One considers the correlation:

(2) $$\log X_i/A_i = -\alpha \log \log \mu K_R/A_i + \log a \quad (K_R = 1000)$$

μ is chosen to maximize the correlation coefficient R.

3. Determination of a and μ Corresponding to a Given Series of N Observations for a Given Value α^* of α

μ is chosen to minimize σ^2 with

(3) $$\sigma^2 = \sum_i (\theta_i - \theta_m)^2/N$$

(4) $$\theta_i = \log(X_i/A_i) + \alpha^* \log \log(\mu K_R/A_i) \quad (K_R = 1000)$$

(5) $$\theta_m = \left(\sum_i \theta_i\right)/N \quad (a = e^{\theta_m})$$

4. Determination of μ Corresponding to a Series of N Observations (A_i, X_i) for Given Values α^* and α^* of α and a

μ is chosen to minimize E with

$$(6) \qquad E = \sum_i (\log X_i - \log X_i^*)^2/N$$

$$(7) \qquad X_i^* = a^* A_i/(\log K/A_i)^{\alpha^*} \quad K = \mu K_R$$

5. Fittings

For all the considered data one verifies *a posteriori* that it is sufficient to consider only the component f_2 of f (T VI), i.e. relation (1) above of the generating function since we always find for the considered data

$$(8) \qquad A_i/\mu \geq A_{1R}$$

VIII. INVARIANT CARDINAL UTILITY MODEL DETERMINATION OF THE CARDINAL UTILITY FUNCTION FROM THE GENERATING FUNCTION[14]

1. Hypotheses

$$(1) \qquad (a) \qquad s(X) = 2s(A)$$

for

$$(2) \qquad X = A(2 + A/W') \quad \text{for} \quad A \leq A_1 \quad X \leq X_1$$

$$(3) \qquad X = \alpha A/(\log K/A)^\alpha \quad \text{for} \quad A \geq A_1 \quad X \geq X_1$$

$$(4) \qquad (b) \qquad s = m' \log(1 + X/W') \quad \text{for} \quad X \leq X_1$$

2. Determination of s for $X \geq X_{1R}$ for the Reference Subject

To any point $\hat{M}_1$

$$(5) \qquad \left(\begin{array}{l} u_1 = \log(1 + \hat{X}_1/W_R') \\ s_1 = m' u_1 \end{array} \right.$$

of the straight line (b) corresponds a series of points $\hat{M}_n$

$$(6) \qquad \left(\begin{array}{l} \hat{X}_n = a\hat{X}_{n-1} / (\log K/\hat{X}_{n-1})^\alpha \\ s_n = 2^{n-1} s_1 \end{array} \right.$$

Asymptote: $n - 1 = p$

(7) $s_p = M/2 \quad \text{for} \quad \hat{X}_p = K$

(8) $M = 1.9 \quad 2pm' \log(1 + \hat{X}_1/W'_R) = M/2 = 0.95$

where $\hat{X}_1$ corresponds to $\hat{X}_p = K$. The coefficient m' results from (8).

IX. INVARIANT CARDINAL UTILITY MODEL FUNDAMENTAL PROPERTIES OF THE CARDINAL UTILITY FUNCTION[15]

1. Invariance

(1) $s = s(X/U_0) = s(X_R/U_{0R})$

The function s is the same for every subject.

2. Log-linearity for Small Values of X

(2) $s = m'u' \quad \text{for} \quad X \leq X_1$

(3) $u' = \log(1 + X/W') = \log(1 + X/\mu W'_R)$

3. Approximative Log-linearity Over a Very Large Domain

(4) $s \sim mu \quad \text{for} \quad A_2 \leq X \leq X_2$

(5) $u = \log(1 + X/W) = \log(1 + X/\mu W_R)$

A_2 and X_2 are defined by equations (7) and (11) of T VI.

4. Interpretation of the Parameters W and W′ in the Framework of the Model

(6) $\boxed{U'_0 = W' = \mu W'_R}$

(7) $\boxed{U_0 = W = \mu W_R}$

5. Invariance Conditions

(8) $$\frac{W'}{W'_R} = \frac{W}{W_R} = \frac{K}{K_R} = \frac{A}{A_R} = \frac{X}{X_R} = \frac{A_1}{A_R} = \frac{X_1}{X_{1R}} = \frac{A_2}{A_{2R}} = \frac{X_2}{X_{2R}} = \mu$$

Characteristic Parameters

The parameters W'_R, W_R, A_{1R}, X_{1R}, A_{2R}, X_{2R} are determinate functions of α, a and K_R (T VI, 3–4).

X. INVARIANT CARDINAL UTILITY MODEL FOR $\alpha = \alpha^* = 1 \qquad A = A^* = 21.671$ INTRINSIC INVARIANT MODEL[16]

1. Generating Function

$$(1)\qquad \boxed{f_1 : X = A(2 + A/W') = A(2 + A/\mu W'_R) \text{ for } A \leq A_1 \;\; X \leq X_1}$$

$$(2)\qquad \boxed{f_2 : X = a^* A/\left(\log \frac{K}{A}\right)^{\alpha^*} = a^* A/\left(\log \frac{\mu K_R}{A}\right)^{\alpha^*} \text{ for } A \geq A_1 \;\; X \geq X_1}$$

2. Reference Subject

$$(3)\qquad \boxed{\mu = 1 \qquad K_R = 1000}$$

3. Characteristics Coefficients α^* and a^*

- The value $\alpha^* = 1$ corresponds to a mathematical property of the generating function ($\zeta\zeta' = \zeta + \zeta' = a^*/2$).
- For $a = a^* = 21.671$ the iteration process (3) of T VIII (determining the cardinal utility function from the generating function) leads to

$$(4)\qquad \hat{X}_8 = A_2 \quad \text{for} \quad \hat{X}_1 = A_1$$

4. Associated Parameters for $\alpha = \alpha^* = 1$; $a = a^* = 21.671$; $K = K_R = 1{,}000$; $M = 1.9$ (T VI, 3–4 and T VIII, 2)

$$\left(\begin{array}{l} \zeta' = 9.721 \\ A_{1R} = 0.0600 \\ X_{1R} = 0.1338 \\ W'_{1R} = 0.2617 \\ m' = 0.02636 \end{array}\right. \quad \left(\begin{array}{l} \zeta = 1.115 \\ A_{2R} = 328.0 \\ X_{2R} = 6377 \\ W_{2R} = 18.81 \\ m = 0.2390 \end{array}\right. \quad \left(\begin{array}{l} s_1 = m \log(1 + A_{2R}/W_R) = 0.6966 \\ \quad = 2^7 m' \log(1 + A_{1R}/W'_R) \\ s_2 = m \log(1 + X_{2R}/W_R) = 1.393 \\ \quad = 2 s_1 = 2^8 m' \log(1 + A_{1R}/W'_R) \\ (s_2 - s_1)/M = 36.6\% \end{array}\right.$$

The values of all these parameters are derived from the considered values of α, a, K and M (T VI, 3–4).

XI. FUNDAMENTAL PROPERTIES OF THE INTRINSIC INVARIANT MODEL[17]

$$\alpha = \alpha^* = 1 \qquad A = A^* = 21.671$$

1. Components of the Generating Function

Component f_1: it results from *Postulate IV* (T III)
Component f_2: its *mathematical form* results from the *empirical analysis* of the (1952) data (T VI).

2. Purely Mathematical Definition of α^* and a^*

The coefficients $\alpha = \alpha^*$, $a = a^*$ correspond to purely mathematical properties of the generating function and of the corresponding utility function (T X,3).

3. Approximative Log-linearity of the Cardinal Utility Function for $A_2 \leq X \leq X_2$

$$(1) \qquad s \sim mu \quad \text{for} \quad A_2 \leq X \leq X_2 \quad (s_1 \leq s \leq s_2)$$

$$(2) \qquad \left| \frac{s}{mu} - 1 \right| \leq 0.4\%$$

$$(3) \qquad u = \log(1 + X/W) = \log(1 + X/\mu W_R)$$

4. Interpretation of the Parameters W and W' in the Framework of the Intrinsic Invariant Model

$$(4) \qquad \boxed{U_0' = W' = \mu W_R'}$$

$$(5) \qquad \boxed{U_0 = W = \mu W_R}$$

Invariance Conditions

$$(6) \qquad \frac{K}{K_R} = \frac{W'}{W_R'} = \frac{W}{W_R} = \frac{A}{A_R} = \frac{X}{X_R} = \mu$$

$$(7) \qquad \frac{A_1}{A_{1R}} = \frac{X_1}{X_{1R}} = \frac{A_2}{A_{2R}} = \frac{X_2}{X_{2R}} = \mu$$

6. *Charts*

Generating function of the reference subject: Chart VIII.
Cardinal utility function reference subject: Chart IX.

XII. INTRINSIC INVARIANT MODEL EMPIRICAL VERIFICATIONS AND ILLUSTRATIVE RESULTS[18]

1. *Fittings*

The fitting depends only of *one parameter* μ for a given Group of subjects and N observations (T VII,4)

$$(1) \qquad e = \sqrt{E} \quad E = \Sigma(\log X_i - \log X_i^*)^2/N$$

2. *Empirical Data of the 1952 Experiment*

Group fittings:
Results: Charts XII and XIII as illustrations.

Group	I	II	III	IV	V	All
Number of subjects n	4	5	3	5	2	19
Number of observations N	4	4	4	4	3	
μ	7.2	1.5	0.24	0.14	0.084	
$e(\%)$	11.5	7.9	11.9	15.7	15.9	11.7

Individual fittings:
Value of e corresponding to relations (1) for the 19 subjects = 34.3%
Illustrative subjects: Charts XIV and XV.

3. *Empirical Data of the 1975 Experiment*

Group fittings:
Results: Charts XVII and XVIII as illustrations
Group E: $n = 5$; $N = 10$; $\mu = 1.03$; $e = 13\%$

Individual fittings:
Value of e corresponding to relations (1) for the six subjects of Group $E = 40.5\%$.

4. *Two Illustrative Subjects of the 1952 and 1975 Experiments*

Results: Charts XXI and XXII
Rabussier (1952) ($N = 3$) $\quad \mu = 0.077 \quad e = 4.1\%$

Anonymous I (1975) ($N = 10$) $\mu = 4.6$ $e = 8.4\%$.

5. Fittings

As a matter of fact one verifies *a posteriori* that all the fittings depend only of the component f_2 of the generating function (T VII,5).

XIII. INDICES OF PSYCHOLOGICAL INDETERMINATION

Answers X to the Questions of the Experiments

The answers were "yes" or "no" for different values of X for each value of A with the following mentions:

BH	much hesitation
H	hesitation
PAH	almost with no hesitation
AH	without hesitation

Index of Psychological Indetermination

Considering the values X_1 and X_2 separating the mentions AH or PAH from the mentions H or BH, and

$$(1) \qquad \delta s = \frac{ds}{du} \frac{\delta X}{U_0 + X} = \frac{ds}{du} \delta u$$

$$(2) \qquad u = \log(1 + X/U_0) \quad \delta u = \log(1 + X_2/U_0) - \log(1 + X_1/U_0)$$

the index of psychological indetermination is taken as

$$(3) \qquad \pi = \frac{\delta s}{M} = \frac{1}{2M} \frac{ds}{du} [\log(U_0 + X_2) - \log(U_0 + X_1)]$$

$$(4) \qquad \frac{ds}{du} = \frac{ds}{du}(U_0 + X) \quad M = 1.9$$

3. Results for the 1952 Experiment

For all the 14 subjects j of the 1952 experiment who have effectively given indications of § 1 above the values of π_{ij} for the different Questions i are remarkably consistent and of the same order of magnitude: 7%.

4. Estimate of the Standard Value σ_p of the Psychological Errors on X

$$\sigma_p = \frac{1}{1.96} \text{ average of } \left|\frac{1}{2} \log \frac{X_2}{X_1}\right| = 36.6\%$$

This value corresponds to the 14 subjects considered.
The calculation of σ_p is totally independent of any hypothesis on the cardinal utility function.

REFERENCES

Allais, Maurice (1952a) 'Fondements d'une théorie positive des choix comportant un risque et critique des postulats et axiomes de l'Ecole Américaine' (Foundations of a positive theory of choice involving risk, and a criticism of the postulates and axioms of the American School), Econométrie, Colloques Internationaux du Centre National de la Recherche Scientifique, Vol. XL, Paris, 1953, pp. 257–332. (See also pp. 34–35, 37–39, 40, 47–48, 151–163, 194–197 and 245–247.)
This memoir was republished in Vol. 144 of the *Annales des Mines*, special issue, 1955, and again as a separate volume, under the same title by the Imprimerie Nationale 1955.

Allais, Maurice (1952b) 'Le comportement de l'homme rationnel devant le risque: Critique des postulats et axiomes de l'Ecole Américaine' (The behavior of rational man facing risk: Criticism of the postulates and axioms of the American School) in *Econometrica*, **21** (4), October 1953, pp. 503–546 (summarised version of the 1952 Memoir).

Allais, Maurice (1952c) 'La psychologie de l'homme rationnel devant le risque – La théorie et l'expérience', *Journal de la Société de Statistique de Paris*, January–March 1953, pp. 47–73.

Allais, Maurice (1976) *The Foundations of a Positive Theory of Choice Involving Risk and a Criticism of the Postulates and Axioms of the American School*, English translation of the (1952) Memoir, in Allais and Hagen, 1979, pp. 27–145.

Allais, Maurice (1977) 'The so-called Allais' paradox and rational decisions under uncertainty', in Allais and Hagen, 1979, pp. 437–699.

Allais, Maurice (1983) 'The foundations of the theory of utility and risk; some central points of the discussions at the Oslo Conference', in Hagen and Wenstop (Eds.), *Progress in Decision Theory*, Reidel, 1984, pp. 3–131.

Allais, Maurice (1984), 'The cardinal utility and its determination, hypothesis, methods and empirical results', *Theory and Decision*, forthcoming.

Allais, Maurice and Hagen, Ole (1979) *Expected Utility Hypotheses and the Allais' Paradox; Contemporary Discussions and Rational Decisions under Uncertainty with Allais' Rejoinder*, Reidel, Dordrecht, 1979, p. 715.

Pieron, Henri (1927) *Psychologie Expérimentale*, A. Colin, Paris, p. 220.

MAURICE ALLAIS

CARDINAL UTILITY

History, Empirical Findings, and Applications. An Overview

December 29, 1993

> Many will object, no doubt, that the notions which we treat . . . are incapable of any measurement . . .
>
> The popular opinions . . . tend to deter any man from attempting tasks which, however difficult, ought, some day, to be achieved . . . If we trace the history of other sciences, we gather no lessons of discouragement. In the case of almost everything which is now exactly measured, we can go back to the age when the vaguest notions prevailed . . .
>
> It seems strange indeed that economists have not bestowed more minute attention on a subject which doubtless furnishes the true key to the problem of economics . . .
>
> It is very curious that in this subject, which reaches to the very foundations of political economy, we owe more to early than later writers . . .
>
> Having no means of ascertaining numerically the variation of utility, Bernoulli had to make assumptions of an arbitrary kind, and was then able to obtain reasonable answers to many important questions. – W. STANLEY JEVONS*

The purpose of this paper is to present briefly an overview on the concept of cardinal utility in its relations with the literature since the beginning of the 18th century (Part I); an estimate of the cardinal utility function for its negative values, thus completing the estimate of this function for its positive values given in my 1984 Venice paper (Part II); and finally different applications on the one hand to the theory of choices in the presence of risk and on the other hand to the wealth transfer problem, applications which imply the knowledge of the negative as well as the positive values of the cardinal utility function.

The reader will find all necessary justifications and appropriate comments in my forthcoming paper 'Cardinal utility' (Allais, 1988 b).

For sake of brevity the main mathematical formulas and numerical results are presented below in tables and charts.

M. Allais and O. Hagen (eds.), Cardinalism, 65–103.

1. CARDINAL UTILITY AND THE LITERATURE

1.1. The Utility Concept as a Cardinal Utility

1.1.2. The Literary Theories

Since the beginning of the 18 century at least the economic literature has been dominated by the utility concept, but generally, in literary theories, in a rather vague and confused manner, using words like 'value', 'usefulness', 'satisfaction', 'pleasure and pain', 'happiness', etc.

In fact, its meaning has shifted continually over time, but in any case the term was used in a *cardinal sense* although the word 'cardinal' was not used.

For the utilitarians like Bentham (1789) the possibility of interpersonal comparisons was assumed, the object of the social action being to promote *the greatest happiness of the greatest number*.

1.1.3. The Concept of Cardinal Utility as a Foundation of the Theories of General Economic Equilibrium

The concept of cardinal utility, associated with the principle of decreasing marginal cardinal utility, was extensively used by Gossen (1854), Jevons (1871), Menger (1871) and Walras (1874–1877), and their immediate successors, especially Edgeworth (1881) and Irving Fisher (1892), to found the general economic equilibrium theory.

1.1.4. The Welfare Function Defined as the Sum of Cardinal Utilities

For the utilitarians the welfare function to be maximized is defined as the sum of cardinal utilities.

In his *Mathematical Psychics* (1881),[1] following the formulation of Fechner (1860), Edgeworth defines cardinal utility by the principle that *just-perceivable increments of pleasure, of all pleasures for all persons, are equatable* (p. 60) and he considers the *Economical* and the *Utilitarian* calculus.

Economical calculus. The state of equilibrium may be considered as such the utility of any one contractor must be a maximum *relative* to the utilities of the other contractors being constant, or not decreasing (p. 27). This definition of a *relative maximum* is identical to the definition of maximum efficiency later used by Pareto (Allais, 1968, p. 404).

Utilitarian calculus. An absolute maximum corresponds to the maximum of the sum of all cardinal utilities, *the greatest possible* sum of universal happiness (p. 11).

Without income and wealth transfers such an absolute maximum cannot evidently be realized by the general economic equilibrium of a market economy (§ 3.2 below). This question has been discussed by Launhardt (1885), Irving Fisher (1892), and Wicksell (1901).

Edgeworth (1897, 1899, 1910, 1919 and 1920) applied the concept of cardinal utility and the utilitarian calculus to the taxation problem.

1.1.5. Two Basic Problems

In all the above literature two basic problems are involved: Can utility be measured cardinally or simply ordinally? And is it possible to make interpersonal comparisons of utility?

1.2. Attempts to Measure Cardinal Utility

The Daniel Bernoulli Log-linear Formulation of Cardinal Utility

The concept of psychological value (or cardinal utility) was introduced by Daniel Bernoulli in 1738 to explain the *St Petersburg Paradox.* Arguing that incremental utility is inversely proportional to current fortune (and directly proportional to the increment in fortune), Bernoulli concluded that utility is a linear function of the logarithm of the fortune monetary value. That was really *a breakthrough* not only in the theory of risky choices, but also in psychology.

A century *later* Ernest Heinrich Weber (1834) stated that *equal relative increments stimuli are proportional to equal increments of senseation.* This law led to the Fechner law (1860), in fact the Weber–Fechner law: The magnitude of the sensation is proportional to the logarithm of the fundamental stimulus value.

Later this log-linear formulation was revised and completed by the Weber–Fechner successors for the small and large values of the stimulus (Allais, 1943, pp. 163–165, and 1984, § 4.3 and Chart III, pp. 91 and 119).

The Bernoulli formulation was used again by Laplace (1812 and 1814) in his theory of moral expectations, and in most treatises on probability by the 19 century.

1.2.2. Computation of Cardinal Utility from the Analysis of Demand Laws

Many attempts have been made to compute cardinal utility from an analysis of demand laws. They generally could not succeed. The reason is because the equations of general economic equilibrium only involve ordinal preference indexes (Allais, 1943, pp. 158–159, nos. 4 and 5, and 1951, Annexe III, § 75).

Fisher (1927) developed a method of computing the marginal utility as a function of the income, under the assumption that the goods consumed may be classified into independent groups. It boils down to admitting the hypothesis

$$(1) \qquad u(A, B, \ldots, C) = \psi_A(A) + \psi_B(B) + \ldots + \psi_C(C)$$

Frisch (1926 and 1932) assumes that the cardinal utility $u = u(A, B, \ldots, C)$ is a function $u = u(R, P)$ where R stands for nominal income and P for the price level. René Roy (1942, 1944, 1948 and 1949) worked on a similar hypothesis. But this hypothesis is only valid under the Allais condition

$$(2) \qquad A\,\frac{\partial u}{\partial A} + B\,\frac{\partial u}{\partial B} + \ldots + C\,\frac{\partial u}{\partial C} = K$$

where K is a constant.

A thorough critical analysis of the Frisch–Roy formulation is given in Allais (1988).

1.2.3. The Theory of Games

In their *Theory of Games* von Neumann and Morgenstern asserted that it is possible to determine cardinal utility by the observation of the choices made among random prospects. But this assertion was completely false since it confused two distinct effects, the curvature of cardinal utility and the preference for risk or security (Allais, 1952 and 1977).

1.3. The Progressive Abandonment of the Concept of Cardinal Utility in the Contemporary Literature

1.3.1. The Pareto Theory

Departing from his predecessors, Pareto founded his theory of general economic equilibrium and economic efficiency on the only consideration of ordinal preference indexes. This was really a major contribution to economic theory.

By he did not make the mistake of discarding cardinal utility from economic theory. On the contrary, he made it a major part of his *Treatise on Sociology*. As he wrote 'the public authorities have necessarily to compare the different utilities' (Allais, 1968, p. 405).

1.3.2. The Progressive Abandonment of the Concept of Cardinal Utility

Since Pareto the concept of cardinal utility has been progressively discarded, and for different reasons:

(1) the possibility to elaborate a valid theory of general economic equilibrium and maximum efficiency using only ordinal utilities, as Pareto showed;

(2) the failures of the attempts to measure cardinal utility (§ 1.2 above);
(3) a strong underestimation of the role of cardinal utility to explain government policies, and especially fiscal policy;
(4) and last, but not least, the incapacity of the neo-Bernoullians to maintain the neo-Bernoullian formulation (i.e. the so-called 'expected utility theory') once the very existence of cardinal utility is admitted (Allais, 1952 and 1977).

This refusal of cardinal utility attained its climax with Savage's statement that the very existence of cardinal utility is nothing else but a myth (Allais, 1984, p. 34).

Today, given the positions taken by some eminent economists, which, with some rare exceptions, are as spectacular as they are dogmatic, an intolerant orthodoxy has banished, almost totally, cardinal utility, and, in general, any psychological introspection from economic science.

1.3.3. The Necessity of Cardinal Utility for Economic Theory

Whatever the objections against the use of cardinal utility, this concept is essential for any general theory of society, because the distribution of income within a given family, and all political decisions concerning, *directly or indirectly*, the distribution of incomes and the people's welfare, *do imply interpersonal comparisons.* It is also essential for any valid theory of choices involving risk.

Indeed what is the real validity of the dogma of the interpersonal noncomparability of cardinal utilities? In fact it is really difficult to deny the greater psychological value of a dollar for a poor man than for a rich man. As Jevons said "It is almost self-evident that the utility of money decreases as a person's total wealth increases" (Allais, 1984).

1.4. My Own Works

As regards cardinal utility, my works[2] rest on five strong convictions:

(1) It is possible to elaborate a complete theory of general economic equilibrium and maximum efficiency without any use of the concept of cardinal utility.
(2) The discussion of the properties of the fields of choices and of the laws of demand is also possible without any use of cardinal utility, but this discussion is *much easier, and much more psychologically and economically significant*, if we consider this concept.
(3) The consideration of cardinal utility and interpersonal utility comparisons is absolutely necessary and really irreplaceable for any realistic theory

    (a) of the distribution of income among the members of a family.

(b) of the government policies as regards the distribution of incomes and the fiscal policy, and generally the public choices,
(c) of choices involving risk.

(4) It is possible to determine cardinal utility by appropriate questions relating to the intensity of preferences, and the cardinal utility function of any subject can be represented, at least as a first approximation, by a single invariant function in space and over time of the ratio X/U_0, U_0 being the psychological capital *he is accustomed to*, and X a *virtual* change of this capital, considered at the time at which he is taking a decision concerning the future.

(5) The data of our introspection are as real as our "revealed preferences" since, before being taken, any decision concerning the future cardinally takes into account all possible virtual changes of our psychological capital we are accustomed to, and not only the particular one which is finally revealed by the decision we take.

2. THE CARDINAL UTILITY FUNCTION

THEORETICAL ANALYSIS AND EMPIRICAL FINDINGS

In my 1984 Venice Memoir the cardinal utility function was deduced from the answers to the Questions of the *1952 Questionnaire*. However, only designed in relation to the examples discussed during the 1952 Conference which basically covered the psychological assessment of gains of positive values, this Questionnaire unfortunately does not comprise any set of questions from which the cardinal utility can be estimated for negative variations X of the psychological capital U_0. The purpose of the present Memoir is to fill this gap.

2.1. Invariant Cardinal Utility Function Corresponding to Positive Virtual Variations of Psychological Capital

The determination of the cardinal utility function

$$(3) \qquad u = u(1 + X/U_0) = u(1 + y) \text{ for } y = X/U_0 \geq 0$$

is derived from the consideration of equivalent psychological intervals $(U_0, U_0 + A)$ and $(U_0 + A,\ U_0 + X)$, U_0 representing the psychological capital of the considered subject (Allais, 1984, Table I, p. 93).

The fundamental assumption is that the function $u(1 + y)$ is the same for every subject (invariance postulate).

The gauging of the cardinal utility function (Table I and Chart I) is determined by the two conditions:[3, 4]

(4) $u(y=0)=0 \qquad u(y=+\infty)=1$

These conditions are the same for every subject and consequently all cardinal utility functions are comparable.

2.2. *Determination of the Negative Values $u^*(y^*)$ of the Invariant Utility Function from its Positive Values $u(y)$*

To determine the negative values $u^*(y^*)$ of the invariant cardinal utility function from its positive values $u(y)$ one considers the equivalent psychological intervals $[(1-k)\,U_0, U_0]$, and $[U_0, (1+K)\,U_0]$, and the generating function $K(k)$.

The function $u^*(y^*)$ is determined by the condition:

(5) $u^*(-k) = -u(K)$

The function $u^*(y^*)$ is assumed to be invariant (invariance postulate).

The two functions $u(y)$ and $u^*(y^*)$ being assumed to be invariant, the generating function $K(k)$ is also invariant.

The interpolation formulas used for the derivation of the functions $K(k)$ and $u^*(y^*)$ are given in Table II.

2.3. *Analysis of Cardinal Utility for its Negative Values, 1985–1987*

Table III presents the estimates of the generating function $K(k)$ nd the cardinal utility function $u^*(y^*)$ I deduced at different times from my own introspection and theoretical considerations from October 1985 to September 1987 *before* the analysis of the answers to the *1987 New Questionnaire*.

2.4. *The August 1987 New Questionnaire*

Table IV A presents the August 1987 new Questionnaire sent in September–October 1987 to a few people in its French version. As an illustration, the answers of Bertrand Munier to Questions III ($k = 0.10$) are given in Table IV B.

2.5. *General Characteristics of the Answers to the 1987 New Questionnaire*

Table V A presents the 18 sets of answers to the 1987 new Questionnaire. The answers can be distributed in two very different classes. The first class includes (Groups I, II and III. Allowing for the inevitable psychological errors, the answers present strong similarities. Group IV is indeed very different. It is characterized by very great values of K, at least for $k \geq 0.25$.

It seems that the very marked differences of the Group IV relative to Groups I, II and III arise from the fact that the subjects of Group IV realize perfectly the consequences of possible losses (especially in the case of an important indebtness) whereas they are not very able, if not absolutely unable, to imagine what would be the changes in their life resulting from a considerable increase of their assets (see Allais 1988a).

As regards Groups I, II and III, the comparison of the estimated standard deviations σ', σ, and σ_1 of log K, deduced from my own estimates (§ 2.3 above), from the answers K of the subjects, and from their comments is presented in Table V B. These estimates, obtained in very different ways, show a remarkable coherence.[5] The values of σ as functions of k are represented on Chart V A.

We can deduce from these results that the errors on the generating function $K(k)$ are certainly small relative to the psychological errors, and that the *invariance hypothesis* (§ 2.1 above) is justified, at least as a first approximation.

On Chart V B the geometric averages $\bar{K}$ of the observed K of Table V B corresponding to the five considered values of k are represented relative to my last estimate of the generating function of September IV, 1987, deduced from my own introspection and theoretical considerations (Table III).

If we consider that the estimate of the generating function of September 4, 1987, was made *before* the 1987 experiment and the April–May 1988 analysis of the answers to the *1987 New Questionnaire* the agreement shown by Chart V B is certainly very remarkable.

2.6. Estimate of the Generating Function $K(k)$ for $0 \leq k \leq 0.9$ from the 1987 Experiment

Chart VI A represents the fitting of 53 pairs of values (K, k) to the interpolation formula of Tabel II and the 95% confidence belt limits.

Charts VI B and VI C represent respectively the geometric averages K of K for the whole set of 13 subjects of Groups I, II and III, and for the three Groups I, II and III considered separately.

Although the psychological errors are very great, a striking underlying regularity appears as soon as averages are considered.

Indeed Charts VI B and VI C show that the invariance hypothesis is completely justified, at least as a first approximation.

The estimates of the numerical values of the generating function $K(k)$ are given in Table VI.

2.7. Estimate of the Cardinal Utility Function $u^*(y^*)$ for $-0.9 \leq y^* \leq 0$ from the 1987 Experiment

Chart VII A represents the fitting of the 5 pairs of values (k, u^*) to the interpolation formula of Table II. Chart VII A shows the existence of an underlying regularity.

The corresponding values of the cardinal utility function $u^*(y^*)$ are presented in Table VII.

Charts VII B and VII C represent the cardinal utility function using linear and semi-loglinear scales on different intervals.

Considering Tables I and VII, and Charts I, VII A, VII B and VII C, the cardinal utility function $u^*(y^*)$ for the negative values of y^* presents six main features:

(a) The cardinal utility function is decreasing very rapidly as y^* decreases, showing that the subjects are much more sensitive to decreases than to increases of their psychological capital.

(b) The marginal cardinal utility du/dy is always decreasing for all values, positive or negative, of y except in the interval $-0.19 < y < 0$.[6]

(c) The *invariance hypothesis* of the function $u^*(y^*)$ appears as completely justified by the invariance of the generating function (§ 2.6 above), at least as a first approximation.

(d) Chart VII C gives a representation of the cardinal utility function in the whole field

$$(6) \qquad 0.065 \leq 1 + y^* \leq 1 \leq 1 + y \leq 15{,}000$$

under the two gauging conditions

$$(7) \qquad u(y^* = y = 0) = 0 \qquad u(y = +\infty) = 1$$

The functions $u^*(y^*)$ and $u(y)$ are the same for every subject with

$$(8) \qquad y^* = X^*/U_0 \quad y = X/U_0 \quad (X^* \leq 0;\ X \geq 0)$$

So long as new data do not invalidate it, the general shape of the cardinal utility function *in the whole interval* $-0.90 \leq y^* \leq 0 \leq y \leq 15{,}000$ *corresponding to empirical data* must be considered as corresponding to the real nature of things. Indeed this shape will be modified in the future, but my firm belief is that the orders of magnitude will not change very much.

(e) To correctly interpret the effective meaning of these results, it must be recalled that the psychological capital U_0 includes at least some part of the present value of future incomes and that the X and X^* represent *virtual* variations of the psychological capital to which the considered subject is accustomed.

(f) Chart VII C shows that the *Bernoullian loglinear hypothesis*

$$(1) \qquad u = \omega \log(1 + y) \quad y = x/U_0 \quad -1 < y < +\infty$$

where ω is an arbitrary constant is absolutely incompatible with the empirical data.

Indeed we may take approximately

$$(10) \qquad u = r \log(1+y) \text{ with } r = 0.9971 \text{ for } |y| \le 1$$

$$(11) \qquad u = m \log(1+y) \text{ with } m = 0.1258 \text{ for } 17.4 \le y \le 339$$

(Chart I above). But these two approximations are only valid in very limited domains. We have also

$$u \sim \lambda \log(1+y^*) \text{ with } \lambda = 0.365 \text{ for } 0.01 \le 1+y^* \le 0.065$$

(Table II and Chart VII C). But this approximation results only in a likely hypothesis.

3. APPLICATIONS OF THE CARDINAL UTILITY FUNCTION

3.1. Application to the Theory of Choices Involving Risk – Illustration by the (U, θ) Model

In the framework of the (U, θ) Model the knowledge of the cardinal utility function in its whole domain of variation allows to be *illustrated qualitatively and quantitatively* the problem of the purchase at the same time by the same subject, insurance policies and lottery tickets (see Table VIII below).[7]

3.2. Application to the Wealth Transfer Problem

(1) The problem of wealth transfer is a very old and indeed fundamental problem.

In considerating cardinal utility, it is absolutely essential to regard all the questions relating to the distribution of income, especially the fiscal policy.[8]

The question is generally no longer studied in the contemporary literature since it implies interpersonal cardinal utility comparisons.

(2) Two different problems must be considered:

(a) The "absolute optimum of welfare" for a given real gross national product, assuming that the efficiency of the economy is independent of the income distribution.
(b) The distribution of an increase of real gross national product which would secure a maximum increase of the welfare function.

(3) As regards the first problem (a), its solution depends on the respective shape of cardinal utility for positive or negative increases of individual psychological capital, and it is absolutely different in the case of a Bernoullian log-linear formulation which would imply an equality of the wealth distribution and thus a much greater equality (Table IX, § 1e, below).

Chart IX represents the lines of maximal possibilities in the cardinal utilities space for different values concerning the increase of the global consumption.[9]

As regards the second problem (b), the solution is totally independent of the particular expression of the cardinal utility function $u(1 + x/U_0)$ (Table IX, § 2, below).

(4) Indeed it is certain that a greater equality in wealth distribution would lead ultimately to a reduction in the production total amount to be distributed. Thus there is some trade-off to be found by the political power.

(5) In any case I must underline that for any application of the cardinal utility formulation given above (Part II) it must be recalled that:

(a) U_0 is the psychological capital, one is accustomed to.
(b) The variation ΔU_0 of U_0 are virtual changes as they are felt.

(6) Finally, the concept of "happiness" is absolutely different from the concept of cardinal utility, and, as far as we can judge, and from an economical point of view, it is related to the changes over time of cardinal utility, i.e. to the changes of psychological capital we are accustomed to.

NOTES

* *The Theory of Political Economy* (1871), pp. 81, 105, 179, and 183.

[1] A book of genius from many points of view but which, if published today, would be open to mockery and would certainly discredit his author (Allais, 1974).

[2] See in particular: Allais (1943), (1951), (1961), (1968 a), (1981), (1986 b), (1987), (1987 a), (1988 b), and (1988 c).

[3] For sake of brevity I design the cardinal utility function by $u(y)$ as well as $u(1 + y)$. No confusion is possible.

[4] In Appendix C of Allais (1977), and for lack of space I have considered only the log-linear approximation of the cardinal utility function (§ C.7 and C.21).

[5] In the calculations we have considered only the finite values of the answers (see Allais, 1988 b).

[6] For the analysis of increasing marginal cardinal utility see Allais (1968 a), pp. 135–137.

[7] To explain this possibility Friedman and Savage (1948) admitted a cardinal utility function which is nothing but extravagant.

[8] See for instance Edgeworth (1897), (1899), (1910), (1919) and (1920).

[9] On these lines see Allais (1943), pp. 641–643. The paternity of this concept has been wrongly attributed to Paul Samuelson. On this point see Allais (1986 b), pp. 165–166, note 5.

TABLE I – INVARIANT CARDINAL UTILITY FUNCTION. TABLE OF NUMERICAL VALUES[A]

$u = u(1 + X/U_0)$ U_0 = psychological capital
$u(1) = 0$ $u(\infty) = 1$ $0 \leq X/U_0 \leq 15,000$[b]

$1 + \frac{X}{U_0}$	u
10	0.2963
10.5	0.3018
11	0.3070
12	0.3169
13	0.3260
14	0.3345
15	0.3425
16	0.3500
17	0.3570
18	0.3638
19	0.3701
20	0.3762
23	0.3930
25	0.4030
30	0.4254
35	0.4446
40	0.4614
45	0.4763
50	0.4897
60	0.5131
70	0.5331
80	0.5504
90	0.5657
100	0.5794
110	0.5918
120	0.6030
130	0.6134
140	0.6229
150	0.6318
170	0.6478
180	0.6550
190	0.6619
200	0.6684
230	0.6858
250	0.6961
270	0.7055
300	0.7183
340	0.7332
350	0.7366
400	0.7521
450	0.7654

$1 + \frac{X}{U_0}$	u
500	0.7771
600	0.7967
700	0.8126
800	0.8258
900	0.8370
1,000	0.8467
1,100	0.8551
1,200	0.8626
1,300	0.8692
1,400	0.8752
1,500	0.8806
1,600	0.8855
1,700	0.8900
1,800	0.8941
1,900	0.8978
2,000	0.9013
2,300	0.9104
2,500	0.9155
2,700	0.9200
3,000	0.9259
3,500	0.9338
4,000	0.9401
4,500	0.9452
5,000	0.9495
6,000	0.9561
7,000	0.9610
8,000	0.9649
9,000	0.9680
10,000	0.9705
11,000	0.9726
12,000	0.9744
13,000	0.9759
15,000	0.9784
17,000	0.9803
20,000	0.9825
25,000	0.9850
30,000	0.9868
40,000	0.9890
50,000	0.9903
60,000	0.9912
70,000	0.9918
100,000	0.9930
∞	1.0000

[a] Allais (1986 a), § 1.2, pp. 237–239; § A.2 pp. 263–264; Tables B1 and B2, pp. 277–278. The interpolation formulas are given on Table B2 for $M = 1.9$ (id., p. 278).
[b] Empirical validity domain (Allais, 1984 a, p. 113).

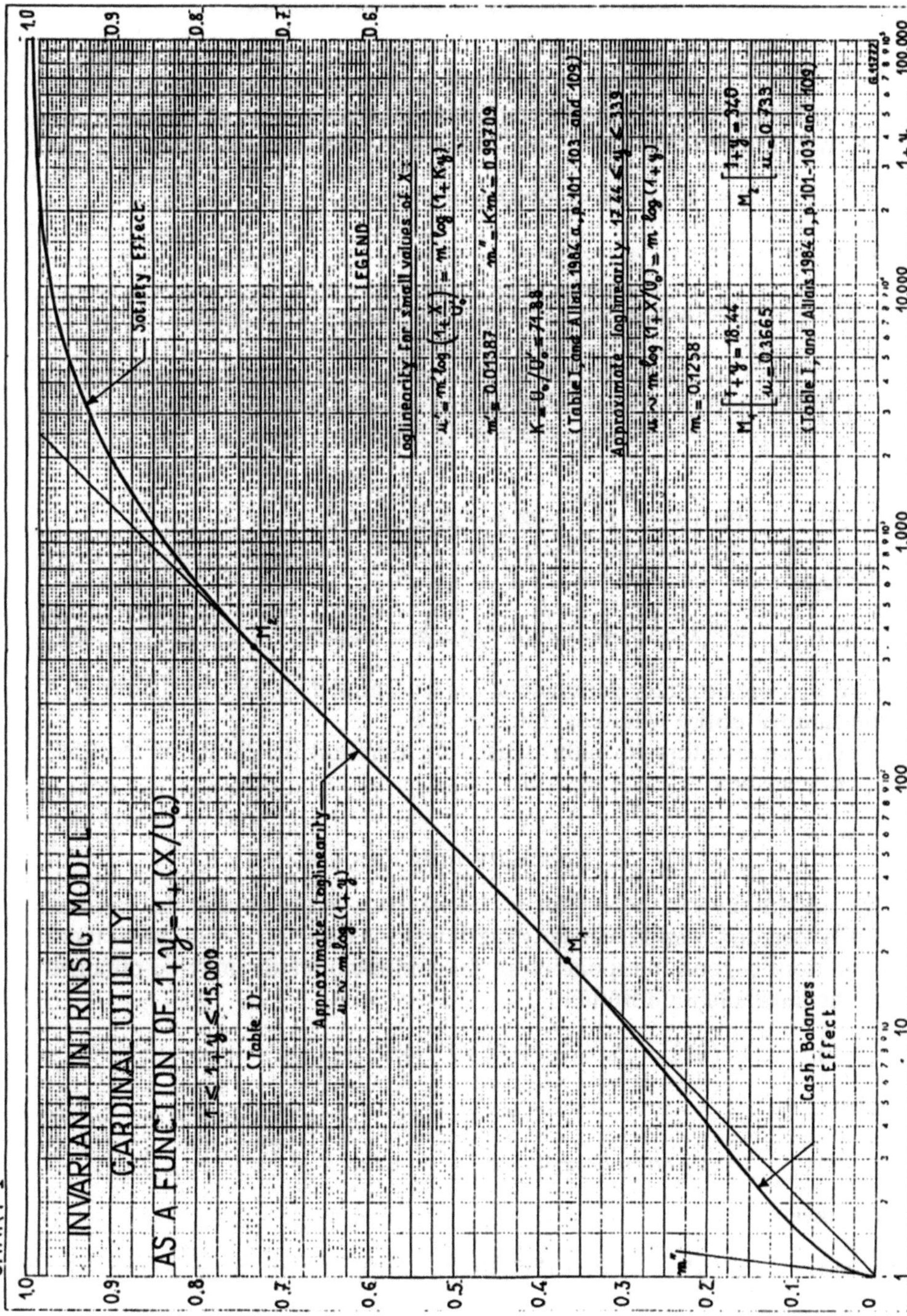
CHART I
INVARIANT INTRINSIG MODEL
CARDINAL UTILITY
AS A FUNCTION OF 1 + y = 1 + (X/U₀)
1 ≤ 1 + y ≤ 15,000
(Table I)
Satiety Effect
Approximate loglinearity
u ~ m log (1 + y)
Cash Balances Effect
LEGEND
Loglinearity for small values of X
u' = m' log (1 + X/U'₀) = m' log (1 + Ky)
m' = 0.01387
m'' = Km' = 0.99709
K = U₀/U'₀ = 71.88
(Table I, and Allais 1984 a, p.101-103 and 109)
Approximate loglinearity 17.44 ≤ y ≤ 339
u ~ m log (1 + X/U₀) = m log (1 + y)
m = 0.1258
1 + y = 18.44
u = 0.3665
1 + y = 340
u = 0.733
(Table I, and Allais 1984 a, p.101-103 and 109)
1 + y
1
10
100
1,000
10,000
100,000
0
0.1
0.2
0.3
0.4
0.5
0.6
0.7
0.8
0.9
1.0

Chart I.

TABLE II – INTERPOLATION FORMULAS

1. Generating Function

A good interpolation of the empirical results may be obtained by the interpolation formula

$$(1) \qquad \log(K^* + q) = \log(K_1 + q) - \alpha\omega - \beta\omega^2 - \gamma\omega^3$$

with

$$(2) \qquad \omega = \log\left(\frac{l+p}{k+p} - 1\right) \quad \omega_0 = \log\frac{l}{p} \quad k \leq l$$

$$(3) \qquad q = \frac{plr}{(\alpha + 2\beta\omega_0 + 3\gamma\omega_0^2)\,(l+p)}$$

$$(4) \qquad \log\left(1 + \frac{K_1}{q}\right) = \alpha\omega_0 + \beta\omega_0^2 + \gamma\omega_0^3$$

We have

$$(5) \qquad K^*(k=0) = 0 \quad \mathrm{d}K^*/\mathrm{d}k(k=0) = r \quad K^*(k=l) = +\infty$$

p, α, β, γ are arbitrary parameters; l is determined by the consideration of the cardinal utility values as function of k.

The same fitting formula is used to represent the limits of the 95% confidence belt.

2. Cardinal Utility Function

We should have $u^* = -1$ for $y^* = -l$. It is assumed that the cardinal utility function is approximately log-linear for $1 + y^* < 1 - l$. Under these conditions a good interpolation of the empirical results may be obtained by the interpolation formula

$$(6) \qquad u^*(y^*) = (\lambda + (r - \lambda)\, e^{z\theta(z)})\, z$$

with

$$(7) \qquad \theta(z) = a + bz + cz^2 + dz^3 + ez^4 \quad z = \log(1 + y^*)$$

We have

$$(8) \qquad u^*(y^* = 0) = 0 \;\; \mathrm{d}u^*/\mathrm{d}y^*(y^* = 0) = r \;\; u^*(y^* = -l) = -1$$

$$u^*(y^*) \sim \lambda z \;\text{ for }\; y^* \sim -1 \quad u^*(y^* = -1) = -M^* = -\infty$$

TABLE III

Three significant estimates of the generating function $K(k)$ before the October 1987 experiment values of K

k	A. November 12, 1986			B. August 6, 1987 (New Questionnaire)			C. September 4, 1987		
	$M^a = 1$		$l = 1$	$M^a = 1$		$l = 1$	$M^a = +\infty$		$l = 0.9$
(1)	(2)	(3)	(4)	(5)	(6)	(7)	(8)	(9)	(10)
0.10	0.30	0.35	0.40	0.11	0.31	0.60	0.18	0.31	0.55
0.25	1.5	2	2.7	0.33	1.85	8	1.10	2	4.5
0.50	5.5	9	15	1	10.5	100	3.10	15	74
0.75	25	45	80	3	43.8	400	25	155	980
0.90	400	700	1200	9	127	3000	∞	∞	∞
1	$+\infty$	$+\infty$	$+\infty$	$+\infty$	$+\infty$	$+\infty$	-	-	-

Notes:
$M^a = u^a(y^a = -1) \quad u^a(y^a = -l) = -1$

Estimate A: col. (3): psychological estimates; col. (2) and (4): extreme possible psychological values.

Estimate B: col. (6) corresponds to the estimate $u^a = (u_l^a + u_d^a)/2$ of the cardinal utility function $u^a(y^a)$: u_l^a corresponds to the log-linear correspondence $\log(1 + K) = -\log(1 - k)$; u_d^a is defined by $u_d^a = ry^a$. col. (5) and (7): correspond to the extreme values of K considered in the *1987 New Questionnaire.*

Estimate C: col. (9): estimate of the cardinal utility function $u^a(y^a)$ obtained from psychological estimates of the generating function $K(k)$ for $-y^a = k \leq 0.5$, and an approximate log-linear hypothesis of the cardinal utility function $u^a(y^a)$ for $y \leq -0.9$. col. (8) and (10): 95% confidence belt limits of the fitting value (9).

Comment: It is impossible to describe here the long process of successive inductions and deductions which finally led me to the estimates of the generating function $K(k)$ and the cardinal utility function $u^a y^a)$ of Tables VI and VII (see Allais, 1988b). But it is certainly interesting and useful to present on this Table three *particularly* significant estimates I considered in November 1986, August 1987, and September 1987. They display the importance of my psychological errors in estimating my *generating function* $K(k)$ and my *cardinal utility function* $u^a(y^a)$ for its negative values (see Table V B below).

TABLE IV A – CARDINAL UTILITY
THE AUGUST 1987 NEW QUESTIONNAIRE

(1) The purpose of the *New Questionnaire* is to determine the cardinal utility $u(X)$ for the negative values of X from the knowledge of the cardinal utility for the positive values of X as has been determined in my preceding works (Table I above).

(2) The aim of the questions is to determine the generating function $K(k)$ corresponding to intervals of psychologically equal value $(-kC, 0)$ and $(0, KC)$.

The assets' global value C of a subject corresponds to the sum of the global value of all his property plus the global value of *all his future incomes and pensions, as he anticipates them to be.*

Five values of k are considered: 0.1; 0.25; 0.5; 0.75; 0.90.

(3) For each answer, the subject should indicate the intensity of his answers:

BH : Much Hesitation
H : Hesitation
PAH : Almost Without Hesitation
AH : Without Hesitation

The purpose of this indication is to assess the firmness of the conviction with which the choice is made between "yes" and "no", *after the subject has fully perceived the meaning of the question.*

This information is essential for the appreciation of the psychological errors (see Allais, 1977, p. 616; and Allais, 1984a, § 3.4, p. 89, and Table XIII, p. 105).

(4) As an illustration we may consider Questions III ($k = 0.10$) and Bertrand Munier's answers as indicated on Table IV B.

For the processing of the analysis we have taken $K(k = 0.10) = 0.45$ for Munier (see Table V A).

TABLE IV B – QUESTIONS III ($K = 0.10$)
(REPRODUCTION OF THE QUESTIONNAIRE)
MUNIER'S ANSWERS

Case A

Assume that you are responsible for an accident which caused damage only to property. As a result, you are sentenced to compensate for loss sustained, up to a fraction $k = 10\%$ of your assets' global value C^1, that is:

$$kC = C/10 = \text{ dollars }^1$$

Case B

Assume now that your lawyer told you yesterday that you would receive a legacy equal to K times your assets' global value C, and that he tells you today that he had mistaken you for someone else, and that you actually inherit nothing at all.

You would again feel disgruntled.

Questions

Would you be more disgruntled in case (A) than in case (B) for the following values of K:

K (1)	KC^1 (2)	Answer (3)	Intensity of your answer (4)
0.1		Yes	AH
0.2		Yes	AH
0.3		Yes	PAH
0.4		Yes	H
0.5		No	BH
0.6		No	H

Indicate the approximate value of K for which your answer changes.

$K =$

Munier's answer: "I am not able to answer".

[1] To facilitate your answer you should compute this figure, but *it is not necessary to join it to your answer.*

TABLE V-A

Answers to the 1987 new questionaire values of K

Subjects / k	GROUP I ($n = 4$) 1	2	3	4	GROUP II ($n = 6$) 11	12	13	14	15	16	GROUP III ($n = 3$) 21	22	23
0.1	0.35	0.5	0.2	1	0.45	0.4	0.4	0.35	0.5	0.3	0.2	0.4	0.35
0.25	5	3	0.8	3	3	5.7	2	1.5	2	2	0.9	4	0.80
0.50	12	9	5	20	15	32	15	35	20	20	15	50	1.5
0.75	120	18	50	300	50	200	30	250	200	250	> 400	+∞	+∞
0.90	5,000	150	500	5,000	> 3,000	> 3,000	+∞	> 3,000	> 3,000	> 3,000	+∞	+∞	

Subjects / k	GROUP IV ($n = 5$) 31	41	42	51	52
0.1	2	0.8	≥ 10	> 0.6	> 0.6
0.25	10	+∞	[a]	> 8	> 8
0.50	10^3	+∞	[a]	> 100	> 100
0.75	10^6	+∞	[a]	> 400	> 400
0.90	∞	+∞	> 3,000	> 3,000	

[a] no value of K

Observations	Group I	:	4	subjects	;	20	answers
	Group II	:	6	subjects	;	24	answers
	Group III	:	3	subjects	;	9	answers
	Total	:	13	subjects	;	53	answers

Subjects			
1	Bethenod	21	Bagiotti
2	Bouyssou	22	Jaffray
3	Montesano	23	McCord
4	Prat		
11	Berthier	31	Y_1
12	Munier	41	Cohen
13	Villemur	42	Y_2
14	Mme Villemur	51	Batteau
15	X_1	52	Bernard
16	X_2		

TABLE V B – 1. COMPARISON OF THE STANDARD DEVIATIONS σ', σ AND σ_1

The following table presents – the standard deviations σ' of the Allais's psychological errors in log K estimated from his different estimates over time (Allais 1988b); the standard deviations σ in log K for the different questions (Table V A and Chart V A); the standard deviations σ_1 of the subject's psychological errors in log K estimated from their comments on their answers (Tables IV A and IV B above, and Allais 1988b).

k	σ'	σ	σ_1	σ'/σ	σ_1/σ	σ'/σ_1
0.10	0.29	0.39	0.27	0.74	0.71	1.06
0.25	0.41	0.63	0.63	0.65	1.00	0.65
0.50	0.81	0.87	0.77	0.93	0.89	1.05
0.75	0.94	0.96	1.00	0.98	1.04	0.94
0.90	1.18	1.51	1.05	0.78	0.70	1.12

Incontestably this table displays very strong regularities, and it is impossible not to be struck by the remarkable coherence of all these estimates obtained in very different ways.

We can deduce from these results that the error on the generating function $K(k)$ is certainly small relatively to the psychological errors, and that the *invariance hypothesis* of § 2.1 above is justified, at least as a first approximation.

2. *Last Estimate of the Generating Function Before the 1987 Experiment and the Answers to the 1987 Questionnaire*

On Chart V B the geometric averages $\bar{K}$ of the observed K of Table V A corresponding to the five considered values of k are represented relatively to my last fitting of September 4, 1987 deduced from my own introspection and theoretical consideration (Table III). If we consider that the fitting was made before the 1987 experiment and the April–May 1988 analysis of the answers to the *1987 New Questionnaire*, the agreement shown by Chart V B is certainly very remarkable.

CHART VA

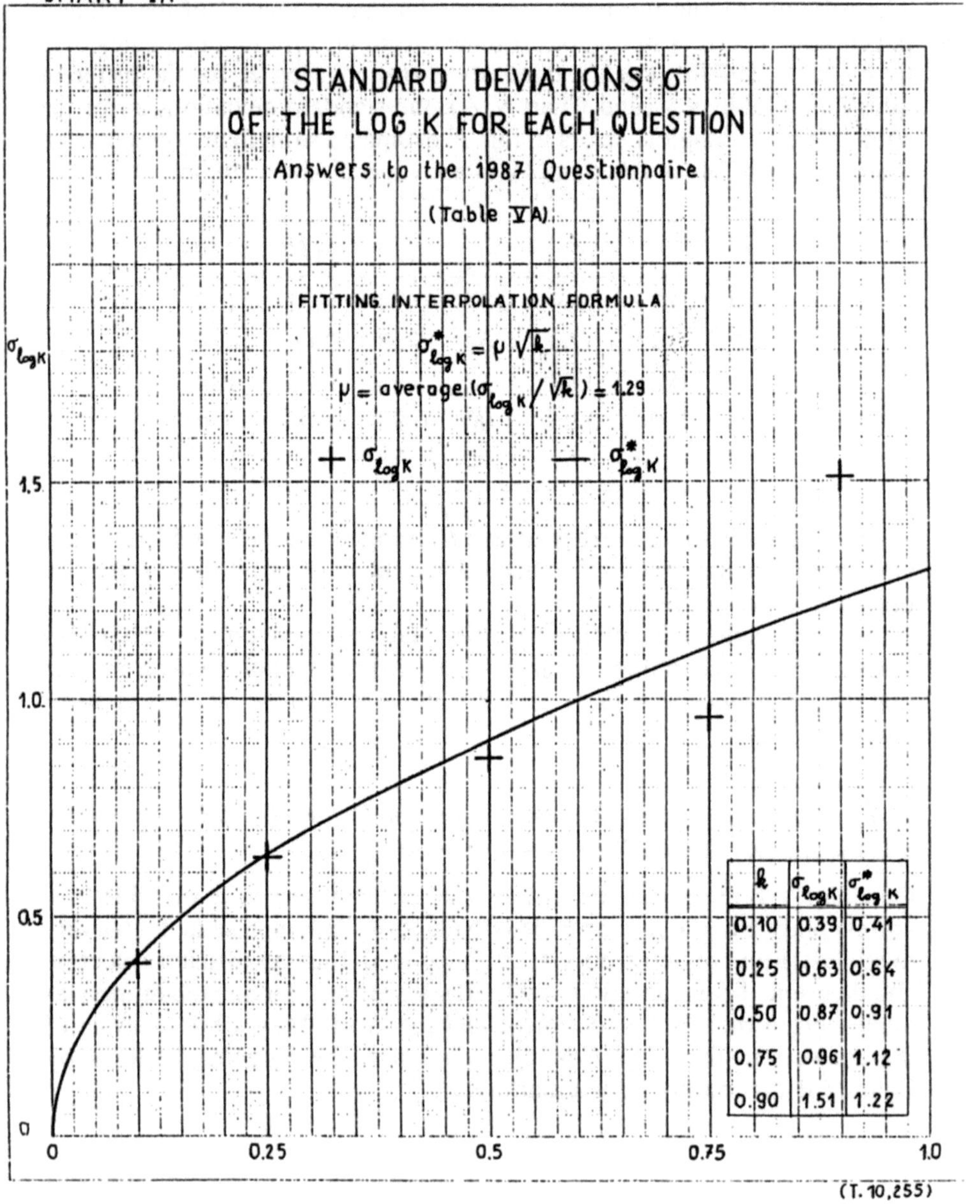

Chart V-(A).

CHART V B

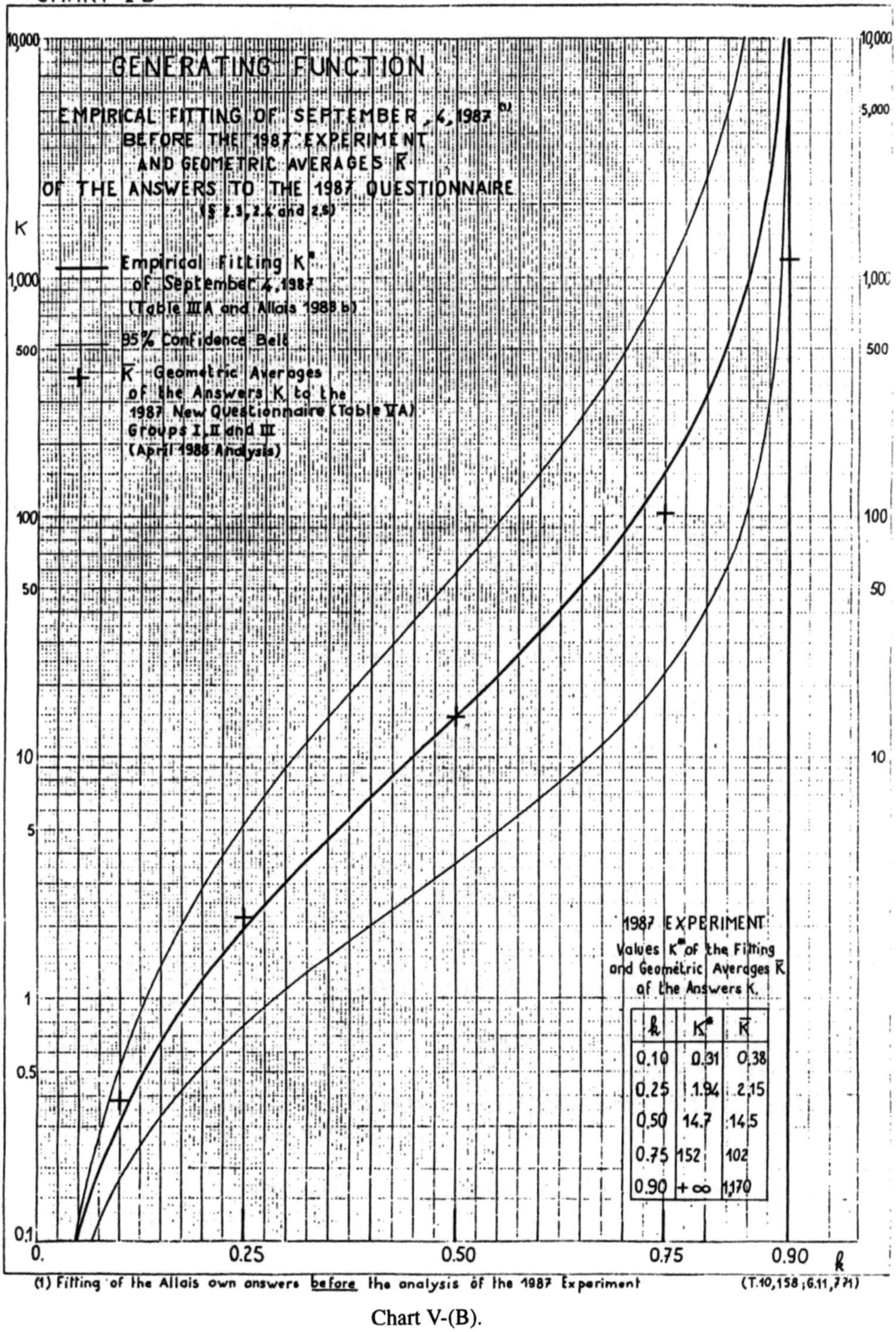

k	K*	K̄
0.10	0.31	0.38
0.25	1.94	2.15
0.50	14.7	14.5
0.75	152	102
0.90	+∞	1,170

Chart V-(B).

TABLE VI – GENERATING FUNCTION $K(K)$
TABLE OF NUMERICAL VALUES
$0 \leq K \leq 0.9$

k	K	k	K	k	K
0	0	0.20	1.38	0.60	29.1
0.01	0.0128	0.21	1.53	0.62	33.8
0.03	0.0546	0.22	1.69	0.64	39.3
0.04	0.0833	0.23	1.85	0.66	45.9
0.05	0.117	0.24	2.04	0.68	54.0
0.06	0.156	0.25	2.23	0.70	63.9
0.07	0.201	0.26	2.43	0.72	76.2
0.08	0.251	0.27	2.65	0.74	91.9
0.09	0.307	0.28	2.89	0.76	112
0.10	0.369	0.29	3.13	0.78	139
0.11	0.437	0.30	3.40	0.80	176
0.12	0.512	0.32	3.98	0.82	228
0.13	0.593	0.34	4.64	0.84	307
0.14	0.682	0.36	5.39	0.86	435
0.15	0.777	0.38	6.23	0.88	666
0.16	0.881	0.40	7.19	0.90	1,178
0.17	0.992	0.42	8.28	0.91	1,734
0.18	1.11	0.44	9.52	0.92	2,935
0.19	1.24	0.46	10.9	0.93	7,042
		0.48	12.5	0.935	$+\infty$
		0.50	14.4		
		0.52	16.5		
		0.54	19.0		
		0.56	21.9		
		0.58	25.2		

Empirical fitting formula: $0 \leq k \leq 0.90$ (Table II)

$$\log(K^* + q) = \log(K_1 + q) - \alpha\omega - \beta\omega^2 - \gamma\omega^3 \quad \omega = [\log(l + p)/(k + p) - 1]$$

$K_1 = 11.11$ $\quad p = 0.0102$ $\quad q = 0.00672$ $\quad r = 0.9971$

$\alpha = 1.63$ $\quad \beta = 0.0364$ $\quad \gamma = -0.00757$ $\quad l = 0.935$

This interpolation formula has no validity outside the interval $0 \leq k \leq 0.9$. (Source: T.10152)

CHART VIA

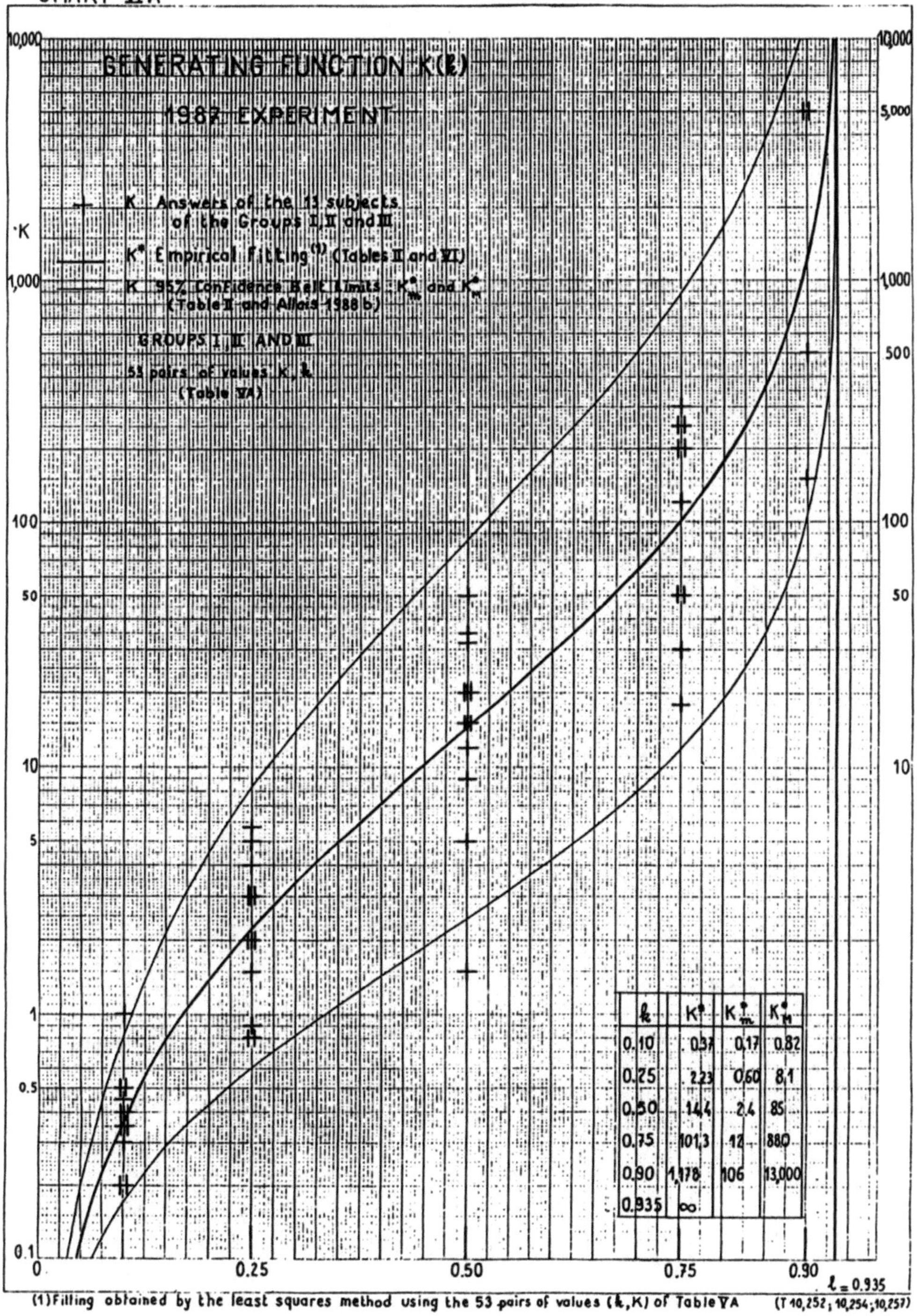

Chart VI-(A).

CHART VIB

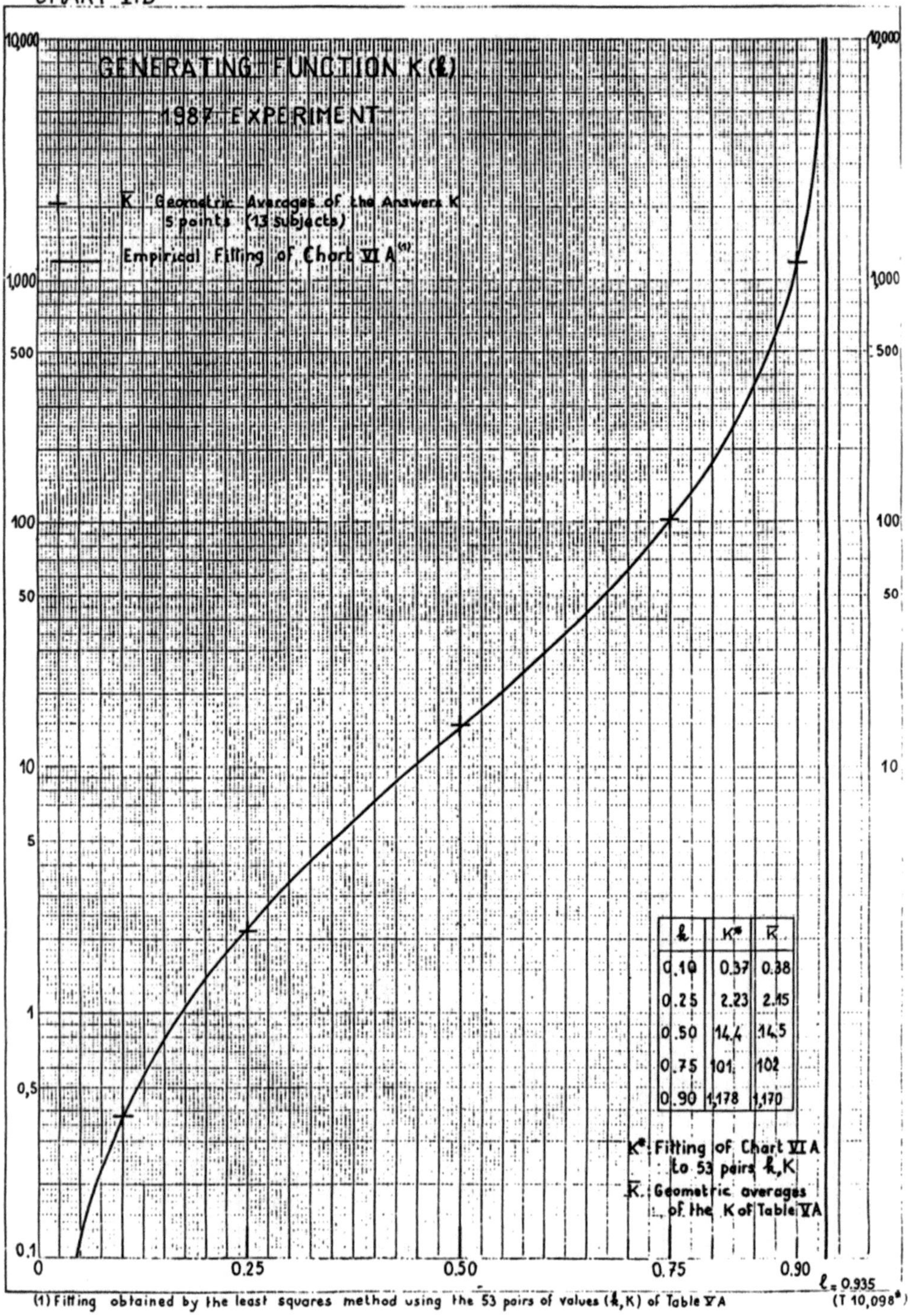

Chart VI-(B).

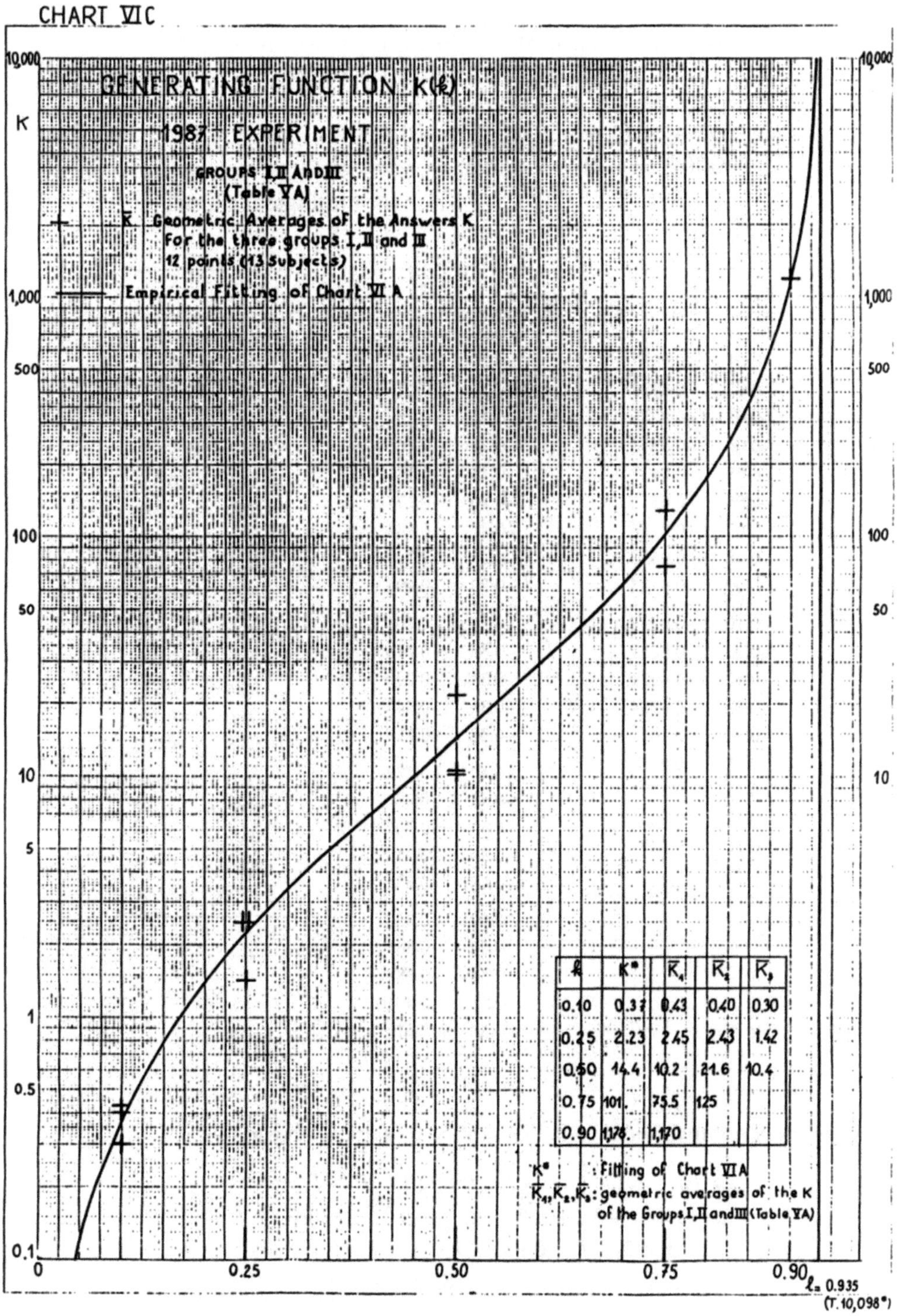
CHART VI C
GENERATING FUNCTION K(k)
1987 EXPERIMENT
GROUPS I,II AnD III
(Table V A)
K̄ Geometric Averages of the Answers K
For the three groups I, II and III
12 points (13 Subjects)
Empirical Fitting of Chart VI A
K
10,000
1,000
500
100
50
10
5
1
0.5
0.1
0
0.25
0.50
0.75
0.90
l= 0.935
(T. 10,098*)
k | K* | K̄1 | K̄2 | K̄3
0.10 | 0.37 | 0.43 | 0.40 | 0.30
0.25 | 2.23 | 2.45 | 2.43 | 1.42
0.50 | 14.4 | 10.2 | 21.6 | 10.4
0.75 | 101. | 75.5 | 125
0.90 | 1,178. | 1,170
K* : Fitting of Chart VI A
K̄1, K̄2, K̄3 : geometric averages of the K of the Groups I, II and III (Table V A)

Chart VI-(C).

TABLE VII - INVARIANT CARDINAL UTILITY FUNCTION
TABLE OF NUMERICAL VALUES

$$u^* = u^*(1 + y^*) \quad u^*(y^* = 0) = 0$$
$$u^*(y^* = -l) = -1 \quad u(y = +\infty) = 1$$
$$y^* = 1 + X^*/U_0 \qquad U_0 = \text{psychological capital}$$

y^*	u^*
0	0
–0.01	–0.0097
–0.02	–0.0188
–0.03	–0.0275
–0.04	–0.0358
–0.05	–0.0437
–0.06	–0.0513
–0.07	–0.0586
–0.08	–0.0656
–0.09	–0.0725
–0.10	–0.0792
–0.11	–0.0857
–0.12	–0.0921
–0.13	–0.0984
–0.14	–0.105
–0.15	–0.111
–0.16	–0.117
–0.17	–0.123
–0.18	–0.129
–0.19	–0.135

y^*	u^*
–0.20	–0.141
–0.21	–0.147
–0.22	–0.153
–0.23	–0.159
–0.24	–0.165
–0.25	–0.171
–0.26	–0.177
–0.27	–0.184
–0.28	–0.190
–0.29	–0.196
–0.30	–0.203
–0.32	–0.216
–0.34	–0.229
–0.36	–0.243
–0.38	–0.257
–0.40	–0.272
–0.42	–0.287
–0.44	–0.302
–0.46	–0.318
–0.48	–0.334
–0.50	–0.350
–0.52	–0.367
–0.54	–0.384
–0.56	–0.401
–0.58	–0.418

y^*	u^*
–0.60	–0.437
–0.62	–0.454
–0.64	–0.472
–0.66	–0.490
–0.68	–0.580
–0.70	–0.528
–0.72	–0.548
–0.74	–0.569
–0.76	–0.591
–0.78	–0.617
–0.80	–0.645
–0.82	–0.676
–0.84	–0.712
–0.86	–0.754
–0.88	–0.803
–0.90	–0.860
–0.91	–0.894
–0.92	–0.931
–0.93	–0.975
–0.935	–1.000

Empirical fitting formula: $-0.935 \leq y^* \leq 0$ (Table II above)

$$u^*(y^*) = (\lambda + (r - \lambda)\, e^{z\omega(z)})\, z \quad u^*(-l) = -1$$
$$\omega(z) = a + bz + cz^2 + dz^3 + ez^4 \quad z = \log(1 + y^*)$$
$$r = 0.9971 \quad l = 0.935 \quad \lambda = 0.365$$
$$a = 5.56 \quad b = 9.34 \quad c = 8.55 \quad d = 3.44 \quad e = 0.5156$$

(Source: Table 10227.)

CHART VII A

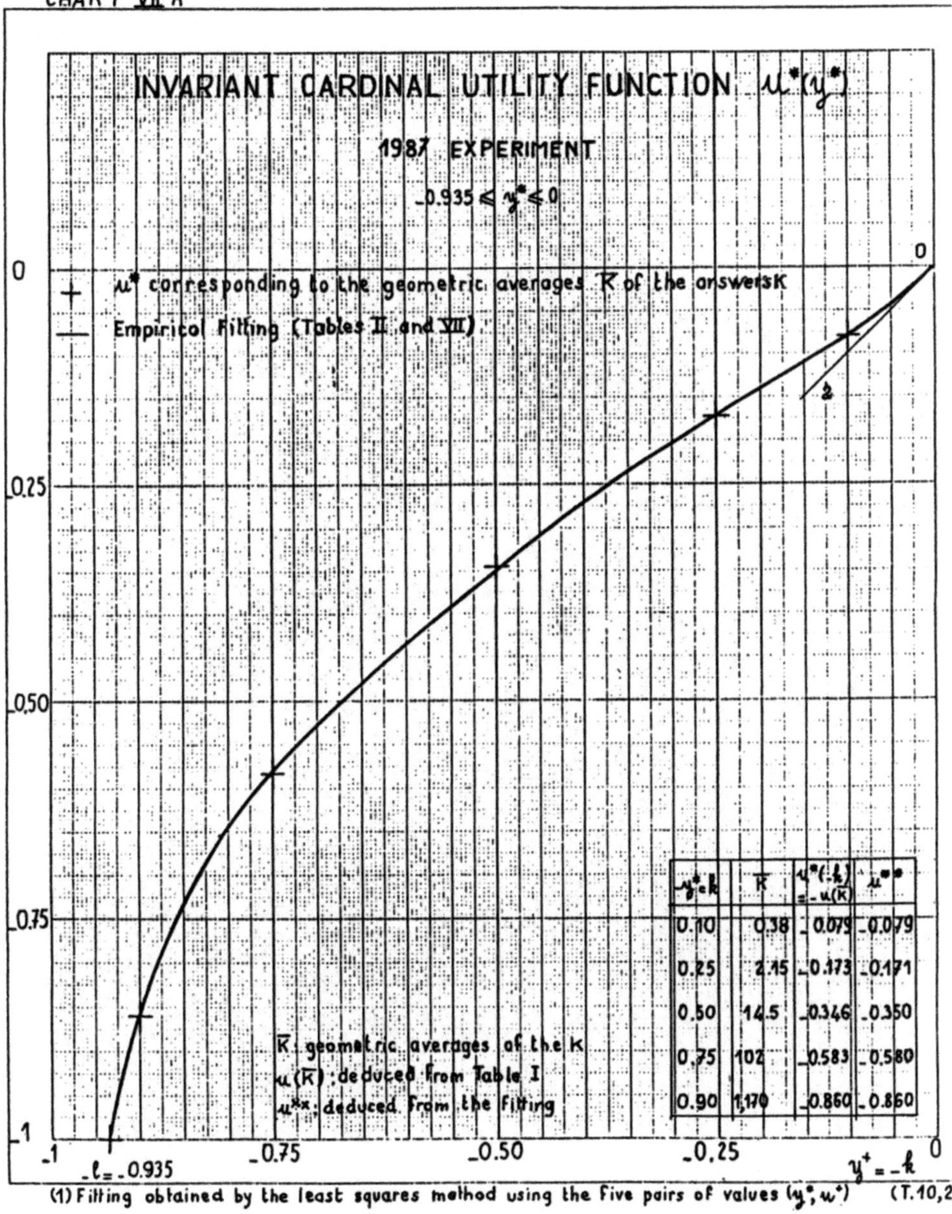

$-y^* = k$	$\overline{K}$	$u^*(-k) = -u(\overline{K})$	u^{**}
0.10	0.38	-0.079	-0.079
0.25	2.15	-0.173	-0.171
0.50	14.5	-0.346	-0.350
0.75	102	-0.583	-0.580
0.90	1,170	-0.860	-0.860

Chart VII-(A).

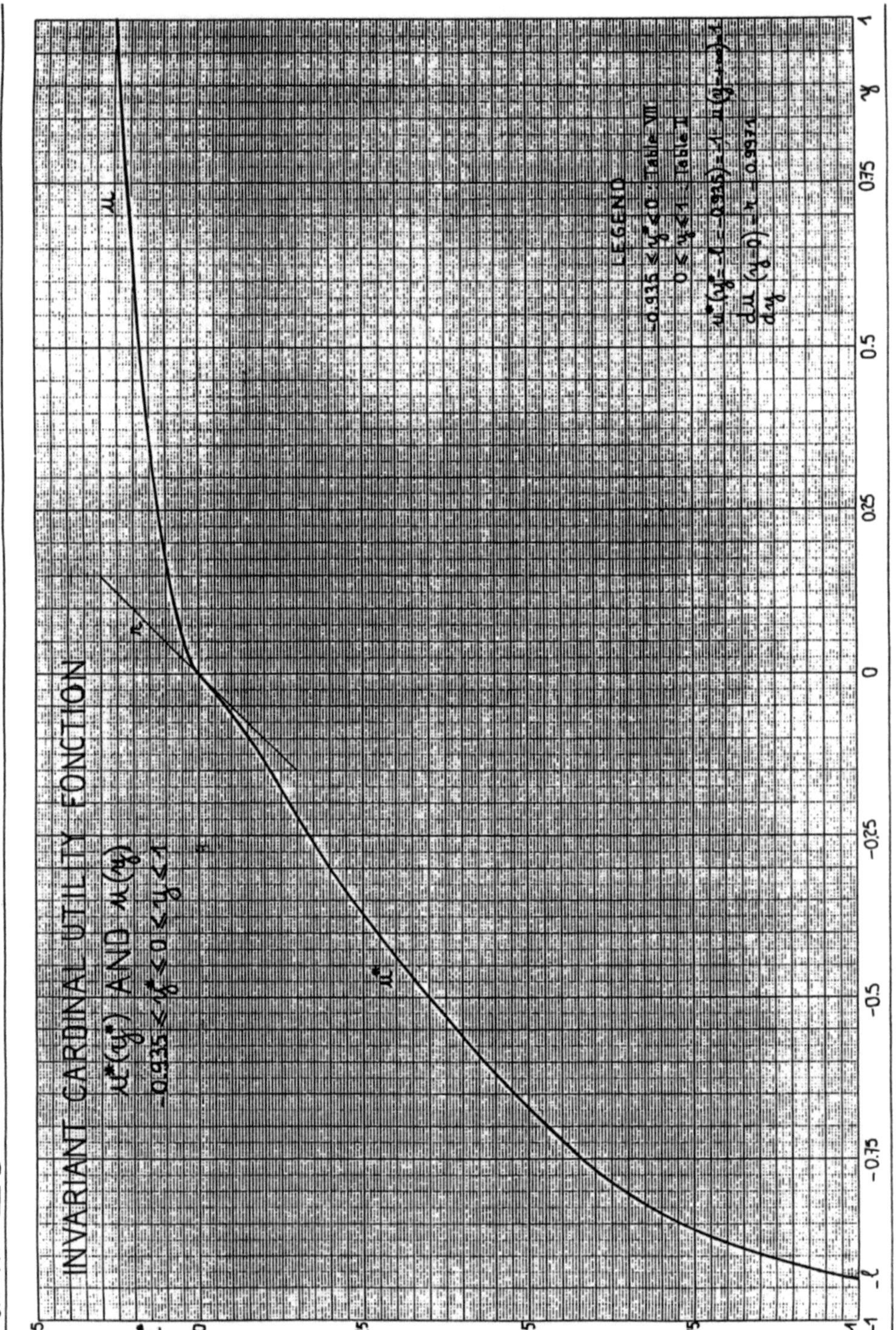

Chart VII-(B).

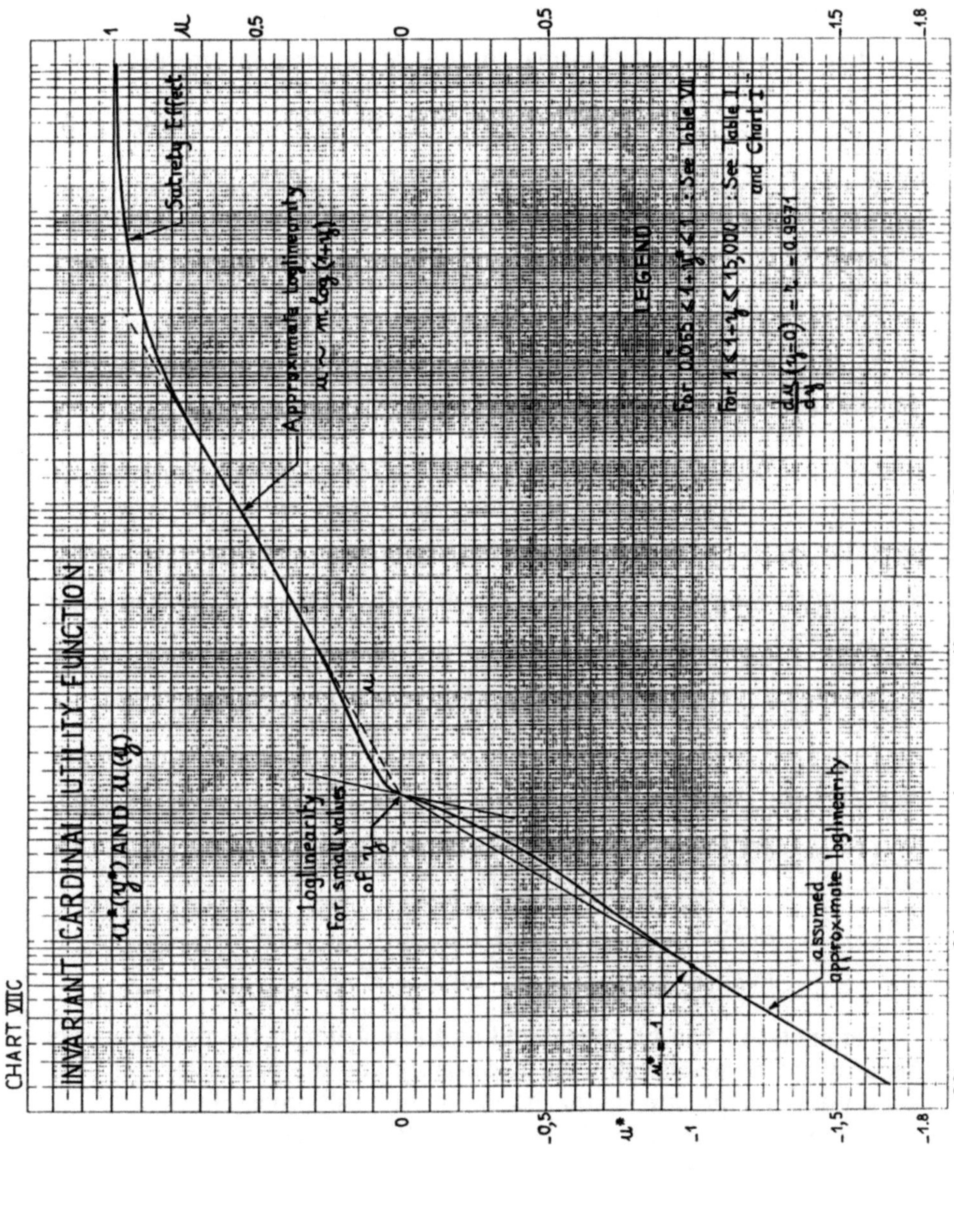
CHART VIIC
INVARIANT CARDINAL UTILITY FUNCTION
Satiety Effect
Approximate loglinearity
LEGEND
For 0.065 ≤ 1+y* ≤ 1 : See Table VII
For 1 ≤ 1+y ≤ 15,000 : See Table I and Chart I
Loglinearity for small values of y
assumed approximate loglinearity
0.01
0.1
1
10
100
1,000
10,000
100,000

Chart VII-(C).

TABLE VIII - PURCHASE OF INSURANCE POLICIES AND LOTTERY TICKETS
ILLUSTRATION BY THE (U, θ) MODEL

1. The (U, θ) Model in the Case of Discrete Distributions

(a) Let $U(P)$ be the cardinal utility of a random prospect (P): $x_1, x_2, \ldots, x_n,\ p_1, p_2, \ldots, p_n$, with $0 < x_1 < x_2 < \ldots < x_n$; $p_1 + p_2 + \ldots + p_n = 1$, the p_i representing the probabilities of the gains x_i.

For a given subject let $u = u(x/U_0)$ be his cardinal utility U_0 representing his psychological capital, and x a potential increase of the psychological capital. We have

$$(1) \qquad u_i = u(x_i/U_0) \qquad u_1 < u_2 < \ldots < u_n$$

According to the (U, θ) Model the psychological monetary value v of the random prospect considered is defined by the condition

$$(2) \qquad \begin{aligned} u(v/U_0) = u(P) = \theta(F_1)\, u_1 + \theta(F_2) \\ (u_2 - u_1) + \theta(F_3)\,(u_3 - u_2) \\ + \ldots + \theta(F_n)\,(u_n - u_{n-1}) \end{aligned}$$

where $\theta(F)$ represents the specific probability function of the considered subject with

$$(3) \qquad \begin{aligned} &F_1 = p_1 + p_2 + p_3 + \ldots p_n\,, \quad F_2 = p_2 + p_3 + \ldots + p_n \\ &F_3 = p_3 + \ldots + p_n, \ldots\,, \quad F_n = p_n \end{aligned}$$

(b) The $\theta(F)$ function. We have

$$(4) \qquad \begin{aligned} &\theta(0) = 0 \;\; \theta(1) = 1 \;\; \mathrm{d}\theta/\mathrm{d}F\ (F = 0) = \\ &\quad m' \;\; \mathrm{d}\theta/\mathrm{d}F\ (F = 1) = m \end{aligned}$$

$$(5) \qquad \begin{aligned} &\theta(F) \sim m'F \;\text{ for }\; F \ll 1\,; \\ &\theta(F) \sim 1 - m(1 - F) \;\text{ for }\; 1 - F \ll 1 \end{aligned}$$

Parameter m can be considered as an indicator of the preference for security int he neighbourhood of certainty and the parameter m' as an indicator of the preference for risk about the small probabilities.

For the 19 subjects considered in the *1952 Experiment* (Allais, 1984a, Table XII) we have found: $5.6 \leq m \leq 2{,}500$; $0.15 \leq m' \leq 17$. The averages are $\bar{m} = 191$, $\bar{m}' = 2.36$. These 19 subjects can be distributed in three groups: A (8 subjects): $\bar{m} = 133$; $\bar{m}' = 4.66$; B (5 subjects): $\bar{m} = 190$, $\bar{m}' = 1.06$; C (6 subjects): $\bar{m} = 272$, $\bar{m}' = 0.376$ (Allais, 1988b).

(c) The cardinal utility function. The values of the cardinal utility function $u(x/U_0)$ are given in Tables I and VII. In the following discussion two functions will be considered

$$(6) \qquad f(x/U_0) = \frac{-u(-x/U_0)}{x/U_0} \quad g(x/U_0) = \frac{u(x/U_0)}{x/U_0} \quad (x > 0)$$

From Table VII we find

$$(7) \qquad 0,675 < f(x/U_0) < r = 0,99907 \text{ for } 0 < x/U_0 < 0.32$$

According to Table I the function $g(x/U_0)$ is rapidly decreasing:

x/U_0	0	0,01	0,1	1	5	10	25	100
$g(x/U_0)$	1	0,75	0,37	0,12	0,048	0,031	0,016	0,0058

Assuming the validity of the (U, θ) model (Allais, 1986a, § 4, pp. 261–262), these results facilitate discussion of the purchase of insurance policies and lottery tickets.

2. *Purchase of Insurance Policies*

Let x be the insured value, p the probability of loss, and v the *psychological value* of this risk. The cases to be considered are

$$(8) \qquad \begin{aligned} u_1 &= u(-x/U_0) \text{ with probability } p_1 = p \\ u_2 &= u(0) = 0 \text{ with probability } p_2 = 1 - p \end{aligned}$$

Thus from relation (2) we have

$$(9) \qquad u(v/U_0) = u_1 + \theta(F_2)\,(u_2 - u_1) = [1 - \theta(1-p)]\; u(-x/U_0)$$

The purchase of an insurance policy *is advantageous if*

$$(10) \qquad u(v/U_0) < u(-¶/U_0) \qquad ¶ = (1+c)\,px$$

where ¶ represents the cost of the insurance policy and c the working cost of the insurance company. Since $p \ll 1$, $¶/U_0 \ll 1$ we have according to Table VII and § 1b: $1 - \theta(1-p) \sim mp$; $u(-¶/U_0) \sim -¶/U_0$. Thus according to (3) and (9), condition (10) writes as a first approximation

$$(11) \qquad 1 + c < mf(x/U_0)$$

Assuming for instance $c = 0,2$, $x/U_0 < 0,3$, and considering the data of § 1b and condition (10), we see that for the subjects of the 1952 Experiment the *purchase of insurance policies is always advantageous.* The reason why is the strong preference for security in the neighbourhood of certainty (i.e. $m \gg 1$).

3. Purchase of Lottery Tickets

Generally the lotteries give the possibility of receiving many prizes, but to simplify we will consider only two extreme cases, each corresponding to a single prize x of probability p. Let

$$(12) \qquad ¶ = (1+c)\,px$$

the price of the lottery ticket, c corresponding to the working cost of the lottery. The possibilities to be considered are as follows:

$$(13) \qquad u_1 = u(-¶/U_0) \text{ with probability } 1-p$$

$$(14) \qquad u_2 = [u(x-¶)/U_0)] \text{ with probability } p \quad (p \leq 1)$$

Let v be the *psychological monetary value* of the lottery ticket. We have according to relation (2)

$$(15) \qquad u(v/U_0) = u_1 + \theta(F_2)\,(u_2-u_1) = u_1 + \theta(p)\,(u_2-u_1)$$

Since $p \ll 1$, $¶ \ll 1$, and generally $v/U_0 \ll 1$ we have from Tables I and VII, and § 1b

$$(16) \qquad \theta(p) \sim m'p,\ u(v/U_0) \sim v/U_0,\ u_1 \sim -¶/U_0,\ u_2 \sim u(x/U_0)$$

and assuming $m'p \ll 1$, equation (15) becomes according to (3),

$$(17) \qquad \frac{v}{¶} \sim \frac{m'}{1+c}\,g(x/U_0) - 1$$

(a) First case $x/U_0 \ll 1$, $p \ll 1$– As $g(x/U_0) \sim 1$ the purchase of the lottery ticket is advantageous if $m' > 1+c$. Assume for instance $c = 0.2$, we see from § 1b that this condition is verified by the subjects of Group A.

(b) Second case $x/U_0 \gg 1$, $p \ll 1$ (a grand size with a small probability). According to (15), the purchase of the lottery ticket is advantageous if $v > 0$, i.e.

$$(18) \qquad m' > (1+c)\,/\,g(x/U_0)$$

For $x/U_0 > 5$ we have $g(x/U_0) < 0.048$ and assuming $1+c = 1.2$ we should have $m' > 25$, a condition which is not met by the subjects of the 1952 Experiment (§ 1b above).

For given values of c, x and m', relation (18) and the Table of the values of $g(x/U_0)$ (§ 1c above) show that the purchase of the considered lottery ticket is *the more diadvantageous, the poorer is the subject*, result which is contrary to a commonly accepted view.

(c) Ordinary lottery: intermediate case between (a) and (b).

TABLE XI – THE WEALTH TRANSFER AND TAX QUESTIONS

1. The Welfare Function – Illustrative Model

Consider two groups: poor and rich people

	Population	Wealth initial values	Cardinal Utilities	Wealth variations
Poor	n'	C'	u'	$\Delta C'$
Rich	n''	C''	u''	$\Delta C''$

(a) Let us put

(1) $n'\,C' + n''\,C'' = C$ $\qquad n = n'/n''$

(2) $n'\,\Delta C' + n''\,\Delta C'' = \Delta C$ $\qquad i = C''/C'$

(3) $y' = \Delta C'/C' \quad y'' = \Delta C''/C''$ $\quad \rho = \Delta C/C$

From equations (1), (2) and (3) we have

(4) $ny' + iy'' = \rho(n+i)$

$\Delta C'$ and $\Delta C''$ represent the variations of C' and C'', the result of the global increase of C and of the transfers.

The final inequality coefficient is:

(5) $i^* = (C'' + \Delta C'')/(C' + \Delta C') = (1 + y'')\,i\,/\,(1 + y')$

(b) If ΔC would be equally distributed we would have: $(\Delta C') = \Delta C/N$; $\Delta C'' = \Delta C/N$ with $N = n' + n''$. Thus we can define the transfers as: $\Delta V' = \Delta C' - \Delta C/N$; $\Delta V'' = \Delta C'' - \Delta C/N$ with $n'\Delta V' + n''\Delta V'' = 0$. Positive values of $\Delta V'$ correspond to transfers from the rich to the poor.

(c) The welfare function can be defined as:

(6) $F = n'\,u'(y') + n''\,u''(y'')$

The function $u(y)$ is given by Table I for $y > 0$ and by Table VII for $y < 0$. For given values of n' and n'', and under the condition (4), the welfare function F is maximum for

(7) $\mathrm{d}u''/\mathrm{d}y'' = i\,\mathrm{d}u'/\mathrm{d}y'$ $\qquad \partial u''/\partial u' = -n$

(d) Chart IX represents for different values of ρ the lines of maximal possibilities (§ 3.2.3 above) defined by the functions $u'' = G(u', n, i, \rho)$ for $n = 10$, $i = 5$, as defined by the parametric condition (4). For $\rho = 0$,

$\rho = -0.1$, and $\rho = +0.1$, the function F is maximum in M, M' and M'' as indicated on Chart IX.

(e) To illustrate the pure transfer problem let us consider the case $\rho = 0$. According to equation (5) we have $ny' + iy'' = 0$. For $n = 10$, the values of y', y'' and i^* corresponding to the *maximum of the welfare function F* for different values of i are as follows:

i	2	3	4	5	10	25	100
y'	0.050	0.099	0.152	0.210	0.540	1.75	7.70
y''	–0.250	–0.330	–0.380	–0.420	–0.540	–0.700	–0.770
i^*	1.43	1.83	2.15	2.40	2.99	2.73	2.64
u'	0.0237	0.0363	0.0468	0.0563	0.0926	0.159	0.281
u''	–0.171	–0.223	–0.257	–0.287	–0.384	–0.528	–0.604

In the case of a log-linear formulation $u' = \log(1 + y')$, $u'' = \log(1 + y'')$ with $-1 < y' < +\infty$, $-1 < y'' < +\infty$, the maximum of F under the condition $ny' + iy'' = 0$ implies $(1 + y'')\, i = (1 + y')$, i.e. $i^* = 1$, that is a total equality.

2. *Taxes Involving an Equal Psychological Burden on the Tax-Payers*

Let us consider n subjects j with psychological capital $U_{0,j}$ and let T_j be the tax paid. According to the invariance hypothesis (§ 2.2 above) we have

$$(8) \qquad u_j = u(-T_j / U_{0,j})$$

An equal psychological burden of the tax would imply

$$(9) \qquad u_j = v$$

v being a constant. Consequently we should have

$$(10) \qquad \frac{T_1}{U_{0,1}} = \frac{T_2}{U_{0,2}} = \ldots = \frac{T_n}{U_{0,n}} = \frac{\sum_j T_j}{\sum_j U_{0,j}} = \frac{T}{W}$$

For given values of T and W, that means that *to insure an equal psychological burden, the tax on a given subject should be proportional to his total wealth* (net worth + present value of future income). This result depends only of the invariance and homogeneity hypothesis (§ 2.1 above). It remains valid whatever the particular mathematical expression of the function u.

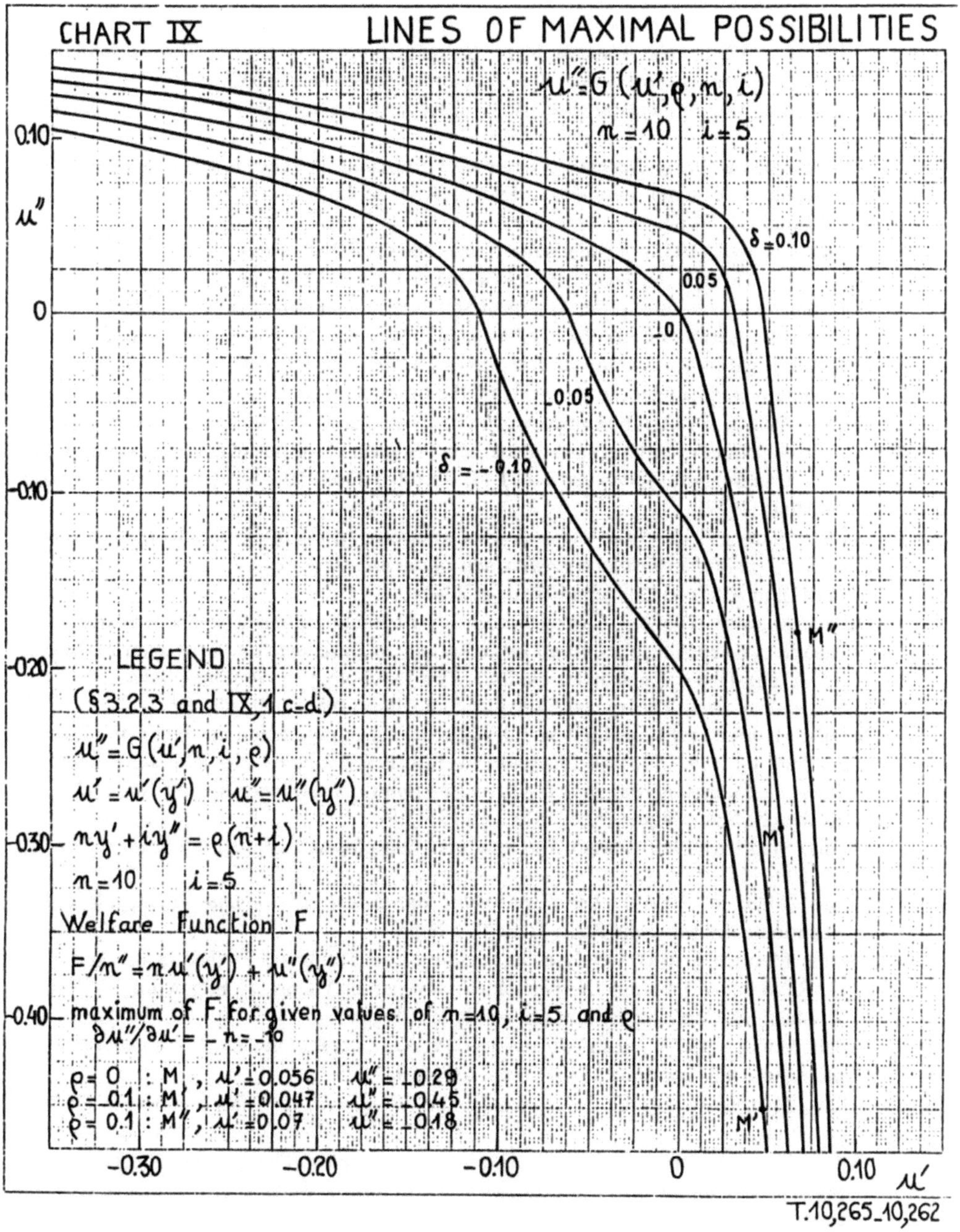
CHART IX
LINES OF MAXIMAL POSSIBILITIES
u″=G(u′,ρ,n,i)
n=10 i=5
δ=0.10
0.05
0
-0.05
δ=-0.10
M″
M
M′
LEGEND
(§3.2.3 and IX,1 c-d)
u″=G(u′,n,i,ρ)
u′=u′(y′) u″=u″(y″)
ny′+iy″=ρ(n+i)
n=10 i=5
Welfare Function F
F/n″=nu′(y′)+u″(y″)
maximum of F for given values of n=10, i=5 and ρ
∂u″/∂u′=-n=-10
ρ=0 : M , u′=0.056 u″=-0.29
ρ=-0.1 : M′, u′=0.047 u″=-0.45
ρ=0.1 : M″, u′=0.07 u″=-0.18
0.10
u″
0
-0.10
-0.20
-0.30
-0.40
-0.30
-0.20
-0.10
0
0.10
u′
T.10,265-10,262

Chart IX.

REFERENCES

Allais, Maurice (1943), *A la Recherche d'une Discipline Economique*, Première Partie: L'Economie Pure. (*In Quest of an Economic Discipline*, Part I, Pure Economics). Ateliers Industria, 852 pp. and Annexes, 68 pp. Second edition under the title *Traité d'Economie Pure (Treatise on Pure Economics)*, Impremerie Nationale (1952), 5 Vol., 1000 p. (the second edition is identical to the first, apart from the addition of a new introduction, 63 pp.).

Allais, Maurice (1951), *Notes théoriques sur l'incertitude de l'avenir et le risque*, Mémoire présenté au Congrès européen d'Econométrie de Louvain; 1951, Centre d'Analyse Economique, 74 pp.

Allais, Maurice (1952) 'Fondements d'une Théorie Positive des Choix comportant un Risque et Critique des Postulats et Axiomes de l'Ecole Américaine' (Foundations of the postulates and axioms of the American School), *Econométrie*, Colloques Internationaux du Centre National de la Recherche Scientifique, Vol. XL, Paris, 1953, pp. 257–332. Republished in Vol. 144 of the *Annales des Mines*, special issue, 1955, and again as a separate volume under the same title by the Imprimerie Nationale, 1955.

Allais, Maurice (1952a) 'Le comportement des postulats et axiomes de l'Ecole Américaine' (The behaviour of rational man facing risk: criticism of the postulates and axioms of the American School), *Econometrica* **21** (4), October 1953, 503–546 (summarised version of Allais, 1952).

Allais, Maurice (1952*) *The foundations of a Positive Theory of Choice involving Risk and a Criticism of the Postulates and Axioms of the American School*, english translation of (1952), in Allais and Hagen (1979), pp. 27–145.

Allais, Maurice (1952b), 'La psychologie de l'homme rationnel devant le risque – La théorie et l'expérience', *Journal de la Société de Statistique de Paris*, January–March 1953, pp. 47–73. English translation: The Psychology of Rational Behavior in the Presence of Risk. Theory and Experience, in Allais (1988c), Chapter IV.

Allais, Maurice (1961) 'L'Influence des besoins sur la production des biens de consommation', pp. 139–140, 149–150, and 178–180: in *L'Evolution et le Rôle des Besoins de Biens de Consommation dans les Divers Régimes Economiques*, Centre National de la Recherche Scientifique, Paris, 1963, pp. 133–194.

Allais, Maurice (1968) Pareto, *International Encyclopedia of Social Sciences*, Vol. II, pp. 399–411.

Allais, Maurice (1968a), *Les Fondements du Calcul Economique*, Ecole Nationale Supérieure des Mines de Paris, Tome II, 282 pp.

Allais, Maurice (1974) 'Analyse de quelques contributions à la théorie des surplus': D. Ricardo, A. Cournot, H. Gossen, S. Jevons, L. Walras, F. Edgeworth, I. Fisher, A. Marshall, Centre d'Analyse Economique, 100 pp.

Allais, Maurice (1977) *The so-called Allais' Paradox and Rational Decisions under Uncertainty*, in Allais and Hagen (1979), pp. 437–699.

Allais, Maurice (1978) *Editorial Introduction, Foreword*, in Allais and Hagen (1979), pp. 3–11.

Allais, Maurice (1981) *La Théorie Générale des Surplus* (The General Theory of Surplus), Economie et Sociétés, Jan.–May 1981, Institut de Sciences mathématiques et économiques appliquées, 2 vols., 716 pp.

Allais, Maurice (1983), 'The foundations of the theory of utility and risk', in O. Hagen and F. Wenstop, *Progress in Decision Theory*, pp. 3–131, Reidel, Dordrecht (1984), 279 pp.

Allais, Maurice (1984), *L'Utilité cardinale et sa détermination – Hypothèses, Méthodes et Résultats empiriques*. Memoir presented to the *Second International Conference on Foundations of Utility and Risk Theory* under the heading 'La détermination d l'utilité cardinal suivant un Modèle invariant', C–4248***, Venice (June 5–9, 1984), 200 pp.

Allais, Maurice (1984*), *The Cardinal Utility and its Determination – Hypotheses, Methods and Empirical Values*, English version of 1984, to be published in Allais (1989).

Allais, Maurice (1984a), 'Determination of cardinal utility according to an intrinsic invariant model', Very abridged version of (1984) in *Recent Developments in the Foundations of Utility and Risk Theory* (L. Daboni *et al.*, Eds.) (Proceedings of the 1984 Venice Conference), Reidel (1986), pp. 83–120. Also this book, pp. 31–64.

Allais, Maurice (1985) 'Three theorems on the theory of cardinal utility and random choice'. In *Essays in Honour of Werner Leinfellner, Theory and Decision*, Gerald Heberlein and Hall Berthel, (Eds.), 205–221, D. Reidel, Dordrecht, 1987.

Allais, Maurice (1985a) 'The Allais paradox', *The New Palgrave, A Dictionary of Economics*, Vol. 1, pp. 78–80, Macmillan, 1987.

Allais, Maurice (1986) *La Théorie générale des choix aléatoires en relation avec la fonction invariante d'utilité cardinale et la fonction spécifique de probabilité*, with seven Annexes, Centre d'Analyse Economique, 260 pp., March–April 1986.

Allais, Maurice (1986*) English translation of Allais (1986). To be published in Allais (1989).

Allais, Maurice (1986a), 'The general theory of random choices in relation to the invariant cardinal utility function and the specific probability function, the (U, θ) model. A general overview', in *Risk, Decision and Rationality*, B. Munier (Ed.), Reidel, Dordrecht, 1987 (very abridged version of Allais, 1986).

Allais, Maurice (1986b), 'The concepts of surplus and loss, and the reformulation of the general theory of economic equilibrium and maximum efficiency', in *Foundations of Economics*, pp. 135–174, M. Baranzini and R. Scazzieri (Eds.), Blackwell, Oxford, 454 pp.

Allais, Maurice (1987), 'The equimarginal principle, meaning, limits and generalisation', *Rivista Internationale di Scienze Economiche E Commerciali* **34** (8), 689–750.

Allais, Maurice (1987a), 'Economic Surplus and the Equimarginal Principle', *The New Palgrave, A Dictionary of Economics*, Macmillan, Vol. 2, pp. 62–69.

Allais, Maurice (1988), 'La théorie des choix dans l'oeuvre de René Roy – une analyse critique', *Revue d'Economie Politique*, 98th year, (3), May–June 1988, 315–357.

Allais, Maurice (1988a) *The Negative Values of Cardinal Utility – Theoretical Analysis, Empirical Findings and Applications*. Fourth International Conference on the Foundations and Applications of Utility, Risk, and Decision Theory, Budapest, June 1988, Centre d'Analyse Economique, C–4611*****, 31 May 1988.

Allais, Maurice (1988b) 'Cardinal utility – history, empirical findings, and applications', to be published in *Theory and Decision*. Also this book, pp. 65–103.

Allais, Maurice (1988c) *Scientific Papers on Risk and Utility Theory – Theory, Experience, and Applications*, Kluwer, 1000 pp.

Allais, Maurice (1988d) *New Applications of the (U, θ) Model*. To be published in Allais (1989).

Allais, Maurice (1989), *Cardinal Utility and Random Choice Theory*. Kluwer, this volume will include: Allais 1984*, 1986*, 1988b and 1988.

Allais, Maurice and Hagen, Ole (1979) *Expected Utility Hypotheses and the Allais' Paradox; Contemporary Discussions and Rational Decisions under Uncertainty with Allais' Rejoinder*, Reidel, Dordrecht, 715 pp.

Bentham, Jeremy (1789) *An Introduction to the Principle of Morals and Legislation*, Athlone Press, London, 1970.

Bernoulli, Daniel (1738) 'Exposition of a new theory on the measurement of risk', *Econometrica* **22** (1954), 23–36. First published as *Specimen theoria novae de mensura sortis*. Contains notes by Louise Sommer and footnotes by Carl Menger.

Collison Black, R.D. (1987) 'Utility', *The New Palgrave, A Dictionary of Economics*, Macmillan, Vol. 4, pp. 776–779.

Cureton, Edward E. (1968) 'Psychometrics', in *International Encyclopedia of Social Sciences*, McMillan and Free Press, Vol. 13, pp. 95–112.

Edgeworth, Francis Y. (1881) *Mathematical Phsycics: An Essay on the Applications of Mathematics to the Moral Sciences*, C. Kegan Paul, London, 152 pp., and Kelly, New York, 1953.

Edgeworth, Francis Y. (1897) 'The pure theory of taxation', in *Papers relating to Political Economy*, Vol. II, pp. 63–125, Burt Franklin, New York.

Edgeworth, Francis Y. (1899) 'Answers to questions put by the local taxation commission', id., Vol. II, pp. 126–149.

Edgeworth, Francis Y. (1910) 'Minimum sacrifice versus equal sacrifice', id., Vol. II, pp. 234–242.

Edgeworth, Franic Y. (1919) 'Graduation of taxes', id., Vol. II, pp. 243–270.

Edgeworth, Francis Y. (1920) 'Formulae for graduating taxation', id., Vol. II, pp. 260–270.

Fechner, Gustav Theodor (1860) *Elements der Psychophysik*, 2 vol. Engl. transl., *Elements of Psychophysics*, Vol. I, 1866.

Fisher, Irving (1892) *Mathematical Investigations in the Theory of Value and Price*, Yale University Press, 1965, pp. 1–126.

Fisher, Irving (1927) 'A statistical method for measuring "Marginal Utility" and testing the justice of a progressive income tax", in *Economic Essays: Contributed in Honor of John Bates Clark*, J.H. Hollander (ed.), Macmillan, New York, pp. 157–193.

Friedman, Milton, and Savage, L. John (1948) 'The utility analysis of choices involving risk', *Journal of Political Economy*, 279–304.

Frisch, Ragnar (1926) 'Sur un problème d'économie pure', *Norsk mathematisk forenings skrifer*, Series 1, no 16, pp. 1–40.

Frisch, Ragnar (1932) *New Methods of Measuring Marginal Utility*, Tübingen, Germany.

Georgescu-Roegen, Nicholas (1968) 'Utility', in *International Encyclopedia of the Social Sciences*, vol. 16, pp. 236–267.

Georgescu-Roegen, Nicholas (1987) 'Ophelimity', *The New Palgrave, A Dictionary of Economics*, Macmillan, Vol. 3, pp. 716–718.

Gossen, Hermann Heinrich Von (1854) *Entwickelung der Gesetze des menschlichen Verkehrs und der daraus fliessender Regeln für menschlichen Handeln*, 3th edition, 1927, Präger, Berlin.

Jevons, W. Stanley (1871) *The Theory of Political Economy*, 5th edition, Kelley, 1957.

Laplace, Pierre-Simon (1812) *Théorie Analytique des Probabilités*, Livre II, Chapitre X, De l'Espérance morale. Oeuvres de Laplace, Tome VII, Imprimerie Royale, Paris, 1847, pp. 474–488.

Laplace, Pierre-Simon (1814) *Essai Philosophique sur les Probabilités*, 2 vols., Paris, Gauthier-Villars, 1921, Engl. transl.: *A Philosophical Study on Probabilities*, 1951, Dover, New York.

Launhardt, Wilhelm (1885) *Mathematische Begründung der Volkswirtschaftslehre*, Engelmann, Leipzig.

Lopes, Lola (1986) 'Economics as psychology: a cognitive assay of the French and American schools of risk theory', in *Risk, Decision and Rationality*, B. Munier (Ed.), Reidel, pp. 405–416.

Menger, Carl (1871) *Grundsätze der Volkswirtschafslehre*, Engl. transl.: *Principles of Economics: First General Part*, Free Press, 1950.

von Neumann, John, and Morgenstern, Oskar (1947) *Theory of Games and Economic Behavior*, Princeton University Press.

Pareto, Vilfredo (1906–1909) *Manuale d'Economia Politica*, Societa Editrice, Milano, 1906. French translation: *Manuel d'Economie Politique*, Droz. Geneva, 1966, 696 p.

Pareto, Vilfredo (1911) 'Economie Mathématique', *Encyclopedie des Sciences Mathématiques*, Gauthier-Villars, pp. 591–641; in Vilfredo Pareto, *Statistique et économie mathématique*. Oeuvres complètes, Vol. 8, Geneva, Droz, pp. 319–368; Engl. transl.: International Economic Papers, no 5, Macmillan, 1955, pp. 58–102.

Pareto, Vilfredo (1916) *Trattato di Sociologia General (Treatise of General Sociology)* Barbera, Firenze, 2 vols. Published in French as: *Traité de Sociologie*, Payot, Paris, 1919, 2 vols., 1763 pp. (Droz, Geneva, 1818 pp.) Published in English as: *The Mind and Society*, Dover, New York, 1935, 2 vols., 2033 pp.

Roy, René (1942) *De l'utilité*, Actualités Scientifiques et Industrielles, no 930, Hermann, Paris, 47 pp.

Roy, René (1944) 'Note sur son ouvrage "*De l'utilité*"', *Journal de la Société de Statistique de Paris*, May–June 1944, (5–6), 134–138.

Roy, René (1948) 'Remarques et suggestions relatives aux nombres indices', *Econometrica* **16** (4).

Roy, René (1949) 'Les nombres indices', *Journal de la Société de Statistique*, (1–2), 15–34.

Savage, Leonard (1954), *The Foundations of Statistics*, New York, Wiley, 294 pp.

Stigler, George J. (1950) 'The Development of Utility Theory', *Journal of Political Economy*, Aug.–Oct. 1950, pp. 307–327 and 373–39?.

Walras, Léon (1874–1877) *Eléments d'Economie Politique Pure – Théorie de la Richesse Sociale*, 6th edition, Guillaumin, Paris, 408 pp. Engl. transl. of the 6th edition: *Elements of Pure Economics*, W. Jaffé (Ed.), Allen and Unwin, London, 1954, 620 pp.

Weber, Ernst Heinrich (1834) *De tactu: annotationices et physiologicae.*

Welch, C. (1987) 'Utilitarianism', *The New Palgrave, A Dictionary of Economics*, Macmillan, Vol. 4, pp. 770–776.

Wicksell, Knut (1901–1906) *Vorlesungen über Nationak Ökonomie*. Engl. transl.: *Lectures on Political Economy*, 1934, Routhledge.

Zabell, S.L. (1987) 'Bernoulli, Daniel', *The New Palgrave, A Dictionary of Economics*, Macmillan, Vol. 1, pp. 231–232.

TORE ELLINGSEN

CARDINAL UTILITY: A HISTORY OF HEDONIMETRY

ABSTRACT. The paper chronicles the scientific use and abuse of cardinal utility during more than two centuries. Surveying the contributions from moral philosophers, economists, psychologists and mathematicians, it is shown that cardinal utility is used as a name not only for one but for a large number of formally distinct concepts. Throughout the years these have become extensively confused, and still are.

Lack of conceptual precision is argued to be the main reason why scientists have disagreed over whether pleasure can be measured, and if so whether such measures can be used for policy purposes.

1. INTRODUCTION

> I'd like to be utilitarian, but the only problem is I have nowhere those utilities come from.
>
> Kenneth J. Arrow
>
> interviewed by J.S. Kelly in *Social Choice and Welfare* **4**, 1987).

In the history of economic science few concepts have been more controversial than that of utility. Whereas some economists have regarded utility as measurable as distance and as real as their morning jam (which, according to Samuelson, 1947, p. 206, is an adequate description of Edgeworth's position), others have insisted on its ordinality and abstractness.

For a while after 1950 it seemed that the issue was closed, most of the economics profession adhering to the latter point of view. Cardinalism was declared dead, and only a few stubborn members of Sir Dennis Robertson's cardinal club kept wearing their club ties – proclaiming that the grave was empty (see Robertson, 1951, 1954). But just as ordinalism seemed to be the universal gospel, cardinal utility found its way into economic models and the best of journals again. Interestingly, this has happened without many serious attempts to justify the measurability assumption *per se*. The last extensive treatments of cardinal utility being those of Stigler (1950), Majumdar (1958), Adams (1960), Luce and Suppes (1965), Georgescu–Roegen (1968) and Fishburn (1968, 1970a, 1976), there may be some benefits from a fresh look at the topic.[1]

1.1. Motivation

Before going into the details, we should be quite clear about the kind and importance of the economic questions to which cardinal utility might con-

M. Allais and O. Hagen (eds.), Cardinalism, 105–165.

stitute (part of) an answer. By Occam's razor, we can rule out all theories where cardinality can be dispensed with without changing the conclusions. Almost a century ago Antonelli, Fisher and Pareto realized that this was the case in price theory (at least as long as individual consumers have no market power). This leaves mainly the problem of group decision making. And indeed it is recent developments within the theories of social choice, cooperative games and bargaining that have accelerated the rehabilitation of cardinal utility.[2]

The reappearance of cardinalism within social welfare analysis can roughly be split into three different lines of development. First, there are those who seriously consider the possibility of making science-aided distributional decisions, arguing that measuring and comparing suitably defined aspects of individual welfare can actually be carried out. A representative work is that of Simon (1974) and also of Ng (1975) which is based upon such a view. Another and less controversial line of research is that carried out by, among others, Amartya Sen (1970, 1974, 1977) investigating the possibilities for constructing a reasonable social choice mechanism under various assumptions about measurability and comparability of utility.[3] The validity of these contributions remain beyond dispute, mainly because the problems are reduced to exercises in formal logic. While the analysis indicates that cardinal utility may be necessary in order to ensure the existence of reasonable social choice mechanisms, most writers within this tradition leave interpretation and application of the results to others.

This division of labour in the economics profession is even more accentuated by the third line of development in social welfare analysis; mathematical modelling of specific distributional issues like progressive income taxation. Two typical examples from the recent literature are Kaneko (1982) and Young (1987, 1990), both failing to give reasons why the so-called von Neumann–Morgenstern utility is adequate for their research (although it is not obvious why behaviour under uncertainty should have any impact on the taxation of non-random incomes).

It seems that a firm understanding of the first development is necessary to evaluate the relevance and make practical use of the mathematical theorems of the second and third: Are there reasonable and operational definitions of cardinal utility which can be used as a basis for distributional judgments?

1.2. Overview and Organization of the Paper

The word utility has a long history. Section 2 gives an account of the uses of the word before 1920. A key to understanding later confusion is the fact that such different disciplines as moral philosophy, statistics and psychology did all use the same term, and that it was adopted by economists at an early stage of economic science.

Section 3 is dedicated to clarifying the meaning of measurement. First, a number of scale types are defined, corresponding to successively higher degrees (i.e. higher precision) of measurement. Next, I discuss some methodological issues arising in connection with measurement of human sensations. Finally, I explain why a measurement operation is always invented and never discovered. Although the chapter contains very little which could not have been written 40 years ago (and certainly contains a lot which has been repeatedly emphasized by other authors since that time), these basic and general insights, applying so directly to the issue at hand, seem to have been ignored by many contemporary economists writing about them. The viewpoint that feelings cannot be measured is also argued to be mistaken.

Section 4 is an overview of the different ways of constructing cardinal utility, indicating that – according to the scientific ideal presented in the preceding section – cardinal utility may be split into at least six or seven different concepts.

Since one word has been used to convey so many different meanings, much confusion has persisted. The two dominant fallacies are the "fallacy of identity" and the "fallacy of unrelatedness". Many of those who have warned against the former are exposed to the latter, drawing the false conclusion that when two concepts are not identical they must be unrelated. Section 5 is called "connections and confusion". Besides a survey of mistaken arguments for logical identity between some of the utility concepts, it lends a support to the idea that logical and empirical relationships should be explored.

Variations over the theme *science-aided distributional decision making* are presented in Section 6. Here the ideas of Sections 3 and 5 prove useful, both for evaluating empirical studies of individual well-being and for a proper understanding of different approaches to utilitarianism as an ethical criterion.

2. EARLY HISTORY

> If I had to live my life over again I should have devoted it to psychology. Economics has too little to do with ideals.
>
> Alfred Marshall.

Although it is possible to go further back in history, there are good reasons for beginning the history of utility with a brief account of 18th century moral philosophy.[4] However, utility theory did not rise from moral philosophy alone. Much of the popularity of the concept rests on the behavioral underpinnings offered by such diverse sciences as statistics and psychophysics. The solution to a paradox in statistics, the St. Petersburg paradox, seemed to prove that to most people marginal utility of wealth is decreasing. Similarly, psychophysical experiments indicated that the human ability to recognize differences in physical stimuli is inversely related to the initial level of the stimulus, which was taken as another evidence of decreasing returns to scale in pleasure production. This chapter describes the three origins of cardinal[5] utility and demonstrate their impact on neoclassical economic thinking.

2.1. Utilitarianism

Utilitarianism is the branch of moral philosophy where public decisions are judged by the implied changes in individual satisfaction.[6] Although Jeremy Bentham (1748–1832) is commonly held to be the father of this "hedonistic" approach to moral questions, the ideas are quite clearly formulated by his predecessors, Richard Cumberland (1631–1718) and Francis Hutcheson (1694–1746). Especially Hutcheson (1728, p. 34) states his position unequivocally, defining *good* as pleasure and *good objects* as objects which create pleasure. The novelty of Bentham's approach is the treatment of utility (satisfaction, pleasure, felicity are synonyms) as a measurable quantity, thus making the utilitarian doctrine directly applicable to specific issues such as legislation[7] and tax policy:

> The quantity of happiness produced by a particle of wealth (each particle being the same magnitude) will be less and less every particle.
>
> Stark (1952, vol. 1, p. 103)[8]

The law of decreasing marginal utility of wealth can hardly be stated more concisely.

In fact, Bentham did not only argue that individual happiness was measurable. He also indicated that pleasures of different persons could be compared.

> Fortunes unequal: by a particle of wealth, if added to him who has least, more happiness will be produced, than if added to the wealth of him who has most.
>
> Stark (1952, vol. 1, p. 113)

These two quotations capture the essence of utilitarianism, and reflect Bentham's bold aspirations to be "the Newton of the moral world" (Mitchell, 1918). The measurability of happiness has been a controversial issue ever since.

2.2. The St. Petersburg Paradox

In my view, the Swiss mathematician Daniel Bernoulli (1700–1782), of whom Bentham probably had never heard, compares better to Newton than Bentham does. That Bernoulli anticipates Bentham's conclusions, is demonstrated by the following passages from his 1738 paper:[9]

> Thus there is no doubt that a gain of one thousand ducats is more significant to a pauper than to a rich man though both gain the same amount (p. 24).

and

it is highly probable that any increase in wealth, no matter how insignificant, will always result in an increase in utility which is inversely proportionate to the quantity of goods already possessed (p. 25).

Contrary to Bentham, Bernoulli also (unintentionally!) offers a theoretical argument for the law of decreasing marginal utility of wealth, since he finds this law to be an explanation to the intriguing *St. Petersburg puzzle*, originally invented by his cousin Nicolas Bernoulli twenty-five years earlier. The puzzle goes like this: *Peter tosses a coin and continues to so until it lands "heads" on the ground. He agrees to give Paul one ducat if he gets "heads" on the very first throw, two ducats if he gets it on the second, four if on the third, eight if on the fourth, and so on, so that with each additional throw the number of ducats he must pay is doubled.* Since the probability of "heads" turning up in each toss is 0.5, the expected pay-off to Paul is infinitely many ducats;

$$(2.1) \qquad \sum_{i=1}^{\infty} \frac{1}{2^i} 2^{i-1} = \frac{1}{2} + \frac{1}{2} + \ldots = \infty$$

But, as Nicolas Bernoulli rightly remarks, it has to be admitted that any fairly reasonable man would sell his chance, with great pleasure, for twenty ducats. This then is an example that maximization of expected monetary gain may not be a good rule of thumb for decision making, an observation which at the time was considered to be paradoxical. Daniel Bernoulli proposed the following solution to the paradox:[10]

If the utility of each possible profit expectation is multiplied by the number of ways in which it can occur, and we then divide the sum of these products by the possible cases, a mean utility will be obtained, and the profit which corresponds to this utility will equal the value of the risk in question (p. 24).

Thus, there is no doubt that Bernoulli advocated maximization of expected utility as a rational goal for decision making under uncertainty. Nor is there any doubt that his conception of utility was the same as Bentham's.

Now we can reverse the argument. If it is rational to maximize expected utility, and if people are willing to sell their opportunity to participate in the St. Petersburg gamble for a finite amount of money, then their marginal utility as a function of wealth must somewhere be decreasing. This reversion remained for other writers to do, but Bernoulli would certainly agree to it (as it is an easily proved theorem).

It took an even longer while before anyone asked the crucial question: *is it necessarily rational to maximize the expectation of ex post*[11] *utility?* If it is not, then gambling behaviour is no longer such a good evidence that marginal utility of wealth is a decreasing function. But for the moment, let us proceed chronologically.

2.3. Psychophysical Laws

Neither Bentham nor Bernoulli regarded decreasing marginal utility of wealth as a doctrine in need of scientific justification. The interpretation of the St. Petersburg paradox as being such evidence was made later, almost *en passant*, as a corollary to the psychophysical laws discovered by Weber (1834, 1846) and generalized by Fechner (1860).

In the *International Encyclopedia of the Social Sciences* psychophysics is defined as "the study of physical stimuli and their relation to sensory reactions" (J.C. Stevens, 1968; see also Bergmann and Spence, 1944, p. 14ff., for a more detailed discussion). Of the questions posed by psychophysicists, one is particularly relevant for our purpose, viz. what is the functional link between different degrees of a given stimulus and a given sensation? The first thorough investigation of this problem was carried out by the German psychologist E.H. Weber, who attempted to measure the smallest detectable change[12] in stimuli such as weight, heat and pitch. His experiments revealed a remarkable regularity, which was later formalized by another German psychologist, G.T. Fechner. This is the so-called

> *Weber's law:* The relative increase of a stimulus needed to produce a just noticeable change is constant.

Fechner's contribution was to take a just noticeable difference (jnd) as a unit of measurement, thereby constructing a scale for subjective magnitude (sensation). Mathematically, increase in sensation (S) is a linear function of relative increase in stimulus (R):

$$(2.2) \qquad \mathrm{d}S = c\,\mathrm{d}R/R$$

Integrating, we obtain

$$(2.3) \qquad S = a + c \log R$$

which is also referred to as

> *Fechner's law:* The magnitude of sensation is a logarithmic function of the stimulus.

Forgetting for the moment methodological problems associated with psychophysical measurement (to which we will return in the next chapter), the similarity between this model and Benthamite utility theory is striking; if wealth is a stimulus, then utility must be the corresponding sensation. Fechner recognized this parallel[13] and considered behaviour in the St. Petersburg game to be just one materialization of his law (see Fechner, 1860, pp. 236–237). Thus, it was only after his work that the interpretation of the St. Petersburg paradox as evidence of decreasing marginal utility became popular.

2.4. Notions of the Neo-classicals

The marginalist revolution paved the way for an ordinal concept of utility. Gossen, Menger, Jevons and Walras all developed ideas of decreasing marginal utility of goods which were perfectly valid without considerations of the utility of wealth. Gossen's law[14]

$$(2.4) \qquad u_1(\mathbf{x})/p_1 = u_2(\mathbf{x})/p_2$$

which seems to depend on cardinal utility, can equally well be written as

$$(2.5) \qquad u_1(\mathbf{x})/u_2(\mathbf{x}) = p_1/p_2$$

involving only the ordinal concept of a marginal rate of substitution. This was not noted explicitly until Fisher (1892, pp. 86–89 and 98–99) made it clear that price theory only depended on ratios between marginal utilities.

Most of the marginalists play a minor role in cardinal utility theory. Jevons and Marshall largely accepted the existing doctrine of diminishing marginal utility of money, and carried it through to later generations without major additions or subtractions[15] (see Jevons, 1965, pp. 147–148 and 160, and Marshall, 1920, pp. 152–153, and for an extensive documentation, Stigler, 1950).

Far more interesting from our point of view are the writings of Edgeworth (1881) and Pareto (1906). Departing from very different assumptions and arriving at equally different conclusions, they still made very similar contributions to cardinal utility theory.

Edgeworth christened his mathematical approach to utilitarianism *hedonimetry*, an illustrative term which later economists unfortunately did not pick up. Marrying utilitarianism and psychophysics, Edgeworth synthesized the works of Bentham and Fechner. Following Fechner, he postulated the unit of utility to be a just perceivable increment of pleasure. But he went further. In order to be able to compare the welfare of different persons, he also chose a just perceivable increment to be an *interpersonal* unit of utility. Edgeworth was fully aware that these two postulates were value judgements, or – in his own terminology – "incapable of proof", but he felt strongly that comparison of happiness between persons and groups of persons was an important scientific task:

> Such comparison can no longer be shirked, if there is to be any systematic morality at all. It is postulated by distributive justice. It is postulated by the population question.
>
> F.Y. Edgeworth (1881, pp. 7–8)

Edgeworth did however not endorse the claim that utilitarian ethics (maximization of total happiness) would necessarily lead to equal distribution of wealth, even if incentive problems are ignored and marginal utility is decreasing everywhere. This would be so only if every person's *capacity for happiness* was the same. Differences in such capacity could favour aristocractical privilege – the privilege of man above brute, of civilised above savage, of birth, of talent, and of the male sex.

op.cit. p. 77.

One may easily attack Edgeworth for being arrogant and male chauvinist,[16] but nevertheless, in this passage he goes right to the heart of utilitarianism. Allocating a pound between two persons, utilitarianism prescribes giving it to the person who would "light up" most, rather than, for example, the person initially less happy.

The Italian economist Vilfredo Pareto denied that interpersonal comparisons of utility was a meaningful operation (Pareto, 1971, p. 192). Still his construction of a cardinal utility index resembles that of Edgeworth:

a man can tell fairly well whether in passing from combination I to combination II, he experiences a greater pleasure than in passing from combination II to another combination III. If his judgement could be of sufficient precision, he would be able, at the limit, to know whether in passing from I to II this man experiences a pleasure equal to that which he experiences in passing from II to III. And consequently, in passing from I to III he would experience a pleasure double that which he gets in passing from I to II. That would be enough to permit us to consider the pleasure or ophelmity as a quantity.

op.cit. p. 191.

On the same page Pareto argues that such perfect precision is not attainable. Pleasure[17] is only *imperfectly* measurable.[18]

Note that Edgeworth's and Pareto's ways of defining measurable utility/ophelmity are not identical. For example, Pareto's method is valid without assumptions of limited sensibility, and even if positive jnd's are assumed, *the two definitions may not coincide.* This is a point which will be elaborated in the next sections. But before leaving the neo-classicals, a few words on applications of cardinal utility is in order.

Already before the neo-classical period (which I loosely define as the epoch starting with the marginalists around 1855–71 and ending sometime in the 1930s), John Stuart Mill (1848) had attempted to formulate policy directives in terms of cardinal utility. Specifically, he argued that taxation should inflict the same loss of utility upon every person (op.cit. § 2, par. 1).[19] Obviously, this does not follow from utilitarianism. As Edgeworth (1897) pointed out, equal *marginal* sacrifice of utility is the condition which guarantees a minimum total sacrifice from taxation. Another interesting contribution is that by Cohen Stuart (1889), who investigates the connection between the shape of utility functions and basic principles of taxation (such as "equal proportionate sacrifice") on the one hand and optimal tax progression on the other.

3. THE MEANING OF MEASURABILITY

> Probably more nonsense is talked about measurement than of any other part of physics.
>
> N.R. Campbell.

In the first two sections, the words "measurement" and "measurability" are not given precise definitions. This has facilitated a discussion of the early writings on their own terms – or at least has not been *too* contaminated by wise answers to questions the authors never asked. However, in the 1930s a battle broke out over mathematical and semantical issues, a debate that has continued with shifting force until the present day. To disentangle the threads, it will be beneficial to make a brief digression into the philosophy of science.

In the section we will first introduce formal definitions of scales. From this theory of *measures*, we then turn to problems of *measurability*, using examples from the physical sciences. This choice of examples is motivated by the convenience of a separation between purely semantical questions from the inherent, methodological problems of psychophysics. After a description of some elementary procedures for psychophysical measurement, the section closes with an assessment of methodological problems of psychophysics in general and of experimental utility measurement in particular.

3.1. The Mathematical Theory of Scales

Although the development of the foundations of measurement is not a major subject matter here, the cardinalist debate will look rather ridiculous unless it is remembered that measurement theory itself was in a pretty confused state until after World War 2. Hence, many of the controversies had solutions that became transparent once a taxonomy of scales was established.[20] The main definitions are as follows:

Definition 3.1. A scale is a rule for the assignment of numbers to aspects[21] of objects or events.

Scales are commonly divided into five types, according to the kinds of transformations permitted. Let $x_i \in X$ be possible manifestations of some aspect, and let $g : X \rightarrow \mathbb{R}$ be a scale.

A *nominal scale* is the least restrictive – every one-to-one substitution of numbers will do equally well as the original scale (e.g. numbering of football players). Nominal scales will not be of our concern.

Ordinal scales are such that every number $g(x_i)$ can be replaced by another number $f(x_i) = F_1(g(x_i))$, where $F_1 : \mathbb{R} \rightarrow \mathbb{R}$ is any increasing monotonic function. Or formally

$$(3.1) \qquad f(x_1) > f(x_2) \Longleftrightarrow g(x_1) > g(x_2)$$

We see that ordinal scales constitute a subset of nominal scales.

More restricting is the *ordered metric scale*,[22] which in order for F_2 to be a permissible transformation requires that if $f(\bullet) = F_2(g(\bullet))$, then

$$(3.2) \qquad f(x_1) - f(x_3) > f(x_2) - f(x_4) \Longleftrightarrow g(x_1) - g(x_3) > g(x_2) - g(x_4)$$

In other words, permissible transformations leave the ranking of differences invariant. Setting $x_3 = x_4$, we see that (3.2) implies equation (3.1). A characterization of this class of transformations – which is anything but simple – can be found, for example, in Krantz *et al.* (1971, Theorem 2, p. 431).

The ordered metric scale is sometimes confused with the *interval scale*, where permissible transformations F_3 are those for which we require for all c, that

$$(3.3) \qquad \frac{f(x_1) - f(x_2)}{f(x_3) - f(x_4)} > c \Longleftrightarrow \frac{g(x_1) - g(x_2)}{g(x_3) - g(x_4)} > c$$

where now $f(\bullet) = F_3(g(\bullet))$. Condition (3.3) implies equation (3.2), but not vice versa. (If $c = 1$, (3.3) will be the same as equation (3.2).) Hence equation (3.3) is a stronger condition. Also the class of transformations corresponding to interval scales is much simpler, viz. the positive affine class. That is, if F_3 is permissible, then $F_3(t) = a + bt$, $b > 0$. Fishburn (1976) associates cardinal utility with interval scales, and defines as quasi-cardinal the ordered metric scales of utility.[23] Here, I will refer to the scale type whenever the difference between ordered metric scales and interval scales becomes important.

Finally, there is the *ratio-scale*, requiring

$$(3.4) \qquad f(x_1) > cf(x_2) \Longleftrightarrow g(x_1) > cg(x_2)$$

This scale permits only transformations of the kind $F_4(t) = bt$, $b > 0$.

3.2. The Meaning of Measurement

The definitions of scales do not of course answer the fundamental question of measurability. The mathematical theory need not refer to any "real-world" actions or processes. (This may be a trivial observation, but even in this century scales have been defined in terms of operations. For reference, see Krantz *et al.*, 1971, p. 7.) So, how do we know what kind of scale is suitable for measuring a given aspect? Everyone agrees that distance can be measured on a ratio-scale. There is a natural zero point, and it makes sense to say that the distance between A and B is twice the distance between C and D. But ask a person on the street on what scale he would measure hardness of minerals, or colour! How come that this question is so much more difficult?

A tentative answer is that everyone has a common notion with regard to the measurement procedure (operation) in the first case, but not in the second. Distance can be measured by laying sticks of identical size end-to-end, and the standard size of such sticks do not influence arguments concerning relative distance, nor what is regarded as a zero measure (a point). Hence, distance is measurable on a ratio-scale.

But what we have done is to *define* (the measure of) distance in terms of a concatenation operation! Since it has taken mankind such a long time to understand that measures are *always* invented (and never discovered), let me dwell a little bit on this point.

In general, *operationalism* embodies the idea that the meaning of a concept is given by a set of operations. In physics, operationalism was the natural consequence of relativity theory. Einstein's insight that observed simultaneity should not be viewed as a property of a pair of events – simply because the position of an observer would also influence the observer's impression of timing – necessitated essentially new definitions of such a basic entity as time (now explicitly in terms of the operation by which it is measured). In Bridgman's words:

> If we have more than one set of operations, we have more than one concept, and strictly there should be a separate name to correspond to each different set.
>
> Bridgman (1927, p. 10)

But this seems a little inconvenient. It is impossible to measure the distance between two planets by concatenating sticks, but we would still like to have a concept called distance applying to relations between planets. The question naturally arises whether one should not after all allow for more than one operational definition of distance. Bridgman ingeniously answered:[24]

> If we deal with phenomena outside the domain in which we originally defined our concepts, we may find physical hindrances to performing the operations of the original definition, so that the original operations have to be replaced by others. These new operations are, of course, to be chosen so that they give, within experimental error, the same numerical results in the domain in which the two sets of operations may be both applied; but we must recognize in principle that in changing the operations we have really changed the concept.
>
> op.cit. p. 23.

Thus Einstein's new concept of length is entitled to its name only because

> within our present experimental limits a numerical difference between the two sorts of operations has not been detected.
>
> op.cit. p. 16.

Obviously there is a two-way interaction between scientific and everyday vocabulary. Measurement of heat (temperature) would not have been invented if there had been no *a priori* notion of it, but surely the present everyday notions are also shaped by the Kelvin, Celsius and Fahrenheit scales. I would guess that rankings of "temperature" differences were carried out before the invention of the scales (which had as an important consequence the notion that statements about differences in temperature were made scientifically testable), but that such rankings afterwards may have been influenced by the scales themselves. A statement such as "today is a little hotter than yesterday, but the difference is not nearly as great as between Sunday and Monday las week" may not carry the same meaning now as it did five centuries ago. In a strict sense, people living at the time, did not speak about temperature at all! Here, however, the distinction between the old and new notions is so unimportant that it was not *economical* to invent an extra word in order to avoid confusion.[25]

Let me press this last point home with an example from economic science, viz. the word *money*. Today there are more definitions (i.e. operational measurements) of money than there are fingers on a normal hand. For many purposes we need not distinguish between them. In some scientific applications it is however important to keep money I from money II, bonds from cash and credit cards from certificates. It is sensible to use the word money whenever all the definitions overlap, it is unscientific to do so whenever differences between them do not leave the interpretation invariant. Because of the ambiguity in one word allowing to have many possible precise meanings, the question what money *is* can only be answered properly by a listing of the different definitions. A main feature of Sections 4 and 5 is to show that this very same reasoning is valid for *utility* as well.

3.3. Psychophysical Measurement

Physical science has gone a long way in defining operational measures of such aspects as loudness, brightness, temperature etc. Psychophysics is concerned with the subjective assessment of these aspects.

The fundamental methodological problem is of course to make people report their sensory reactions to different stimuli without any "error-correction", i.e. their answers should not be biased by their knowledge of the objective scale. Psychophysical experiments are concerned not with people's ability to approximate objective measures, but with the responsiveness of their bodies and minds. Subjects are supposed to report reactions, not to make guesses (see S.S. Stevens, 1951, pp. 41–42). If this problem can be overcome, such experiments represent the most direct and natural test of the assumptions underlying classical utilitarianism, viz. that the subjective value of money is increasing at a decreasing rate.

In order to evaluate the merits of psychophysics and its relevance to utility theory, we must consider the procedures applied. Determining "minimum perceptible thresholds" was the original approach of Weber and Fechner.[26] Scales obtained by using *jnd*'s as units need however not correspond to people's explicit ranking of differences. Two other procedures that (from our point of view) suffer from similar deficiencies are *number matching* and *cross modality matching*. As the name indicates, number matching is based on asking the subjects to assign numbers to the stimuli offered to them. Cross modality matching is a little more subtle, in that the subjects associate (differences in) intensities of one stimulus with (differences in) intensities of another in such a way that (differences in) both stimuli are perceived equally intensely. It has been proposed (Ekman, 1964) that number matching is only a variant of cross modality matching, and that people may exhibit a non-linear number sensation as well. If this is the case, then the sensation function for a stimulus created by either of these methods will only have meaning relative to other sensation functions created the same way.[27]

This leaves us with the method of *interval estimation*,[28] where the subject is asked to rank changes in the stimulus directly, i.e. an increase in stimulus from one level to another is compared to an increase in the same stimulus from a third level to a fourth, and so on. As noted earlier, this method will not in general give rise to more precise scales than ordered metrics. Hence, it may be desirable to have people report *ratios* of differences so that an interval scale can be constructed.

Is psychophysical measurement meaningful? Or, to stay within the framework of the preceding paragraph, is psychophysics compatible with operationalism? (In social sciences *behaviourism* and *operationalism* are often used interchangeably, a practice that I will also adopt.) Many writers argue that it is:

> Operational psychology deals with experience only as it is indicated by the operation of differential behaviour, ***including verbal report.***
>
> S.S. Stevens (1962)
> (italics are mine)

This classification of verbal report as part of behaviour is strongly advocated by the British philosopher Gilbert Ryle (1949) who distinguishes first-person utterances like "I am in pain" from their third-person counterparts ("he is in pain"). First-person utterances, termed *avowals*, should be taken as part of behaviour, whereas the third-person utterance is an information-giving statement open to doubt. The main problem with this approach, as I see it, is that it is difficult to treat *lying* within the theory. A person who claims that he is very much in pain will *by definition* be very much in pain. Thus, in order to evaluate first-person utterances the context in which they are made are of prime importance. One possible way of solving this problem would be to have one concept of pain corresponding to each context (just like Bridgman would have one concept of distance for each method of measurement). This is obviously going too far. For psychophysical experiments it should suffice if honest answers could be separated from the dishonest ones.

A more extreme form of behaviourism would be to disregard utterances in general and introspective judgements especially as part of behaviour. The statement "I am in pain" will then be meaningful only if it has observable physical consequences (i.e. pain behaviour).

Although there are positions between these two, e.g. Wittgenstein's, I think that many of the controversies in cardinal utility theory can be explained sufficiently well by recognizing that the opponents adhere to different standards of behaviourism. "Extreme" behaviourists abandon most psychophysical methods, whereas "ordinary" behaviorists accept them, Thus, before making up one's mind about subjective versions of utility, one might as well take a stand in this more fundamental controversy belonging in the philosophy of language or in epistemology.

Personally, I tend to fall down on the side of the "ordinary" behaviourists. Numerous experiments have proven people's ability to answer the psychophysicists' questions promptly and consistently. This is in itself an indication that the language is rich enough to communicate more than ordinal information about the many aspects of life.

4. AXIOMATIZATIONS OF CARDINAL UTILITY

> "When I use a word", Humpty Dumpty said in a rather scornful tone, "it means just what I choose it to mean – neither more nor less".
>
> "The question is", said Alice, "whether you *can* make words mean so many things".
>
> "The question is", said Humpty Dumpty, "which is to be master – that's all".
>
> Lewis Carroll
>
> *(Through the Looking Glass.)*[29]

The term cardinal utility is about as precise as that of "travelling time". Saying that the travelling time between A and B is twice the travelling time between C and D is meaningless without reference (explicit or implicit) to the means of transportation – unless, of course, these destinations are located so that all imaginable means of transportation are equally effective, which would be a rare case indeed. Analogously, saying that the difference in terms of utility of options A and B is greater than the difference in utility between the options C and D is ambiguous without reference to a particular definition of utility – unless we speak of the utility to a person for whom all definitions give rise to exactly the same utility scale. Whether such a person would be a rare case or not will, I hope, be clearer in this section and the next.

Since the development of different definitions of utility has proceeded throughout many decades, it is difficult to determine a "correct" chronological order of presentation. Hence, in what follows I have tried to find a logical ordering of the axiomatizations. Each approach is however treated chronologically.

The chapter contains some terminology of binary relations. For definitions of basic concepts the non-expert reader may consult, for example, Fishburn (1970a).

4.1. Interval Comparisons

The most direct way of constructing sensation functions is to let people rank sensation differences. A *utility* function (or should I say, *one* utility function) is obtained when the stimulus is wealth and the sensation is the corresponding happiness. The first economist who explicitly noticed the possibility of performing such experiments in order to obtain a more than ordinal measure of utility was, as mentioned in paragraph 2.4, Vilfredo Pareto. Although he had some doubts whether a person could actually have a complete ranking of such differences, his reservations were not more serious than those shared by a majority of economists with regard to the completeness axiom in ordinal utility theory. Thus, Pareto was an "ordinary" behaviourist, not demanding that the ranking of differences must also be manifest in non-verbal behaviour.

Ragnar Frisch (1926a) was the first to formulate the interval comparison approach axiomatically. In the 1930s a debate over the "determinateness" of the utility function, involving in particular Oscar Lange (1934a, 1934b) and Franz Alt (1936), provided an even sounder mathematical foundation.

Frisch postulated two kinds of axioms. His "axioms of the first kind" pertained to the preferences of the consumer, and his "axioms of the second kind" were restrictions on the ordering of changes from one position to another (sometimes referred to as the *intensity* of preference). The preference axioms completeness, transitivity and a regularity condition, are all necessary for the existence of a differentiable utility function representing the preferences.[30] Intensity axioms are similar in structure and necessary for the existence of an interval scale measurable utility. With this, Frisch had laid down an important principle in modern utility theory: Instead of the tautologous phrase, "A is chosen over B because A yields higher utility", is put "a utility function must, in order to be representative of the preferences involved, assign at least as high a value to the preferred alternative A as to the rejected alternative B". The time was now ripe for searching a full characterization of the relationship between orderings and cardinal utility.

Unfortunately, Frisch's article was published in French in a Norwegian mathematical journal. This impeded its impact. Ten years were to pass before Franz Alt made the next major step along this path (in German in a German journal!). Actually, Alt himself explicitly refrained from relating his contribution to Frisch's work. Instead, he addressed a debate in the freshly founded *Review of Economic Studies* initiated by an article by Oscar Lange (1934a).[31] Let us therefore, in the name of chronology, make a digression into this debate.

Let P be a strict preference relation defined on the set of alternatives and let G be the corresponding relation ordering differences. The statement xPy is read "x is strictly preferred to y", whereas $xyGrs$ is read "x is more preferred to y than r is preferred to s", or rather, "a change from y to x is felt to be greater than a change from s to r". Two important assumptions are

$$(4.1) \qquad yPyx \Longleftrightarrow u(y) > u(x), \; \forall x, y$$

$$(4.2) \qquad yxGwz \Longleftrightarrow u(y) - u(x) > u(w) - u(z), \; \forall x, y, w, z$$

The central argument in Lange's article can then be formulated as:

Theorem 4.1. If there exists a differentiable utility function $u : \mathbb{R} \to \mathbb{R}$ such that conditions (4.1) and (4.2) both hold, then only positive affine transformations of that utility function represent the given preferences P and rankings G.

For a proof, see Lange (1934b), and for a very simple exposition, Samuelson (1938).

Before taking up the question of *existence* of the function u, some remarks about the theorem are in order. First, differentiability can be dispensed with. This is hinted at already in Lange's own graphical analysis. More surprising is perhaps that a version of the theorem can be proved without assuming continuity of $u(\bullet)$. This is done in Basu (1982). Here Basu makes clear a distinction between cardinality in Lange's framework and cardinality in the "modern" sense: In Theorem 4.1 it is an implicit assumption that the domain of the transformations F is that of the real numbers (since this is the range of u). In the modern framework, every representative utility function u has a range $U = \{u(x) : x \in X\}$ (where X is the set of alternatives), but the range is usually only a *subset* of the real numbers. The crucial assumption for cardinality in the modern context is that this subset is *connected*.[32] The more general version of Lange's theorem is thus:

Theorem 4.2. If there exists a utility function u, satisfying conditions (4.1) and (4.2), its range U being a connected subset of $\mathbb{R}$, then any other function $f(\bullet) = F(u(\bullet))$ represents the same preferences P and rankings G if and only if F is a positive affine transformation.[33]

Now to the problem of existence. Samuelson (1938), in a rather arrogant[34] comment on Lange's articles, regarded the existence of a utility function à la Lange as "infinitely improbable" (p. 70). If he had read Alt's article before writing his own, I suspect his judgement would have been considerably more modest. In his now celebrated article, Alt, inspired by the writings of Lange, tried to find necessary and sufficient conditions for cardinal utility based on preferences and interval comparisons.

His first axioms, axioms I, II and III, are mostly stating clearly what had until then been only implicitly assumed (e.g. asymmetry and irreflexivity of P and G etc.). Alt's next four axioms on the other hand represent a remarkable anticipation of what has later been written on this topic (see Chipman's, 1971, pp. 327–329, evaluation of Alt's contribution). In sum, his set of axioms constitute the necessary and sufficient conditions for the existence of a continuous utility function unique up to a positive affine transformation. His proof relates to Theorem 4.2 via his assumption that the set X of alternatives is connected. Since $u(\bullet)$ is required to be continuous, the range of u must then be connected as well (see e.g. Rudin, 1976, Theorem 4.22). Translated into the language introduced in paragraph 3.1, Alt has established the conditions for utility to be measurable on an *interval scale*. In a sense that is more than Lange asked for, since from (3.2) we know that an *ordered metric scale* is sufficient for conditions (4.1) and (4.2) to hold true.

Hence, it is of some interest to find the necessary and sufficient conditions for the existence of an ordered metric scale of utility. As long as the conditions are required to be open,[35] this task is not easy. For finite sets of alternatives it was first accomplished by Scott (1964), and for infinite sets by Tversky (1967). Whether the number of alternatives is finite or not, the required number of open conditions is itself infinite. For this reason openness is often given up in favour of simpler sets of sufficient conditions (like those of Suppes and Winet, 1955, Scott and Suppes, 1958 and Debreu, 1960). Probably, the persistent identification of cardinal utility with the interval scale rather than the ordered metric scale is explained by the fact that most "simple" and sufficient sets of axioms lead to representations that are unique up to a positive affine transformation.[36] Thus, it is tempting to argue that the difference between interval scales and ordered metric scales is only esoteric mathematics. Should we not agree with Lange (1934a) that

> From the assumption that the individual is able to know *whether* one increase in utility is greater than another increase in utility the possibility of saying *how many times* this increase is greater than another follows necessarily.

I think not. This argument hinges on two assumptions, which can be stated formally as (for all $x, y, z, w \in X$)

(4.3) $\exists s \in X;\ xsEsy$

(4.4) $\exists s \in X;\ (xPy, xyGzw) \Longrightarrow (xPsPy, xsGEzw)$

where E is transitive, reflexive and symmetric, and GE is transitive and reflexive. The first condition says that for any pair (x, y) of alternatives there will always be an alternative which lies midway between. The second condition says that if the "distance" between x and y exceeds that between two other alternatives z and w, then there will be an alternative s between x and y, but which is not closer to x than is w to z. (Obviously, none of these conditions are "open".) From an economist's or a psychophysicists's view both conditions are questionable.

An example that violates (4.3) is the stamp-collector lacking only one stamp in order to complete his collection. If the stamp costs him exactly one thousand pounds, there may be no amount s between $x = £\ 1.000$ and $y = £\ 990$ which fulfills condition (4.3). Either he can afford to buy the stamp – in which case he will be very happy – or he cannot.

It is easy to construct examples violating (4.4) as well. Let me give one in a more serious tone, illustrating that a person living on the subsistence level will not in general have preferences representable by an interval scaled utility: The change from y (below the subsistence level) to x (on the subsistence level) may be greater than the change from w to z (both above the subsistence level), and yet there will be no alternative s between x and y such that the movement from x to s is of any importance at all. Note however that neither of the conditions (4.3) and (4.4) are necessary for an ordered metric utility.

Before closing this subsection, I will briefly comment on some empirical investigations based on the notion of utility differences. The earliest experiment that I am aware of was carried out by Maurice Allais in 1952, but is reported first in Allais (1979b, 1986). Here the subjects respond to questions of the type: "Is your preference for an inheritance of 10 millions rather than no inheritance stronger than your preference for X millions rather than 10 millions?" The subject reports various degrees of agreement to the question corresponding to levels of freely chosen amounts of inheritance X. It is noteworthy that the respondents – students and scientists – were able to answer the questions (found them "meaningful") and that for most subjects the resulting index of psychological value was approximately logarithmic.

Another approach, suggested by Dyer and Sarin (1979), is applied by Krzysztofowicz (1983). Here, the analyst elicits "indifference points" s such that the decision maker is indifferent between exchanging x for s and s for y.

4.2. *Least Noticeable Differences*

Among the less direct constructions of measurable utility, the approach of least noticeable differences has the longest traditions. Bentham himself gave a clear statement:

> The degree of intensity possessed by that pleasure which is the faintest of any that can be distinguished to be pleasure, may be represented by unity.
>
> see Stigler (1950, p. 310).

As mentioned in paragraph 2.4, Edgeworth also advocated the concept of a just noticeable difference.

The idea was picked up again in our century by W.E. Armstrong (1939, 1948, 1951, 1955, 1958), who persistently claimed that intransitivity of the indifference relation is an empirical fact, and that utility for this reason has to be cardinally measurable:

> it is a well known fact that it is possible to be indifferent as between two alternatives A and B and as between B and C, while there is preference for A over C, i.e. the relation of indifference is not transitive.
>
> Armstrong (1939, p. 457).

> All we have to assume is that there is indifference between alternatives, between the utilities of which there is less than a certain difference.
>
> Armstrong (1939, p. 461).

At first glance, it seems that this approach *must* yield a utility function which is unique up to a positive affine transformation (since we can order differences by counting jnd's)[37]. Indeed, this assertion has seemed so obvious that it has gone without proof for a century (see e.g. Allais, 1979a, p. 98, Ng, 1984, p. 179, and even Fishburn, 1970b, p. 217). Formally, however, the assertion is wrong. If P is a strict preference relation reflecting finite sensibility,[38] and $u(\bullet)$ is a corresponding utility function, then for all x and y

$$yPx \Longleftrightarrow u(y) - u(x) > k, \; k > 0 \tag{4.5}$$

But (4.5) allows for a more general class of transformations than the positive affine! This result is recently proved by L.G. Svensson who also gives a characterization of the class of permissible transformations (Svensson, 1985, proposition 1). If u is a representative utility function with a jnd level of k, then all transformations

$$f(x) = a + bu(x) + p(u(x)) \tag{4.6}$$

where

$$p(0) = 0$$
$$p(t + k) = p(t)$$
$$\|p\| \leq bk$$

are permissible. The jnd level of $f(\bullet)$ is bk, and $p(\bullet)$ is a periodic function which repeats itself once within every jnd.

The point is that if the numbers of jnd's between pairs of alternatives (x, y) and (w, z) are not both integers, then the relation between utility functions u and f may satisfy neither condition (3.3) nor condition (3.2). Thus, this "approximately cardinal" utility need not be an ordered metric scale.

As far as I know, no attempt has been made to establish empirically utility functions based on the notion of just noticeable differences.

4.3. Additive Utility

Up to this point, the concern has been with one-variable utility functions, although both interval comparisons and just noticeable differences can be obtained without this dimensionality assumption. Another way of obtaining cardinal utility is to put restrictions on a multi-dimensional function

$$(4.7) \qquad u(\mathbf{x}) = u(x_1, x_2, \ldots, x_n)$$

Incidentally, economists before Edgeworth (quite arbitrarily) assumed that utility was *additive*, i.e.

$$(4.8) \qquad u(\mathbf{x}) = u_1(x_1) + u_2(x_2) + \ldots + u_n(x_n)$$

This assumption was probably due to lack of mathematical sophistication, but has as a by-product that $u(\mathbf{x})$ is defined uniquely up to a positive affine transformation. (Cardinality follows directly from the assumption that the cross-derivatives of the utility function are identically zero, an insight that goes back to Fisher, 1892. For a simple proof, see Samuelson, 1947, pp. 174–175.)

For our purpose, the important feature of additive utility is that the *elasticity of marginal utility of income* is invariant under positive affine transformations of the utility function (Frisch, 1932). Let us establish this more precisely. The first-order condition for utility maximization is

$$(4.9) \qquad \frac{\partial u}{\partial x_i} = \lambda p_i$$

where p_i is the price of commodity i and λ is the Lagrange multiplier, interpreted as the marginal utility of income (I). Differentiating with respect to income yields

$$(4.10) \qquad \frac{\partial^2 u}{\partial x_i^2}\frac{\partial x_i}{\partial I} = p_i \frac{\partial \lambda}{\partial I}$$

(since the cross-derivatives are zero). The elasticity of marginal utility of income is defined as

$$(4.11) \qquad \varepsilon_I \equiv \frac{\partial \lambda}{\partial I}\frac{I}{\lambda} = I\varepsilon_i \frac{\partial x_i}{\partial I}$$

where

$$\varepsilon_i = \frac{\partial^2 u/\partial x_i^2}{\partial u/\partial x_i}$$

is the elasticity of marginal utility of commodity i. Since ε_i is invariant to positive affine transformations of the utility function, ε_I must be so too. The virtue of the additivity assumption is claimed to be that in principle it is possible to estimate ε_I from consumer expenditure data (see e.g. Frisch, 1959, or Houthakker, 1960). This observation was made early by Fisher (1927) and Frisch (1926, 1932), and Fisher optimistically argued that sufficiently reliable statistical data

> would enable us to determine a juster system of income taxation than that now in vogue based purely on arbitrary judgment of guesswork.
>
> Fisher (1927, p. 171).

There are two difficulties with this argument. First, additivity implies that the marginal rate of substitution between every pair of goods is independent of the consumption of other goods. But at least this is a property which can be tested on market data. Much more devastating is the question: why be concerned with the *additive* representations only? Remember that we are concerned with the cardinal properties of utility. All positive monotonic transformations of the utility function impose the same restrictions on the demand function, but they do not leave the elasticity of marginal utility invariant. Hence, focussing on the additive representations and their corresponding elasticity of marginal utility is *not* warranted from demand data alone. These data give only necessary and not sufficient information to test the additivity assumption (an argument which was made very forcefully by Vickrey, 1945, pp. 322ff.). To check whether the cross-derivatives of the utility function is zero, only survey data will do.[39] We need to know whether the pleasure from consuming a unit of commodity x is dependent upon the consumption of commodity y. Without such information the selection of the additive representation is, for our purposes, essentially arbitrary.

The above argument is one of the reasons why the empirical estimates of ε_I obtained by Barten (1964), Johansen (1958) and Pearce (1961) must be taken with a grain of salt.[40] Another reason is that additive preferences are an extremely restrictive assumption, ruling out among other things complementarity between commodity groups.[41] Furthermore, in empirical work inferior goods are often ruled out as well, as the component functions $u_i(\bullet)$ are all assumed to be concave.[42] This last assumption by itself generates an elasticity of marginal utility of income which must be negative (a sum of concave functions is itself concave). Finally, estimations of additive utility models typically take the budget in the observed period to be exogenously given; there are no intertemporal decisions (saving decisions) to be made. However, including time in the model allows for additive preferences in another, less objectionable way.

Paul Samuelson early recognized under what circumstances one might, in principle, obtain a cardinal utility index from commodity market data. In his first published paper (Samuelson, 1937), he argued that observations of an individual's distribution of consumption through time gave the sufficient information if

(1) Utility at one point in time is independent of consumption at other points of time.
(2) The utility function is not subject to change through time.
(3) The individual maximizes the discounted sum of utilities, applying a constant (and known) discount factor (capital markets are "perfect").
(4) Prices are constant and correctly anticipated.[43]

Although Samuelson gave the earliest precise statement of the argument,[44] Frisch had already spelled out its underlying logic. A small-scale experiment for constructing individuals' utility functions for wealth is reported by him (Frisch, 1926b, pp. 330ff.). Assuming stable preferences for commodities and zero utility discounting, he asked the question:

> Suppose that you would this year have an income x lower than the average (a) and that you would next year earn equally much more. You cannot have credit from any other person than me. I am offering you a certain amount y this year. How much (z) would you maximally be willing to pay me back the next?

Frisch seems to have interpreted this question to mean: find z such that

$$u(a-x+y)-u(a-x)=u(a+x)-u(a+x-z) \tag{4.12}$$

Frisch refers to the measure $\log(z/y)/\log((a+x)/(a-x))$ as "the speed of decline in the marginal utility of money". (If this "global" measure is positive, the marginal utility of money is declining.) In the spirit of our earlier analysis, we shall instead consider the elasticity of income, which can indeed also be proven to be invariant under all positive affine transformations of the utility function. To get the idea, consider the function

$$v_t(\mathbf{x})=\sum_{i=t}^{T}\frac{u(\mathbf{x}_i)}{(1+r)^{i-t}} \tag{4.13}$$

which is maximized under Samuelson's assumptions (r is the utility discount rate). Again, since cross-derivatives are zero by definition, $u(\bullet)$ is determined up to a positive affine transformation. However, the budget constraint under this specification is an intertemporal one. Thus, the expenditure in each period need not equal the income. If we let Y_t denote expenditure in period t and let I denote the present value of the intertemporal budget, we can now measure both $\varepsilon_I\equiv(\lambda'/\lambda)\,I$, and $\varepsilon_{Y_t}\equiv(\mu'/\mu)\,Y_t$, where λ denotes the shadow price of *discounted* income, λ' is the derivative of λ with respect to I, μ denotes the (implicit) shadow price of expenditure in period t, as viewed from that period and μ' its derivative with respect to Y_t. The first measure is not independent of positive monotonic transformations of $v(\bullet)$. (However, as argued below, the criticism may not be as devastating here as in the case of atemporal additivity.) The second measure is however independent of such transformations.[45] What happens is that the intertemporal maximization allocates income to the various periods (a decision which is of course independent of the p.m. transformations of $v(\bullet)$), whereafter the single-period elasticity of marginal utility ε_{Y_t} is uniquely determined (since $u(\bullet)$ itself is left unchanged).

Unfortunately, Frisch never really seems to have grasped the fundamental difference between additive preferences over bundles of goods consumed within the same period and additivity with respect to consumption at different points of time. Thus, in his paper "Dynamic utility" from '1964 he refers to empirical measurements of ε_I obtained under the first assumption *as if* it was ε_{Y_t} obtained under the second (see Frisch, 1964, p. 188). Even if his additivity assumption had been fulfilled, this would be correct only if people *said* that their utility of one group of commodities is independent of all other groups. The validity of the measure ε_{Y_t} on the other hand, can be verified from market data alone, by checking whether the demand for a commodity today depends on previous consumption of this or other commodities.

Another point to be made is that Samuelson's theorem is in the same vein as Lange's (Theorem 4.1), in the sense that it applies only if a utility representation exists. It is not immediately obvious precisely what restrictions must be put on the preferences in order to obtain the representation (4.13). The gap was filled, by Fishburn (1970, Theorem 7.5). Considering preference relations for inter-temporal consumption, he asked what conditions are needed in order for these preferences to be representable by a time-additive utility function. He demonstrated that, besides standard assumptions, stationarity of the inter-period preferences is the only condition needed for the desired utility representation to exist.[46] Fishburn also gives a stationarity condition on intra-period preferences under which interval comparisons result in additive utility.

Finally, let me take this opportunity to place in perspective two papers by Camacho (1979, 1980). Camacho's story goes like this: Imagine that a *choice situation* is repeated a number of times, i.e. you face the same set of alternatives, and your preferences are identically the same each time (an assumption which underlies the revealed preference approach as well).

> The decision maker, when imagining a sequence of the two *same* choice situations, can determine whether the satisfaction obtained by making choice x in one of the choice situations and choice x''' in the other same choice situation is greater than, equal to, or less than the satisfaction obtained by making choice x' in one choice situation and choice x''

in the other.

Camacho then proves that if sequences of outcomes (in identical situations) can be ranked completely and transitively, there exists a utility function which is unique up to a positive affine transformation.[47] Clearly, the assumption that choice situations are identical is reminiscent of the stationarity assumption employed by Fishburn. The main difference seems to be that Fishburn considers actual intertemporal choice whereas Camacho studies hypothetical choices. Thus, in order to establish originality of his research, Camacho should have compared his existence theorem with that of Fishburn (1970, Theorem 7.5), rather than with the results of Alt and Herstein and Milnor.

4.4. Stochastic Choice

Transitive indifference in a theory of stochastic choice is modelled by letting all feasible alternatives belonging to an indifference set be chosen with equal probability. If a certain feasible indifference set contains n elements each will be chosen with probability zero or $1/n$. With intransitive indifference, as assumed in paragraph 4.2, the possibility arises that two alternatives may be chosen with positive, but different probability. There is nothing artificial about this. Small "errors of perception" commonly occur in psychophysical experiments. Imagine, for example, comparing the weight of two approximately similar objects. Only by repeating the experiment a number of times can one draw valid conclusions regarding the subject's ability to discriminate between the two weights. The lower the frequency of correct responses, the less sensitive is the person and the more concave is his response function. Using similar logic, we can define *degrees of preference* by means of the relative frequency of choice. A person is defined to be indifferent with respect to two alternatives a and b if and only if they are chosen equally often, the context being fixed.

There are two traps here. First, we must be careful using the assumption of constant preferences over time (constant sensory abilities are more likely). Secondly, it is necessary that the subject is not able to remember his previous responses, so that the experimental situations are reasonably constant. To quote Luce and Raiffa (1957, p. 372):

> Our ideal would be an individual who immediately forgets his choice upon making it [. . .]. Since our ideal is unreal, we will have to resort to dodges.

In an experimental situation, such a dodge could be for instance blind testing, precluding the possibility that the desire for consistency induces the subject to make the same choice every time, or variations in "framing" of the alternatives.

But even though dodges may work in some situations, I doubt that the stochastic choice approach will be of much value for social choice.

If the alternatives between which the subject chooses represent unequal wealth, it is hard to see how they could be framed in a way so that the best alternative is not always chosen *without* casting serious doubt on the validity of the experimental procedure.

A set of sufficient conditions for a probabilistic preference ordering that is able to be represented by an interval scale utility function is given by Debreu (1958). This article also has some references to the limited amount of other works on stochastic choice.

4.5. Expected Utility

Until 1930, economic analysis of decision making under uncertainty[48] and its relation to cardinal utility was very simple. A rational person was an expected utility maximizer, and since both direct introspection and the St. Petersburg paradox indicated that utility was a concave function of wealth, gambling was morally wrong and insurance was morally right.

> Gambling involves an economic loss, even when conducted on perfectly fair and even terms [. . .] A theoretically fair insurance against risks is always an economic gain.
>
> Marshall (1920, p. 135).

Since gambling was indeed observed, it had to be admitted that this theory was not a perfect description of reality. But then, of course, reality should be changed!

> It is true that this loss of probable happiness [from gambling] need not be greater than the pleasure derived from the excitement of gambling, and we are the thrown back upon the induction that pleasures of gambling are in Bentham's phrase "impure"; since experience shows that they are likely to engender a restless feverish character, unsuited for steady work as well as for the higher and more solid pleasures of life.
>
> op.cit. p. 843.

However, there is a serious drawback attached to accepting this argument. If decisions under uncertainty are not indicative of cardinal utility in any of the classical senses, the St. Petersburg paradox loses its force as an empirical verification of the diminishing marginal utility of wealth. The cardinalist/moralist will have to decide which foot to stand on; whether to define individual choices as expected utility maximization (allowing for a utility function which is convex in some interval) or to give some other "evidence" of diminishing marginal utility of wealth.

The works of Ramsey (1926), von Neumann and Morgenstern (1947) and Savage (1954) represent a watershed in the theory of decision making under uncertainty. But like most revolutionary ideas they were neither promptly understood nor given a uniform interpretation. One reason why contemporary economists did not instantaneously grasp the new ideas was the underlying change of perspective. Basically their theories are positive. The authors are not concerned about the moral questions which are so important to the utilitarians. All three works strongly emphasize the importance of simple and consistent *definitions*, thus adopting an operationalist approach. Also, the definitions of utility they introduce are auxiliary rather than basic. A short review of these important contributions may shed some light on the issue.

Frank Ramsey's posthumously published essay, "Truth and probability", is primarily an "inquiry into the logic of partial belief" (p. 159), debating central points in Keynes's probability theory.

> We must [. . .] try to develop a purely psychological method of measuring belief. It is not enough to measure probability; in order to apportion correctly our belief to the probability, we must also be able to measure our belief (p. 66).

Apart from the somewhat confusing line of division between probability and belief (inducing later writers to make an analogous distinction between objective and subjective probability), this quotation gives a useful reminder of the conceptual relationship between degrees of belief and classical cardinal utility. The "psychogalvanometer" of Ramsey (p. 161) and the "hedonimeter" of Edgeworth both belong in the dictionary of psychophysics. But contrary to Edgeworth, Ramsey sacrifices introspection (and forgets about the psychogalvanometer) right away. Instead he chose to *define* a person's degree of belief in an event by the person's willingness to bet that the event will occur. Being very explicit that a degree of belief "has no meaning unless we specify more exactly how it is to be measured" (p. 167), he avoids also the semantical fallacy that betting behaviour is *indicative* of the degree of belief (a statement which would make sense only after the degree of belief had been properly defined). Thus, Ramsey is among the first social scientists who explicitly adhere to the operationalist programme as described in subsection 3.2.

I will not go into Ramsey's arguments here against introspection based upon definitions of numerical belief, but rather turn to his treatment of value (utility).

> We have to explain what is meant by the difference between α and β being equal to that between γ and δ; and we define this to mean that if ρ is an ethically neutral proposition believed to degree 1/2, the subject has no preference between the options (1) α if ρ is true, δ if ρ is false, and (2) β if ρ is true, γ if ρ is false (p. 177).

Formally, this can be translated into the statement

$$(4.14)\quad w(\alpha) - w(\beta) = w(\gamma) - w(\delta) \Longleftrightarrow (\alpha, \delta, 1/2, 1/2)\, I(\gamma, \beta, 1/2, 1/2)$$

where $w(\bullet)$ is Ramsey's value function[49] and I is the indifference relation. Rearranging, we can write

$$(4.15)\quad (1/2)w(\alpha) + (1/2)w(\delta) = (1/2)w(\beta) + (1/2)w(\gamma) \Longleftrightarrow (\alpha, \delta, 1/2, 12/)\, I(\gamma, \beta, 1/2, 1/2)$$

Ramsey then goes on to show how values can be "correlated one-one with real numbers" essentially establishing axioms under which a value function $w(\bullet)$ will exist. He ascribed no intuitive interpretation to his value function. On the contrary

> It should be remembered, in judging my system, that in it value is actually defined by means of mathematical expectation (p. 183).

Using this function $w(\bullet)$ he then defines a measure of belief using a method which was later to be refined by Savage (1954).

Both Ramsey and Savage were primarily occupied with probability theory, and neither of them would have entered into the history of hedonimetry were it not for the unlucky choice of terminology made by von Neumann and Morgenstern (hereafter vNM) in their extremely influential "Theory of Games and Economic Behavior".

> I have chosen to use the name "utility" in preference to any other, in spite of some unfortunate connotations with economic theory, because it was adopted by von Neumann and Morgenstern when they revived the concept to which it refers.
>
> Savage (1972, p. 69).

In the next section I will return briefly to the ambiguities in vNM's verbal treatment of utility. Right now the concern will be only with their mathematical definition of it. Let $(\mathbf{x};\mathbf{p}) = (x_1, x_2, \dots, x_n; p_1, p_2, \dots, p_n)$ denote a lottery with outcomes $\mathbf{x}$ and corresponding probabilities $\mathbf{p}$, and let R be the weak preference relation. The vNM utility function $w(\bullet)$ is defined so that

$$(4.16) \qquad \sum_{i=1}^{n} p_i w(x_i) \geq \sum_{k=1}^{m} q_k w(y_k) \iff (\mathbf{x};\mathbf{p})\, R(\mathbf{y};\mathbf{q})$$

Or in their own words:

> We have practically defined numerical utility as being the thing for which the calculus of mathematical expectations is legitimate.
>
> vNM (1947, p. 28).

In the second edition of their book, the authors prove that their proposed axioms are indeed sufficient for existence of a utility function unique up to a positive affine transformation. The converse is also true; the vNM axioms are necessary for representing decisions under uncertainty as maximization of expected utility (see Fishburn, 1970a, ch. 8 for a proof).

This is not the right place for discussing the normative and descriptive validity of the vNM model. It should however be mentioned that many decision makers display behaviour which is inconsistent with the vNM axioms, so that their behaviour cannot be modelled as maximization of the expected value of such a utility function.[50]

From now on, the vNM utility will be referred to as an *ex ante* utility concept, whereas the other concepts are referred to as *ex post* utilities.

4.6. Less Formalized Approaches

A problem with axiomatic analysis is that axioms and theorems can have many different interpretations. The non-axiomatic approaches are ridden by another problem; arguments may be internally inconsistent or do not support the conclusions drawn from them. Personally, I believe that in cardinal utility theory "intuitions" and verbal arguments bear most of the responsibility for persistent confusion.[51]

One seducing, but logically mistaken argument in favour of diminishing marginal utility of wealth is articulated by the otherwise eminent economist Abba Lerner:

> With a given income, all the things bought give a greater satisfaction for the money spent on them than any of the other things that could have been bought in their place but were not bought for this very reason. From this it follows that if income were greater the additional things that would have been bought with the increment of income would be the things that are rejected when income is smaller because they give less satisfaction; and if income were greater still, even less satisfactory things would be bought.
>
> Lerner (1944, pp. 26–27)[52]

There is probably no formal way to save this argument. If all commodities are assumed to be (infinitely) divisible, then a person can buy a small amount of each commodity if he is poor and a larger amount if he is rich. Then, of course, the notion of a "less satisfactory thing" is not meaningful. On the other hand, if some commodities are not divisible, they may also be outside the budget constraint of a poor man, but increase his welfare considerably once income becomes sufficiently large to finance the purchase.[53]

Another informal approach to cardinal utility is taken by Pareto:

> If the actions of the individuals had to be determined not only by the sign but also by the amount of the increase in the index function, the choice of this function would be very much more restricted... For example, in order to handle a problem of dynamics, it would be necessary to know not only the direction in which the individual moves, but also the intensity of the movement corresponding to a certain amount of increase in the index function.
>
> Pareto (1955, pp. 63–64).

It is not quite clear what intensity means in this context. Vickrey (1945, p. 323) translates it to rapidity, so that quick responses to unexpected price and income fluctuations are signs of the high marginal utility of wealth. This sounds like a reasonable argument. However, the same phenomenon can alternatively be explained by the fact that expenditure planning takes time and leisure is a normal good.

A last example of criteria for cardinalization of utility is suggested by Coombs and Beardsley (1954), who regard as an indicator the *difficulty of choice*, reported or indirectly observed as time used for decision making.[54] The idea is that the relatively great difficulty of making a choice corresponds to a small utility difference between the alternatives and vice versa.

However, this method is valid only when all choice situations are of similar complexity. And when the complexity goes to zero, e.g. alternatives being expressed in money values, the method becomes useless (cf. also the comments about "dodges" in subsection 4.2).

5. CONNECTIONS AND CONFUSION

What are the connections between the different utility concepts? To this question there seems to be almost as many answers as there are economists who have written about utility theory. For convenience they can be grouped into three categories. In the first category are those who, like the neoclassicals, are not aware that utility is not a uniquely defined concept. Admittedly, many authors of elementary textbooks belong in this category. A recent example that this ill-founded idea occasionally slips into well-reputed journals as well is Montmarquette and Blais (1987) who, without any reservation, "use survey data of individual well-being to measure attitudes toward risk". (See also van de Stadt *et al.*, 1985, for similarly confused ideas.) A radically different position is taken by many of our most distinguished scholars and can be summarized in the words of Baumol (1977, p. 431).[55]

> What relationship, if any, does the N-M cardinal utility theory have to that of the neoclassical utility theorists? It is generally (though not universally) agreed that there is none.

It should be noted that within this category a large number of writers (there are honourable exceptions, like Luce and Raiffa, 1957, and Weldon, 1950) also tend to dismiss the introspective approaches to cardinal utility as "meaningless" (Arrow, 1951, p. 425[56]) or "nonsensical" (Savage, 1972, p. 96), a view which I hope has been discredited in the previous sections. At least, it is not in line with mainstream philosophy of language. In between these two categories is a small group of writers who ask questions like:

> Under what Conditions are the various utility concepts theoretically equivalent?
> And
> What is the empirical relationship between measures of risk aversion and measures of well-being (ex ante and ex post measures of utility)?

These are the questions to which we now turn.

5.1. *A Long-Lived Error*

The idea that for a given person, his vNM utility function $w(\bullet)$, if it exists, must be equal to ex post cardinal utility (as obtained from interval comparisons[57]) has been most vigorously defended by Allais (1953, 1979, 1983). They must be intrinsically the same, so the argument goes, because they are equal under very mild conditions.

Suppose that there is a cardinal utility $u(x)$ defined from intensity comparisons, and let there also be a function $w(x)$ representing the risk preferences. By definition, if x^* is the certainty equivalent of a lottery $(\mathbf{x};\mathbf{p})$, then

$$(5.1) \qquad w(x^*) = \sum_{i=1}^{n} p_i w(x_i)$$

Furthermore, define $u(x^*)$ as the ex post utility of the lottery. In Allais' framework this is a function F of the probability distribution $\mathbf{p}$ over the vector of ex post utilities $\mathbf{u}$. Let $\mathbf{e}$ be the unit vector. Now we can state Allais's *axiom of cardinal iso-variation* as

$$(5.2) \qquad u(x^*) = F(\mathbf{u},\mathbf{p}) \Longrightarrow F((\mathbf{u}+\mathbf{e}k),\mathbf{p}) = F(\mathbf{u},\mathbf{p}) + k$$

In words: If the ex post utility of each possible outcome is increased by the same number k, then the ex post utility of the certainty equivalent is also increased by k.[58] It is easy to check that this axiom is satisfied if ex post utility is a positive affine transformation of the vNM utility (i.e. if $F(\bullet)$ is the expectations operator), but this is – contrary to Allais's belief – not the only case satisfying (5.2). As pointed out by John Broome (1985), the following transformation is also valid:

$$(5.3) \qquad w(x) = a - be^{-cu(x)}$$

Broome's claim can be proved as follows. If this relation is true for all x, it must also be true for the certainty equivalent, x^*. Thus

$$(5.3) \qquad w(x^*) = a - be^{-cu(x^*)}$$

Equating (5.1) and (5.3′), it is straightforward to solve for $u(x^*)$.

$$(5.4) \qquad u(x^*) = \frac{-\ln\left(\sum_{i=1}^{n} p_i e^{-u(x_i)c}\right)}{c}$$

It remains to show that this expression satisfies the axiom of cardinal isovariation. Again, it is a matter of three or four lines to demonstrate

$$(5.5) \qquad \frac{-\ln\left(\sum_{i=1}^{n} p_i e^{-(u(x_i)+k)c}\right)}{c} - \frac{-\ln\left(\sum_{i=1}^{n} p_i e^{-u(x_i)c}\right)}{c} = k$$

This completes the proof that Allais's assertion is wrong.[59] A person who adheres to the vNM axiom, maximizing the expectation of w, and for whom the axiom of cardinal iso-variation is valid with respect to ex post utility, can still maximize a non-linear function of u, such as that given in (5.4). Note in particular that (5.4) is consistent with the decision maker being either risk averse or risk seeking with respect to u. Increasing the spread of (ex post) utility outcomes for a given mean reduces the certainty equivalent of the lottery if c is positive, and increases the certainty equivalent if c is negative.[60 x)]

5.2. Conditions for Identity

Formally, there is only one valid procedure to follow if one wants to compare different definitions of utility, namely to check what axioms are necessary and sufficient for identity. As far as I know, this method has validly been applied only twice [the second case, an article by Sarin (1982), came to my attention only at the proof stage; Sarin presents a condition under which the utility function from interval comparisons equals the vNM utility]: In a recent article, Ng (1984) claims that to an individual the jnd definition is identical to the vNM definition if and only if

$$(5.6) \qquad \forall r, x, y, z;\ (rIx \& zPy) \Longleftrightarrow (r, z; 1/2, 1/2)\, \underline{P}(x, y; 1/2, 1/2)$$

where $\underline{P}$ now denotes an "ordinary" preference relation (being a weak order; asymmetric and negatively transitive), I is an intransitive indifference relation and P is a semiorder, but not a weak order (i.e. it is not negatively transitive, but two levels of preference "dominate" one of indifference).[61] The important thing to note is how the link between the two utility concepts is established. First, the two utility functions are independently constructed from different sets of axioms. The individual is ascribed by both an "underlying" preference, satisfying full transitivity and an explicit preference exhibiting finite sensibility (intransitive indifference). The vNM utility function is constructed from the first set and the jnd function from the other. Secondly, the two sets of preference relations are *tied together* by (5.6).

Since I find it hard to reason about monetary alternatives which differ less than noticeably, let me propose a similar axiom (hereafter referred to as the axiom of identity) in terms of interval comparisons. Let $\underline{G}$ be a weak order (i.e., it ranks differences "the same way" as $\underline{P}$ ranks alternatives). The axiom is

$$(5.7) \qquad \forall r, x, y, z;\ (zy\underline{G}xr) \Longleftrightarrow (r, z; 1/2, 1/2)\, \underline{P}(x, y; 1/2, 1/2)$$

Note that (5.7) is a consequence of (5.6) if the interval comparisons correspond to the number of jnd's between alternatives. In (5.6) there is less than one jnd between r and x, whereas there is more than one jnd between z and y. Translated into the utility representations, this amounts to the requirement

$$u(z) - u(y) > u(x) - u(r) \iff (1/2)w(r) + (1/2)w(z) > (1/2)w(x) + (1/2)w(y)$$

which can be rewritten as

$$u(z) - u(y) > u(x) - u(r) \iff w(z) - w(y) > w(x) - w(r) \quad (5.8)$$

which again is only a restatement of (3.2). This proves the theorem that (5.7) is necessary and sufficient for the two utility representations to be identical (up to the class of transformations defining an ordered metric scale, not – as Ng claims – up to a positive affine transformation).

How reasonable is the axiom? I think it comes close to begging the question: Those who believe that a risk averse person, defined as having a concave $w(\bullet)$, always displays decreasing marginal (ex post) utility of wealth will accept the axiom. What is ruled out by the axiom is, to make a common abuse of language, risk-averseness and risk-proneness with respect to ex post utility. At this particular point I support Allais's view that there is no *prima facie* reason for neglecting the dispersion of psychological values. Empirical work also seems to invalidate the axiom (see references below). On the other hand, the axiom can also be thought of as a norm: Taking a purely result-oriented attitude, the decision maker should neglect the particular ex ante distribution of utility and care about the expected ex post utility only. This is the position of Harsanyi (1978, 1983). However, just like Allais, Harsanyi wrongly believes the vNM axioms to *imply* maximization of expected ex post utility:

> [the compound lotteries axiom and the sure-thing principle] presuppose that the decision maker has no specific utility or disutility for gambling as such, that is, for the nervous tension and the other psychological experiences connected with gambling. In other words, the two postulates assume that the decision maker will take a purely result-oriented attitude toward lotteries, and will derive all his utility and disutility from the prizes he may or may not win through these lotteries, rather than from the act of gambling itself.
>
> Harsanyi (1978, p. 224).

But here Harsanyi confuses necessary and sufficient conditions. Let excitement (or nervous tension) be defined as a *tendency not to maximize expected ex post utility*. The compound lotteries axiom and the sure-thing principle are *necessary* for the decision maker not to be excited, but they are *not sufficient*. The two axioms rule out only two kinds of nervous tension. The compound lotteries axiom does not allow a particular form of "framing" to matter; a two-stage lottery is equivalent to a one-stage lottery with the same probability distribution over outcomes. The sure-thing principle requires insensitivity toward the "importance" of the choice; adding an alternative

x_h with probability p_h to two lotteries (reducing the probabilities of all other outcomes proportionally), should not alter the ranking of the two lotteries. But from this it does not follow that von Neumann and Morgenstern (and Savage) "abstracts from *all* process utilities" as claimed by Harsanyi (1983, p. 307).[62] It is perfectly possible to maximize a non-linear function of ex post utility without violating the vNM axioms (since $u(\bullet)$ and $w(\bullet)$ are in general related only via positive monotonic transformations). Also a person can behave *as if* he maximized the expected value of *some* function defined on outcomes without this function reflecting necessarily his intensity of preference for outcomes. Shoemaker (1982) in his valuable review of expected utility theory articulates this insight clearly:

> preferences among lotteries are determined by at least two separate factors; namely (1) strength of preference for the consequences under certainty, and (2) attitude toward risk. The [vNM] utility function is a compound mixture of these two. (p. 533)

Much confusion would have been avoided if leading economists had taken this position instead of their stubborn refusal to accept avowals as being "meaningful" statements.[63]

Empirical testing is the only way to check whether the "axiom of identity" is correct or not. This task is a rather difficult one however, simply because many people do not rank lotteries according to the vNM/Savage axioms (for evidence, see Allais, 1979b, appendix c, Cohen *et al.*, 1985, Combs and Huang, 1976, Ellsberg, 1961, McCord and de Neufville, 1983, 1984, 1985, and McCrimmon and Larsson, 1979). As a matter of fact, not even rats, to whom mythology ascribes so much rationality, conform to the expected utility theory (see Battalio *et al.* (1985) for evidence).

Comparison between $w(\bullet)$ and $u(\bullet)$ can of course only be carried out for persons who actually conform to the vNM axioms. It is a pity that this elementary point is forgotten or ignored by those who have carried out empirical analysis. The refutation of the "identity axiom" implicit in the works of McCord and deNeufville (1983) and Krzysztofowicz (1983) may be due to subjects violating the vNM axioms.[64] Presently, the question of empirical similarity remains wide open.

5.3. The Fallacy of Unrelatedness

Based on the preceding discussion it is tempting to argue that leading mainstream economists like Baumol, Strotz, Savage and Marschak replaced one error with another. While it was certainly correct that

> this philosophical question of whether utility is intrinsically measurable or not is a spurious one

and

> Crucial to an understanding of this entire subject matter is the realization that measurement is always invented and never discovered!

Strotz (1953, p. 385).

it does *not* logically follow that different "inventions" are unrelated. On the contrary, a plausible explanation why von Neumann and Morgenstern chose the word utility for their invention is that the new concept resembled some of the old ones. This hypothesis is strenghtened by the observation that the authors tend to mix up the concepts, or – as Ellsberg (1954, p. 551) impertinently writes

they are prone to write in large, clear type about comparing differences in preferences and to discard such notions in fine print at the bottom of the page.

Readers doubting that scientists of von Neumann's format can write ambiguously about such elementary matters are referred to this article (esp. pp. 551–553).

As a consequence of these ambiguities some intelligent writers like Allais and Robertson were led astray and started to attack the vNM theory on the false ground that it was only valid for men who are "content to be governed entirely by mathematical expectations" (Robertson, 1952, p. 28). If they had understood the vNM theory correctly, they would have realized instead how well it can be fitted with the modified Marshallian view advocated by Robertson himself that actions under uncertainty are *related* to the relative desirability of the outcomes, but do not necessarily imply maximization of the expected ex post utility. Thus, instead of a discussion of conceptual closeness, which seemed to be the natural outcome of a very lively colloquium in Paris in 1952, with most of the leading researchers in the field as participants (for a summary of the debate, see Frisch, 1953[65]), came a futile war of words, debating whether the classical utility concept is meaningful and whether the vNM concept is useful. The only opinions on the logical relatedness of the concepts came from Allais and de Finetti. Allais's opinion was that the two are the same, whereas de Finetti insisted that they are generally related only via positive monotonic transformations,[66] a view shared by all those who admitted both concepts, but did not hold them to be identical (e.g. Ellsberg, Baumol and Strotz).

While formally right, the latter writers threw the baby out with the bathwater when concluding that the vNM utility would "not seem to be of any relevance in welfare evaluations" (Ellsberg, 1954, p. 556).

6. CARDINALITY AND SOCIAL CHOICE

The "ordinalist revolution" implied a technocratization of economists' role in society. Whereas classical economists considered distributional problems as an important part of economic science, the ordinalists refused to deal with questions involving interpersonal comparisons of welfare.

The scope was narrowed down from devising *correct* policies to devising *consistent* policies, the difference being mainly a reclassification of value judgements like "a dollar is more worth to a poor man than to a rich man". All value judgements were exported to politics, now being unquestionable constraints for economic analysis rather than scientific statements. Only the apparently uncontroversial value judgement that expressed individual preferences should count in collective decision making (the Pareto principle) was not exorcized from welfare economics.[67]

However, rules for collective decision making relying solely on ordinal and noncomparable properties of individual preferences soon proved to be unattractive. Arrow's impossibility theorem and further research along the same lines (see Sen, 1986, for a survey of the literature) made it abundantly clear that

> armed with only an n-tuple of individual orderings, we can hardly expect to say much of interest on inequality.
>
> Sen (1974, p. 390).

One way of phrasing the problem is that quite weak consistency requirements are nevertheless very limiting when the number of possible individual rankings which are to be treated consistently is large. Therefore, admitting *more* information than that represented by n-tuples of individual orderings (or n-tuples of ordinal utility functions) reduces the number of permissible transformations of utility and hence makes it more likely that a reasonable[68] social welfare functional will exist. But as it turns out, *cardinal* utility does not by itself impose enough structure on the problem (see Sen, 1970, Theorem 8*.2). Only by admitting *comparable* utility will the existence of a reasonable social decision rule be guaranteed.

Reading the literature, it appears that questions of cardinality and comparability are so controversial that they can only be discussed in mathematical terms: It is legitimate to investigate *what kind* of information (degrees of measurability and comparability of utility) is needed to obtain a well-functioning social decision rule, but not to discuss how the information can practically be obtained.

The section starts with a justification of empirical welfare measurement. Then we go on to ask how individual welfare measurement and interpersonal comparisons can be distinguished from value judgements, i.e. how to avoid confusion between politics and science. In section 6.3 the differences between ex ante and ex post utilitarianism are spelled out, before we close with some brief considerations on tax policy.

6.1. Empirical Welfare Measurement

The statement that utility cannot be cardinally measured is without content as long as utility is not precisely defined and wrong for a number of precise definitions (see section 3.3). Similarly, once welfare is properly defined,

TABLE I

Cardinality assumption	Data		
	Market	Survey	Experimental
Intensity comparisons		×	
Additive preferences	×	+	
Time independent preferences	×	+	
Stochastic choice			×
Least noticeable differences			×
Behaviour under uncertainty	×	×	
Speed of adjustment	×		

Explanation: The entries marked with an × indicates that this is and adequate type of data. The "+" entries are made where this kind of data must supplement the main source.

it is possible to measure it from data.[69] Essentially, the question is; what kind of information is relevant for distributional and other social choices?

Simon (1974) argues that the natural definition of welfare may well be a *composite measure* of various types of data. A welfare measure defined on income (other parameters like, for example, race and education held constant) could be based on the correlation between income and personal reports of well-being, risk behaviour, suicide and health statistics etc. The value of such a definition is that it facilitates science-aided distribution decisions without mixing up the roles of scientists and politicians: Scientists' role is to analyse the logical and empirical relationship between various indices (concepts),[70] whereas the politicians' domain are the basic value judgments; deeming what information is relevant for distributional decisions as well as the weight to be put on each index composing the welfare measure.

The utility concepts characterized in Section 4 are all potential components of such a welfare measure. The rest of this paragraph investigates the applicability of various utility information for welfare analysis.

The suitable data sources for empirical measurement of the utility functions are indicated in Table I. In Section 4 I gave some references to the empirical work carried out under each of the cardinality assumptions. There are however reasons for being sceptical with respect to the usefulness of this work for distributional decisions. Recapitulating, the utility models whose estimation require experimental data, i.e. stochastic choice and least noticeable differences, do not lend themselves to measurement at all. Methods which are perfectly sound when the stimulus is a physical magnitude (rather than a number), and when it is a question of perception rather than of preference, seem to be neither valid nor reliable in this case. Even upon acceptance of the stimulus-response doctrine of man as a pleasure-machine, it is doubtful whether a convincing experiment can be constructed for eliciting least noticeable increments of wealth. The major methodological weakness attached to the additive preference approach is that market data are necessary but not sufficient to build a cardinal index of utility. Survey data are needed to assure that the classification of commodities not only satisfies additivity of preference, but also independence according to Edgeworth's sense of it (i.e. cross-derivatives of the utility function being zero). Also time independent cardinal utility cannot be found from market data alone. Only if it is approximately true that utility in period t does not depend on consumption in previous or future periods[71] will saving decisions give indications of the marginal utility of wealth.[72] Whether these obstacles justify the young Samuelson's negative conclusion that

> The idea that the results of such a statistical investigation could have any influence upon ethical judgments of policy is one which deserves the impatience of modern economists.
>
> Samuelson (1937, p. 161).

I leave it for the reader to decide. At any rate, modern economists have followed Samuelson's advice to the extent that not a single empirical investigation has been carried out along these lines. Nor have I seen empirical work attempting to estimate cardinal utility by direct use of Camacho's hypothetical repetitions approach.

This leaves us with the two utility concepts that have been subject to extensive measurement. But, as noted earlier, people seem not to conform to vNM axioms, and also the theoretical foundations for using behaviour under uncertainty as an indicator of welfare are shaky. A satisfactory empirical investigation of the relationship between ex post utility and the vNM utility concept remains to be done. (In subsection 6.3, however, an argument is presented where risk aversion is relevant for distributional decisions without postulating any direct link between vNM utility and ex post utility.) Therefore, as I see it, the only practicable empirical welfare measurements which to some extent correspond to the classical utilitarian idea are those carried out explicitly in terms of rankings of utility differences. Some surveys of this kind have been referred to earlier (sections 4.1 and 5.2), but recent large scale surveys have been almost exclusively carried out by the "Leyden school", whose methods and results will now be examined.

The "Leyden school" method,[73] as described by, for example, van Heerwarden and Kapteyn (1981), Kapteyn and van Praag (1977) and van Praag (1971), is to have respondents answer questions of the following type: "I would call my net yearly income [some adjective, e.g. *good*] if it were between . . . and . . . ". The blank spaces are filled in by the respondent, and there are usually about nine adjacent categories, ranging from *very bad* via *good* to *excellent*. In order to interpret the results as indications of strength of preference, one assumption is crucial: Respondents must try to "maximize informational content" by letting the perceived difference in welfare between any two adjacent labels be equal. In particular this means that answers should be insensitive to the actual labelling; replacing *very bad* by *horrible* as the label covering the worst income interval should not alter the elicited answers. This hypothesis is actually rejected by Buyze (1982), but may nevertheless provide a "reasonable approximation to reality" (for a discussion, see Kapteyn and Wansbeek, 1985a, b, and Ratchford, 1985). Three central results obtained by Leyden school authors can be summarized as follows:

- individual welfare functions are convex for low incomes and concave for normal and high incomes,
- most people regard themselves to be at the concave segment of the curve, and
- reference group phenomena and habit formation strongly influence people's evaluation of income.

The latter result has been pointed out earlier by a number of sociologists, notably Bradburn (1969), Bradburn and Caplowitz (1965), Cantril (1965), Inkeles (1960) and Wilson (1967). For a review of these works, see Easterlin (1974), and for an intriguing discussion of the "Easterlin paradox" that reported happiness correlates positively with income *within* a country, but not necessarily *between* countries or between points in time, see Abramovitz (1979). The two first results are however not captured by these earlier sociological surveys, as these are mainly concentrated on (the ordinal property of) correlation between happiness and income.

6.2. Value Judgements Vs. Judgements of Fact

A Bergson–Samuelson welfare function

$$(6.1) \qquad W = W(u_1, u_2, \ldots, u_n)$$

does not, according to its originators, rely on a cardinal concept of utility:

> there are an infinity of equally good indicators [of social welfare] which can be used. Thus, if one of these is written as $W = F(u_1, u_2, \ldots)$, and if we were to change from one set of cardinal indexes to another set $(v_1, v_2, \ldots)$, we should simply change the form of the function F so as to leave all social decisions invariant.
>
> Samuelson (1947, p. 228).

With this formulation, the government's value judgements are reflected in the *combination* of $W(\bullet)$ and the chosen cardinalization of utilities. Following the articles of Parks (1976) and Kemp and Ng (1976), there was widespread disagreement concerning the existence of a "reasonable" Bergson–Samuelson welfare function. Some authors, notably Kemp and Ng (1977, 1982) and Ng (1982, 1985, 1986), have argued forcefully that cardinal utility is necessary, whereas Samuelson (1977), Mayston (1982) and Seidl (1986) take the opposite view. I will now briefly summarize the lessons to be drawn from the debate.

First, if a social welfare functional of the Bergson–Samuelson type is not subject to any consistency requirement,[74] existence will not be a problem. Second, it can be proven (Parks, 1976, Kemp and Ng, 1976) that imposition of an ordinalist condition like "single-profile neutrality" (if every person ranks alternatives a and b in the same order as he ranks x and y, then society should rank a and b in the same order as x and y) leads to an impossibility theorem similar to Arrow's. However, according to Samuelson "to understand this condition is to reject it". For example, one consequence of the condition is that in matters of income distribution involving only two persons in the society (the others being indifferent), if the society decides to take a dollar from person 1 and give it to person 2, then the whole of person 1's wealth should be given to person 2. Samuelson is probably right that this condition must be rejected, but the real question is: when rejecting it, do we not also give up ordinalism? If the planner thinks that a one dollar transfer is warranted whereas a thousand dollar transfer is not, does not an *interpretation* in terms of cardinal and comparable utility become even more relevant? A refusal of this interpretation amounts again to the (dubious) denial that cardinal utility is a meaningful concept and a stubborn insistence that to scientists judgements of welfare must necessarily be a "black box".

In the previous subsection an argument was presented in favour of science-aided distribution decisions. I will now, using the concept of a Bergson–Samuelson social welfare functional, try to follow the argument to its logical conclusion (an exercise which of course must not be taken too literally).

Remember that cardinal utility is not enough to avoid Arrow-type impossibility theorems. Some comparability of utility is also necessary.[75] The question is how to introduce comparability non-arbitrarily, and leaving a role to play for the (scientifically determined) individual utility functions, i.e. we must lay down some rules for comparing individual welfares. I suggest the following procedure: Assume that the planner has defined (and scientists have cardinally measured) an index of individual welfare/utility. Now let the planner decide on an income vector $\mathbf{Y_t}$ at which everybody enjoys equal total utility and another vector $\mathbf{Y_m}$ where everybody's marginal utility is the same (in the planner's eyes). Clearly, these decisions reflect *value judgements* in the sense that they are disputable. However, they are a kind of value judgements which are familiar, thus facilitating public discussion. The equalization of total utility is implicitly what a (utilitarian) society does, for example, when establishing a poverty line depending on family size etc. (with better information, individual poverty lines would be a natural consequence), and the equalization of marginal utilities means that there must exist *some* (not necessarily feasible) income distribution where the planner, *if he put equal weight on everybody's welfare*, would want to make no redistribution.

The idea is the following: Assume that the planner has decided on the income vector $\mathbf{Y_t} = (y_{1t}, y_{2t}, \ldots)$ which *in his opinion* yields everybody the same total utility, k_1, and the vector $\mathbf{Y_m} = (y_{1m}, y_{2m}, \ldots)$ yielding everybody the same marginal utility, k_2. Select arbitrarily a utility representation $\mathbf{U} = (u_1(\bullet), u_2(\bullet), \ldots)$. For each person i, find the positive affine transformations $v_i(\bullet)$ fulfilling

$$v_i(y_{it}) = a + bu_i(y_{it}) = k_1 \tag{6.2}$$

and

$$v_i'(y_{im}) = bu_i'(y_{im}) = k_2 \tag{6.3}$$

(where u' and v' denotes derivatives). Solving for a and b, we obtain

$$a = k_1 - k_2 \frac{u_i(y_{it})}{u_i'(y_{im})}$$

and

$$b = \frac{k_2}{u_i'(y_{im})}$$

Implying

$$v_i(y_i) = k_1 + \frac{k_2}{u_i'(y_{im})}(u_i(y_i) - u_i(y_{it})) \tag{6.4}$$

Here we see that changing k_1 and k_2 amounts to making the same positive affine transformation of each of the selected utility functions $u_i(\bullet)$, i.e. we have obtained what in the social choice literature is called cardinal full comparability (see Sen, 1986, p. 1113).[76] There are no Arrowian impossibility theorems for this rich informational structure. Furthermore, cardinal full comparability corresponds to the framework of Bentham and Mill, facilitating, for example, a discussion of progressive taxation à la Cohen Stuart (1889).

The important thing to note is that cardinalization itself is not a value judgement here. The planner is thus forced to make distributive choices based on publically observable information. Political discussion (value judgements) boils down to three matters: the definition of individual welfare indices, the selection of the vectors $\mathbf{Y_m}$ and $\mathbf{Y_t}$, and the "just" shape of the Bergson–Samuelson social welfare functional.[77]

6.3. Ex Post Vs. Ex Ante Welfare

With the works of Vickrey (1945, 1960) and Harsanyi (1953, 1955), the old utilitarian idea, that maximization of an unweighted sum of individual utility should be the goal of social planning, enjoyed a sudden renaissance.[78] Harsanyi's work has had greater impact than Vickrey's , which is regrettable because Harsanyi, as mentioned in section 5.2, confuses ex ante with ex post utility. Vickrey on the other hand makes himself perfect clear:

> If utility is defined as that quantity the mathematical expectation of which is maximized by an individual making choices involving risk, then to maximize the aggregate of such utility over the population is equivalent to choosing that distribution of income which such an individual would select were he asked which of various variants of the economy he would like to become a member of, assuming that once he selects a given economy with a given distribution of income he has an equal chance of landing in the shoes of each member of it.
>
> Vickrey (1945, p. 329).

A little bit more formally: Let S_i be a social state, and x_{ji} the position of individual j in state i. These positions are objectively observable *and are unanimously compared.* (This last assumption demands a lot of empathy.) Having equal probability of becoming each of the n persons in the society ("the principle of impersonal choice"),[79] a person k satisfying the vNM rationality postulates will choose the social state i which maximizes

$$(6.5) \qquad W_{ki} = \frac{1}{n} \sum_{j=1}^{n} w_k(x_{ji})$$

where $w_k(\bullet)$ is the vNM utility function of person k. In other words, the state is chosen which maximizes the utility sum or, equivalently, the average utility.[80] But, as recognized by Pattanaik (1968), we have now got as many welfare functions are there are individuals, and in general only if their risk preferences are identical will their rankings of social states be the same. So how can consensus be brought about? Vickrey (1961) proposes that in a case with differing welfare judgements one can apply *repeated averaging*, or as explicitly suggested by Mueller (1973) and Mueller, Tollison and Willett (1974), the functions W_{ki} can enter as arguments into a second round of evaluations where each person maximizes

$$(6.6) \qquad U_{ki} = \frac{1}{n} \sum_{j=1}^{n} w_k(W_{ji})$$

Again of course we have to make the heroic assumption that W_{ji} is comparable across individuals j. If such a process of repeated averaging converges, unanimity is reached.[81]

Let us now, in the spirit of Harsanyi, let the position of individual j in state i be represented by his ex post utility in that state. Formally, this is only a renaming of variables, x_{ji} becoming u_{ji} (comparable positions becoming comparable utility). Then, if we accept Harsanyi's view that vNM utility and ex post utility are the same, by definition no person will have risk aversion with respect to outcome utilities, and everyone will have identical welfare functions

$$W_{ki} = \frac{1}{n} \sum_{j=1}^{n} u_{ji} \tag{6.7}$$

But this is just another way of saying that all persons have the same risk aversion – if not, there would have been disagreement establishing comparable utility at the outset! This way of phrasing the problem sheds some light on a dispute between Sen (1977) and Harsanyi (1975, 1977). In particular, Harsanyi's insistence that

> it would make no sense whatever to assume a law of decreasing marginal utility for utility
> Harsanyi (1975, p. 322)

must be understood as a consequence of his mistaken view that the two utility concepts are identical. But as we have seen, the utility-sum theorem does not automatically follow if people have different risk aversion (in which case repeated averaging may or may not lead to a utilitarian rule).

If the vNM utility differs from ex post utility, we may obtain a vNM utility-sum theorem without maximization of ex post utility. Ethically this is a dilemma, since two seemingly utilitarian rules lead to different conclusions. Risk aversion with respect to ex post utility combined with the doctrine of impersonal choice typically leads to preference for a social state with more equality and less total ex post utility than the state picked by the Benthamite utility-sum criterion which is "risk-neutral with respect to ex post utilities" (This follows straightforwardly from the risk of aversion (Rothschild-Stiglitz, 1970): of two mean-preserving spreads, the one with less dispersion is mostly preferred. Thus for any non-degenerate lottery A there exists a less risky lottery B with a lower expected outcome which is preferred to A.) Note in particular that Sen's argument in Sen (1973) in favour of taking into account the dispersion of utilities – and not only the average – does *not* contradict the idea of ethics in terms of hypothetical alternatives. A crucial moral question is therefore what kind of welfare society should maximize.[82] Personally, I find the principle of impersonal choice very appealing. Here ethical judgement follows directly from rationality postulates once people agree in their judgement of fact. The classical utility-sum criterion lacks an independent moral foundation, and the very relevant criticism which might be directed against it is exactly the possibility that it contradicts the principle of impersonal choice.[83]

A related issue arises when in a social state people make risky decisions. The result, despite initial equality, may be gross inequality. Should society care? Friedman (1953, 1962) argues to the contrary:

> Consider a group of individuals who initially have equal endowments and who agree voluntarily to enter a lottery with very unequal prizes. The resultant inequality of income is surely required to permit the individuals in question to make the most of their initial equality.
>
> Friedman (1962, p. 162).

We see that consumer sovereignty leads directly to acceptance of the ex ante view. As long as actual risk-bearing is freely agreed upon by those involved, society should be concerned with ex ante inequality only. Still, many countries have compulsory insurance against a variety of accidents, and publicly financed rescue squads save the lives of uninsured mountain climbers who could easily have insured themselves.[84] It seems safety is a "merit good" (Sandmo, 1983), for which can be found little more justification than Shackle's distrust in human foresight:

> I do not think, in human terms, knowledge can be so perfect that tomorrow's hunger can be felt today.
>
> (quoted after Kanbur (1987)).

On the other hand, how praisworthy are the egalitarian tendencies of those who have bet on a long shot – and lost? The Biblical tale of the prodigal son is not for Paretians!

How can the preceding discussion be applied to the question of a fair income taxation? A few simple results follow directly. First, *ceteris paribus*, risk aversion and concave ex post utility (as functions of wealth) are jointly sufficient for the impersonal choice principle to support progressive lump-sum taxation. Second, if ex ante and ex post utility in fact correlate strongly and society is run according to ex post utilitarianism, tax rates should be differentiated according to the riskiness of the income source. People who become rich by taking risks display a high marginal utility of wealth, and therefore "deserve" a lower rate than those who build a the same fortune slowly and safely.[85] Conversely, society should not be as concerned about the misery of a gambler as of the truly unfortunate. Note that in both these cases the conclusions effectively depend on information about suitably defined individual utility.[86]

7. CONCLUDING REMARKS

Failure to recognize the diverse meanings of the word "utility" has led to persistent confusion within the economics profession.

The aim of this work has been twofold. First, I have tried to give a picture of the development of cardinal utility theory from the 18th century to the present date. Since earlier surveys have either been mostly concerned with positive theory (e.g. Stigler, 1950) or have been sketchy on the historical parts (e.g. Fishburn, 1986, 1976), an extensive and truly "hedonimetrically" oriented survey has been lacking. Secondly, I have wanted to give a scientifically founded answer to the questions of *meaning* and *relatedness* of the utility concepts. Thus, the emphasis has been on conceptual clarification rather than on the practical relevance of the concepts for policy making. However, in my defence should count that the latter problem can be approached more constructively once the epistemological issues are clarified.

The history of hedonimetry is a story of persistent failures. Jeremy Bentham once wrote about himself "I have planted the tree of utility. I have planted it deep and spread it wide". Regrettably he also rooted some serious ambiguities, which besides spreading widely did also multiply during the centuries. For example, Bentham seems to have been the first to suggest the lnd approach to cardinal utility, and also the first to mix it up with the interval comparisons approach, a mistake which was to be repeated by Fechner almost a century later. Still, an even more devastating fallacy trapped the genius of Daniel Bernoulli, who suggested that decision makers facing an uncertain situation would (and should) make the decision which maximized expected happiness, explaining in this way the fact that people did not seem to maximize the expected *monetary* outcome while choosing between uncertain options. Fechner "generalized the mistake" by noting that behaviour under uncertainty, as in the St. Petersburg game, indicated that marginal utility of wealth was decreasing. Even today many economists seem not to recognize the force of innocent-looking questions like: why should a person want to maximize *expected* happiness (and not some other function of it), or, with a similar effect, if a person acts as if he maximizes the expectation of some function, why the expectation of *happiness*?

These confusions were carried over to our century notwithstanding the cleverness of such innovators as Jevons, Edgeworth, Pareto and Marshall. Frisch and Fisher even managed to invent a failure on their own, by claiming that utility could be measured if preferences were independent (see Section 4.3).

The basic mistake made by all these masterminds was to identify introspective happiness/utility with their ways of measuring it, without noticing that in general *each measuring procedure would lead to a different measure* (and might even correspond to incommensurable scale types, the permissible class of transformations not being the same). As indicated in Section 3.2, this was a kind of error which could hardly have survived long in physics. It has probably done so in economics much because of the familiarity of the utility concept.[87]

Once this first type of failure, the "fallacy of identity", was properly treated, two new errors immediately appeared.

The first error was made by Maurice Allais when he tried to prove the theoretical identity of the interval comparisons approach and the vNM approach.

Secondly, some economists who accepted that the various definitions were not equal got trapped by the "fallacy of unrelatedness". I have argued that both logical and empirical arguments may lead to the conclusion that the various definitions of utility are indeed closely related.

In addition, some leading economists insisted – and still insist – that the classical (ex post) cardinal utility concepts, especially the utility found from interval comparisons, were "meaningless" and "nonsensical". This position is shown not to be grounded in mainstream epistemology, and is therefore not an argument against scientific interest in these concepts. As I see it, the worst that can be said about hedonimetry is that the science is of *little relevance* for distributional decision making. But, according to the analysis of Section 6, the definition of a welfare index is a political rather than a scientific task. A scientist cannot *qua* scientist object to politicians' use of information in social decision making, unless he or she can demonstrate that the information is wrongly interpreted.

The insights contained in the illuminating articles by William Vickrey (1945), Robert Strotz (1953) and Daniel Ellsberg (1954) are far from being commonly recognized. The misconceptions about cardinal utility theory stil flourish in modern textbooks of economics. Precise concepts are necessary for adequate analysis. Thus in my judgement the most fundamental problem of utility theory is not where to go next, but to communicate the established wisdom.

Department of Economics
Stockholm School of Economics
Stockholm, Sweden

NOTES

* Comments and suggestions from Peter Fishburn, Terje Lensberg, Heine Rasmussen and Bjørn Sandvik are gratefully acknowledged. The author is responsible for all remaining errors and shortcomings.

[1] The most recent bibliography, by Aoki *et al.* (1977), is also out of date.

[2] Also many recent theories of individual intertemporal decision making rely heavily on a cardinalistic formulation of utility. I have chosen to treat this topic only sketchily (in section 4.3).

[3] For an excellent overview, see Sen (1986).

[4] Utilitarian reasoning can also be found in Aristoteles' works. See Kraus (1903) for examples. Kauder (1953) provides an alternative starting point to ours.

[5] Before the work of Hicks and Allen (1934), economists spoke of "measurable" and not of "cardinal" utility.

[6] Any reader of pre-1920 utility theory should be aware that utility sometimes is taken to be an attribute of an object and on other occasions refers to the satisfaction enjoyed by the person holding the object. Here we will only discuss the latter use of the word.

[7] A proposal to let the election system reflect intensity of wants originates with de Borda (1781), who must also be reckoned as a pioneering cardinalist.

[8] To give exact bibliographical references to Bentham's work is a non-trivial task. Hence, I make all references to Stark (1952), wherein the interested reader may find further clues as to where the relevant quotation first appeared (Stark, vol. 3, appendix 1).

[9] The references are made to the English translation by Louise Sommer, *Econometrica*, 1954.

[10] A similar suggestion had in fact already been made by the mathematician Gabriel Cramer in a letter to Nicolas Bernoulli in 1728.

[11] The phrase *ex post utility* is used as a synonym for *riskless utility*, i.e. an evaluation of outcomes ("end states") which is independent of any *ex ante* uncertainty. This is done in order to avoid confusion with the (ex ante) utility concepts introduced in section 4.5.

[12] The German phrase "kleinsten noch merklichen Verschiedenheiten" will be variously translated as "smallest detectable change", "just noticeable difference", "least noticeable difference", "minimum perceptible threshold" etc.

[13] Bentham himself came close to the idea when he wrote: "A quantity of the matter of wealth may be assigned so small, that if subtracted from the fortune of a person possessed of a certain quantity of the matter of abundance, no sensible subtraction of happiness would be the result" (op.cit. vol. 1, p. 114).

[14] Here $u(\bullet)$ is a utility function, $\mathbf{x}$ a vector of goods, p_i is the price on good i, and $u_i(\mathbf{x})$ is the partial derivative of u with respect to i.

[15] It should be noted that Jevons had some serious doubts about interpersonal comparisons. "Every mind is inscrutinable to every other mind, and no common denominator seems to be possible" (Jevons 1965, p. 14).

[16] Read, e.g. pp. 77–79 where the author gives a flavour of previous sexism in the poetical mode, quoting Tennyson:

> Woman is the lesser man,
> and her passions unto mine
> are as moonlight unto sunlight
> and as water unto wine

[17] Pareto used the word "ophelmity" for what we have called utility in order to avoid confusion between what is *wanted* and what is generally considered as *useful*. (Fisher, 1918, in his turn suggested that "wantability" was a better term than "ophelmity", whereas Tinnes, 1919, believed that "valure" would suitably describe the phenomenon in question.) This distinction was not always clear in nineteenth century writings. However, the conclusion advanced by Cooter and Rappoport (1984), that "utility" to these writers *in general* meant usefulness (or referred to material welfare), is not warranted. This point is made by Hennipman (1988), but not accepted by Cooter and Rappoport (see Rappoport, 1988). Personally, I think that Fisher (1918) settles the case:

The concept called "final degree of utility" by Jevons, "effective utility", "specific utility" and "marginal efficiency" by J.B. Clark, "marginal utility" and "marginal desirability" by Marshall, Gide and others [. . .], and ophélmité by Pareto. . .

[18] But as we see, Stigler's claim that "Pareto believed the consumer could not rank utility differences" (Stigler, 1950, p. 381) can hardly be upheld. Pareto repeated his views later: "there is no reason for not accepting it [cardinal utility], with the reservation that it must be verified by the results deduced from it" (Pareto, 1955, p. 73).

[19] The statement was qualified so as to be valid in the absence of incentive effects only.

[20] An early attempt to clarify the relevance of measurement theory to issues of measurable utility is Alchian (1953). The treatment here is a bit more up to date.

[21] E.g. length, volume, greyness, hardness, density.

[22] Ordered metrics was first formally treated by Coombs (1950).

[23] Actually Fishburn's definition of quasi-cardinality contains a little more than the ordered metric scales. Hence, elsewhere one can find a grading of quasi-cardinal utility functions (see e.g. Basu, 1980).

[24] The relevance of these quotations for cardinal utility is noted in a lucid article by Ellsberg (1954).

[25] The costliness of precision can be illustrated with the example of education. Low-level teaching often covers a broader range of topics per unit of time than does high-level education. Less precision is the cost of saying something interesting to non-experts.

[26] For a short account of the various methods for determining minimum perceptible thresholds, see J.C. Stevens (1968).

[27] For an elaboration of this psychophysical version of the rule that only relative prices matter, see Sinn (1983, ch. 3).

[28] Sometimes, this method is also referred to as *category estimation* or *interval comparison*.

[29] I would have liked to come across this quotation all by myself, but I have to admit that I have borrowed it from Milton Friedman (1955), who in turn borrowed it from Dennis Robertson.

[30] Had he been explicit about reflexivity of the indifference relation and stated his continuity argument more clearly, he could have obtained a result similar to that of Debreu (1954), proving sufficiency as well.

[31] Other contributions were those by Allen (1935), Bernardelli (1934), Lange (1934b), Phelps-Brown (1934) and Zeuthen (1937).

[32] Connectedness of a set means that the set cannot be written as a union of two disjoint sets A and B where no point of A lies in the closure of B, and no point of B lies in the closure of A.

[33] This is a restatement of Basu's theorem 1, and the reader is referred to this article for a proof.

[34] Samuelson's punchline is much below the belt: "In conclusion, I should like to express

my agreement with Dr. Lange concerning the inconsistencies in the writings of the earlier mathematical economists".

35 Open conditions for existence of a utility function are here defined as conditions which do not require that the function's domain (the set of alternatives) exhibit special properties, like e.g. connectedness (see Luce and Suppes, 1965, p. 269).

36 This is true for the interval comparison approach, but not necessarily for all other approaches to cardinal utility.

37 To Armstrong *existence* of a utility function was not an issue. Some contributions to that literature can be found in Chipman *et al.* (1971).

38 I do not know why, in the literature, the term "sensibility" has been preferred to the more natural "sensitivity".

39 This claim is valid in a one-period context only. Multi-period models are treated below.

40 All the three authors obtain an esitmate of $\varepsilon_I \cong 2$, but as noted below this result is more a product of the model thatn it is an inherent feature of the data.

41 Even with few commodity groups, the additive preference assumption is falsified by data. For references, see Deaton and Muellbauer (1983, paragraph 5.3).

42 If $u(\mathbf{x})$ is to be quasi-concave, at most one of the component functions can be non-concave (see e.g. Debreu and Koopmans, 1982, for a proof). The case where one component is convex looks rather weird, and is always ruled out in empirical analysis.

43 Samuelson presents an odd argument for this assumption: "The marginal utility of income derived will hold only for a given set of prices. This limitation is inherent in the problem, since the concept has meaning only with reference to a fixed set of prices." But the fact that λ is a *function of* the prices does not support this conclusion!

44 For a later statement, see Hillinger (1969) who also analyses the variation of λ with prices, although he does not devise a method for *constructing* the utility function without assuming constancy of prices.

45 For further remarks on Samuelson's approach, see Gabor and James (1958, pp. 8ff.).

46 I am grateful to Peter Fishburn for alerting me to this theorem.

47 Camachos's wording is, I think, a little misleading, since he speaks of ranking sequences of *choices* instead of sequences of *outcomes* – over which utility is defined.

48 We will be concerned with *probabilistic* uncertainty only; neither the Knightian distinction between uncertainty and risk nor the related concept of ignorance will play any role in what follows.

49 Ramsey never confused his construction of value with old fashioned utility, nor did he claim that expected utility should be maximized. On the other hand, he gave a concession to the cardinalists when he stated that "it is universally agreed that money has a diminishing marginal utility". He did not live to regret it.

50 A good place to start if one is interested in a critical appraisal of the model and its proposed alternatives is the survey by Machina (1987).

51 Of course, mathematical analysis can go wrong as well. For instance, the mathematical arguments of Bernardelli (1938, 1952) did not rehabilitate at all the classical theory of marginal utility in the way he believed them to do. On the contrary, the were easily refuted by Samuelson (1939) and Lancaster (1953) respectively. (See Bernardelli, 1939, 1954 and Lancaster, 1954 for the full discussion.) The point is that mathematical errors are often more transparent and easier to correct than errors which are due to verbal imprecision.

52 This argument is repeated in Lerner (1977, p. 239).

53 The possibility of indivisibilities and of complementarity between indivisibilities is noted by Lerner, but rejected on the grounds that he believes substitutes to be at least equally important. The case with full divisibility of commodities he does not comment upon. This

simple point is also overlooked in the critical comment by Marx (1949).

[54] This method does not quite deserve the description of the header; it *is* formalized.

[55] The notion referred to here became more and more explicit during the 1950s through a series of influential works by among others Arrow (1951), Baumol (1958) (not to be confused with his abandoned views set forth in Baumol, 1951), Ellsberg (1954), Friedman (1955), Friedman and Savage (1948, and esp. 1952), Luce and Raiffa (1957), Marschak (1950), Ozga (1956), Savage (1954), Strotz (1953) and Weldon (1950).

[56] Arrow's position is slightly less categorical in the extra Chapter 8 of the second edition.

[57] Allais uses the term "cardinal utility in Jevon's sense", a wording which is hard to justify, since Jevons never explicitly defined his concept. He also sometimes uses the jnd definition of utility as if interval comparisons and the jnd approach were identical.

[58] In Allais' initial formulation only increases k of a magnitude of less than a just noticeable difference was considered. In his paper (1979b) Allais adopted the present formulation, which had earlier been used by Hagen (1972) who attributes it to Leinfellner (1968).

[59] Note that Allais's axiom is analogous to the requirement of constant absolute risk aversion, only the latter is expressed in terms of monetary outcomes. Actually, Pfanzagl (1959) made an identical mistake to Allais, when he claimed that the "axiom of consistency" would imply that the vNM utility would have to be linear in money, a mistake which was pointed out by Mellon (1960).

[60] It should be emphasized that if the vNM axioms are not required to hold, the axiom of cardinal iso-variation allows for a very large class of decision rules under uncertainty. As pointed out by Hagen (1972), the axiom is consistent with maximizing an additive function of the expectation, variance and skewness of ex post utility.

[x)] Editor's note: A different view is found in Hagen: The short step etc. (This book.)

[61] Readers who are unfamiliar with the terminology of binary relations are again referred to Fishburn (1970a, ch. 2).

[62] Fellner (1968, p. 58) does also, like Harsanyi, "conclude that *ideally* the two operational theories should give us identical utility functions". Rothenberg (1961, p. 214) is also trapped: "it is difficult to believe that the hypothetical preference intensities which are weighted linearly to form expected utilities are not essentially the same as those computed from psychometric riskless context".

[63] Bell (1981) and Hansson (1988) also argues in favour of interpreting risk aversion as a conjoint measure of ex post utility of wealth and other psychological factors. Krelle (1968) and Hagen (1969) both belong to the avant garde, adopting the view when it was still very heretical. Bernard (1984, 1986) leaves the impression that things have now changed dramatically in favour of this position, but I think he is a bit too optimistic.

[64] Similarly, the apparent confirmation of the identity axiom in Paine (1975) is open to doubt, as the author does not check whether the result is dependent on the particular probabilities applied.

[65] From this article it is clear that Frisch held the two concepts to be either closely related or identical.

[66] de Finetti confirms his standpoint in de Finetti (1979).

[67] Politics not rooted in the Pareto-principle have been of little interest to economists, who refuse to spend time seriously analysing the consistency of such frameworks. For instance, the concept of "merit wants" is generally taken to be incompatible with the Pareto-criterion, and it is not far-fetched to ascribe the lack of scientific interest in this topic to that fact.

[68] In the social choice literature "reasonable" social welfare function(al)s are those which do not require a dictator of some sort to ensure Pareto-optimality.

[69] Natural as this argument seems, it is by no means an old truth in economic science. In his

influential book, Little (1957, p. 34) writes: "measurement is a precise objective operation, and if something called 'satisfaction' were really measured, then the very precision of the result would destroy its value for helping to decide on ethical issues".

[70] In addition, scientists should aid politicians in formulating their basic value judgements unambiguously, a necessary condition for reaching an internally consistent policy.

[71] Habit formation will typically increase the stability of (instantaneous) preferences, but contrary to learning it may over time decrease the utility obtained from a given collection of goods.

[72] The underlying assumption of "perfect" credit markets may also be violated in reality, making the estimation of the index even more difficult.

[73] This approach originated with van Praag (1968), and active research is mostly carried out in Belgium and in the Netherlands.

[74] There is a great number of possible consistency requirements. Some of them require consistent treatment of different preference profiles (ordinal utility vectors), others require only that the social choice should correspond consistently to a single preference profile.

[75] There is no room here for a thorough discussion of the comparability issue. The literature on comparable utility is recently surveyed by Möller (1983).

[76] Curiously enough, this trivial result seems to have gone unnoted in the literature. Ng (1984a) claimed to have proved the related theorem that comparability of utility levels implies comparability of utility differences. This assertion was wrong, as shown by Jaffray (1985).

[77] I do of course not suggest that this is an exhaustive list of relevant political questions at this level of generality, for example, the question of rights might fall outside the framework applied here.

[78] Despite the close relationship between their works, the two authors have made it an odd custom not to refer to each other's articles. This is one of the reasons why Vickrey's seminal paper (Vickrey, 1945) is virtually unknown.

[79] See Harsanyi (1958) for a general defence of the principle of "ethics in terms of hypothetical alternatives".

[80] A critique against using the sure-thing principle in social choice is raised by Diamond (1967) and is still referred to by some writers. However, it is my opinion that Harsanyi (1975, 1977) rejects the critique convincingly.

[81] Even if the process converges, the outcome may be troublesome. For example, as demonstrated by Mueller *et al.*, if one person is infinitely risk averse and none of the other infinitely risk-seeking, the point of convergence is the maximin solution.

[82] I stress once more that there are several non-welfarist approaches to moral philosophy, although some economists, notably Ng (1981, 1985), argues that all of them ultimately should rest on welfarist grounds. Whether this is a question of true disagreement or only of terminology, I will not judge.

[83] Direct application of the impartial choice idea in empirical research is an interesting possibility. The ex post welfare concept can in principle be avoided by using a suitably worked out procedure where people are actually made to reveal the tax system they would prefer if they had equal chances of landing in anybody's shoes. Similar procedures are also well suited for evaluating other important questions, like intergenerational fairness and immigration policy. In this way social decision making can be based directly on attitudes without invoking the troublesome notion of measurable welfare at all.

[84] Also, there is great reluctance to using randomized taxes, despite the possibility of implementing ex ante Pareto-improvements (see Stiglitz, 1982).

[85] This simple result need not hold true in a second-best context (labour supply and risk-

taking being dependent on tax rates).

[86] A writer who takes measurable utility seriously and applies it in the theory of taxation is Brunner (1986).

[87] It is ironic that it was Irving Fisher who wrote:
"In all sciences, and particularly in one like economics, which appeals to the general public and which uses concepts and terms at least partially familiar, it is a matter of some practical importance to select a suitable terminology." – Fisher (1918, p. 335).

REFERENCES

Abramovitz, M. (1979) 'Economic growth and its dicontents', in Boskin (ed.) (1979).

Adams, E.W. (1960) 'Survey of Bernoullian utility theorey', in Solomon (ed.) (1960).

Alchian, A.A. (1953) 'The meaning of utility measurement', *American Economic Review* **43**, 26–50.

Allais, M. (1953) 'Le comportement de l'homme devant le risque: critique des postulats et axiomes de l'ecole amèricaine', *Econometrica* **21**, 503–546. Reprinted in English as Allais (1979a).

Allais, M. (1979a) 'The foundations of a positive theory of choice involving risk and a criticism of the postulates and axioms of the American school', in Allais/Hagen (eds.) (1979).

Allais, M. (1979b) 'The so-called Allais paradox and rational decisions under uncertainty', in Allais/Hagen (eds.) (1979).

Allais, M. (1983) 'The foundations of the theory of utility and risk. Some central points of the discussions at the Oslo Conference', in Hagen/Wenstøp (eds.) (1983).

Allais. M. (1986) 'Determination of cardinal utility according to an intrinsic invariant model', in Daboni *et al.* (1986).

Allais, M. and Hagen, O., (eds.) (1979) *Expected Utility Hypothesis and the Allais Paradox*, Dordrecht, D. Reidel.

Allen, R.G.D. (1935) 'A note on the determinateness of the utility function', *Review of Economic Studies* **2**, 155–158.

Alt, F. (1936) 'Über die Mäßbarkeit des Nutzens', *Zeitschrift für Nationalökonomie* **7**, 161–169. English translation: On the measurability of utility, in Chipman *et al.* (1971).

Aoki, M., Chipman, J.S., and Fishburn, P.C. (1971) 'A selected bibliography of works relating to the theory of preferences, utility and demand', in Chipman *et al.* (eds.) (1971).

Armstrong, W.E. (1939) 'The determinateness of the utility function', *Economic Journal* **49**, 453–467.

Armstrong, W.E. (1948) 'Uncertainty and the utility function', *Economic Journal* **58**, 1–10.

Armstrong, W.E. (1951) 'Utility and the theory of welfare', *Oxford Economic Papers* **3**, 259–271.

Armstrong, W.E. (1953) 'A reply', *Oxford Economic Papers* **5**, 264–270.

Armstrong, W.E. (1955) 'Concerning marginal utility', *Oxford Economic Papers* **7**, 170–176.

Armstrong, W.E. (1958) 'Utility and the ordinalist fallacy', *Review of Economic Studies* **25**, 172–181.

Arrow, K.J. (1963) *Social Choice and Individual Values*, 2nd edn., New Haven, Yale University Press (1st edn., 1951).

Arrow, K.J., Karlin, S., and Suppes, P. (1959) *Mathematical Methods in the Social Science*, California: Stanford University Press.

Arrow, K.J. and Intriligator, M.D. (eds.) (1986) *Handbook of Mathematical Economics*, Amsterdam, North-Holland.

Barten, A.P. (1964) 'Consumer demand functions under conditions of almost additive preferences', *Econometrica* **32**, 1–38.

Basu, K. (1980) *Revealed Preference of Government*, Cambridge, Cambridge University Press.

Basu, K. (1981) 'Determinateness of the utility function: Revisiting a controversy of the thirties', *Review of Economic Studies* **49**, 307–311.

Battalio, R.C., Kagel, J.H., and MacDonald, D.N. (1985) 'Animals' choices over uncertain outcomes: some initial experimental results', *American Economic Review* **75**, 597–613.

Baumol, W.J. (1951) 'The Neumann–Morgenstern utility index: an ordinalist view', *Journal of Political Economy* **59**, 61–66.

Baumol, W.J. (1958) 'The cardinal utility which is ordinal', *Economic Journal* **68**, 665–672.

Bell, D.E. (1981) 'Components of risk aversion', *Proceedings of the ninth IFORS International Conference on Operational Research*, Amsterdam, North-Holland.

Bentham, J. See Stark (1952).

Bergmann, G. and Spence, K.W. (1944) 'The logic of psychological measurement', *Psychological Review* **51**, 1–24.

Bergson (Burk), A. (1954) 'On the concept of social welfare', *Quarterly Journal of Economics* **68**, 233–252.

Bernard, G. (1984) 'On utility functions. The present state', *Theory and Decision* **17**, 97–100.

Bernard, G. (1986) 'A discussion of the present state of utility theory', *Theory and Decision* **20**, 173–188.

Bernardelli, H. (1934) 'Notes on the determinateness of the utility function', *Review of Economic Studies* **2**, 69–75.

Bernardelli, H. (1938) 'The end of the marginal utility theory', *Economica* **5**, 192–212.

Bernardelli, H. (1939) 'A reply to Mr. Samuelson's note', *Economica* **6**, 86–89.

Bernardelli, H. (1952) 'A rehabilitation of the classical theory of marginal utility', *Economica* **18**, 254–268.

Bernardelli, H. (1954) 'Comment on Mr. Lancaster's "refutation"', *Economica* **21**, 240–242.

Bernoulli, D. (1738) 'Specimen theoriae novae de mensura sortis', *Commentarii Academiae Scientarum Imperialis Petropolitanae* **5**, 175–192. English translation: Exposition of a new theory on the measurement of risk, *Econometrica* **22**, 23–26.

Borch, K. and Mossin, J. (eds.) (1968) *Risk and Uncertainty*, London, Macmillan.

Borda, J-C. de (1781) 'Mémoire sur les élections au scrutin', *Mémoires in l'Académie Royale des Sciences*, pp. 657–665. English translation in Alfred de Grazia (1953): Mathematical derivation of an election system, *Isis* **44**, 42–51.

Boskin, M. (ed.) (1979) *A Festschrift for Tibor Scitovsky*, New York, Academic Press.

Bradburn, N.M. (1969) *The Structure of Psychological Well-being*, Chicago, Aldine.

Bradburn, N.M. and Caplovitz, D. (1965) *Reports on Happiness*, Chicago, Aldine.

Bridgman, P.W. (1927) *The Logic of Modern Psychics*, New York, Macmillan.

Broome, J. (1985) 'A mistaken argument against the expected utility theory of rationality', *Theory and Decision* **18**, 313–318.

Brunner, J.K. (1986) *Zur Theorie der Steuergerichtigkeit. Normative Fundierung und distributive Konsequenzen der Einkommen-besteuerung*, Habilitationsschrift, Linz.

Butts, R. and Hintikka, J. (eds.) (1977) *Logic, Methodology and Philosophy of Science*, Dordrecht, Reidel.

Buyze, J. (1982) 'The estimation of welfare levels of a cardinal utility function', *European Economic Review* **17**, 325–332.

Camacho, A. (1979) 'On cardinal utility', *Theory and Decision* **10**, 131–145.

Camacho, A. (1980) 'Approaches to cardinal utility', *Theory and Decision* **12**, 359–379.

Camacho, A. (1983) 'Cardinal utility and decision making under uncertainty', in Stigum/Wenstøp (eds.) (1983).

Cantril, H. (1965) *The Pattern of Human Concerns*, New Brunswick, Rutgers University Press.

Chipman, J. (1971) 'Introduction to part 2', in Chipman *et al.* (eds.) (1971).

Chipman, J., Hurwicz, L., Richter, M.K., and Sonnenschein, H.F. (eds.) (1971) *Preferences, Utility and Demand*, Harcourt Brace Jovanovich.

Churchman, C.W. and Ratoosh, P. (eds.) (1959) *Measurement: Definitions and Theories*, New York, John Wiley & Sons.

Cohen, M., Jaffray, J.-Y., and Said, T. (1985) 'Individual behaviour under risk and under uncertainty: An experimental study', *Theory and Decision* **18**, 203–228.

Cohen Stuart, A.J. (1989) *Bijdrage tot de theorie der progressieve inkomstenbelasting*, The Hague. Extract translated as: On progressive taxation, in Musgrave and Peacock (eds.) (1967).

Coombs, C.H. (1950) 'Psychological scaling without a unit of measurement', *Psychological Review* **57**, 145–158.

Coombs, C.H. (1959) 'Inconsistency of preference as a measure of psychological distance', in Churchman and Ratoosh (eds.).

Coombs, C.H., and Beardslee, D. (1954) 'On decision-making under uncertainty', in Coombs *et al.* (eds.) (1959).

Coombs, C.H., and Huang, L.C. (1976) 'Test of the betweenness property of expected utility', *Journal of Mathematical Psychology* **13**, 323–337.

Coombs, C.H., Davis, R.L., and Thrall, R.M. (eds.) (1954) *Decision Processes*, New York, John Wiley & Sons.

Cooter, R. and Rappoport, P. (1984) 'Were the ordinalists wrong about welfare economics?', *Journal of Economic Literature* **22**, 507–530.

Daboni, L., Montesano, A., and Lines, M. (eds.) *Recent Developments in the Foundations of Utility and Risk Theory*, Dordrecht, D. Reidel.

David, P.A. and Reder, M.W. (1974) *Nations and Households in Economic Growth*, New York, Academic Press.

Deaton, A. and Muellbauer, J. (1980) *Economics and Consumer Behaviour*, Cambridge, Cambridge University Press.

Debreu, G. (1954) 'Representation of a preference ordering by a numerical function', in Coombs *et al.* (eds.) (1959).

Debreu, G. (1958) 'Stochastic choice and cardinal utility', *Econometrica* **26**, 440–444.

Debreu, G. (1959) 'Topological methods in cardinal utility theory', in Arrow *et al.* (eds.) (1959).

Debreu, G. and Koopmans, C. (1982) 'Additively decomposed quasiconvex functions', *Mathematical Programming* **24**, 1–38.

Diamond, P.A. (1967) 'Cardinal welfare, individualistic ethics and interpersonal comparisons utility. Comment', *Journal of Political Economy* **75**, 765–766.

Dyer, J.S. and R.K. Sarin (1979) 'Group preference aggregation rules based on strength of preference', *Management Science* **25**, 822–832.

Easterlin, R.A. (1974) 'Does economic growth improve the human lot? Some empirical evidence', in David and Reder (eds.) (1974).

Edgeworth, F.Y. (1881) *Mathematical Psychics*, London, Kegan Paul.

Edgeworth, F.Y. (1987) 'The pure theory of taxation', *Economic Journal* **7**, A modified version occurs in Musgrave and Peacock (eds.) (1967).

Ekman, G. (1964) 'Is the power law a special case of Fechner law', *Perceptual and Motor Skills* **19**, 730.

Ellsberg, D. (1954) 'Classic and current notions of "measurable utility"', *Economic Journal* **64**, 528–556.

Ellsberg, D. (1961) 'Risk, ambiguity, and the Savage axioms', *Quarterly Journal of Economics* **75**, 643–669.

Fechner, G.T. (1860) *Elemente der Psychophysik*, Leipzig, Breitkopf und Härtel.

Feiwel, G. (ed.) (1985) *Issues in Contemporary Microeconomics and Welfare*, London, The Macmillan Press.

Fellner, W. (1968) 'Operational utility: The theoretical background and a measurement', in Fellner (ed.) (1968).

Fellner, W. (ed.) (1968) *Ten Economic Studies in the Tradition of Irving Fisher*, New York, John Wiley & Sons.

Finetti, B. de (1977) 'A short confirmation of my standpoint', in Allais/Hagen (eds.) (1979).

Fishburn, P.C. (1968) 'Utility theory', *Management Science* **14**, 335–378.

Fishburn, P.C. (1970a) *Utility Theory for Decision Making*, New York, John Wiley & Sons.

Fishburn, P.C. (1970b) 'Utility theory with inexact preferences and degrees of preference', *Synthese* **21**, 204–221.

Fishburn, P.C. (1976) 'Cardinal utility: An interpretive essay', *Rivista Internazionale di Scienze Economiche e Commerciale* **22**, 1102–1114.

Fisher, I. (1892) 'Mathematical investigations in the theory of values and prices', *Transactions of Connecticut Academy of Arts and Sciences* **9**, 1–124. Reprinted in 1925 by Yale University Press.

Fisher, I. (1918) 'Is "utility" the most suitable term for the concept it is used to denote?', *American Economic Review* **8**, 335–337.

Fisher, I. (1927) 'A statistical method for measuring marginal utility and testing the justice of a progressive income tax', in Hollander (ed.) (1927).

Friedman, M. (1936) 'Marginal utility of money and elasticities of demand', *Quarterly Journal of Economics* **50**, 532–533.

Friedman, M. (1953) 'Choice, chance and the personal distribution of income', *Journal of Political Economy* **61**, 277–290.

Friedman, M. (1955) 'What all is utility', *Economic Journal* **65**, 405–410.

Friedman, M. (1962) *Capitalism and Freedom*, Chicago, University of Chicago Press.

Friedman, M. and Savage, L.J. (1948) 'The utility analysis of choices involving risk', *Journal of Political Economy* **56**, 279–304.

Friedman, M. and Savage, L.J. (1952) 'The expected utility hypothesis and the measurability of utility', *Journal of Political Economy* **60**, 463–474.

Frisch, R. (1926a) 'Sur un problème d'économie pure', *Norsk Matematisk Forenings Skrifter* **16**, 1–40. Reprinted in *Metroeconomica* **9**, 79–111. English translation in Chipman *et al.* (eds.) (1971).

Frisch, R. (1926b) 'En kvantitativ formulering av den teoretiske økonomikks lover', *Statsøkonomisk Tidsskrift*, 299–334.

Frisch, R. (1932) *New Methods for Measuring Marginal Utility*, Tübingen, Verlag von J.C.B. Mohr.

Frisch, R. (1953) 'Discours', *Colloques Internationaux du Centre National de la Recherche Scientifique* **40** (Économétrie), 249–255.
Frisch, R. (1959) 'A complete scheme for computing all direct and cross demand elasticities in a model with many sectors', *Econometrica* **27**, 177–196.
Frisch, R. (1964) 'Dynamic utility', *Econometrica* **32**, 418–424.
Gabor, A. and James, S.F. (1958) 'On measuring utility', *Yorkshire Bulletin of Economic and Social Research* **10**, 1–18.
Georgescu-Roegen, N. (1936) 'Marginal utility of money and elasticities of demand', *Quarterly Journal of Economics* **50**, 533–537. Reprinted in Georgescu-Roegen (1966).
Georgescu-Roegen, N. (1936) 'The pure theory of consumer's behavior', *Quarterly Journal of Economics* **50**, 133–170. Reprinted in Georgescu-Roegen (1966).
Georgescu-Roegen, N. (1958) 'Threshold in choice and in the theory of demand', *Econometrica* **26**, 157–168. Reprinted in Georgescu-Roegen (1966).
Georgescu-Roegen, N. (1966) *Analytical Economics*, Cambridge, MA, Harvard University Press.
Georgescu-Roegen, N. (1968) 'Utility', in *International Encyclopedia of the Social Sciences*, vol. 16, pp. 236–267. The Macmillan Company and the Free Press.
Gärdenfors, P. and Sahlin, N.-E. (1988) *Decision, Probability and Utility. Selected Readings*, Cambridge, Cambridge University Press.
Hagen, O. (1969) 'Separation of cardinal utility and specific utility of risk in theory of choices under uncertainty', *Statsøkonomisk Tidsskrift*, 81–107.
Hagen, O. (1972) 'A new axiomatization of utility under risk', *Teorie A Metoda* **4**, 55–80.
Hagen, O. and Wenstøp (eds.) (1984) *Progress in Utility and Risk Theory*, Dordrecht, D. Reidel.
Hansson, B. (1988) 'Risk aversion as a problem of conjoint measurement', in Gärdenfors and Sahlin (eds.) (1988).
Harsanyi, J. (1953) 'Cardinal utility in welfare economics and in the theory of risk-taking', *Journal of Political Economy* **61**, 434–435.
Harsanyi, J. (1955) 'Cardinal welfare, individualistic ethics and interpersonal comparisons of utility', *Journal of Political Economy* **63**, 309–321.
Harsanyi, J. (1975) 'Nonlinear social welfare functions', *Theory and Decision* **6**, 311–332.
Harsanyi, J. (1977) 'Non-linear social welfare functionals: a rejoinder to Professor Sen', in Butts and Hintikka (eds.) (1977).
Harsanyi, J. (1978) 'Bayesian decision-theory and utilitarianism', *American Economic Review* **68**, 223–228.
Harsanyi, J. (1983) 'Use of subjective probabilities in game theory', in Stigum and Wenstøp (eds.) (1983).
Herstein, I.N. and J. Milnor (1953) 'An axiomatic approach to measurable utility', *Econometrica* **21**, 291–297.
Hicks, J.R. (1954) 'Robbins on Robertson on utility', *Economica* **21**, 154–157.
Hillinger, C. (1969) 'The measurement of utility', *Review of Economic Studies* **36**, 111–116.
Hollander, J.H. (ed.) (1927) *Economic Essays Contributed in Honor of John Bates Clark*, New York, The Macmillan Company.
Houthakker, H. (1960) 'Additive preferences', *Econometrica* **28**, 244–257.
Hurwicz, L., Schmeidler, D., and Sonnenschein, H. (eds.) (1985) *Social Goals and Social Organization: Essays in Memory of Elisha Pazner*, Cambridge, Cambridge University Press.
Hutcheson, F. (1728) *An Essay on the Nature and Conduct of the Passions and Affections*, London, J. Osborn and T. Longman.

Inkeles, A. (1960) 'The relation of status to experience, perception, and value', *American Journal of Sociology* **66**, 1–31.

Jaffray, J.-Y. (1985) 'Interpersonal level comparability does not imply comparability of utility differences – a comment on Ng', *Theory and Decision* **19**, 201–203.

Jevons, W.S. (1871) *The Theory of Political Economy*, London and New York, Macmillan & Co.

Johansen, L. (1958) 'Et sett av etterspørselskoeffisienter for en multi-sektor analyse med variable priser', *Memorandum from Department of Economics*, University of Oslo.

Kauder, E. (1953) 'Genesis of the marginal utility theory: from Aristotle to the end of the eighteenth century', *Economic Journal* **63**, 638–650.

Kauder, E. (1965) *A History of Marginal Utility Theory*, New Jersey, Princeton University Press.

Kanbur, R. (1987) 'The standard of living: uncertainty, inequality and opportunity', in Sen (1987).

Kaneko, M. (1982) 'The optimal progressive income tax', *Mathematical Social Sciences* **3**, 193–222.

Kapteyn, A. and Wansbeek, T. (1985) 'The individual welfare function. A review', *Journal of Economic Psychology* **6**, 333–363.

Kapteyn, A. and Wansbeek, T. (1985b) 'The individual welfare function. A rejoinder', *Journal of Economic Psychology* **6**, 375–381.

Kemp, M.C. and Ng, Y.-K. (1976) 'On the existence of social welfare functions, social orderings and social decision functions', *Economica* **43**, 59–66.

Kemp, M.C. and Ng, Y.-K. (1977) 'More on social welfare functions: The incompatibility of individualism and ordinalism', *Economica* **44**, 89–90.

Kemp, M.C. and Ng, Y.-K. (1982) 'The incompatibility of individualism and ordinalism', *Mathematical Social Sciences* **3**, 33–37.

Kennedy, C. (1954) 'Concerning utility', *Economica* **21**, 17–20.

Krantz, D.H., Luce, R.D., Suppes, P., and Tversky, A. (1971) *Foundations of Measurement*, New York and London, Academic Press.

Kraus, O. (1903) 'Die Aristotelische Werttheorie in ihrer Beziehungen zu den Lehren der modernen Psychologenschule', *Zeitschrift für die gesamte Staatswissenschaft* **61**, 573–592.

Krelle, W. (1968) *Präferenz- und Entscheidungstheorie*, Tübingen, J.C.B. Mohr.

Krzysztofowicz, R. (1983) 'The risk attitude hypothesis of utility theory', in Stigum/Wenstøp (eds.) (1983).

Lancaster, K. (1953) 'A refutation of Mr. Bernardelli', *Economica* **19**, 259–262.

Lancaster, K. (1954) 'Rejoinder to Mr. Bernardelli', *Economica* **21**, 242–243.

Lange, O. (1934) 'The determinateness of the utility function', *Review of Economic Studies* **1**, 218–224.

Lange. O. (1934) 'Notes on the determinateness of the utility function', (3), *Review of Economic Studies* **2**, 75–77.

Lerner, A.P. (1946) *The Economics of Control*, New York, The Macmillan Company.

Lerner, A.P. (1977) 'Marginal cost pricing in the 1930's', *American Economic Review (Papers and Proceedings)* **67**, 235–239.

Leinfellner, W. (1968) 'Generalization of classical decision theory', in Borch and Mossin (eds.) (1968).

Little, I.M.D. (1957) *A Critique of Welfare Economics*, 2nd edn., Oxford, Clarendon Press.

Luce, R.D. (1956) 'Semiorders and a theory of utility discrimination', *Econometrica* **24**, 178–191.

Luce, R.D. (1958) 'A probabilistic theory of utility', *Econometrica* **26**, 193–224.
Luce, R.D. (1959) 'A probabilistic theory of utility and its relationship to Fechnerian scaling', in Churchman and Ratoosh (eds.) (1959).
Luce, R.D., Bush, R.R., and Galanter, E. (eds.) (1965) *Handbook of Mathematical Psychology* vol. 3, New York, J. Wiley & Sons.
Luce, R.D. and Raiffa, H. (1957) *Games and Decision*, New York, J. Wiley & Sons.
Luce, R.D. and Suppes, P. (1965) 'Preference, utility and subjective probability', in Luce, Bush and Galanter (eds.) (1965).
MacCrimmon, K.R. and Larsson, S. (1979) 'Utility theory: axioms versus "paradoxes", in Allais and Hagen (eds.).
Machina, M. (1987) 'The choice under uncertainty: problems solved and unsolved', *Journal of Economic Perspectives* **1**, 121–154.
Majumdar, T. (1957) 'Armstrong and the utility measurement controversy', *Oxford Economic Papers* **9**, 30–40.
Majumdar, T. (1958a) 'Behaviourist cardinalism in utility theory', *Economica* **25**, 26–33.
Majumdar, T. (1958b) *The Measurement of Utility*, London, Macmillan & Co.
Majumdar, T. (1958b) *The Measurement of Utility*, London, Macmillan & Co.
Majumdar, T. (1960) 'A reply', *Economica* **27**, 253–255.
Marschak, J. (1950) 'Rational behavior, uncertain prospects and measurable utility', *Econometrica* **18**, 111–141.
Marshall, A. (1920) *Principles of Economics*, 8th edn., London, Macmillan & Co.
Markowitz, A. (1952) 'Utility of wealth', *Journal of Political Economy* **60**, 151–158.
Marx, W. (1949) 'The law of diminishing marginal utility of income', *Kyklos* **3**, 254–279.
Mayston, D.J. (1982) 'The generation of a social welfare function under ordinal preferences', *Mathematical Social Sciences* **3**, 109–129.
McCord, M.R. and de Neufvill, R. (1983) 'Empirical demonstration that expected utility decision analysis is not operational', in Stigum and Wenstøp (eds.) (1983).
McCord, M.R. and de Neufville, R. (1984) 'Utility dependence on probability', *Large Scale Systems* **6**, 91–103.
McCord, M.R. and de Neufville, R. (1985) 'Assessment response surface: investigating utility dependence on probability', *Theory and Decision* **18**, 263–285.
Mellon, W.G. (1960) 'Comment on "A general theory of measurement – applications to utility"', *Naval Research Logistics Quarterly* **7**, 285–287.
Mill, J.S. (1848) *Principles of Political Economy* (edited with an introduction by W.J. Ashley, 1917), London, Longmans Green.
Mitchell, W.C. (1918) 'Bentham's *felicific calculus*', *Political Science Quarterly* **33**, 161–183. Reprinted in Page (ed.) (1968).
Montmarquette, C. and Blais, A. (1987) 'A survey measure of risk aversion', *Economics Letters* **25**, 27–30.
Mosteller, F. and Nogee, P. (1951) 'An experimental measurement of utility', *Journal of Political Economy* **59**, 371–404.
Musgrave, R.A. and Peacock, A.T. (1967) *Classics in the Theory of Public Finance*, New York, Macmillan.
Mueller, D.C. (1973) 'Constitutional democracy and social welfare', *Quarterly Journal of Economics* **87**, 60–80.
Mueller, D.C., Tollison, R.D., and Willett, T.D. (1974) 'The utilitarian contract: a generalization of Rawls' theory of justice', *Theory and Decision* **4**, 345–367.
Möller, R. (1983) *Interpersonelle Nutzenvergleiche. Wissenschaftliche Möglichkeit und politische Bedeutung*, Göttingen, Vandenhoeck & Ruprecht.

Ng, Y.-K. (1975) 'Bentham or Bergson? Finite sensibility, utility functions and social welfare functions', *Review of Economic Studies* **42**, 545–570.

Ng, Y.-K. (1979) *Welfare Economics, Introduction and Development of Basic Concepts*, London, The Macmillan Press.

Ng, Y.-K. (1982) 'Beyond Pareto optimality: the necessity of interpersonal cardinal utilities in distributional judgements and social choice', *Journal of Economics* **42**, 207–233.

Ng, Y.-K. (1984a) 'Interpersonal level comparability implies comparability of utility differences', *Theory and Decision* **17**, 141–147.

Ng, Y.-K. (1984b) 'Expected subjective utility: is the Neumann–Morgenstern utility the same as the neoclassical's?', *Social Choice and Welfare* **1**, 177–186.

Ng, Y.-K. (1985) 'Some fundamental issues in social welfare', in Feiwel (ed.) (1985).

Ng, Y.-K. (1986) 'Beyond Pareto optimality. A response to Christian Seidl', *Journal of Economics* **46**, 311–315.

Ozga, S.A. (1956) 'Measurable utility and probability – a simplified rendering', *Economic Journal* **66**, 419–430.

Paine, N.R. (1975) 'Introspective utility and the group choice problem', *Theory and Decision* **6**, 357–362.

Page, A.N. (1968) *Utility Theory. A Book of Readings*, New York, J. Wiley & Sons.

Pareto, V. (1911) 'Economie mathématique', in *Encyclopédie des Sciences Mathématiques*, Tome 1, vol. 4, Fasc. 4, Paris. English translation: Mathematical Economics, in *International Economic Papers* **5** (1955), 58–102.

Pareto, V. (1927) *Manuel D'Economie Politique*, 2. printing (1st printing 1909, Italian edition 1906), Paris: V. Giard et E. Brière. English translation: *Manual of Political Economy*, London, The Macmillan Press 1971.

Parks, R.P. (1976) 'An impossibility theorem for fixed preferences: a dictatorial Bergson–Samuelson welfare function', *Review of Economic Studies* **43**, 447–450.

Pattanaik, P.P. (1968) 'Risk, impersonality and the social welfare function', *Journal of Political Economy* **76**, 1152–1169.

Pearce, I.F. (1961) 'An exact method of consumer demand analysis', *Econometrica* **29**, 499–516.

Pfanzagl, J. (1959) 'A general theory of measurement: applications to utility', *Naval Research Logistics Quarterly* **6**, 283–294.

Phelps, E. (ed.) (1973) *Economic Justice*, Harmondsworth, Penguin Education.

Phelps-Brown, E.H. (1934) 'Notes on the determinateness of the utility function', *Review of Economic Studies* **2**, 66–69.

Ramsey, F. (1926) 'Truth and probability', in Ramsey (1931).

Ramsey, F. (1931) *The Foundations of Mathematics and Other Logical Essays*, New York, Harcourt Brace & Co.

Rappoport, P. (1988) 'Reply to Professor Hennipman', *Journal of Economic Literature* **26**, 86–91.

Ratchford, B.T. (1985) 'The individual welfare function. A comment', *Journal of Economic Psychology* **6**, 365–374.

Robbins, L. (1932) *An Essay on the Nature and Significance of Economic Science*, London, Macmillan & Co.

Robbins, L. (1953) 'Robertson on utility and scope: a comment', *Economica* **20**, 99–111.

Robertson, D.H. (1951) 'Utility and all that', *Manchester School of Economic and Social Studies* **19**, 348–385. Reprinted in Robertson (1952).

Robertson, D.H. (1952) *Utility and All That and Other Essays*, London, George Allen & Unwin.

Robertson, D.H. (1954) 'Utility and all what', *Economic Journal* **64**, 665–678.
Rothenberg, J. (1953) 'Marginal preference and the theory of welfare', *Oxford Economic Papers* **5**, 248–263.
Rothenberg, J. (1961) *The Measurement of Social Welfare*, New Jersey, Prentice Hall.
Rothschild, M. and Stiglitz J. (1970) 'Increasing risk I: a definition', *Journal of Economic Theory* **2**, 225–243.
Rudin, W. (1976) *Principles of Mathematical Analysis*, International Student Edition, McGraw-Hill.
Runes, D.D. (ed.) (1962) *Dictionary of Philosophy*, Littlefield, Adams & Co.
Ryle, G. (1949) *Concepts of Mind*, London, Hutchinson.
Sandmo, A. (1983) 'Ex post welfare economics and the theory of merit goods', *Economica* **50**, 19–33.
Samuelson, P.A. (1937) 'On the measurement of utility', *Review of Economic Studies* **4**, 155–161.
Samuelson, P.A. (1938) 'The numerical representation of ordered classifications and the concept of utility', *Review of Economic Studies* **6**, 65–70. Reprinted in Stiglitz (ed.) (1966).
Samuelson, P.A. (1950) 'Probability and the attempts to measure utility', *The Economic Review (Keizai Kenku)* **1**, 167–173. Reprinted in Stiglitz (ed.) (1966).
Samuelson, P.A. (1947) *Foundations of Economic Analysis*, Cambridge, MA, Harvard University Press.
Samuelson, P.A. (1977) 'Reaffirming the existence of "reasonable" social welfare functions', *Economica* **44**, 81–88.
Sarin, R.K. (1982) 'Strength of preference and risky choice', *Operations Research* **30**, 982–997.
Savage, L.J. (1954) *The Foundations of Statistics*, New York, John Wiley & Sons. 2nd revised edition, New York, Dover Publications, 1972.
Schoemaker, P.J.H. (1982) 'The expected utility model: Its variants, purposes, evidence and limitations', *Journal of Economic Literature* **20**, 529–563.
Schultz, H. (1933) 'Frisch on the measurement of utility', *Journal of Political Economy* **41**, 95–116.
Scott, D. (1964) 'Measurement structures and linear inequalities', *Journal of Mathematical Psychology* **1**, 233–247.
Seidl, C. (1986) 'Beyond Pareto optimality? A comment to Yew-Kwang Ng', *Journal of Economics* **46**, 305–310.
Sen, A.K. (1970) *Collective Choice and Social Welfare*, San Francisco, Holden-Day.
Sen, A.K. (1974) 'Informational bases of alternative welfare approaches. Aggregation and income distribution', *Journal of Public Economics* **3**, 387–403.
Sen, A.K. (1977) 'Non-linear social welfare functionals: A reply to professor Harsanyi', in Butts and Hintikka (eds.) (1977).
Sen, A.K. (1979) 'Interpersonal comparisons of welfare', in Boskin (ed.) (1979).
Sen, A.K. (1986) 'Social choice theory', in Arrow and Intriligator (eds.) (1986).
Sen, A.K. (1987) *The Standard of Living*, Cambridge, Cambridge University Press.
Simon, J.L. (1974) 'Interpersonal welfare comparisons can be made and used fro redistribution decisions', *Kyklos* **27**, 63–99.
Sinn, H.-W. (1983) *Economic Decisions under Uncertainty*, Amsterdam, North-Holland.
Sinn, H.-W. (1985) 'Psychophysical laws in risk theory', *Journal of Economic Psychology* **6**, 185–206.
Solomon, H. (ed.) (1960) *Mathematical Thinking in the Measurement of Behavior*, Glencoe.

Stark, W. (1947) 'Diminishing utility reconsidered', *Kyklos* **1**, 312–344.

Stark, W. (ed.) (1952) *Jeremy Bentham's Economic Writings*, vol. 1–3, London, George Allen & Unwin.

Stevens, J.C. (1968) 'Psychophysics', in *International Encyclopedia of the Social Sciences*.

Stevens, S.S. (1951) 'Mathematics, measurement and psychophysics', in Stevens (ed.) (1968).

Stevens, S.S. (1959) 'Measurement, psychophysics and utility', in Churchman and Ratoosh (eds.) (1959).

Stevens, S.S. (1951) *Handbook of Mathematical Psychology*, New York, J. Wiley & Sons.

Stigler, G. (1950) 'The development of utility theory', *Journal of Political Economy* **58**, 307–327 and 373–396.

Stiglitz, J.E. (ed.) (1966) *The Collected Scientific Papers of Paul Samuelson*, Cambridge, MA, The MIT Press.

Stiglitz, J.E. (1982) 'Utilitarianism and horizontal equity. The case for random taxation', *Journal of Public Economics* **18**, 1–33.

Stigum, B. and Wenstøp, F. (1983) *Foundations of Utility and Risk Theory with Applications*, Dordrecht, D. Reidel.

Strotz, R.H. (1953) 'Cardinal Utility', *American Economic Review* **43**, 384–397.

Stuart, H.W. (1895) 'The hedonistic interpretation of subjective value', *Journal of Political Economy* **4**, 64–84.

Suppes, P. and Winet, M. (1955) 'An axiomatization of utility based on the notion of utility differences', *Management Science* **1**, 259–270.

Svensson, L.-G. (1985) 'The utilitarian criterion, finite sensibility, and the weak majority preference principle. A further analysis', *Social Choice and Welfare* **2**, 23–35.

Tinnes, D.J. (1918) 'Why not valure?', *American Economic Review* **8**, 585–586.

Tversky, A. (1967) 'A general theory of polynomial conjoint measurement', *Journal of Mathematical Psychology* **4**, 1-20.

Van de Stadt, H., Antonides, G., and van Praag, B.M.S. (1984) 'Empirical testing of the expected utility model', *Journal of Economic Psychology* **5**, 17–29.

Van Heerwarden, F.G. and Kapteyn, A. (1981) 'Empirical comparison of the shape of welfare functions', *European Economic Review* **15**, 261–286.

Van Praag, B.M.S. (1968) *Individual Welfare Functions and Consumer Behavior*, Amsterdam, North-Holland.

Van Praag, B.M.S. (1985) 'Linking economics with psychology. An economist's view', *Journal of Economic Psychology* **6**, 289–311.

Vickrey, W.S. (1945) 'Measuring marginal utility by reaction to risk', *Econometrica* **13**, 319–333.

Vickrey, W.S. (1960) 'Utility, strategy, and social decision rules', *Quarterly Journal of Economics* **74**, 507–535.

Vickrey, W.S. (1961) 'Risk, utility and social policy', *Social Research* **28**, 205–217. Reprinted in Phelps (ed.) (1973).

Viner, J. (1925) 'The utility concept in value theory and its critics', *Journal of Political Economy* **33**, 369–387 and 638–659.

Von Neumann, J. and Morgenstern, O. (1947) *Theory of Games and Economic Behavior*, 2nd edn., Princeton, Princeton University Press.

Waldner, I. (1972) 'The empirical meaningfulness of interpersonal utility comparisons', *The Journal of Philosophy* **69**, 87–103.

Wakker, P. (1984) 'Cardinal coordinate independence for expected utility', *Journal of Mathematical Psychology* **28**, 110–117.

Weber, E.H. (1846) *Die Lehre vom Tastsinne und Gemeingefühle auf Versuche gegründet*, Braunschweig, F. Wieweg und Sohn.

Weldon, J.C. (1950) 'A note on measures of utility', *Canadian Journal of Economics and Political Science* **16**, 227–238.

Wilson, W. (1967) 'Correlates of avowed happiness', *Psychological Bulletin* **67**, 294–306.

Young, H.P. (1987) 'Progressive taxation and the equal sacrifice principle', *Journal of Public Economics* **32**, 203–214.

Young, H.P. (1990) 'Progressive taxation and equal sacrifice', *American Economic Review* **80**, 253–266.

Zeuthen, F. (1937) 'On the determinateness of the utility function', *Review of Economic Studies* **4**, 236–239.

ERIK GRØNN

CARDINALISM AND DYNAMIC ANALYSIS IN ECONOMIC THEORY[1]

ABSTRACT. This paper discusses the contention of Professor Ragnar Frisch that cardinal utility has a place in dynamic analysis. As for the necessity of cardinal utility in dynamic analysis we note that ordinal utility is incapable of treating the case of calendar-time dependent preferences and we also question whether an ordinal approach can grasp the content of Böhm-Bawerk's rate of pure time preference. In examining the meaningfulness of cardinal utility in dynamic analysis we look for a canonical way of selecting a set of representations of the preferences which are linear transformations of each other. This may be possible if the preferences admit a concave representation, because there is a result by Debreu that such preferences have a least concave representation, and all such representations are linear transformations of each other. Our methods of analysing this problem do not, however, reach conclusions that will support the claim that cardinal utility is easier to define in a dynamic than in a static framework.

1. INTRODUCTION

Suppose, one day, the temperature in Oslo is 15°C, the temperature in Rome is 30°C, and the temperature in Cairo is 40°C. Then everybody will agree that it is hotter in Rome than in Oslo, and still hotter in Cairo. This conclusion will be reached regardless of the way different people have learned to *measure* temperature. Will we further say that the temperature-difference between Oslo and Rome is greater than the temperature-difference between Rome and Cairo? We probably will. But how many will insist that it is twice as hot in Rome as in Oslo? Probably very few.

The usual way to measure a quantity is to attach a numerical value (a real number) to the quantity, with the tactical understanding that we intend to employ the *ordering-property* ("a is less than b") of the system of the real numbers to the measures.

But now we must be careful: The difference and the ratio between two numbers are also numbers, but this does not mean that we are automatically willing to apply the concepts of the ordering-relation of the real numbers to the differences between (the measures of) two quantities or the ratios between (the measures of) two quantities. We will in this paper try to delineate exactly what "we can do" with the measures of measurable quantities. Our first task is then to settle what we shall mean by the term "measurable quantities". An absolute requirement for measurements to be meaningful is that the ordering between (the measures of) two quantities should be independent of every (acceptable!) way of measuring the two quantities. Then the quantities are said to be *measurable*. Thus, the

M. Allais and O. Hagen (eds.), Cardinalism, 167–208.

temperature at a certain place, at a certain time is measurable, because at a fixed point in time the temperature at place A, measured in degrees Celsius, is greater than the temperature at place B, measured in degrees Celsius if and only if the temperature at place A is greater than the temperature at place B measured in any other acceptable way of measuring temperature.

We can characterize measurable quantities further according to whether or not the ordering properties of the real numbers can be applied to certain combinations of the measures of measurable quantities. If the differences between the measures of two quantities is ranked independent of every acceptable measure, we say that the quantities are cardinally measurable or just cardinal. If not, the measurable quantities are ordinally measurable or just ordinal. (These definitions will be refined in the next section.) Thus, temperature should be termed a cardinal variable. This is in the final analysis more a convention, a reflection of how people have become accustomed to think about these matters, than a statement about how the world "really is". The convention is based upon a compromise between what is relevant and what is objectively attainable. In many cases we are interested in what the temperature *means to us*. Then two temperature-differences of equal Celcius-size do not necessarily mean the same thing: On a normal winter day in Oslo a change in temperature from −2°C to −6°C could be far less important than a change from, say, −20°C to −24°C. We can accordingly, for a single individual, imagine a temperature-scale based on "intensities of dislike/like", "willingness to pay", etc., that cannot be transformed linearly into the Celsius-scale. The resort to the usual ways of measuring temperature represents an improvement in scientific objectivity and facilitates interpersonal comparisons, but something may have been lost in essentially.

If also the ratio between the measures of two quantities is always greater than the ratio between the measures of two other quantities, independent of the methods of measurements, the quantities will be called *purely cardinal.* Temperature is not a purely cardinal quantity;[2] a sack of potatoes is. Suppose we measure sacks of potatoes in kilograms. If sack A weighs 50 kg and sack B weighs 25 kg, the weight of sack B is just half the weight of sack A, irrespective of the method of measurement. Accordingly, the ratio between the weights of sacks A and B is fixed, so is the ratio between the weights of sacks C and D, and the result, that sacks of potatoes are purely cardinally measurable, follows.

Is there a place for these distinctions in economic theory, and are they important in that theory? The answer to the first question is an unequivocally yes; the answer to the second question is more debatable. The technical term for a person's well-being, satisfaction, happiness etc. from consuming a certain commodity-bundle is called the person's utility. An old debate is whether utility is measurable as a cardinal quality or only as an ordinal quantity. It was realized by Irving Fisher already in 1892 that a cardinal utility concept was not *necessary* in order to devleop economic theory and derive all (almost all?) interesting, testable theorems. It was further questioned whether it was possible to make *meaningful* in an empirical sense the evaluation of the intensities of the preferences which seemed necessary for a cardinalistic utility measure. Accordingly, cardinalistic concepts were gradually expelled from economic theory, particularly after the "Hicks–Allan revolution" in the 1930s. This is, however, not an accurate description of the *practice* of economic theorists: Cardinal utility is used freely, with the apology, when pressed, that it is only used for "illustrative purposes", the emphasize more effectually a point which is also valid with only ordinal utility, etc. Anyhow, as the saying goes, the distinction between cardinal and ordinal utility is not an important distinction.

But it can be argued that this distinction is not necessarily entirely innocuous. Is it true that the ban on cardinal utility really represented a scientific progress? As pointed out by Cooter and Rappoport (1984), economic theory did not provide better answers to old questions when cardinal utility went out of fashion; instead economic theory posed new questions and deemed some of the old questions meaningless, not worthy of scientific inquiry. For instance, many economists around the turn of the century were passionate about income distribution and economic welfare. They wanted, among other things, to find out what better housing really "was worth" and sought justifications for redistributing income. If differences in utility levels could be compared, within a person and between persons, we can find a scientific basis for an activist welfare policy. But this seems to require a cardinalistic utility concept; ordinalists will judge these endeavours as being "unscientific". Cooter and Rappoport (1984) listed some of the questions the cardinalists wanted to answer and the ordinalists claimed were unanswerable by economics: Is a dollar more valuable to the average poor person than to the average rich person? Should economists give different weight to additional income for the rich and poor when doing cost–benefit analysis? Does a hungry person need food more than a bored person needs theater tickets? If income is redistributed to the poor, with no change in total income, does national welfare go up or down? Is there an economic justification for progressive income tax schemes?

Perhaps it is worth the effort to take a fresh look at what cardinal utility is really all about?

In *Econometrica* (1964) Professor Ragnar Frisch stated he was "in complete agreement" with Sir Roy Harrod's point of view that "cardinal utility is necessary in dynamic analysis". Frisch continued: "To me, the idea that cardinal utility should be avoided in economic theory is completely sterile. It is derived from a very special and indeed narrow part of theory, viz. that of static equilibrium". And further on he wrote "...there are many domains of economic theory where it is absolutely necessary to consider the concept of cardinal utility if we want to develop an sensible sort of analysis".

He then developed a formula for the so-called "incentive-free rate of interest", but in a later issue of *Econometrica* Morishima and Pollak set out to prove "that the incentive-free rate of interest depends only on the characteristics of the indifference map (i.e. the marginal rate of substitution) and not on the utility function we choose to represent the indifference map" (Pollak, 1965).

In Appendix I we comment on this discussion and conclude, in accordance with Morishima and Pollak, that Frisch had not been able to identify a situation where cardinal utility was necessary. But we still want to explore the question left open by Frisch: has cardinal utility a place in dynamic analysis? We in particular want to find out whether cardinal utility is *necessary* or *meaningful* in that branch of economic theory.[3] The necessity of cardinal utility is established if we can single out real and important concepts and problems that can only be properly treated within a cardinalistic framework. One candidate may be the case of so-called calendar-time dependent preferences, which means that two future dates have different utility-weights when looked upon from the present (24th of December, my birthday, 17th and 18th May, Norway's national holiday, and the "day after"). But still more critical for an ordinalist is the fact that ordinalists seem to be, in principle, incapable of getting hold of Böhm–Bawerks concept of the rate of pure time preference. For instance, Morishima in his criticism of Frisch is trying to measure the Böhm–Bawerk factor by going along the 45°-line. But this will not isolate the rate of pure time preference if preferences are calendar-time dependent. These points are taken up more fully in Section 3 where we also try to show that these questions are serious questions.

Our concept of meaningfulness of cardinal utility is the following: Cardinal utility is *meaningful* if there is a *canonical* way of picking out a subset, closed under only positive *linear* transformations, of representations of the preference field. Well known examples are the different forms of separability properties, mentioned for instance by Debreu (1960) and Koopmans (1960). Their results are briefly commented upon in Section 4, where we also refer to results by Fishburn (1978), which succeeds in generating a cardinalistic utility concept from certain axiomatizations governing the individual's behaviour when the individual's lifetime is uncertain.

Section 5 takes as its point of departure a theorem of Debreu (1976) which says that if the preference field admits a concave representation then there is a least concave representation, and this representation is unique up to a positive linear transformation. We are then looking for sufficient conditions that will guarantee that preferences are more likely to be concavable when the time perspective is widening – results which will give some credibility to the statement that cardinal utility is meaningful in a dynamic setting. It must be admitted, however, that the results so far are less than convincing. In fact we reach conclusions that are almost opposite to those sought.

Section 2 gives some definitions of the main concepts of the paper, cardinalism and ordinalism, and Section 6 offers some conclusions. Appendix II contains a proof of a characterization of cardinal utility due to Oscar Lange from way back in 1933, and the proofs of Proposition 1 and 2 from Section 5 are in Appendix III.

2. CARDINALISM AND ORDINALISM

We will in this section develop definitions which will convey the idea that ordinalism means that only the sign, not the numerical value, of the partial derivatives of the first order of the utility functions has any meaning. The sign of the second order partial derivates has no meaning for the ordinalist. A person who is comparing more than the sign of marginal utilities is accordingly a cardinalist.

An *object* has certain *attributes*. For instance: a person has a certain weight, height, colour of eyes, sense of humour etc. A *quantity* is an attribute by an object which can, by an impartial observer, be put uniquely in a one-to one correspondence with a subset of the real numbers, through the employment of a well-defined rule. The essential point is that the rule is well-defined and well understood. Thus, a person's colour of eyes is a quantity: his or her sense of humour is not a quantity. We are seeking definitions of measurable quantities. What is embedded in the definition of quantities is a certain *one-dimensionality*. Measurable quantities are both one-dimensional and have in a sense a natural direction, a natural ordering: Consider all quantities which are *the same attribute* by all objects under consideration (for instance the colour of eyes for all persons in the population). These are called *quantities of the same type*. Let M, M' be generic terms for the acceptable rules of putting quantities of a certain type into a one-to-one correspondence with a subset of the real numbers. By "an acceptable rule" we mean a rule which some people find useful; it gives them insight or a guide to better performance by applying that rule. Let Q, Q' be generic symbols for quantities of the same type. Then a type of quantities is *measurable* if and only if

$$M(Q) \geq M(Q') \text{ implies } M'(Q) \geq M'(Q')$$

for all acceptable measures M, M' and all quantities Q, Q' of the type under consideration. Thus, a person's colour of eyes is not a measurable quantity. (To be more precise, it does not belong to a measurable type of quantities.)

We will now insert a warning regarding the additivity of a measure. Suppose, if Q, Q' denote two quantities of the same type, that it is in some way possible to combine Q and Q' into a third quantity of the same type. Denote this combined quantity by the symbol $Q + Q'$. If M is a measure of quantities of this type, $M(Q)$, $M(Q')$ and $M(Q + Q')$ are all real numbers, but it will be a pure coincidence if the relation:

$$M(Q) + M(Q') = M(Q + Q') \text{ holds.}$$

The reason why we often take this additivity-relation to be true is that we, as pointed out by Strotz (1953) many years ago, tend to visualize any measure as analogous to the measuring of the length of an iron rod. If we have two iron rods and we want to measure the length of "the two iron rods", we put them down, the one after the other in a straight line, and measure the length of the configuration of two iron rods, the one following the other. The additivity of the measure follows.

But suppose we want to "measure" oranges, and suppose further that oranges are perfect spheres, with the only difference between two oranges being the radii. Then an acceptable measure of the oranges may be their weight. If $M(Q)$ is the weight of an orange Q with radius r, we have for some fixed positive number A:

$$M(Q) = A \cdot r^3$$

The number $M(Q)$ contains all relevant information regarding the oranges, since everything is known as long as the radius is known. But suppose we do not want to eat the oranges: we are only interested in the peel (for jam, maybe). The peel is proportional to the surface, so that an orange with radius r has a quantity of peel at a size of Br^2, with B a positive number. Since $r = (M(Q)/A)^{1/3}$ we have, if $Q_1 + Q_2$ denote (the peel of) two oranges with radii, r_1 and r_2, respectively:

$$M(Q_1 + Q_2) = \frac{B}{A^{2/3}} \cdot \left[M(Q)^{2/3} + M(Q_2)^{2/3}\right]$$

The measure M is not additive, but it *is* an acceptable measure. We will for the rest of this paper speculate about the properties of the measure of a person's utility from consuming a certain commodity-bundle. Let Y be the set of alternatives facing the individual, and let R be the set of real numbers. There are at least three different ways of representing the consumer's preferences. The perhaps most fundamental approach is to start with the preference-relation "not liked less than" defined over Y. We will, however, take as our point of departure the utility functions representing the preferences. By a *utility function* we mean a function U from Y to R, and by a *transformation* we mean a function f from R to R:

$$U : Y \to R, \quad f : R \to R$$

The traditional setting defines an individual as a pair (U, Ω), where U is a reference utility function and Ω is the set of permitted transformations.

Ω contains the identity transformation. The *permitted representations* (or the *permitted utility-functions*), $L(U, \Omega)$, consists of all transformations of the reference utility function, U, with transformations from the permitted set of transformations, Ω:

$$L = L(U, \Omega) = \{f \circ U;\ f \in \Omega\}$$

The individual is supposed to have those preferences which are implied by *all* the utility functions in $L(U, \Omega)$. It is clear that the structure of the representation of the preferences is dependent upon the structure of Ω.

The modern setting starts with a set L of permitted utility functions, and the individual is again supposed to have those preferences which are implied by *all* the utility functions in L. The difference between the traditional and the modern setting is that the traditional setting *starts* with a reference utility function and then develops the permitted representations, whereas the modern setting employs as its basic concept the set of permitted representations. As will be shown later, this distinction is not entirely harmless. The above definitions have been treated in a series of works by K. Basu (Basu, 1980, 1982, 1984). From either of these definitions it is possible to define the preference relation of the individual over the set Y. Let F be a permitted utility function, $F \in L$, in the modern or in the traditional setting. The preference relation R, meaning "not liked less than", is defined by the property that for $x, x' \in Y$:

$$xRx' \text{ if and only if } F(x) \geq F(x') \text{ for all } F \in L$$

The relations P, "liked more than", and I, "indifferent to", could also be defined. (For typographical reasons the symbol "R" denotes both the set of real numbers and the preference relation "not liked less than".)

It should be noted that the relation R so defined is reflexive (xRx for all $x \in Y$) and transitive (xRx' and $x'Rx''$ implies xRx'' for all $x, x', x'' \in Y$), but not complete. (It is not true that either xRx' or $x'Rx$ for all $x, x' \in Y$.) We will now introduce the concept ordinal utility.

The individual is in the traditional setting said to have ordinal utility if all transformations in Ω are monotone increasing: If for all $f \in \Omega$ and all $u_1, u_2 \in R$, $u_1 \geq u_2$ if and only if $f(u_1) \geq f(u_2)$, then the utility is called ordinal (in the traditional setting). Note carefully that we are not assuming that Ω contains *all* monotone increasing transformations.

In the modern setting the utility is called ordinal if all representations $F, G \in L$ rank the commodity-bundles in the same order:

If for all $F, G, \in L$ and all $x, x' \in Y$ it is true that $F(x) \geq F(x')$ if and only if $G(x) \geq G(x')$, then the utility is called ordinal (in the modern setting). We finally note that if the utility is ordinal the preference relation R is also complete, in both the traditional and the modern setting.

Now to definitions of cardinal utility. In the traditional setting the utility is cardinal if all $f \in \Omega$ are linear increasing functions: If for all $f \in \Omega$

there exist numbers $a, b, b > 0$, such that $f(r) = b \cdot r + a$ for all $r \in R$, then the utility is called cardinal (in the traditional setting). Note that, under cardinal utility, two functions $f, g, \in \Omega$ are linear transformations of each other. This is the basis for the definition of cardinal utility in the modern setting: If for all $F, G, \in L$ there exist numbers $a, b, b > 0$, such that $F(x) = bG(x) + a$ for all $x \in Y$, then the utility is called cardinal (in the modern setting). One consequence of these definitions is that cardinal utility implies ordinal utility.

We will now comment on the old discussion from the 1930s regarding the connection between cardinal utility and the ability "to compare first-differences in utility". Our main source will be the works of K. Basu already referred to. An individual is in the traditional framework able to *compare first-differences in utility* if for all $f \in \Omega$ and all $x_1, x_2, x_3, x_4 \in Y$

$$U(x_1) - U(x_2) \geq U(x_3) - U(x_4)$$

if and only if

$$f(U(x_1)) - f(U(x_2)) \geq f(U(x_3)) - f(U(x_4))^4$$

It is quite clear that if the utility is cardinal, then the first-differences in utility can be compared, which means that the ranking between all such differences is invariant under all permitted transformations $f \in \Omega$. It was Oscar Lange's old conjecture that the opposite implication is also true. This created quite a controversy in the 1930s, but the correctness of Lange's deductions was finally proved by K. Basu in 1982 – if we assume that O. Lange operated in the traditional setting and if the space $U(Y)$ is connected:

Theorem 1. (Lange, 1933; Basu, 1982)
If $U(Y)$ is a connected subset of R, then the ability to compare first-differences in utility implies cardinal utility – in the traditional setting.[5, 6]
(Notice that there are no continuity-assumptions in this theorem.)

One important point should now be noted: Under the assumptions of Theorem 1 the ratio between the utility-differences is a well-defined real number, because

$$\frac{U(x_1) - U(x_2)}{U(x_3) - U(x_4)} = \frac{f(U(x_1)) - f(U(x_2))}{f(U(x_3)) - f(U(x_4))}$$

for all $f \in \Omega$ (if $U(x_3) \neq U(x_4)$).
In Lange's own words: "From the assumption that the individual is able to know *whether* one increase of utility is greater than another increase of utility the possibility of saying *how many times* this increase is greater than another one follows necessarily." (Lange, 1933–1934, p. 220.) Recently Morey (1984) stated (on p. 166), with a reference to Phelps-Brown

(1934–1935), that this assertion of Lange is incorrect. The reason for this confusion may be threefold:

(1) Lange seemingly stumbled in his *proof* in 1933–1934. In Phelps-Brown's presentation (on p. 68 in Phelps-Brown, 1934–1935): "[Lange] asks us to consider three combinations of goods I, II, III such that 'the individualfinds that the change of utility due to transition from II to III is equal to the change of utility due to transition from combination I to combination II'. It is clear" [Lange concludes] "that in this case we may say that the change of utility due to transition from I to III is twice the change of utility due to transition from I to II or from II to III". Of course, this is close to assuming what should be proved.

(2) It was not at all clear to all participants in the discussion that O. Lange was probably operating within what we have called the traditional setting – which among other things takes for granted the existence of a (reference) utility function. As correctly pointed out by Morey (1984) the existence of a (reference) utility function necessitates some continuity-assumptions.

(3) Interestingly enough Phelps-Brown's concept of measurability is at variance with ours. He states, on p. 66, "... measurability (...) consists in the possibility of expressing one magnitude as a multiple of another. It may be possible to arrange terms in an order, so that we can tell whether any one precedes or succeeds another, but we have not reached measurement, until we can express one as a multiple of another". This seems to be what we called a *purely cardinal measure* in the Introduction, and implies among other things that temperature is not measurable. Referring to the definition of cardinal utility, we see that we have a purely cardinal measure if all transformations $f \in \Omega$ are straight lines *through the origin.* Has anyone ever suggested something like that?

Loosely speaking the restriction on Ω to only monotone increasing transformations determines the sign of the first order partial derivatives of the utility functions, the ability to compare first-difference in utility determines the sign of the second order partial derivatives. This interpretation is in accordance with the flavour of Lange's original two proofs where he assumed first (implicitly) the continuity of the utility function and in the second proof he also assumed U to be differentiable. It should then be reasonably clear that a cardinalist is willing to compare (the size of) marginal utilities, but an ordinalist is not.[7]

What Lange actually did in the 1930s was to assume only the ability to compare those utility-differences in the definition of the ability to compare first-differences in utility where $U(x_1) = U(x_4)$. That this is sufficient for cardinal utility can now be proved with the help of Theorem 1 if we also assume that the preferences are continuous. The continuity of the preferences is expressed by the continuity of the (real-valued) reference function U.

Theorem 2. If the reference function U is continuous, and if $U(Y)$ is a connected subset of R and if for all $x_1, x_2, x_3 \in Y$ and all $f \in \Omega$

$$U(x_1) - U(x_2) \geq U(x_3) - U(x_1)$$

if and only if

$$f(U(x_1)) - f(U(x_2)) \geq f(U(x_3)) - f(U(x_1)),$$

then for all $f \in \Omega$

there exist $a, b \in R$, $b > 0$ such that $f(r) = a + b \cdot r$, for all $r \in R$. The proof is in Appendix II.

We will now demonstrate that the ability to compare first-differences in utility *does not* imply cardinal utility in the modern setting. We employ the following definition:
If for all $F, G \in L$ and all $x_1, x_2, x_3, x_4 \in Y$

$$F(x_1) - F(x_2) \geq F(x_3) - F(x_4)$$

if and only if

$$G(x_1) - G(x_2) \geq G(x_3) - G(x_4)$$

the individual is said to be able to compare first-differences in utility (in the modern setting). It is again clear that this property is fulfilled if the utility is cardinal, but the opposite implication is not valid, as the following example from Basu (1980) shows: Let there be three individuals, no. 1, no. 2, no. 3, and let each individual face only three alternatives, x, y, z, and let for each individual L consist of only two functions, F, G. Consider the following tables of "utilities":

	F	G		F	G		F	G
x	4	8	x	4	9	x	4	9
y	2	6	y	2	5	y	2	5
z	1	2	z	1	3	z	1	2
	No. 1			No. 2			No. 3	

All individuals have ordinal utility. Since $G = 2F + 1$ for no. 2, he has cardinal utility. No. 1 cannot compare first-differences in utility.

$$(2 = F(x) - F(y) > F(y) - F(z) = 1, \text{ but}$$
$$2 = G(x) - G(y) < G(y) - G(z) = 4)$$

No. 3 can compare first-differences in utility, but the utility is not cardinal. (It is not true that there exist $a, b, b > 0$ such that $F = b \cdot G + a$.)

It is then natural to define utility-scales *between* cardinal and ordinal utility. A utility will be called *quasi-cardinal of degree* n, $n \geq 1$, if the so-called utility-differences of degree n can be compared. It can be proved that the utility is cardinal if and only if the utility-difference of degree n can be compared for every natural number n. For details see Basu (1980).

To start with the set of reference-representations, in one way or another, as we have done, is efficient and elegant but the procedure may circumvent some crucial points. For instance, the so-called lexicographic ordering is a well-defined and interesting ordering, but as is well known it does not admit a utility-function representation. Can the concepts cardinality and ability to compare first-differences in utility be applied to that type of ordering?

Let the set of alternatives be R_{2+}. The lexicographical ordering, P, is defined by:

$$(x, y)P(a, b) \text{ if and only if } (x > a) \text{ or } (x = a \text{ and } y > b)$$

The ordering P is reflexive, complete and transitive, but there does not seem to be any meaningful way of attaching the terms "ordinal" or "cardinal" to this ordering. It is easy enough to define the ability to compare first-differences in utility, however. Here is an example:

By $((x_1, x_2), (y_1, y_2))\ P^1((a_1, a_2), (b_1, b_2))$

We want to mean that the increase in utility-level by a movement from the point (y_1, y_2) to the point (x_1, x_2) is greater than the utility-level increase by a movement from the point (b_1, b_2) to the point (a_1, a_2), and the following definition is possible:[8]

$$((x_1, x_2), (y_1, y_2))\ P^1((a_1, a_2)\ (b_1, b_2)) \text{ if and only if:}$$
$$(x_1 - y_1 > a_1 - b_1) \text{ or } (x_1 - y_1 = a_1 - b_1 \text{ and } x_2 - y_2 > a_2 - b_2)$$

We close this section with the following remarks:

(1) All that can be deduced from market data, at least in the first analysis, is the fact that the commodity bundle x is preferred to x' (if this is the case). The intensity of preferences, how "much" x is preferred to x', or if x if preferred "more" to x' than x^* is preferred to x° can possibly not be determined by looking at behaviour in the market; the only thing we will see is that x is always chosen before x'. The true pattern of preferences can only be identified if the individuals provide, under interrogation, what Samuelson (1974), p. 1258, refers to as "introspective information" on the intensity of their preferences. Of course, this is the reason why the foundations of any cardinality-concept has been questioned.

(2) The context will not always make it clear whether or not we are operating with a cardinal or an ordinal utility-concept. Suppose we consider pairs of goods, (x_1, x_2), and have arrive at the conclusion that the utility function $U(x_1, x_2)$ is additive separable, that is there exist functions u_1 and u_2 so that:

$$U(x_1, x_2) = u_1(x_1) + u_2(x_2), \text{ with } u_1' \neq 0 \text{ and } u_2' \neq 0$$

Do we then have cardinal utility? The answer is that it depends on what transformations we are permitting. If we are willing to use all monotone increasing transformations of U we are ordinalists, if we are only willing to use those monotone increasing transformations that preserve the property of additive separability we are cardinalists. The reason is that if the marginal utility with respect to x_1 is assumed to be independent of x_2, then for all transformations f:

$$\frac{\mathrm{d}}{\mathrm{d}x_2}\left(f'(u_1(x_1) + u_2(x_2)) \cdot u_1'(x_1)\right) =$$
$$f''(u_1(x_1) + u_2(x_2)) \cdot u_1'(x_1) \cdot u_2'(x_2) = 0$$

which implies $f''(\ ) = 0$, that is: $f(r) = a + b \cdot r$.

(3) From the preceding remarks it is reasonably clear what will be needed to make cardinal utility *meaningful*. First of all it may seem fruitless to seek for any philosophical or psychological connotations in a cardinalistic utility concept. What we should be looking for is some *structure* in the preferences that we happen to believe in, either through logical deductions from more or less "self-evident" axioms or through observations from market behaviour. And then this structure should be invariant under linear transformations. This procedure enables us to pick out in a canonical, well-defined and meaningful way a "cardinalistic subset" out of the manifold of possible utility-representations.

3. ON THE NECESSITY OF CARDINAL UTILITY IN DYNAMIC ANALYSIS

We will say we have established the necessity of cardinalism if we can locate "real" and important concepts and propositions that can only be properly treated with the use of cardinalistic concepts. In short, we are trying to challenge the idea, expressed for instance by Arrow (1963), p. 9: that "... the proponents of measurable utility have been unable to produce any proposition of economic behaviour which could be explained by their hypothesis and not by those of the indifference-curve theorists". We will look in another direction than Frisch, however.

Consider a representative consumer (individual, agent) facing a consumption program $x_1, \ldots, x_n$, where x_1 = consumption in period i, $i = 1, \ldots, n$. There is only one kind of consumption-good in the economy. The consumer has well-defined (ordinal) preferences over consumption programmes as *viewed from the beginning of period 1*, represented by the utility-function U^1:

(1) $\qquad U^1 = U^1(x_1, \ldots, x_n)$

Suppose $n = 3$. Define the marginal rate of substitution between period 2 and period 3 (viewed from period 1), S^1_{23}, by equation (2), when U^1_i, $i = 2, 3$, denote partial derivatives:

$$(2) \qquad S^1_{23}(x_1, x_2, x_3) = \frac{U^1_2(x_1, x_2, x_3)}{U^1_3(x_1, x_2, x_3)}$$

Given a consumption programme (x_1, x_2, x_3) there are three reasons why a small increase in x_2 should be valued differently than a small increase in x_3 – that is why $S^1_{23} \neq 1$:

1. x_2 may be different from x_3.
2. x_3 is consumed later than x_2. This effect is attributed to the Böhm–Bawerk–factor.
3. Period 2 and period 3 are different, not of equal importance. Examples of this effect abound: 17th May (Norway's national holiday) is something entirely different from the 18th May (the "day after"), we should have some extra purchasing power just before Christmas eve, the days our exams are taking place have been dreaded a long time in advance, etc. etc.
   If this effect 3 is in force we will talk about calendar-time dependent preferences (c.t.d.p.).

It should be a task for theory to identify and isolate these three effects. Our first point is the following:

Point 1. The case of c.t.d.p. cannot be treated within an ordinalistic framework. This is obvious because if we have c.t.d.p. we are in effect comparing utility-differences (an extra glass of beer the 17th of May gives a greater increase in utility than an extra glass of beer the 18th of May), and Oscar Lange's theorem is then implying that utility is cardinal. It may be the case, however, that c.t.d.p. is not deemed to be an important concept, worthy of serious study.

Point 2 is fare worse for the ordinalists:

Point 2. Ordinalists cannot isolate Böhm–Bawerks rate of pure time preference, it they accept the existence of c.t.d.p. (which they should do!) – even though they may be willing to live with the fact that c.t.d.p. exist beyond the grasp of their conceptual framework.

This could be called a serious problem because of the time-honoured and prominent standing of Böhm–Bawerks rate of pure time preference in economic theory. We are not pretending to "prove" that ordinalists cannot identify the Böhm–Bawerk factor, but by going through for instance Morishima's reasoning it is clear that the ordinalists have a problem here – on their part rests the burden of proof if they want to incorporate the

Böhm–Bawerk–factor. Morishima (1965), in his criticism of Frisch, seems to overlook the fact that the consumer may have c.t.d.p.: "The Bawerkian factor $1 - \beta_t$ may, from the viewpoint of the ordinalists, be interpreted as the marginal rate of substitution between future and present income at a stationary state where the growth rate of income = 0". Thus, Morishima wants to measure the Böhm–Bawerk factor by going along the 45°-line. But if we, for instance, are comparing the 17th and 18th of May there are entirely different reasons for evaluating a glass of beer on the 18th as being lower than a glass of beer on the 17th than the fact that the 18th of May is later than 17th of May.

If there is something like perspective shortening – what comes later is valued less because it is later – Morishima's method seems inadequate to cope with this effect in the presence of c.t.d.p. We will now suggest how the Böhm–Bawerk factor could be defined within a cardinalistic framework – given the existence of c.t.d.p.

Suppose there are over the set of all consumption programmes (x_1, x_2, x_3) well-defined (ordinal) preferences, evaluated at the beginning of period 1 given by $U^1(x_1, x_2, x_3)$; *evaluated at the beginning of period 2*, given by $U^2(x_1, x_2, x_3)$; and evaluated at the beginning of period 3, given by $U^3(x_1, x_2, x_3)$. Some examples could be:

$$U^1 = U^1(x_1, x_2, x_3) = u_1(x_1) + \frac{1}{r_1(1)} u_2(x_2) + \frac{1}{r_2(1)} \cdot u_3(x_3) ,$$

$$U^2 = U^2(x_1, x_2, x_3) = K + u_2(x_2) + \frac{1}{r_1(2)} \cdot u_3(x_3) ,$$

$$U^3 = U^3(x_1, x_2, x_3) = K^1 + u_3(x_3) .$$

These are *only* examples; intended only to give some support to the imagination. The interpretation of $r_i(j)$, $i, j = 1, 2$ is the following:

$\frac{1}{r_i(j)}$ = the discount-factor, attributed to Böhm–Bawerk's rate of pure time preference, *over i periods*, as seen from the beginning of period j. $j = 1, 2$.

Accordingly, $1/r_1(1)$ is the factor by which we underestimate the value of period 2's consumption, as seen from the beginning of period 1, $1/r_2(1)$ is the factor by which we underestimate the value of period 3's consumption, as seen from the beginning of period 1 and $1/r_1(2)$ is the factor by which we underestimate the value of period 3's consumption, as seen from the beginning of period 2. To get hold of the Böhm–Bawerk factor between period 2 and period 1, as seen from the beginning of period 1, we should accordingly imagine a situation where the marginal utility of period 1's consumption is equal to the marginal utility of period 2's consumption – if only the marginal utility of period 2 could be "cleansed" from the fact that period 2 is later than period 1. A comparison of U^3 and U^2 is doing the trick:

Definition 1. The consumer has a *rate of pure time-preference* between period 1 and period 2 – as seen from the beginning of period 1 – if for all consumption programs (x_1, x_2, x_2) the following is the case:

$$\frac{U_1^1(x_1, x_3, x_3)}{U_2^2(x_1, x_2, x_3)} = 1 \Longrightarrow \frac{U_1^1(x_1, x_2, x_3)}{U_2^1(x_1, x_2, x_3)} \geq 1$$

and there is at least one program (x_1, x_2, x_3) such that the last inequality is a strong inequality.

The point is that if the marginal utility of consumption in period 1, as seen from the beginning of period 1, is equal to the marginal utility of consumption in period 2, *as seen from the beginning of period 2* – that is cardinalism – then there is a rate of pure time-preference if the marginal rate of substitution between period 1 and 2, as seen from the beginning of period 1, is at least equal to 1.

Definition 2. Suppose the consumer has a rate of pure time-preference between period 1 and period 2, as seen from the beginning of period 1. For a point (x_1, x_2, x_3) where $U_1^1(x_1, x_2, x_3) = U_2^2(x_1, x_2, x_3)$ *the Böhm–Bawerk discount-factor* $1/r_1(1)$ is given by:

$$\frac{1}{r_1(1)} = \frac{U_2^1(x_1, x_2, x_3)}{U_2^2(x_1, x_2, x_3)} = \frac{1}{r_1(1)(x_1, x_2, x_3)}$$

We will assume that $r_1(1)$ is constant, independent of (x_1, x_2, x_3), wherever it is defined. Similar definitions for $r_2(1)$ and $r_1(2)$ can easily be constructed. We see that the gist of the definition is to measure how much consumption in period 2 is degraded, as seen from period 1, given a situation where consumption in period 2, as seen from period 2, is marginally valued to be equal to consumption in period 1, as seen from period 1.

To get a feeling for whether or not these distinctions are important we will discuss some problems within "intertemporal consistency".

Suppose a certain income or consumption-quantity is to be distributed over 3 periods. As seen from the beginning of period 1 the consumer has to solve the following problem:

$$\underset{x_1, x_2, x_3}{\text{Max}}\, U^1(x_1, x_2, x_3), \text{ subject to } x_1 + x_2 + x_3 = \bar{x}$$

The optimal interior solution $x^* = (x_1^*, x_2^*, x_3^*)$ is given by:

$$S_{13}^1(x^*) = S_{23}^1(x^*) = 1 \;\&\; x_1^* + x_2^* + x_3^* = \bar{x}. \tag{3}$$

x_1^* is consumed, period 1 passes by, then comes period 2. The consumer is then solving the following problem:

$$\underset{x_2, x_3}{\text{Max}}\, U^2(x_1^*, x_2, x_3), \text{ subject to } x_1^* + x_2 + x_3 = \bar{x}$$

If we assume that these problems have unique solutions, then we have intertemporal consistency (people do not change their plans) if and only if:

$$(4) \qquad S_{23}^1(x^*) = S_{23}^2(x^*)$$

with S_{23}^2 defined in an obvious way. (4) means that the marginal evaluation between period 2 and period 3, at the consumption program x^*, is unaffected by whether we stand at the beginning of period 1 or at the beginning of period 2 (pure ordinalism so far).

It should be of considerable interest to study the reasons why (4) is not fulfilled – that is, to study why the marginal evaluation changes with time. The main problem will be to establish reasonable connections between the preference given by U^1 and U^2, but it should be stressed that there is nothing irrational about the non-fulfilment of (4); things like that happen all the time.

Some reasonable and non-arbitrary possibilities for intertemporal inconsistency may be:

(1) The two-period Böhm–Bawerk factor is not equal to the product of the appropriate one-period Böhm–Bawerk factors.
This can be formulated by assuming that the "time-independent-aspects" of the preferences represented by U^1 and U^2 are equal; that is the evaluation of consumption in the different periods, "cleansed" for the Böhm–Bawerk factor is the same in both periods.
Thus, let us assume:

$$r_1(1) \cdot U_2^1(x^*) = U_2^2(x^*)$$
$$r_2(1) \cdot U_3^1(x^*) = r_1(2) \cdot U_3^2(x^*)$$

In these formulae we are first, with the help of the Böhm–Bawerk factors, "upgrading" the marginal utility of consumption in the various periods to the beginning of period 2 and the beginning of period 3, respectively. Then we are equalizing the "upgraded" marginal utilities given by U^1 to the "upgraded" marginal utilities given by U^2. These conditions imply:

$$\frac{r_1(1)}{r_2(1)} \frac{U_2^1(x^*)}{U_3^1(x^*)} = \frac{1}{r_1(2)} \cdot \frac{U_2^2(x^*)}{U_3^2(x^*)}$$

so that the consistency condition (4) is equivalent to:

$$(5) \qquad r_2(1) = r_1(1) \cdot r_1(2)$$

And there is nothing in the concept of a rate of pure time preference that will guarantee that equation (5) is valid.[9] To the extent that the Böhm–Bawerk factor cannot be defined within an ordinalistic framework, the ordinalists will not be able to formulate this point.

(2) The periods are of different importance, but we tend to "forget" this difference until it is almost too late.
This point is completely trivial, but is still an important characteristic of human behaviour. It is not connected to "learning" – we know at which date is Christmas eve 1990 – but our actions reveal almost as a tautology that we almost always have to rush in the last minute. Another example: We know in January that we have to pass our exams in May, so that we should have some spare time to prepare in April, but come April we have too much else to do! How this point should be formulated is somewhat arbitrary. Let for instance U^2 represent the "true" preferences. Suppose U^1 is such that:

$$U_2^1(x_1, x_2, x_3) = U_2^2(x_1, x_2, x_3)$$
$$U_3^1(x_1, x_2, x_3) = U_2^2(x_1, x_3, x_2)$$

which means that at the beginning of period 1 period 2 is evaluated "correctly", but period 3 is evaluated approximately as period 2. We have a case of intertemporal inconsistency if $U_2^2(x_1, x_3, x_2) \neq U_3^2(x_1, x_2, x_3)$. Of course, this point can only be formulated by a cardinalist.

(3) The preference towards a period are becoming "sharper" the closer the period.
Let us suppose that far away – from period 1 – period 2 and period 3 look (exactly) the same, so that $S_{23}^1(x)$ is constant. One non-arbitrary candidate for S_{23}^1 is $r_2(1)/r_1(1)$. At the beginning of period 2 we have become wiser, we know more definitely what we want to do, and as a rule: $S_{23}^2(x^*) \neq S_{23}^1(x^*)$.
This point is partly dependent upon the existence of the Böhm–Bawerk factor.

4. SOME AXIOMATIZATIONS TO ESTABLISH THE MEANINGFULNESS OF CARDINAL UTILITY IN DYNAMIC ANALYSIS

4.1. General Remarks

First of all we will contemplate the fact that there is indeed a short step from ordinal to cardinal utility. Suppose the commodity-space is composed of all vectors (x_1, x_2) with non-negative real components. Given the preferences in the (x_1, x_2)-space we will indicate some of the comparisons an ordinalist

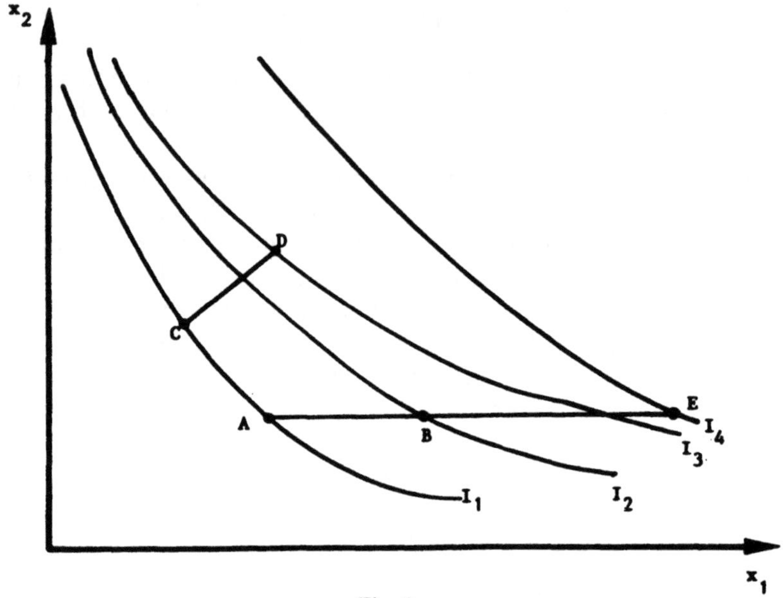

Fig. 1.

can do, and some he/she cannot do. In Figure 1, let I_1, I_2, I_3 and I_4 be four indifference–curves.

An ordinalist will be able to settle whether or not the movement from A to B gives a greater or smaller increase in utility than the movement from C to D, but – remember Lange's conjucture – the ordinalist is not able to decide whether or not the movement from A to B gives a smaller or greater increase in utility than the movement from B to E. There are some indications in Frisch's earlier works, for instance (1947), that if we give x_1 and x_2 an intertemporal interpretation (x_1 is consumption in period 1, x_2 is consumption in period 2), then we are able to make judgements of this second kind. The idea is apparently that it is easier to ascertain that we prefer an extra bottle of beer on Tuesday more than an extra bottle of beer on Wednesday than to ascertain that we prefer an extra bottle of beer today more than an extra loaf of bread today. We are, according to Frisch, constantly living with these intertemporal evaluations, in the sense that these judgements influence our daily decisions all the time. In short: the intertemporal interpretation is giving the mind some support to perform comparisons of first-differences in utility. It must be admitted, however, that it is extremely difficult to make any sense of this. One possible justification for the superiority of being able to make comparisons of utility-differences in an intertemporal framework may be that the situations in the future which we contemplate when we make our decisions today are situations that *will actually be realized, later on*, but the reader is not asked by the present author to find this convincing. We have to look in different directions.[10]

In searching for a cardinal utility function one point must be "perfectly clear": If we somehow *have* a utility-function which we happen to *believe* in, the cardinal/ordinal controversy is settled – dynamic or non-dynamic analysis. There may be procedures that through empirical investigations may give rise to a utility-function with some empirical content, but the problem for the cardinalist is to ensure that all *arbitrariness* has been eliminated in the construction of the utility function. What we should be looking for when we try to find a utility-function is some *general principles* which stand above the particular assumptions we are making. To be more specific, consider the following utility representation, which has been used by many authors, perhaps first by Herman Wold (1943):

If the preferences are continuous and strictly monotone (with a suitable interpretation), it can be showed that for each $(x_1, \ldots, x_n)$ in the set of alternatives Y there exists a unique t such that $(x_1, \ldots, x_n)$ is indifferent to $(t, \ldots, t)$. Then put $U(x_1, \ldots, x_n) = t$

This U is a continuous representation of the preferences, and perhaps it can be arrived at through empirical investigations. The problem is, however, that the value of U is dependent on the choice of units of measurement of the x_i's. If there is some universal acceptance of some "natural units" we have a general principle to generate a (cardinal) utility function. (And then we could fix Ω, the set of permitted transformations, to include only the indentity mapping, in which case we will be able to say for instance that A gives twice as much utility as B.) But this is of course only nonsense; the choice of units is completely arbitrary. To arrive at a cardinal utility concept through *general principles* we could employ Herman Wold's construction as outlined above and examine whether or not the different utility-representations which are emerging through the different choice of units are linear transformations of each other. The argument runs as follows: Let U and V be two "Herman Wold" – utility functions arrived at by using two sets of units of measurement, and let, say U, be the reference representation. The permitted transformation f from U to V is given by: $f(u) = V(a)$, where $U(a) = u$. We have a cardinal utility concept only if f is linear. If f is linear it is possible to compare first-differences in utility, that is, for all A, B, C in Y we have:

$$V(A) - V(B) \geq V(B) - V(C)$$

if and only if

$$U(A) - U(B) \geq U(B) - U(C)$$

It is completely trivial, however, to give examples such that this equivalence is not valid:

Let $Y = R^2_+$ and let *in the units of meaurement used for the construction of* U the points, A, B, C and some respective indifferent points A^*, B^*, C^* be given by:

$$\begin{aligned} A &= (14, 14) \quad I \quad (1,\ 100) &&= A^* \\ B &= (9, 9) \quad I \quad (0.8,\ 80) &&= B^* \\ C &= (7, 7) \quad I \quad (0.5,\ 50) &&= C^* \end{aligned}$$

We then have: $U(A) = 14, U(B) = 9, U(C) = 7$.

Suppose V is arrived at through the following change in units: 1 unit of good number 1 in the old system (the U-system) is 10 units of good number 1 in the new system (the V-system), and 10 units of good number 2 in the new system is 1 unit of good number 2 in the old system.

Then *in the new system* the points A^*, B^*, C^* will be written:

$$A^* = (10,\ 10)\ ,\quad B^* = (8, 8)\ ,\quad C^* = (5, 5)$$

Thus, accordingly:

$$\begin{aligned} V(A) &= V(A^*) = 10, \\ V(B) &= V(B^*) = 8, \\ V(C) &= V(C^*) = 5, \end{aligned}$$

and we have:

$$U(A) - U(B) = 5 > U(B) - U(C) = 2,$$

and

$$V(A) - V(B) = 2 < V(B) - V(C) = 3$$

We have then showed that Herman Wold's construction is generally not a way to proceed if we want to arrive at a cardinal utility function.

There is a presumption in the literature that the search for intensities of preferences, which seems necessary to develop cardinal utility, is empirically unsound, whereas indifference-curve analysis has a sound footing. As a general rule this may be true, but it has turned out that indifference-curve analysis is less perfect than many people have been accustomed to believe.

What we would want, in order to have a "good theory", is to be able to pinpoint a consumer's preferences by an empirical study of his demand functions. Given enough data it should be possible to plot the indifference map – so goes the saying. But this is not literally true. The most that can be hoped for – given the best of all circumstances – is to find the value of the marginal rate of substitution at every point in the set of alternatives. It has then turned out that *complete knowledge* of the different marginal rates of substitution at all points is *not sufficient to uniquely determine* the

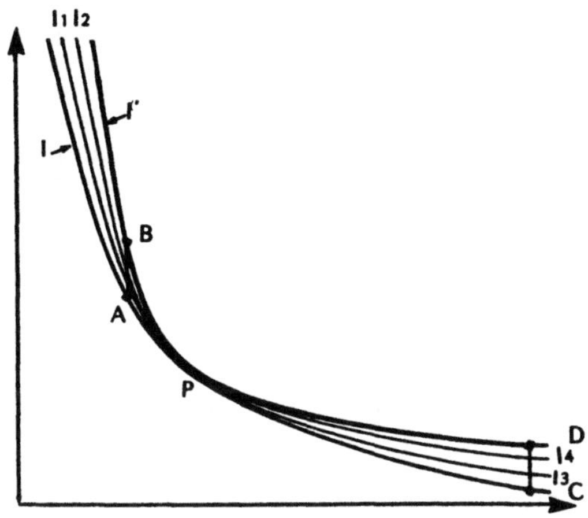

Fig. 2.

set of indifference-curves. There are two types of results in this direction, the first involves a kind of discontinuity, the second does not.

Suppose the study of the marginal rates of substitution gives rise to a configuration as in Figure 2. The curves I and I' are tangent to each other at the point P, otherwise they do not intersect. The same is also true for all curves between I and I'. Can the indifference-curves now be identified? Let the curves between I and I' and to the left of P, but not including P, like I_1, and I_2 represent curves of indifferent points. And let the curves between I and I' to the right of P, but not including P, like I_3 and I_4, represent curves of indifferent points. But how can we match indifference-curves to the left and to the right of P? Empirical analysis gives us no clues as to how to proceed. This is shown as follows: We index the indifference-curves to the left of P by the distance from A of the intersection with the line-segment AB. Likewise for the indifference-curves to the right of P, with the use of the line-segment CD. Both AB and CD are of unit length. One possible way of matching the indifference-curves is to put those with an intersection within 1/3 from A into a one-to-one correspondence with those within 1/2 from C. Another possibility is to match those within 1/2 from A with those within 1/2 from C. Empirical investigations will not be able to tell how to perform the matching, and we conclude that there is no way to deduce the consumer's preferences by a study of market data.

A discontinuity as in point P has been called a "pole" by Gorman (1971). Still more striking is a result by Mas-Colell (1977), which is mentioned in Rader (1972) and partly attributed to Shapley. Mas-Colell postulates that the underlying preference relation "is a continuous, monotone, convex one". He then poses the problem: "does the given demand function identify uniquely a monotone, convex, continuous preference relation?" The answer is that "... such a contention is false. There are two distinct continuous, monotone, strictly convex preference relations, defined in the non-negative orthant of R^l $(l \geq 2)$, giving rise to identical demand functions". There seems to be a consequence of this result that the notion of indifference between two points can never, in principle, be verified empirically without further postulates regarding human behaviour. Is this a disturbing fact?

4.2. Additive separability

Various types of considerations (axioms, empirical generalizations etc.) may give rise to utility structures that are additive separable, that is:

$$U(x_1, \dots, x_n) = \sum_{i=1}^{n} U_i(x_i)$$

According to Houthakker (1960) "additivity assumptions appear most promising (...) when we are dealing with large aggregates such as clothing, food etc. The interrelations between such aggregates probably follow largely from their competition for the consumer's dollar, rather than from any more specific connection, such as exists between butter an margarine, or between cars and gasoline". By some stretching of the imagination it could be defended to assume that the very large aggregates which are consumptions in the various periods are well suited for an additive separable utility-representation. Anyhow, Koopmans (1960) has given a set of sufficient conditions for additive separability in an intertemporal framework:

Denote a consumption program for the infinite future by ${}_1x = (x_1, x_2, x_3, \dots) = (x_1, {}_2x) =$ etc. We will stand by the simplification, which Koopmans is not using, that there is only one kind of consumption good in each period. Three postulates are of main interest: We need "that the preference ordering within a class of programmes ${}_1x$ with a common first-period consumption vector x_1 does not depend on what that vector x_1 is". Koopmans requires further "that that preference ordering be the same as the ordering of corresponding programs obtained by advancing the timing of each future consumption vector by one period. ( ). This expresses the idea that the passage of time does not have an effect on preferences". The final and essential postulate is the following:

Postulate 3′ (3′a and 3′b). For all $x_1, x_2, {}_3x, x'_1, x'_2, {}_3x'$

(3′a) $U(x_1, x_2, {}_3x) \geq U(x'_1, x'_2, {}_3x)$ implies $U(x_1, x_2, {}_3x') \geq U(x'_1, x'_2, {}_3x')$.

(3′b) $U(x_1, x_2, {}_3x) \geq U(x'_1, x_2, {}_3x')$ implies $U(x_1, x'_2, {}_3x) > U(x'_1, x'_2, {}_3x')$.

It then follows, by using a result of Debreu (1960), that there exists α, $0 < \alpha < 1$, and *a one-period* utility function $u(\,)$, so that for all $(x_1, x_2, x_3, \ldots)$:

$$(6) \qquad U(x_1, x_2, x_3, \ldots) = \sum_{t=1}^{\infty} \alpha^t \cdot u(x_t)$$

Koopmans' postulate 3 can then be used as a basis for defining a cardinal utility function, since as is showed in Section 2 of the present paper, a form like (6) is destroyed by any other transformations than increasing linear ones.

The theory of choice under uncertainty is particularly relevant to dynamic analysis and it offers a wide choice of different forms of cardnalizations. We will not go into these models in any detail, but only mention an interesting twist made by $P.$ Fishburn (1978), which obtains cardinal utility without resort to any kind of expected-utility maximization à la von Neumann–Morgenstern. The uncertainty in Fishburn's model pertains to the length of the individual's lifetime. Suppose the (finite) future is divided into n periods. There is a well-behaved (unconditional) preference relation R defined over consumption streams over the n periods "which aknowledges the possibility that the individual may die after any period if he survives beyond the present". There are further well-behaved (conditional) preference relations $R_1, \ldots, R_n$ defined over consumption streams up to period $1, \ldots, n$, respectively, "that (are based on the hypothesis that death will occur at the end of period i", $i = 1, \ldots, n$. The interesting point now is how the ordering R is related to the orderings $R_1, \ldots, R_n$. Two key axioms are employed: The first says "that if x is preferred to y on the hypothesis that death will occur at the end of period i, and if this is true for each i, then x is unconditionally preferred to y. The second is an indifference-independence axiom". Fishburn is then able to prove that if the orderings R_i are represented by the functions $U_i(x_1, \ldots, x_1), i = 1, \ldots, n$, the ordering R is represented by the function $U_1(x_1) + U_2(x_1, x_2) + \ldots + U_i(x_1, \ldots, x_i) + \ldots + U_n(x_1, \ldots, x_n)$, where $(x_1, \ldots, x_i)$ is a consumption stream over the first i periods. $i = 1, \ldots, n$. Moreover, when the axioms hold and $U_i^!(\,)$ also represent R_i, $i = 1, \ldots, n$, there are real numbers $a > 0$, $b_1, \ldots, b_n$ such that $U_i^!(\,) = a \cdot U_i(\,) + b_i$, for all $i = 1, \ldots, n$. Thus, the representation of R is a cardinal utility function: it is unique up to a positive linear transformation.

5. CONCAVE REPRESENTATIONS IN DYNAMIC ANALYSIS

Another possibility for finding a cardinal structure can be sought by using a theorem of Debreu that "concavable preferences admit a least concave representation". Denote the preference relation by the symbol R, with the usual interpretation (if $a, b \in Y$, the commodity-space, aRb means that b

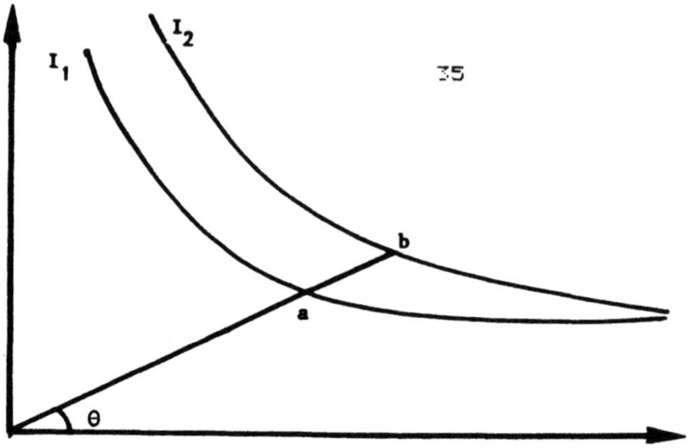

Fig. 3.

is not preferred to a, aPb means that a is preferred to b, aIb means that a is indifferent to b).

Theorem (Debreu 1976). If the preferences R can be represented by a *concave* continuous function U (R is concavable), there exists *a least concave representation* of R, that is there exists a concave representation U such that if V is any concave representation of R, then there exists a concave function f, from $U(R)$ to R, such that:

$$V = f \circ U$$

Least concave representations are unique up to increasing *linear* transformations.

In light of this theorem a fruitful avenue of research into the question left open by Frisch could be to examine whether or not the obstacles to admit concave representations are less severe in a dynamic setting, or are less severe as the time perspective goes to infinity. If this much could be established there is at least some credibility to the claim that cardinal utility is more natural in a dynamic setting – since Debreu's theorem permits a canonical way of picking out some cardinal representations of the preferences, if they are concavable. Let us first study why preferences may not admit a concave representation.

In Figure 3 I_1 and I_2 are two indifference-curves and $a(\theta) = a$ and $b(\theta) = b$ are the respective intersections between I_1 and I_2 with a straight line from the origion with an angel θ with the abscisse-axis.

Let the preferences be *monotone* so that $U(a(\theta)) < U(b(\theta))$ for all representations U if $a(\theta) < b(\theta)$, $0 < \theta < \frac{\pi}{2}$, and all representations U.

Define $r(\theta) = r$ by $a = r \cdot b$, $0 < r < 1$.

Assume that:

$$r \to 1 \text{ when } \theta \to 0$$

Then there is no concave representation of the preferences. This is so because if U is a concave representation we have:

$$U(a) = U((1-r)\cdot 0 + r \cdot b) \geq (1-r)\cdot U(0) + r \cdot U(b)$$

But $((1-r)\cdot U(0) + r \cdot U(b) \to U(b)$ as $\theta \to 0$, thus $U(a) \geq U(b)$, a contradiction.

We will call a situation like this, where "the distance" between two fixed, separate indifference-curves is zero, for non-concavity of the first kind. To give a precise definition of this concept we will first introduce some assumptions which we will stand by for the rest of this paper.

The set of alternatives Y will be the non-negative ortant R^n_+ of the Euclidian space R^n. The preference relation R is reflexive (i.e. aRa, for every $a \in Y$), transitive (i.e. aRb, bRc implies aRc), complete (i.e. for every $a, b \in Y$, either aRb or bRa), and continuous (i.e. $\{a' \in Y;\ a'Ra\}$ and $\{a' \in Y;\ aRa'\}$ are closed in Y for every $a \in Y$). We will also assume that R is strictly monotone (i.e. if $a = (a_1, \ldots, a_n)$ and $b = (b_1, \ldots, b_n)$, and $a_i \geq b_i$ for all $i = 1, \ldots, n$ and $a \neq b$, then aPb).

By $I(a)$ we mean all consumption programmes in Y which are indifferent to a:

$$I(a) = \{a' \in Y : a'Ia\}$$

By $K^n(0)$ we mean the coordinate planes:

$$K^n(0) = \{(a_1, \ldots, a_n) \in Y; \text{ there exists } i,\ 1 \leq i \leq n;\ a_i = 0\}$$

The distance, $d(a, b)$, between $a = (a_1, \ldots, a_n)$ and $b = (b_1, \ldots, b_n)$ is the Euclidean norm:

$$d(a, b) = ((a_1 - b_1)^2 + \ldots + (a_n - b_n)^2)^{1/2}$$

Given two subsets Y_1, Y_2 of Y the distance between Y_1 and Y_2, $d(Y_1, Y_2)$, is given by:

$$d(Y_1, Y_2) = \inf \{d(y_1, y_2);\ y_1 \in Y_1,\ y_2 \in Y_2\}$$

Definition 3. The preference relation R has *non-concavity of the first kind* if there exist $a, b \in Y$ and a positive number $\delta > 0$ such that (i) bPa, (ii) $d(I(b);\ K^n(0)) = \delta$, (iii) $d(I(b),\ I(a)) = 0$.

The condition (ii), that $I(b)$ has a positive distance from the coordinate planes, is needed to avoid "a Cobb–Douglas case": If $U(x_1, x_2) = x_1 x_2$

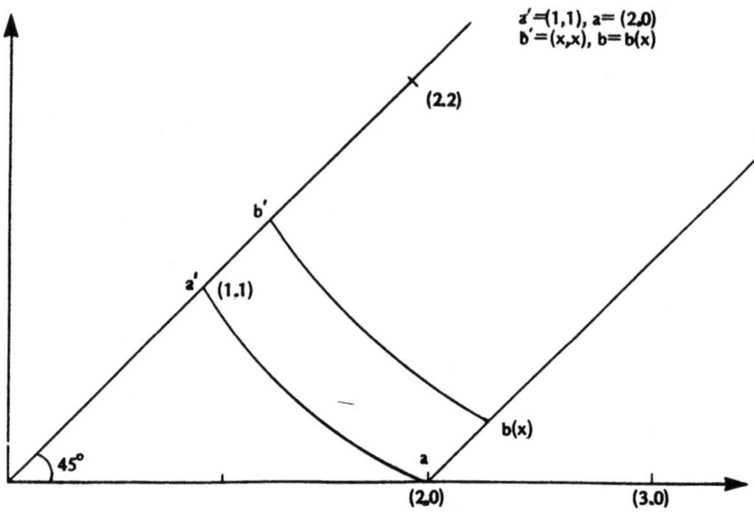

Fig. 4.

the representation U is concave, and $d(I(a),\ I(b)) = 0$ for all $a, b, \in Y$, but all indifference-curves are asymptotic to the coordinate planes.

Proposition 1. If the preference relation R has non-concavity of the first kind, it is not concavable. (The proof is in Appendix III.)

A non-concavity of the first kind is a very straightforward instance of preference not being able to be represented by a concave function; the odd thing happens "in the infinite". More subtle forms of non-concavable preferences can be arrived at by employing T. Rader's concept uniform sensivity.

Definition (Rader, 1972). Let $d(a,\ I(b)) = \inf\ \{d(a, c);\ cIb\}$. The preferences R are *uniformly sensitive* if there exist $\varepsilon > 0$ and $t > 0$ such that for all $a, b \in Y$:

$$d(a, b) < \varepsilon \Rightarrow d(a', b') \geq t \cdot d(a,\ I(b)) \text{ for all } a'Ia,\ b'Ib\ ^{11}$$

This definition is meant to capture the idea that indifference curves are fitting together not too wildly. If preferences have non-concavity of the first kind they are not uniformly sensitive, but we can construct examples where the non-fulfilment of uniform sensivity is happening "in the finite".

In Figure 4 L is a fixed straight line from the point $a = (2, 0)$. For each $x \in [1, 2]$ mark a point on the line L in a distance $\sqrt{x - 1}$ from a, and call this point $b = b(x)$.

Suppose the preferences are such that:

(i) $(x,x)Ib(x)$, for all $x \in [1,2]$, in particular (1,1) Ia,

(ii) $d(a,b(x)) = d(a,\ I(b(x)),$

(ii) means that the shortest distance from a to the indifference-curve through $b(x)$ and (x,x) can be found by going along the line L.

For each x we let $b'(x) = b'$ be equal to (x,x). If the preferences are uniformly sensitive then, if only a and b are close enough there exists $t > 0$ so that:

$$d(a',b') \geq t \cdot d(a,\ I(b))\ , \quad \text{for } a'Ia \text{ and } b'Ib$$

We have for the present example, with $a' = (1,1)$

$$\frac{d(a',b')}{d(a,\ I(b))} = \frac{\sqrt{2}\cdot(x-1)}{\sqrt{x-1}} = \sqrt{2}\cdot\sqrt{x-1} \underset{x\to 1}{\longrightarrow} 0$$

thus the preferences are not uniformly sensitive; we can say that a' is infinitely more sensitive than a.

The relevance of this concept for the present discussion stems from a result of Mas-Colell:

Theorem (Mas-Colell, 1977). If the preferences are continuous, monotone, strictly convex and concavable they are uniformly sensitive. There exist continuous, monotone, strictly convex and uniformly sensitive preferences that are not concavable.

Mas-Colells' theorem justifies the following.

Definition 4. Preferences that are not uniformly sensitive have *non-concavity of the second kind.*

It is clear that preferences that have non-concavity of the first kind also have non-concavity of the second kind, but the opposite is not generally true.

We will now outline an approach for studying the question of whether preferences are more likely to be concavable as the time perspective is widening. Let the future be divided into n periods, and let consumption in the various periods be denoted by $x_1, \ldots, x_n$. Suppose the consumer has well-defined preferences over pairs (x_1, x_2), with consumption x_1 in the first period and consumption x_2 in the second period. We will then say that this consumer has 2-preferences. If the consumer also has preferences over triples (x_1, x_2, x_3) we say that the consumer has 3-preferences. Thus, one and the same consumer can possibly have a whole series of intertemporal preferences: 2-preferences, 3-preferences, ..., k-preferences, $k \leq n$. One interpretation of these concepts may be that the type of preferences a consumer is operating with depends upon *the information* available to the consumer. The consumer is using his or her 2-preferences in the choice between consumption in period 1 and period 2 when what is coming after period 2 is unknown. But if the consumer knows or believes that consumption in period 3 is x_3, his or her choice between period 1 and period 2 is determined by the 3-preferences. If he or she also knows the consumption in period 4, he or she will use 4-preferences etc. It may perfectly well be the case that the consumer is not able to predict what will happen 5 or 6 periods hence, so that he or she is only able to operate with 4-preferences. Of course, these different preferences are in some way connected. We would in particular want to know how the uncertainty regarding the future should be modelled. At the end of this section we return to these questions, but for the moment we take the different k-preferences as basic concepts and will look for conditions that will guarantee that the $k+1$-preferences are more likely to be concavable than the k-preferences. To make it simple we only study the case where $k = 2$. We would like to have results in the following direction:

- If the 2-preferences can be represented by a concave utility-function, the same is true of the 3-preferences.
- If the 2-preferences cannot be represented by a concave utility-function, the obstacle against such a representation are less severe for 3-preferences.
- If only k is large enough, the k-preferences can be represented by a concave utility-function.

We start by introducing the concept of a transformation between 2-preferences and 3-preferences.

Definition 5. A preference-preserving transformation (p.p.t.) T from 3-preferences to 2-preferences is a pair of real-valued functions.

$T = (f, g)$, such that for all $x = (x_1, x_2, x_3)$ and
$x' = (x'_1, x'_2, x'_3)$ we have:
(i) $xIx' \Rightarrow (f(x),\ g(x))\ I\ (f(x'),\ g(x'))$
(ii) $xPx' \Rightarrow (f(x),\ g(x))\ P\ (f(x'),\ g(x'))$.

(The symbols I and P are used in (i) and (ii) first for 3-preferences, then for 2-preferences.

We see that if there exists a $T = (f, g)$ as in Definition 5 we can from knowledge of the 2-preferences deduce the 3-preferences. This is so because if the 2 preferences are given by a function $U^2(x_1, x_2)$, $(x_1, x_2) \in R^2_+$, the 3-preferences can be determined by defining: $U^3(x_1, x_2, x_3) = U^2(f(x),\ g(x))$ for all $x = (x_1, x_2, x_3) \in R^3_+$.

We should in the ensuing discussion not lose track of the following fact:

Fact 1. If $T = (f, g)$ is a p.p.t. from 3-preferences to 2-preferences and if the functions f and g are continuous and concave, then the 3-preferences are concavable if the 2-preferences are concavable.

Proof. Put $U^3(x) = U^2(f(x), g(x))$.

In light of the next proposition we will be looking for p.p.t.'s that are *uniformly continuous*.

Proposition 2. If there exists a uniformly continuous p.p.t. from 3-preferences to 2-preferences, which maps indifference curves not asymptotic to the coordinate planes into indifference curves not asymptotic to the coordinate planes and if the 3-preferences have non-concavity of the first kind, then the 2-preferences have non-concavity of the first kind.

Proposition 2 identifies some circumstances where 2-preferences are *not more likely* to be concavable than 3-preferences. Accordingly, if we can find uniformly continuous p.t.t.'s from 3-preferences to 2-preferences there is at least some credibility to the claim that if 3-preferences are not concavable then 2-preferences are not concavable.

Example 1. Only minor assumptions are needed for the existence of a continuous p.t.t. from 3-preferences to 2-preferences: If all preferences are monotone and if for all (x_1, x_2, x_3) there exists x such that $(x_1, x_2, x_3) \sim (x, x, x)$, then $T = (f, g)$ is a continuous p.t.t. from 3-preferences to 2-preferences, if $f(x_1, x_2, x_3) = x = g(x_1, x_2, x_3)$. This T may not be uniformly continuous, however.

We next explore some consequences of assuming T to be differentiable. It is fairly easy to give necessary conditions for the existence of a differentiable p.p.t. from 3-preferences to 2-preferences. Let the 3-preferences be represented by the function $U^3(x_1, x_2, x_3)$, and the 2-preferences be represented by the function $U^2(y_1, y_2)$. Use the following definitions for the respective marginal rates of substitution:

$$S_{1j} = S_{1j}(x) = \frac{U_1^3(x)}{U_j^3(x)}, \; j = 2, 3, \; \text{ where } x = (x_1, x_2, x_3)\,,$$

$$S = S(y) = \frac{U_1^2(y)}{U_2^2(y)}\,, \; \text{ where } y = (y_1, y_2)$$

We then have the following:

Fact 2. If $T = (f, g)$ is a differentiable p.p.t. from 3-preferences to 2-preferences, we have for all $x = (x_1, x_2, x_3)$:

$$\text{(7)} \qquad S_{12}(x) = \frac{g_1(x) + S(f(x), g(x)) \cdot f_1(x)}{g_2(x) + S(f(x), g(x)) \cdot f_2(x)}$$

and

(8) $$S_{13}(x) = \frac{g_1(x) + S(f(x), g(x)) \cdot f_1(x)}{g_3(x) + S(f(x), g(x)) \cdot f_3(x)}$$

where $g_i(x)$ and $f_i(x)$, $i = 1, 2, 3$ are the respective partial derivatives of g and f. (The proof is more messy than difficult.)

The ordinal properties of the preferences are given by their marginal rates of substitution, here S_{12}, S_{13} and S. We will now give two examples of "not-unnatural" connections between S_{12}/S_{13} and S, consistent with (7) and (8) which will give rise to uniformly continuous p.p.t.'s.

Example 2. Suppose there exists $\rho, 0 < \rho < 1$, such that for all (x_1, x_2, x_3):

(9) $$S_{12}(x_1, x_2, x_3) = S(x_1, x_2 + \rho x_3)$$

(10) $$S_{13}(x_1, x_2, x_3) = \frac{1}{\rho} \cdot S(x_1, x_2 + \rho x_3)$$

The transformation from 3-preferences to 2-preferences consists of treating the pair (x_2, x_3) in the vector (x_1, x_2, x_3) (almost) as if $x_2 + \rho x_3$ is coming in period 2, when we look at the 2-preferences. But when we are comparing period 1 and period 3 we think we deserve something extra for the giving up of one unit of consumption in period 1, (x_2, x_3) is really "on the average", consumed a bit later than period 2. By putting $f(x_1, x_2, x_3) = x_1$ and $g(x_1, x_2, x_3) = x_2 + \rho x_3$, $T = (f, g)$ is a uniformly continuous p.t.t., and we see that (9) and (10) are fulfilled.[12]

Example 3. Suppose there exists a real-valued *concave* function $\phi(t)$, defined for non-negative t's, where: $\phi(0) = 0$, $\phi(t) > t$ for $t > 0$, $\phi'(t) > 0$ and $\phi''(t) < 0$ for $t > 0$, such that, for all (x_1, x_2, x_3):

(11) $$S_{13}(x_1, x_2, x_3) = \phi'(x_1) \cdot S(\phi(x_1) + x_2, x_3)$$

(12) $$S_{12}(x_1, x_2, x_3) = \phi'(x_1)$$

The interpretation here is that by going from 3-preferences to 2-preferences x_1 is "upgraded", but at an decreasing rate. By putting $f(x_1, x_2, x_3) = \phi(x_1) + x_2$ and $g(x_1, x_2, x_3) = x_3$, we again see that $T = (f, g)$ is a uniformly continuous p.p.t. and that (11) and (12) are fulfilled.[12]

These three examples have the merit of showing that it may not be totally unreasonable to assume the existence of a uniformly continuous p.t.t. from 3-preferences to 2-preferences. By Proposition 2 this is a (very) small step towards claiming that 3-preferences are more likely to concavable than 2-preferences. But when we explore the possibility of a p.p.t. *from 2-preferences to 3-preferences* this tentative conclusion seems unfounded. Let us start this discussion by speculating over a possible connection between 2-preferences and 3-preferences.

Suppose the consumer has well-defined preferences over the whole time horizon; that is over n-tuples of the form $(x_1, \ldots, x_n)$. Let the function $F(x_1, \ldots, x_n)$ represent these preferences. How do the preferences over the first $n-1$ periods look? These preferences could be derived from the function F if only the consumer knew that would happen in the last period. The consumer is accordingly guessing, and we may suggest that the $n-1$-preferences can be represented by the function U^{n-1} in equation (13):

$$U^{n-1}(x_1, \ldots, x_{n-1}) = \int F(x_1, \ldots, x_{n-1}, x)\, \phi(x)\, \mathrm{d}x \,, \tag{13}$$

where $\phi(x)$ is a density function for consumption x in the last period, possibly dependent upon the pre-history $x_1, \ldots, x_{n-1}$. We will now make the heroic assumption that the consumer has constant point estimates as to the consumption in future "unknown" periods. He assumes that what he receives when he is not told what he receives is something constant, x_0, equal to some average level of consumption in the past. Accordingly, we can express the 3-preferences and the 2-preferences by the functions U^3 and U^2 where:

$$U^3(x_1, x_2, x_3) = F(x_1, x_2, x_3, x_0, \ldots, x_0) \tag{14}$$

$$U^2(x_1, x_2) = F(x_1, x_2, x_0, \ldots, x_0) \tag{15}$$

Given these assumptions it is fairly easy to establish that the 2-preferences are *more likely* to be concavable than the 3-preferences. First of all we note that the transformation $T = (f, g, h)$, where $f(x_1, x_2) = x_1$, $g(x_1, x_2) = x_2$ and $h(x_1, x_2) = x_0$, is a uniformly continuous p.p.t. from 2-preferences to 3-preferences. By the same reasoning as in the proof of Proposition 2 we deduce that if the 2-preferences have non-concavity of the first kind, then the 3-preferences have non-concavity of the first kind. We also have:

Proposition 3. Given the assumption in (14) and (15) we have:

(i) If the 2-preferences have non-concavity of the second kind, then the 3-preferences have non-concavity of the second kind.

(ii) If the 3-preferences are concavable, then the 2-preferences are concavable.

Proof.

(i) With $T(a) = T(x_1, x_2) = (x_1, x_2, x_0)$, when $a = (x_1, x_2)$, we have $d(a, b) = d(T(a), T(b))$ for all $a, b \in R^2_+$ and the result follows.

(ii) By (14) and (15) we have as a representation of the 2-preferences.

$U^2(x_1, x_2) = U^3(f(x_1, x_2), g(x_1, x_2), h(x_1, x_2))$, if U^3 is a representation of the 3-preferences and $f(x_1, x_2) = x_1$, $g(x_1, x_2) = x_2$, $h(x_1, x_2) = x_0$.

Then, if U^3 is concave, U^2 is also concave, q.e.d.

As a final verdict it may be said that this examination failed to give any support to Frisch's claim that cardinal utility is natural in a dynamic setting; on the contrary, by trying to utilize Debreu's result on concavable preferences, we could get a suspicion that it becomes *more difficult* to define a cardinal utility concept as the time-perspective is widening.

6. CONCLUSION

A motivation behind this study is that the distinction between cardinalism and ordinalism is an important one. This is a point of view apparently not shared by all economists. Many economists have a rather sloppy attitude towards the whole problem: they use cardinal concepts freely when it suits them. But this, in contrast to a serious study of cardinalism, can only by called "closet cardinalism" – by the arbitrary use of cardinal concepts at will we will never be able to understand exactly what is the role of cardinalism in economic theory. Cardinal concepts may have a very small place in economic theory, but *the place is not necessarily void.* So according to this author the theoretical enemy is not cardinalism itself, but the restricted and uncritical use of cardinal concepts.

One justification for cardinal concepts, not discussed hitherto, is the use for illustrative, pedagogic purposes. A case in point, mentioned by Oscar Lange in 1933, may be the Gossen-conditions in the theory of consumer's choice. It is more suggestive to the students to explain that the consumer's optimum is characterized by the property that an extra krone spent on a consumption-good will give equal marginal utility irrespective of what consumption-good it is spent on, than to explain that the marginal rates of substitutions are equal to the price-ratios.

Ordinalism, from the point of view of the "theory of science", could be called extreme behaviourism – in so far as it only interested in behaviour that can be verified in the market. In other sciences this methological basis is routinely questioned, not so in economics where the ordinalists have had a "free lunch" for almost 50 years. For instance Chomsky (1973) has given a criticism of Skinner's behaviourism in psychology with the intention of pointing out that concepts like *freedom* and *dignity* are not only empty forms, but do have a *meaning* for many people. (Have we parallels in economic theory? Is there something like *justice* in income-distribution, *joy* in the working-place, *decency* in the way of living?) Chomsky's theory in the science of language is also well known; he point out that experience in itself is insufficient to explain the learning of a language (every day a child is constructing a sentence never constructed before). In the philosophy of mathematics people are living comfortably with the fact that there may be meaningful propositions beyond their reach: Gödels's famous incompleteness theorem says that there exist true propositions within mathematics for which there is no proof. It is further a meta-mathematical theorem that if the theory of real numbers is consistent, it cannot be proved to be consistent.

Is there a fruitful possibility of a non-empiricist economic theory? Is it a case that there may be meaningful theorems out there, beyond the reach of empirical verification, which it is our task to go out and get? The possibility seems far-fetched, but one may wonder, for instance, if a proper understanding of the working of the labour-market can only be arrived at by going beyond the outer veil of appearance, and study the *intentions* behind our choice of working and not working.

APPENDIX I: FRISCH VS. MORISHIMA/POLLAK

If an individual is confronted with income Y_t in period t, the most general form of utility-representation of the income stream $\ldots, Y_{t-1}, Y_t, Y_{t+1}, \ldots$ is given by (1):

$$U = U(\ldots, Y_{t-1}, Y_t, Y_{t+1}, \ldots) \tag{1}$$

Frisch (1964) is making the two basic assumptions of additive separability so that any maximizations of equation (1) over the periods t and $t+1$ is equivalent to the maximization of a function ϕ of the following form:

$$\phi(Y_t, Y_{t+1}) = \phi_t(Y_t) + \phi_{t+1}(Y_{t+1}) \tag{2}$$ [13]

The link between ϕ_t and ϕ_{t+1} is provided by the one-year perspective shortening factor β_t (β for Böhm–Bawerk):

For all income Y we have:

$$\phi_{t+1}(Y) = \phi_t(Y) \cdot (1 - \beta_t) \tag{3}$$

β_t may depend on t, but is assumed to be independent of Y.

The exogenous growth rate from period t to period $t+1$ for the individuals income is given by Y_t:

$$Y_{t+1} = (1 + \gamma_t) \cdot Y_t \tag{4}$$

Further there is a possibility to lend or borrow any amount of money from period t to period $t+1$ at a fixed rate of interest ρ_t. If the individual saves a fraction π of his income in year t, $\pi \overset{>}{\underset{<}{=}} 0$, the actual incomes in the two years become:

$$(5)\quad \begin{array}{l} \text{In the year } t: \ (1-\pi)\,Y_t \\ \text{In the year } t+1: \ [1 + \gamma_t + (1+\rho_t)\pi] \cdot Y_t \end{array}$$

When we put this into equation (2) and utilize equation (3) the maximization problem becomes:

$$\underset{\pi}{\text{Max}} \ \{(1-\beta)\cdot\phi((1+\gamma+(1+\rho)\pi)Y)+\phi((1-\pi)Y)\}$$

where the subscript t has been dropped.

Frisch further assumes that the optimal π can be found by simple derivation with respect to π and that it is a sober procedure to develop the $\phi(\ )$ – functions around the point Y in a power series up to the second power. By assuming $\phi' \neq 0$ and by defining the flexibility of the marginal utility of income $\breve{\omega}(Y)$ by equation (6):

$$(6) \qquad \breve{\omega}(Y) = \frac{\phi''(Y)\cdot Y}{\phi'(Y)}$$

the optimal π is given by a formula of the following form:

$$(7) \qquad [-1+(1-\beta)(1+\rho)(1+\gamma\cdot\breve{\omega}(Y))]\cdot\phi'(Y)\cdot Y+[A]\cdot\pi = 0\,,$$

where A is some function of Y and the parameters.

The incentive free rate of interest ρ is determined by the condition that the optimal π is zero, which means that $(1-\beta)(1+\rho)(1+\gamma\cdot\breve{\omega}(Y)) = 1$. Accordingly:

$$(8) \qquad \rho = \frac{1-(1-\beta)\cdot[1-\gamma\cdot(-\breve{\omega}(Y))]}{(1-\beta)\cdot[1-\gamma\cdot(-\breve{\omega}(y))]}$$

This is Frisch's result. It *is* a beautiful formula, bringing together four different concepts, but Frisch does not claim that formulae of this form are dependent upon the particular representation (2) or some kind of cardinalization of the utility function.

Morishima (1965) is then quick to point out that equation (8), or something like (8), can be developed in a more general framework than Frisch employed in his 1964 paper. No form of additive separability or (implicit) cardinalization is necessary – in fact Morishima is operating with a formulation like equation (1), and is explicitly stating that "any arbitrary function $F(U)$ with $F'(U) > 0$ may serve as a utility function". Of course the concept of the flexibility of marginal utility of income has to be sacrified, but by using Frisch's assumption "that the perspective of the representative man is limited to periods t and $t+1$", and by keeping only the first two terms in a Taylor series expansion around the point (Y_t, Y_t), Morishima arrives at a formula for the incentive free rate of interest ρ_t, given by equation (9):

$$(9) \qquad 1+\hat{\rho}_t = \frac{1}{1-\beta_t}\cdot\frac{1}{1+\gamma_t\cdot\sigma(Y_t,Y_t)}\,,$$

which may be compared to Frisch's formula:

$$(10) \qquad 1+\hat{\rho}_t = \frac{1}{1-\beta_t} \cdot \frac{1}{1+\gamma_t \cdot \breve{\omega}(Y_t)}$$

$\sigma(Y_t, Y_{t+1})$ is called the flexibility of substitution with respect to an increase in future income and is defined by (11):

$$(11) \qquad \sigma(Y_t, Y_{t+1}) = \frac{\mathrm{d}S(Y_t, Y_{t+1})}{\mathrm{d}Y_{t+1}} \cdot \frac{Y_{t+1}}{S(Y_t, Y_{t+1})}$$

where $S(Y_t, Y_{t+1})$ is the marginal rate of substitution between future and present income.

There is a connection between σ and $\breve{\omega}$ given by

$$(12) \qquad \sigma(Y_t, Y_t) = \breve{\omega}_{F_{t+1}} - \breve{\omega}_{F_t}$$

where $\breve{\omega}_{F_t}$ is the flexibility of the marginal utility of present income with respect to an increase in future income, and $\breve{\omega}_{F_{t+1}}$ is the flexibility of the marginal utility of future income with respect to an increase in future income. Even though the cardinalist's concepts $\breve{\omega}_{F_{t+1}}$ and $\breve{\omega}_{F_t}$ are not invariant under monotone transformations of the utility function, their difference $\sigma(Y_t, Y_t)$ is unaffected by such transformations and is accordingly an ordinalistic concept. The special formula (2) which Frisch is employing has the property that $\breve{\omega}_{F_t} = 0$, but Morishima sees "no gain here, however, in choosing a utility function with a property so special that it cannot remain unchanged under a monotonic transformation of the utility function; the result is the same as the ordinalist's".

Pollak (1965) arrives at the same conclusion, but questions further the soundness of terminating the Taylor series expansion after only two terms. If, in the specification $U(y_1, y_2) = u(y_1) + (1-\beta)\, u(y_2)$, for instance $u(y_2)$ is developed in a Taylor series around y_1 with only terms to the second power, we get:

$$u(y_2) = u(y_1) + (y_2 - y_1) \cdot u'(y_1) + \frac{(y_2 - y_1)^2}{2} \cdot u''(y_1)$$

By taking the derivatives on both sides with respect to y_2 we have:

$$u'(y_2) = u'(y_1) + (y_2 - y_1) \cdot u''(y_1)\,, \quad \text{and}$$

further on: $u''(y_2) = u''(y_1)$, which means that the second derivative of the function $u(y)$ must be a constant. This leaves us with a general form for $u(y)$ like

$$(13) \qquad u(y) = ay^2 + by + c$$

which is a far cry from being any arbitrary well-behaved utility function. Pollak also notes that Frisch's formula (10) (or (8)) does not hold when the indifference map is additive and homothetic and that a specification like $U(y_1, y_2) = u(y_1) + (1 - \beta)\, u(y_2)$ together with equation (13) is inconsistent with the assumption that the marginal utility of income is independent of the level of income.

APPENDIX II: PROOF OF THEOREM 2

Let the points in the set of alternatives Y be designated by capital letters: x_i, A, B, C, D. Define for all $f \in \Omega$ and all $x_j \in Y$, $i = 1, 2, 3, 4$ $\Delta(f, x_1, x_2, x_3, x_4)$ by:

$$\text{(1)} \qquad \Delta(f, x_1, x_2, x_3, x_4) = f(U(x_1)) - f(U(x_2)) - f(U(x_3)) + f(U(x_4))$$

The hypothesis of Theorem 2 is that the sign of $\Delta(f, x_1, x_2, x_3, x_4)$ for each vector (x_1, x_2, x_3) is independent of $f \in \Omega$. Theorem 1 tells us that to establish cardinality it is sufficient to prove that the sign of $\Delta(f, x_1, x_2, x_3, x_4)$ for each vector (x_1, x_2, x_3, x_4) is independent of $f \in \Omega$. This trivial unless $U(x_1) > U(x_2)$ and $U(x_3) > U(x_4)$ (or $U(x_1) < U(x_2)$ and $U(x_3) < U(x_4)$).

Let A, B, C, D be four arbitrary points in Y where $U(B) > U(A)$ and $U(D) > U(C)$. We want to show that the sign of $\Delta(f, B, A, D, C)$ is independent of f. Assume first that $U(B) \leq U(C)$.

By $L(A, B, C, D)$ we mean the (broken) curve connecting A, B, C and D with straight line-segments. Consider two points x_1 and x_0 on this curve, with $U(x_1) > U(x_0)$. Because of the continuity of U there exists a point x_2 on this curve, between x_0 and x_1 such that:

$$\text{(2)} \qquad U(x_2) - U(x_0) = U(x_1) - U(x_2)$$

If there is more than one point x_2 satisfying (2), which for instance may happen if the "indifference-curves are concave towards the origin" give the curve between x_0 and x_1 a parametrization and choose as x_2 the "first" point satisfying equation (2). The hypothesis of Theorem 2 implies that $\Delta(f, x_2, x_0, x_1, x_2) = 0$ for all $f \in \Omega$. This is easily seen by noting that (2) gives that $\Delta(f, x_2, x_0, x_1, x_2) \geq 0$ and $\Delta(f, x_2, x_0, x_1, x_2) \leq 0$ for all $f \in \Omega$. Thus it can be defended to say that "the point x_2 is independent of f".

We have by the construction of x_2 for all $f \in \Omega$:

$$\text{(3)} \qquad f(U(x_2)) - f(U(x_0)) = 2^{-1} \cdot (f(U(x_1)) - f(U(x_0)))$$

By repeating this construction with x_2 instead of x_1 we get a point x_3 between x_0 and x_2 with the property that the utility-difference between x_0 and x_3 is half the utility-difference between x_0 and x_2. Employing this method further on we get accordingly a sequence $\{x_n\}$ with the following property:

$$(4) \qquad f(U(x_{n+1}) - f(U(x_0)) = 2^{-n} \cdot (f(U(x_1)) - f(U(x_0)))$$

We will use this technique to divide the utility-difference between A and B in finer and finer segments, and for each division we will "walk" along $L(A, B, C, D)$ from A towards (and behind) D, with "each step of the walk" measuring out a distance so that the utility-difference between two consecutive points is equal to the appropriate (small) segment of the interval $[U(A), U(B)]$.

Let for each integer n the utility-interval $[U(A), U(B)]$ be divided in 2^n segments, with each segment representing a utility-difference equal to $2^{-n} \cdot (U(B) - U(A))$ (or to $2^{-n} \cdot (f(U(B)) - f(U(A)))$, $f \in \Omega$), $n \geq 0$.

We then define recursively, for each n, $n \geq 0$, the sequence $\{x_k(n)\}$ by:

$$(5) \qquad \begin{aligned} &x_1(n) = A \\ &f(U(x_{k+1}(n))) - f(U(x_k(n))) = 2^{-n} \cdot (f(U(B)) - f(U(A))) \end{aligned}$$

(The sequence $x_1(n), x_2(n), \ldots, x_k(n), x_{k+1}(n), \ldots$ is for each $n \geq 0$ well-defined, independent of $f \in \Omega$, by the assumptions of Theorem 2.) Define the numbers $a(n) = a$ and $b(n) = b$ by

$$(6) \qquad a(n) = \inf \{k;\ f(U(x_k(n))) \geq f(U(C)),\ f \in \Omega\}$$

$$(7) \qquad b(n) = \sup \{k;\ f(U(x_k(n))) \leq f(U(D)),\ f \in \Omega\}$$

$a(n)$ and $b(n)$ are independent of f.

If $a(n) > b(n)$, it follows from the definitions:

$$(8) \qquad f(U(x_a(n))) > f(U(D)) \& f(U(C)) > f(U(x_b(n))), \text{ for all } f \in \Omega$$

We must in this case also have $a(n) = b(n) + 1$, so that we get:

$$(9) \qquad f(U(x_a(n))) - f(U(x_b(n))) = 2^{-n} \cdot (f(U(B)) - f(U(A))), \text{ for all } f \in \Omega, \text{ and}$$

$$(10) \qquad f(U(D)) - f(U(C)) < f(U(x_a(n))) - f(U(x_b(n))), \text{ for all } f \in \Omega$$

Thus $\Delta(f, B, A, D, C) > 0$ for all $f \in \Omega$.

If $a(n) \leq b(n)$, define $m = m(n)$ by:

(11) $m(n) = b(n) - a(n)$

($b(n) < \infty$ since $U(D) - U(A) < \infty$, by the continuity of U).
We have for all $n \geq 0$ and all $f \in \Omega$:

$$(12) \quad m \cdot 2^{-n} \cdot (f(U(B)) - f(U(A))) \leq f(U(D)) - f(U(C)) < (m+2) \cdot 2^{-n} \cdot (f(U(B)) - f(U(A)))$$

Consider now three cases:

(i) There exist $n \geq 0$ such that $m(n) > 2^n$.
From (12) we get for all $f \in \Omega$:

$$f(U(B)) - f(U(A)) < f(U(D)) - f(U(C))$$

(ii) There exist $n \geq 0$ such that $m(n) + 1 < 2^n$.
From (12) we get for all $f \in \Omega$:

$$f(U(D)) - f(U(C)) < f(U(B)) - f(U(A))$$

(iii) For all $n \geq 0$, we have: $2^n - 1 \dot{\leq} m(n) < 2^n$.
From (12) we then get for all $f \in \Omega$:

$$(12) \quad \left(1 - \frac{1}{2^n}\right) \cdot (f(U(B)) - f(U(A))) \leq f(U(D)) - f(U(C)) < \left(1 + \frac{1}{2^{n-1}}\right) \cdot (f(U(B)) - f(U(A)))$$

(13) is valid for all $n \geq 0$ and all $f \in \Omega$ only if
$f(U(B)) - f(U(A)) = f(U(D)) - f(U(C))$

Thus we see that the sign of $\Delta(f, B, A, D, C)$ is determined independent of $f \in \Omega$ in all three cases.

If $U(A) \leq U(C) < U(B)$, we use the same technique to construct a sequence $\{x_k(n)\}$ with utility-difference of each step equal to a (small) segment of the interval $[U(A), U(B)]$, but this time we "walk" along the straight line-segments connecting only A, C and D.

If $U(C) < U(A)$, reverse the roles of C and A and of B and D.

Theorem 2 is thus proved.

APPENDIX III: PROOF OF PROPOSITION 1

Let a, b be as in Definition 3. Then there exist two sequences $\{a_n\}$ and $\{b_n\}$ where $a_n I a$, $b_n I b$ for all n, such that:

$$d(a_n, b_n) \to 0\,, \quad \text{as } n \to \infty$$

For all n there exists a number λ_n, $0 \leq \lambda_n < 1$, and a point c_n in the coordinate planes, such that:

$$a_n = \lambda_n \cdot b_n + (1 - \lambda_n) \cdot c_n$$

It then follows by our definition of distance that:

$$d(a_n, b_n) = (1 - \lambda_n) \cdot d(c_n, b_n)$$

But from condition (ii) in Definition 3 we have for all n:

$$d(c_n, b_n) \geq \delta > 0, \text{ so that}$$
$$d(a_n, b_n) \geq (1 - \lambda_n) \cdot \delta, \text{ for all } n$$

This implies that $\lambda_n \to 1$ as $n \to \infty$ since $d(a_n, b_n) \to 0$ as $n \to \infty$.

Suppose now U is a concave representation of R. With no loss of generality we assume $U(a) \geq 0$ for all $a \in Y$. (By monotonicity $U(0) = \min U(a)$, when $a \in Y$, and $U^*(a) = U(a) - U(0)$ is a non-negative representation of R which is concave if U is concave.)

We then have:

$$U(a) = U(a_n) = U(\lambda_n b_n + (1 - \lambda_n) c_n) \geq$$
$$\lambda_n U(b_n) + (1 - \lambda_n) \cdot U(c_n)$$

by concavity of U.

Thus:

$$U(a) \geq \lambda_n \cdot U(b_n) = \lambda_n \cdot U(b)$$

which implies $U(a) \geq U(b_n)$, since $\lambda_n \to 1$ as $n \to \infty$.

This is a contradiction since bPa, and accordingly R permits no concave representation, q.e.d.

PROOF OF PROPOSITION 2

Let $T: R^3_+ \to R^2_+$ be a uniformly continuous p.p.t. as in the proposition. Let $a, b \in R^3_+$ be such that:

(i) bPa, (ii) $d(I(b), K^3(0)) > 0$, and (iii) $d(I(a), I(b)) = 0$

By hypothesis $T(b)\, P\, T(a)$ and $d(I(T(b)), K^2(0)) > 0$.

By (iii) there exist sequences $\{a_n\}$, $\{b_n\}$, $a_n I a$, $b_n I b$ such that $d(a_n, b_n) \to 0$, as $n \to \infty$.

We have $T(a_n)\, I\, T(a)$ and $T(b_n)\, I\, T(b)$ and $d(T(a_n), T(b_n)) \to 0$, as $n \to \infty$.

This is so because suppose $d(T(a_n), T(b_n)) \geq \delta_1 > 0$ for all n. By uniform continuity there exists $\varepsilon > 0$ such that:

$$d(a', b') < \varepsilon \Rightarrow d(T(a'), T(b')) < \delta_1, \text{ for all } a', b' \in R^3_+$$

It is possible to choose a_n, b_n from the sequences $\{a_n\}$, $\{b_n\}$ such that $d(a_n, b_n) < \varepsilon$, and accordingly $d(T(a_n), T(b_n)) < \delta_1$, a contradiction, q.e.d.

Norwegian School of Management
Sandvika, Norway

NOTES

[1] In writing this paper I have benefited from discussions with Arne Amundsen and Trygve Haavelmo.

[2] If the temperature in Oslo, Rome and Cairo is 15°C, 30°C, 55°C, respectively, measured in degrees Celsius, the temperature in the same places is 59°F, 86°F and 131°F measured in degrees Fahrenheit. Since $\frac{86}{59} < \frac{131}{86}$, but $\frac{30}{15} > \frac{55}{30}$, temperature is not a purely cardinal quantity. It is also a fact that in a question of life and death, a rise in temperature from 37°C to 42°C for a human being represents an increase in temperature of 13,5% measured in degrees Celsius, but *the same phenomenon* is described as an increase in temperature of only 9,5% measured in degrees Fahrenheit.

[3] It would be a sad fact to all parties if cardinal utility turned out to be both necessary and meaningless.

[4] O. Lange (1933–1934) interpreted this definition in the following manner, on p. 219: "The (...) postulate (of ordinal utility) defines the meaning of the sign of the first derivatives of the utility function whereas the (...) postulate (of the ability to compare first differences in utility) defines the meaning of the sign of its second derivatives."

[5] The assumption that $U(Y)$ is connected can be dispensed with if more structure is put on Ω in the definition of the ability to compare first-differences in utility. Basu (1984) defines the ability to compare first-differences in utility for an individual (U, Ω) by the property that for all $f \in \Omega$ and all $r_1, r_2, r_3, r_4, \in R$

$$r_1 - r_2 \geq r_3 - r_4 \text{ if and only if } f(r_1) - f(r_2) \geq f(r_3) - f(r_4)$$

and then proves that this property implies cardinal utility.

[6] An earlier and quite rigorous presentation of results along these lines is also contained in Frisch (1926).

[7] I was reminded by Ole Hagen that this statement is not precise; even for an ordinalist it is perfectly legitimate to compare marginal utilities starting from the *same* indifference curve. On this somewhat overlooked fact see Mayston (1976).

[8] Morey (1984) calls the ability to compare first-differences in utility for weak cardinality. We do not employ that terminology.

[9] This point can also be found in Strotz (1955–1956), but he is using a utility-function of the following form:

$$\phi_\tau = \int_0^T \lambda(t - \tau) \cdot u(C(t), t)\, dt$$

which really begs the question of cardinality vs. ordinality.

10 A point was made to me by Tore Thonstad that if x is the consumption of *generation number* i then a welfare-comparison over different generations *necessitates* a cardinal utility-concept.

11 Mas-Colell (1977) calls uniformly sensitive preferences Lipschtizian preferences.

12 To prove that $T = (f, g)$ now actually is a p.p.t. we need some "recoverability" conditions to insure that the marginal rates of substitution do really determine the preferences. On this point see Mas-Colell (1977).

13 In light of Remark 2, Section 2 it will be more correct to say that Frisch is working with a special form of representation than to say that he has through the formulation (2) revealed himself as a cardinalist.

REFERENCES

Arrow, K.J. (1963) *Social Choice and Individual Values*, 1st edn. Yale University Press.

Basu, K. (1980) *Revealed Preference of Government*, Cambridge University Press.

Basu, K. (1982) 'Determinateness of the utility function: revisiting a controversy of the thirties', *The Review of Economic Studies*, April.

Basu, K. (1984) 'Utility measurement: a direct proof of Lange's conjecture', *Economics Letters* **15**.

Camacho, A. (1979) 'On cardinal utility', *Theory and Decision* **10**.

Camacho, A. (1980) 'Approaches to cardinal utility', *Theory and Decision* **12**.

Chaudhuri, A. (1985) 'Formal properties of interpersonal envy', *Theory and Decision* **18**.

Chomsky, N. (1973) 'Psychology and ideology', Ch. 7 in Chomsky, N., *For Reasons of State*, New York, Vintage Books.

Cooter, R. and Rappoport, P. (1984) 'Were the ordinalists wrong about welfare economics?', *Journal of Economic Literature* **XXII**, June.

Debreu, G. (1960) 'Topological methods in cardinal utility theory', Ch. 2, in Arrow, Karlin, Suppes (Eds.), *Mathematical Methods in the Social Sciences*, 1959, Stanford University Press.

Debreu, G. (1976) 'Least concave utility functions', *Journal of Mathematical Economics* **3**.

Fishburn, P.C. (1978) 'Ordinal preferences and uncertain lifetimes', *Econometrica* **46** (4), July.

Frisch, R. (1926) 'Sur une problème d'economie pure', *Norsk Matem. Forenings skrifter*, Ser. 1, (16). English translation in Chipman, J., Hurwicz, L., Richter, M. and Sonnenschein, H. (Eds.), *Preferences, Utility and Demand*, New York: Harcourt, Brace, Jovanovich (1971).

Frisch, R. (1947) *Notater til Økonomisk Teori*. 4. utgave, 2. Hefte, Oslo.

Frisch, R. (1964) 'Dynamic utility', *Econometrica* **32** (3), July.

Gorman, W.M. (1971) 'Preference, revealed preference, and indifference', in Chipman, J., Hurwicz, L., Richter, M. and Sonnenschein, H. (Eds.), *Preferences, Utility and Demand*, New York: Hartcourt, Brace, Jovanovich.

Houthakker, H.S. (1960) 'Additive preferences', *Econometrica* **28** (2), April.

Jaffray, J.Y. (1985) 'Interpersonal level comparability does not imply comparability of utility differences – a comment on Ng', *Theory and Decision* **19**.

Koopman, T.C. (1960) 'Stationary ordinal utility and impatience', *Econometrica* **28** (2), April.

Lange, O. (1933–1934) 'The determinateness of the utility function', *The Review of Economic Studies* **I**.

Lange, O. (1934–1935) 'A note on the determinateness of the utility functionn', *The Review of Economic Studies* **II**.

Mas-Colell, A. (1977) 'The recoverability of consumers' preferences from market demand behaviour', *Econometrica* **45** (6), September.

Mayston, D.J. (1976) 'On the nature of marginal utility – a neo-Marshallian theory of demand', *The Economic Journal* **86** (343), September.

Morey, E.R. (1985) 'Confuser surplus', *The American Economic Review*, March.

Morishima, M. (1965) 'Should dynamic utility be cardinal?', *Econometrica* **33** (4), October.

Ng. Y.K. (1984) 'Interpersonal level comparability implies comparability of utility differences', *Theory and Decision* **17**.

Phelps-Brown, E.H. (1934–1935) 'Notes on the determinateness of the utility function', *Review of Economic Studies*.

Pollak, R.A. (1965) 'Dynamic utility': a comment', *Econometrica* **33** (4), October.

Rader, T. (1972) *Theory of Microeconomics*, Academic Press, New York and London.

Samelson, P.A. (1974) 'Complementarity. An essay on the 40th anniversary of the Hicks-Allen Revolution in demand theory', *The Journal of Economic Literature* **12**.

Sheng, C.L. (1987) 'A note on interpersonal comparisons of utility', *Theory and Decision* **22**.

Strotz, R.H. (1953) 'Cardinal utility', *The American Economic Review. Papers and Proceedings*.

Strotz, R.H. (1955–1956) 'Myopia and inconsistency in dynamic utility maximiation', *The Review of Economic Studies*.

Wakker, P. (1986) 'The repetitions approach to characterize cardinal utility', *Theory and Decision* **20**.

Wold, H. (1943) 'A synthesis of pure demand analysis', Part II, *Skandinavisk aktuarietidskrift*.

OLE HAGEN

THE SHORT STEP FROM ORDINAL TO CARDINAL UTILITY

1. THE LONG ROAD TO AN ORDINAL PREFERENCE MAP

Let us start with the unrealistic but simple case of a consumer in a two-goods world or, if you prefer, a person whose freedom of choice is limited to allocating a budget between buying two goods. We choose an arbitrary starting point with quantities of the two goods, and by trial and error we find other combinations that the consumer deems equivalent. We can thus construct an approximation of one indifference curve. The process is repeated a number of times with new starting points. We attach numbers to the curves in inverse order of preference. We now have an incomplete ordinal preference function. It does not sound too complicated, but try to actually do it!

An approach apparently more easy to carry out is the revealed preference approach, taking account of the fact that preferences are easier to elicit than indifferences. What is required is then a variation over two out of the three variables, budget and two prices, to provide a sufficient number of preferred points to draw a preference map with reasonable approximation. If we have more than two goods, the difficulties seem to be unsurmountable.

When such a mapping is done, it will still offer an incomplete ordering. We can approximate a continuous preference function by constructing a mathematical function which is compatible with the mapping.

Even this is a difficult task. Still, let us accept the tacit assumption of current ordinalist theory that this can be done. Even if we are wrong, some deductions about the necessary characteristics of an ordinal preference function must be true, also, of course, for any subset we might hold to have cardinal validity (see for example Hagen, 1984).

Before proceeding, let it for practical reasons be known that:
By goods we shall mean consumer activities. When a good is named after a commodity, it means the activity of using that commodity as it is usually used under the given circumstances.

2. AN "INNOCENT" IMPLICATION OF ORDINAL PREFERENCE

Let us consider any ordinal preference function of quantities of n goods consumed in one period, found by changes in monetary spending and in prices:

M. Allais and O. Hagen (eds.), Cardinalism, 209–221.

$$f(q_1, q_2, q_3, \ldots, q_n)$$

where q_i = quantity of good number i.

It is well known (see e.g. Henderson and Quandt, 1980) that if we undertake a positive monotonous transformation:

$$F(f) \ : \ F'(f) > 0$$

then we get the following second order derivatives:

$$(1) \qquad F_{ij} = F'' f_i f_j + F' f_{ij}$$

In the point of maximum satisfaction under a budget constraint:

$$(2) \qquad \frac{f_1}{c_1} = \frac{f_2}{c_2} = \frac{f_3}{c_3} = \cdots = \frac{f_n}{c_n} = w$$

where w is a Lagrange multiplier, sometimes called the marginal utility of money.

Thus, given optimal allocation of total monetary spending, the transformation of second order derivatives, can be written:

$$(3) \qquad F_{ij} = F'' c_i w c j_w + F' f_{ij}$$

The preference structure expressed in f and F can be expressed by a function which is always equal to f, but is not identical because the quantities are expressed in units that makes the price equal to unity.[2]

Below we have no need to vary prices, only income or utility level, so no generality is lost in assuming all prices to be unity.

Let g be a function corresponding to f when units of goods are chosen so that if q means quantity in conventional units, the quantity x is q.c/p (measured in unit: "one dollar's worth") and

$$f(q_1, q_2, \ldots, q_n) = g(x_1, x_2, \ldots, x_n)$$

The new prices will, in the initial situation, be:

$$(4) \qquad p_1, p_2, p_3, \ldots, p_n = 1$$

(3) is then replaced by:

$$(5) \qquad g_1 = g_2 = g_3 = \ldots = g_n = w$$

If g is transformed by G in the same way as f by F above,

$$(6) \qquad G(g) \ : \ G' > 0$$

then (3) will be simplified to:

$$(7) \qquad G_{ij} = G'' w^2 + G' g_{ij}$$

(All $g_i = f_i/c_i = w$, the marginal utility of money which by generally accepted theory is the same in all directions in an optimal point.)

This transformation of the g_{ij}'s is linear and positive because neither $(G''w^2)$ nor G' depends on which pair (i, j) we consider, and G' is positive. Since it obviously does not matter in this context whether we consider f or g we have proved:

Theorem 1. A positive *monotonous* transformation of an ordinal preference function implies a positive *linear* transformation of all second order derivatives in this point of maximum satisfaction.

So far we have only clarified some implications of ordinalistic interpretation of consumer behaviour. Maybe it can facilitate a student's understanding of how the sign of:

$$\mathrm{d}q_i/\mathrm{d}p_j \ (u = \text{constant}),$$

i.e. under an income compensated price change, which determines whether the goods are substitutes (+) or complements (−), can be expressed in determinants of u_{ij}. (A formal proof of this is given in Henderson and Quandt (1980), *without* the above linearity theorem.) This must be a little difficult to appreciate when one is compelled to believe that the elements in the determinants are "meaningless".

This particular partial derivative, is conventionally called *the substitution effect, SE*. Before passing on, a warning about the ambiguous usage of the words complements and substitutes.

The classical cardinalistic usage is:

$$\begin{aligned} u_{ij} &> 0 : i \text{ and } j \text{ are complements} \\ u_{ij} &= 0 : i \text{ and } j \text{ are independent} \\ u_{ij} &< 0 : i \text{ and } j \text{ are substitutes} \end{aligned}$$

The ordinalistic usage is:

$$\begin{aligned} \mathrm{SE}_{ij} &< 0 : i \text{ and } j \text{ are "complements"} \\ \mathrm{SE}_{ij} &= 0 : i \text{ and } j \text{ are "independent"} \\ \mathrm{SE}_{ij} &> 0 : i \text{ and } j \text{ are "substitutes"} \end{aligned}$$

It is a nuisance that ordinalists use terms originally attached to concepts which they consider meaningless for other concepts. If a cardinal utility exists, bread and water are obviously complements in the cardinalistic sense, regardless of the total number of available goods. But if there are only those (or any other) two goods available, in the ordinalistic sense they are "substitutes", since a movement along the indifference curve to fit the new gradient of the budget line can only increase the amount of the good whose price is reduced and decrease the other. This happens even if introspection advises us that if the mouth feels like sandpaper, another mouthful of water might activate a latent desire for more bread, so that the two goods are obviously complements not only in the cardinalistic sense, but also in common usage.

3. THREE PSYCHOLOGICAL HYPOTHESES

I have (Hagen, 1984) extensively argued that the normal consumer can distinguish between pairs of goods that are complements and those that are substitutes. The main point can be summarized in one of the "Bartender's Games": By the pitch of a coin you will get either whisky or gin, also soda or tonic. Do you prefer soda with whisky and tonic with gin, or soda with gin and tonic with whisky?

Tastes differ. I was intrigued watching an Indian lady pour salt over a slice of orange. My horror at seeing her actually eat it with great pleasure can only be compared to that of the English bartender receiving an order for gin and Coca-cola (In the same glass, Sir?!). The diversity in tastes does not diminish the clarity and strength of individual feelings, at least in extreme cases, of what goods go together and what are substitutes or, even stronger, should be kept apart for physiological reasons (alcohol and antabus, apple vinegar and sugar).

Let us revisit the friendly bartender. This time he offers for sure: whisky on odd dates and gin on even dates, but tonic with whisky and soda with gin. We can, however, have soda instead of tonic on m days or tonic instead of soda on n days. A person's choice will tell that not only does he know the sign of his second order derivatives, he also has a pretty good idea of the ratios between them, which implies cardinality. (Of course an ordinal preference function can describe his preferences by adding to the original 4 arguments another 4: the two "normal" and the two "perverse" combinations.)

4. PREPARING THE STEP TO CARDINALITY

I think I can safely present these testable hypotheses:

Hypothesis 1. Present a consumer with a list of pairs of goods that he actually consumes, and ask him to sort them into three classes: A, those which go together; C, those which can substitute for each other or should be kept apart; B, those he feels unable to classify under A or C. *He can do this without difficulty in at least some cases.*

Hypothesis 2. Give each member of the sets A, B and C, the numbers 3, 2 and 1 repectively. Construct an ordinal preference function for the same consumer, and figure out the u_{ij} values at the actual point in the goods space. *There will be positive correlation between class numbers and u_{ij} values.*

Hypothesis 3. In the classified or smoothed frequency distribution over u_{ij} values there will be a mode that will be closer to the mean in class B than to any of the other two means. (This last hypothesis is not strictly necessary for the reasoning, but it makes the whole theory clearly testable in that introspective statements from respondents are tested on a base that is, or should be, acceptable for ordinalists.)

Assume that we have found the mode of the frequency distribution according to Hypothesis 3. If this does not work, we select on the scale of g_{ij} a point which we think really separates the complements from the substitutes. In the latter case the empirical testing will be implicit in the testing of the final conclusions. Assume for expository convenience that there is one actual pair of goods which we consider marks the division between complements and substitutes, being a pair of independent goods. We name these goods r and s.

We return to equation (7) from which we can now deduce the condition for an acceptable approximation to a set of cardinal utility functions:

$$(8) \qquad G_{rs} = 0 \Rightarrow G''w^2 + G'gr_s = 0$$

or

$$(9a) \qquad \frac{G''}{G'} = -\frac{g_{rs}}{w^2}$$

$$(9b) \qquad G'' = -\frac{G'g_{rs}}{w^2}$$

or

$$(9c) \qquad -\frac{G''}{G'}\,w^2 = g_{rs}$$

We can also establish that

$$(10) \qquad G_{rs} = 0 \ \textit{and} \ g_{rs} = 0 \Rightarrow G'' = 0$$

and we have defined a subset of the set of ordinal preference functions, the elements of which are *linear transformations of one another in the neighbourhood of the actual point of maximum budget constrained satisfaction.*

We have not, however, established the cardinal utility function yet, because when we change the budget any h_{ij} may change, and the pair ij

which will play the role of rs may change. Or we have determined the indirect second order derivatives on an interval scale. If we determine its zero, we have *utility* on an interval scale.

5. THE SHORT STEP

One might assume that "bubble-bath" shampoo and Champagne are independent for most people. But suppose the budget increases to a very high level. The consumer might then consider have a bath in champagne rather than water with bubble-bath. But we have above defined the independent variables in the preference function not as commodities, but as consumer activities, such as "bathing in water with bubble-bath" and "drinking champagne". A consumer with no particular inclination to drink in the bath tub could well be expected to consider the two activities independent regardless of his budget. The following hypothesis seems reasonable:

Hypothesis 4. For any consumer there is at least one pair of consumer's activities that are independent in terms of Hypothesis 3, regardless of the budget.

If this is true, we have identified the subset of the set of ordinal utility functions that consists of elements that are positive linear transformations of one another.

This hypothesis implies the existence of a cardinal utility.

The assumption that accepting the existence of a cardinal utility rests solely on belief is something many ordinalists like to believe.

Well. Assume that any one of them comes to his hotel room after having gained some important points in a discussion of utility theory and would like to celebrate before his bedtime bath. In the cooler he finds a suitably dimensioned bottle of champagne. Before he decides whether or not ot enjoy it, does he go look if his bath can be a bubble-bath? I *"believe"* not. If what he finds is gin, will he look for tonic water? *I "believe"* so. And if there is no tonic water, will he look for bitter lemon? Frankly, yet *I "believe"* so. *He believes* that there can in the whole field of human behaviour be no problem which can be profitably discussed by means of a cardinal concept of utility.

If the ordinalist feels that we are discussing the difference between creed and science, he may be quite right.

6. THE SHAPE OF THE CARDINAL UTILITY OF MONEY

Let us temporarily return to the set of ordinal utility functions.

If we increase the budget with unchanged prices, the locus of points of restricted maximum satisfaction will intersect each indifference set once. We can pick any set of numbers for these in inverse order of preference and still have an ordinal preference function, with all implications shown above.

One subset of the set of ordinal functions is one whose value at any point on the expansion path is equal to the budget, 'b' a 'Hotelling function' (Thore, 1983). (Expansion path: locus of restricted maximum satisfaction.) We name this function h and its transformation function $H(h)$.

Now we can deduce from (7):

$$H_{rs} = H'' + H'h_{rs} \tag{11}$$

We assume convexity of indifference curves towards the origin and must of course assume:

$$H' > 0 \tag{12}$$

The sign of h_{rs} is restricted through our assumption that h is equal to the budget along the expansion path. Let us consider the movement from one point, A, to a preferred point, B, both on the expansion path in a two goods diagram. The gain in h will be:

$$\Delta h = h(B) - h(A)$$

Let b_1 and b_2 be the money spent on the two goods, then:

$$\Delta b = \Delta b_1 + \Delta b_2 \tag{13}$$

The simplest possible hotelling function is:

$$b = b_1 + b_2$$

which implies:

$$h_{11} = h_{22} = h_{12} = 0$$

But the convexity condition requires

$$2h_{ij} > h_{11} + h_{22} \tag{14}$$

If we add the condition of constant marginal utility of money in terms of h and non-inferiority (see e.g. Hagen, 1984), the only possible set of relationships that does not exclude one of the two goods (in general all but one) is:

$$h_{11} < 0$$
$$h_{22} < 0$$
$$h_{12} > 0$$

This must apply to any pair of goods (Hagen, 1984), so we assume:

(15) $h_{ii} < 0$ (any i)

(16) $h_{ij} > 0$ (any ij)

We can now deduce from (11), (12), and (15):

(17) $H_{rs} = 0 \Rightarrow H'' < 0$

which is in accordance with classical assumptions concerning a cardinal utility function, bearing in mind that H is now a function of the budget.

We now turn to the dependence of h_{ij} on the budget. We have already assumed (15) $h_{ii} < 0$, and convexity (14). These taken together imply that for any pair ij:

(18) $$\frac{\mathrm{d}h}{\mathrm{d}b} = 1 \Rightarrow \frac{\mathrm{d}h_{ij}}{\mathrm{d}b} > 0$$

Can H_{rs} be valid in a range, not just in one point? It follows from (12), (17) and (18) that this is quite possible. The condition is:

(19) $$\frac{H'''}{H''} < \frac{H''}{H'}$$

which can by no means be considered objectionable. Any assumption that denies (20) is incompatible with our set of hypotheses, so it is really implied in them. The following statements are necessary to preserve (12) and (17) unless we will allow higher derivatives to change signs:

(20) $H''' > 0,\ H^{(4)} < 0,\ H^{(5)} > 0$, a.s.o.

(This coincides with intuitive postulate (Hagen, 1969, 1972) about the cardinal utility of money.)

If there is more than one pair of goods that fills our conditions, then their respective h_{ij} must be equal, and the derived utility functions can only vary in the same way as those based on any one pair: *A positive linear transformation.*

7. SOME HINTS ABOUT APPLICATIONS

Some readers may have seen a TV show where a panel is confronted with some instrument from the obscure store rooms of some museum and asked to guess what was its use. Very often they all failed. I presume that nobody would for that reason doubt the existence of the object they were holding in their hand. Also, since somebody had made it, it would be far fetched to doubt that it had some use.

These questions are actually asked about cardinal utility, with the unspoken implication that if there is no use for it, then, even if it exists, it should not be a theme for research.

In replying to the question of applicability of cardinal utility the first field that attracts attention is that of decisions under risk. The works by Allais, Krystofowicz and Ellingsen in this book clearly show the relevance of the concept in this field. Since my point has so far already been made I shall not comment extensively, but make one remark: I once presented (1969) a model of decisions under risk where the utility of a game was not an expectation of some function of outcomes like in the von Neumann/Morgenstern model but as indicated by Allais, a functional of the whole shape of the probability distribution in terms of cardinal utility. More specifically, in my case:

Value of game = $U(E(u), s, z)$
where: u = cardinal utilities of outcome
s = standard deviation
z = a measure of skewness
= variance: 3. central moment

Later, inspired by a remark from Werner Leinfellner, I added an axiom stating that if all outcomes were improved by the same amount of utility, the utility of the game would increase by the same amount. This made it possible to separate the expectation of the ex post utility and the specific utility of risk in an additive function (Hagen, 1972, repr. 1987):

Value of game = $U = E(u) + f(s, z)$
where $f(s, z)$ represents the specific utility of risk

Obviously, when all u values increase by the same amount, then $E(U)$ increases with that same amount, and $f(s, z)$ remains the same, so U increases with the same amount.

If we make the mental experiment that both cardinal utility exists and that the Neumann/Morgenstern utility index exist (no specific utility of risk), then $f(s, z)$ evaporates, and the two utility concepts must be identical.

Allais has (1979 b) given this axiom a name: *The axiom of cardinal isovariation*, and adopted it and applied it in a similar way.

The above may be taken as a comment on Broome's (1985) comment on Allais's argument.

This book also contains a paper by Kraft and Wiese dealing with business cycles from a cardinal utility approach.

I should think that the cardinal utility theory could be useful as a common conceptual frame for formulating some problems in other sciences such as physiology, psychology and psychiatry.

It is well known that some pairs of elements in any diet have synergy effects. To the health-conscious consumer they are complements. Other pairs can in the same way be classified as independent, or substitutes. There are also those which are mutually detrimental to each other's effect, and can in combination cause damage that none of them could cause alone. Like the substitutes, they would have negative cross derivatives, and I cannot quite see how the distinction could be made in mathematical terms. Maybe someone else can.

One problem which is frustrating the professionals is the nature and possible treatment of alcoholics and other addicts. I think we can suggest a definition of an alcoholic: one whose marginal utility of alcohol is increasing till the level of collapse is reached. The therapy could then be to teach him to consider the ex post utility of the total binge rather than the immediate satisfaction of the next drink. Another question of more far reaching implications is if one can actually change his utility function. One therapy that suggests itself would be to put the patient under control and each day giving him the option of a "normal" amount of alcohol and the resulting frustration, or to suffer abstaining from it completely.

The question of the possibility of changing the utility function/preference structure has been discussed latterly (Elster, 1983). If this is a question of the subject's own decision, we have another example of how sterile the ordinalistic conceptuology is, as shown by: Do I prefer to have other preferences?

8. FINAL REMARKS

We have seen that given the hypotheses, which anybody is invited to test empirically, it is meaningful to work on the theory of consumer's choice from the classical assumption of a cardinal utility function.

On this assumption, supplemented by introspective observation of second order derivatives, it is possible to derive testable predictions.

An ordinalistic preference function can of course always be shaped to conform to the same reality. But it is a sterile description, and it may need more variables than the cardinalistic function. For example: where a cardinalistic theory needs the sign of the cross derivatives between four goods, whisky, gin, soda and tonic water, an ordinalistic preference function would have to add five more goods: whiskey-and-soda, whiskey-and-tonic, gin-and-soda, gin-and-tonic and whiskey-and-gin. If a person has stable preferences, a cardinal utility function of money consumed needs only to be supplemented by a time preference function for utility to *predict* the allocation of money spent over periods.

To apply a time preference function, for example a subjective rate of interest, to a merely ordinal one-period ("this" period) preference function (invariant through periods) would of course be meaningless.

An ordinalistic *description* concerning n goods and m periods would need a preference function over nm arguments.

The rule of dogmatic ordinalism has paralysed the research into the structure of cardinal utility and its applications. There is a vast and probably fertile area in need of cultivation.

ACKNOWLEDGEMENTS

In a central theme like this, which has for a long time been discussed off and on in theory, the author has of course received many impressions from the literature and oral discussions which it is impossible to specify. The first preparation towards this paper was made when I visited Professor Skala's department in the University of Paderborn. I had some very inspiring discussions there, particularly with Dr Kraft and Dr Landes which led to changes, though not always those suggested, so I alone am responsible for all faults and shortcomings. The inspiring time spent in Paderborn and Bonn was made possible by Ruhrgas stipends.

When I was finalizing the manuscript I received some ideas for more precise formulations through a conversation about the topic with Professor Reinhard Selten, who is of course not to blame for any part of its contents.

In the cause–effect chain which lead me to write this article, one important link was a provocative text from the end of the 1960s, entitled "De siste kardinalister" (The Last Cardinalists), which was meant to expose my stupidity, but inadvertently bestowed upon me a much too great honour: The three 'last' cardinalists turned out to be, in order of appearance, Ragnar Frisch, Maurice Allais and myself. From those two (later) Nobel laureates, from Allais in particular, I believe I have learned much. As for being among the last, in the third decennium after the apparent victory of the ordinalistic revolution: If there is anything the world has learned in the 1980s it is that there are times when the wagon of revolution, being on the wrong track, must be reversed.

Norwegian School of Management
and the University of Bonn

REFERENCES

Allais, Maurice (1952) 'Fondements d'une theorie positive des choix comportrant un risque et critique des postulats et axiomes de l'Ecole Americaine', *Colloques Internationaux du Centre National de la Recherche, Vol. XL, Paris 1953.*

Allais, Maurice (1979a) 'Foundations of a positive theory of choices involving risk and a criticism of the postulates and axioms of the American School', see Allais, and Hagen (1979).

Allais, Maurice (1979b) 'The so-called Allais paradox and rational decisions under uncertainty', see Allais and Hagen (eds.) (1979).

Allais, Maurice (1983) 'The foundations of the theory of utility and risk', see Hagen and Wenstoep (eds.) (1984).

Allais, Maurice (1985a) 'Three theorems on the theory of cardinal utility and random choice', Eberlein and Berghel (eds.), Reidel, 1987.

Allais, Maurice (1986) 'The general theory of random choices in relation to the invariant cardinal utility function and the specific probability function. The $(U, 0)$ model', in Munier (ed.), *Risk, Decision and Rationality*. Reidel, 1987.

Allais, Maurice (1988) *Scientific Papers on Risk and Utility Theory – Theory, Experience, and Applications*. Forthcoming, Reidel. Ch. XVIII, Cardinal Utility – History, Empirical Findings, and Applications.

Allais, Maurice and Hagen, Ole (eds.) (1979) *Expected Utility Hypotheses and the Allais Paradox – Contemporary discussions of rational decisions under risk with Allais' rejoinder*, Reidel, Dordrecht.

Bell, D. (1982) 'Regret in decision making under uncertainty', *Operations Research* **33**, 1–27.

Broome, J. (1985) 'A mistaken argument against the expected utility theory of rationality', *Theory and Decision* **18**, 313–318.

Camacho, A. (1979) 'Maximizing expected utility and the rule of long run success'. See Allais and Hagen (1979).

Chew, S. and MacCrimmon, K. (1979) 'Alpha-nu choice theory: a generalization of expected utility theory', *Working Paper 669*, University of British Columbia.

Daboni *et al.* (eds.), *Recent Developments in the Foundations of Utility and Risk Theory*, Reidel, Dordrecht.

Elster, J. (1983) *Sour Grapes*, Cambridge University Press.

Fishburn, Peter C. (1987) 'Reconsiderations in the foundations of decision uncertainty', *The Economic Journal* **8** (97), 825–841.

Hagen, Ole (1972) 'A new axiomatisation of utility under risk, Theorie a Metoda', *Reprint 1987/4 Norwegian School of Management.*

Hagen, Ole (1979) 'Towards a positive theory of decisions under risk', see Allais and Hagen (1979).

Hagen, Ole (1984) 'Relativity in decision theory', see Hagen and Wenstoep (1984), pp. 237–249.

Hagen, Ole (1985) 'Rules of behavior and expected utility theory. Compatibility versus dependence', *Theory and Decision* **18** (1), January, 31–46.

Hagen, Ole and Wenstoep, Fred (eds.) (1984) *Progress in Utility and Risk Theory*, Reidel, Dordrecht.

Hey, John D. and Lambert, Peter J. (eds.) (1987) *Surveys in the Economics of Uncertainty*, Basil Blackwell, Oxford.

Loomes, G. and Sugden, R. (1985) 'Regret theory: an alternative theory of rational choice under uncertainty', *Economic Journal* **92**, 805–824.

Loomes, G. and Sugden, R., 'Some implications of a more general form of regret theory', available from authors.

MacCrimmon, K.R. and Larsson, S. (1979) 'Utility theory: axioms versus "paradoxes"', see Allais and Hagen (1979).

Machina, Mark J. (1983) 'Generalized expected utility analysis and the nature of observed violations of the independence axiom', see Stigum and Wenstoep (eds.) (1983).

Schoemaker, P. (1982) 'The expected utility model: its variants, purposes, evidence and limitations', *Journal of Economic Literature* **20**, 529–563.

Sugden, Robert (1985) 'Regret, recrimination and rationality', *Theory and Decision* **19** (1), July, 77–100.

Sugden, Robert, 'New developments in the theory of choice under uncertainty', see Hey and Lambert (1987).

Stigum, B.P. and Wenstoep, F. (eds.) (1983) *Foundations of Utility and Risk Theory with Applications*, Reidel, Dordrecht.

Ståhl, I. (1980) 'Review of Allais and Hagen (eds.) q. v.', *Scandinavian Journal of Economics*, pp. 413–417.

Thore, S. (1983) 'Hotelling utility functions', in Stigum and Wenstoep (1983).

MANFRED KRAFT AND PETER WEISE

A CARDINAL UTILITY APPROACH TO THE THEORY OF THE BUSINESS CYCLE

ABSTRACT. We use a cardinal utility approach to depict the influence of a business climate on individual producers of investment and consumption goods. Generated by the total of producers, this climate alters its strength and direction in the course of time thus modifying the behaviour of each producer. Cumulative effects, errors of optimism and pessimism, and disproportions of investment goods and consumption goods production may occur. Assuming reasonable values for the parameters, we obtain an asymptotically and structurally stable business cycle.

1. INTRODUCTION

In some theories of the business cycle the following three elements are heavily stressed

- cumulative effects;
- a psychological climate which generates errors of optimism or pessimism;
- disproportions of the investment goods industry and the consumption goods industry.

These elements are well expressed by Keynes:

By a cyclical movement we mean that as the system progresses in, e.g., the upward direction, the forces propelling it upwards at first gather force and have a cumulative effect on one another but gradually lose their strength until at a certain point they tend to be replaced by forces operating in the opposite direction; which in turn gather force for a time and accentuate one another, until they too, having reached their maximum development, wane and give place to their opposite.[1]

And:

it is an essential characteristic of the boom that investments which will in fact yield, say, 2 per cent, in conditions of full employment are made in the expectation of a yield of, say, 6 per cent, and are valued accordingly. When the disillusion comes, this expectation is replaced by a contrary "error of pessimism", with the result that the investments, which would in fact yield 2 per cent in conditions of full employment, are expected to yield less than nothing; and the resulting collapse of new investment then leads to a state of unemployment in which the investments, which would have yielded 2 per cent in conditions of full employment, in fact yield less than nothing.[2]

And:

The Trade Cycle is best regarded, I think, as being occasioned by a cyclical change in the marginal efficiency of capital.[3]

M. Allais and O. Hagen (eds.), Cardinalism, 223–232.

Thus producing over- and under-investment. Many other authors argue in the same vein.[4]

Using a cardinal utility approach, we will try to incorporate the three elements mentioned above in order to show how cyclical movements will occur in an economy comprising many agents which interact with one another.

2. THE MODEL

Consider an economy consisting of $2\,N$ producers, $2\,N_c$ producers of consumption goods and $2\,N_i$ producers of investment goods. Thus

$$2\,N = 2\,N_c + 2\,N_i$$

Each producer can choose between two alternative strategies

s^+: to produce one unit of goods

s^-: not to produce one unit of goods.

Let $n_{\alpha j}(t)$ be the number of producers in industry α, $\alpha = c, i$, choosing at point of time t strategy j, $j = s^+, s^-$. Then

$$n_{cs^+}(t) + n_{cs^-}(t) = 2\,N_c \text{ for all } t$$
$$n_{is^+}(t) + n_{is^-}(t) = 2\,N_i \text{ for all } t$$

Define

$$n_\alpha(t) = n_{\alpha s^+}(t) - N_\alpha \quad (\alpha = c, i)$$

then

$$-N_c \leq n_c(t) \leq N_c \text{ for all } t$$
$$-N_i \leq n_i(t) \leq N_i \text{ for all } t$$

The vector $n(t) = (n_c(t),\ n_i(t))$ then defining a discrete time path describes completely the state of the economy.

We assume that behaviour of the individual producers is determined by transition rates p^α_{kj} describing the probability per unit of time of changing the strategy j to k in the infinitesimally small time interval $[t,\ t + \Delta t]$. Let us assume further that Δt may be set such that only one change of strategies is possible and that the Markovian assumption is fulfilled. Let transition rates p^α_{kj} depend upon the utility assessment of the state of the economy, $n(t)$, at point of time t by producers α and let for the sake of simplicity this dependence be linearly. Then we may write the linear utility functions

$$u(n(t)) = \hat{\kappa}_c n_c(t) + \hat{\sigma}_c n_i(t)$$
$$v(n(t)) = \hat{\kappa}_i n_i(t) + \hat{\sigma}_i n_c(t)$$

for producers of consumption goods and investment goods, respectively.

We assume that the units of consumption goods and investment goods are defined such that $n_c = n_i = 0$ is an equilibrium of the economy. Hence positive and negative n_c and n_i depict the deviation of the state of the economy from its equilibrium value. Cardinal utility of the producers depends positively or negatively on the extent of this deviation, according to the signs of the parameters $\hat{\kappa}_c$, $\hat{\sigma}_c$, $\hat{\kappa}_i$, $\hat{\sigma}_i$, and is supposed to be proportional to the deviation, the degree of proportionality being expressed by the values of the parameters. The cardinal utility functions $u(n(t))$ and $v(n(t))$ give an exact measure for the rather blurred concept of business climate.

It is true that the producers act so as to maximize their profits, but in order to realize this goal they first of all have to generate an estimation of the prospective development of the economy. This estimation is based on successes and failures of other producers, on trends and so on, and is summarized to a point of reference against which the producers value the profitability of investments. This point of reference is the business climate expressed by the utility functions above. We make the basic behavioural assumption that an improvement of the business climate, i.e. an increase of the cardinal utility, raises the probability that a producer changes his strategy from s^- to s^+ and vice versa.[5]

According to concepts in 'logit and probit models'[6] we may specify the transition rates as

$$p_+^c(n) = p_{s^+s^-}^c(n) = \gamma_c e^{u(n)}$$
$$p_-^c(n) = p_{s^-s^+}^c(n) = \gamma_c e^{-u(n)}$$
$$p_+^i(n) = p_{s^+s^-}^i(n) = \gamma_i e^{v(n)}$$
$$p_-^i(n) = p_{s^-s^+}^i(n) = \gamma_i e^{-v(n)}$$

Let us assume that transitions can occur between adjacent states of the economy only, i.e. behaviour of the producers changes sequentially. Then the motion of the economy is described by the master equation

$$\begin{aligned}\frac{\mathrm{d}p(n;t)}{\mathrm{d}t} &= \frac{\mathrm{d}p(n_c,n_i;t)}{\mathrm{d}t} = \\ &= (n_{cs^+}+1)p_-^c(n_c+1,n_i)p(n_c+1,n_i;t) - n_{cs^+}p_-^c(n)p(n;t) \\ &+(n_{cs^-}+1)p_+^c(n_c-1,n_i)p(n_c-1,n_i;t) - n_{cs^-}p_+^c(n)p(n;t) \\ &+(n_{is^+}+1)p_-^i(n_c,n_i+1)p(n_c,n_i+1;t) - n_{is^+}p_-^i(n)p(n;t) \\ &+(n_{is^-}+1)p_+^i(n_c,n_i-1)p(n_c,n_i-1;t) - n_{is^-}p_+^i(n)p(n;t)\end{aligned}$$

If N is very large, in order to describe the state of the economy we can define the quasi-continuous variables $(\bar{x}, \bar{y})$ as

$$\bar{x} = \frac{n_c}{N_c}\,, \quad \bar{y} = \frac{n_i}{N_i}$$

If we can assume further that it is sufficient to consider the motions equations of the means $E(\bar{x}(t)) = x(t)$ and $E(\bar{y}(t)) = y(t)$,[7] we obtain the approximate equations

$$\left\{ \begin{aligned} \frac{dx}{d\tau} &= (\tanh(u(x,y) - x)\ \cosh(u(x,y)) \\ \frac{dy}{d\tau} &= \lambda(\tanh(v(x,y) - y)\ \cosh(v(x,y)) \end{aligned} \right. \tag{1}$$

where

$$\begin{aligned} &\lambda = \frac{\gamma_i}{\gamma_c} \qquad \tau = 2\gamma_c t \\ &u(x,y) = \kappa_c x + \sigma_c y \\ &v(x,y) = \kappa_i y + \sigma_i x \\ &\kappa_\alpha = \hat{\kappa}_\alpha N_\alpha\,, \quad \sigma_\alpha = \hat{\sigma}_\alpha N_\alpha \quad (\alpha = c, i) \end{aligned}$$

We see that the motion of the economy depends on the cardinal utility assessment of the states of the economy by producers in industries c and i. At every point of time utility assessments initiate individual actions resulting in interaction processes which change the states of the economy. In order to further analyse the behaviour of the economy it is necessary to consider the cardinal utility functions more closely.

κ_i, κ_c describe cumulative effects in the investment goods and consumption goods industries, respectively. It is assumed that increasing production generates optimism thus fostering production even more, and vice versa. It is plausible to assume further that the degree of optimism or pessimism is higher in the investment goods industry than in the consumption goods industry.

Thus we postulate

$$\kappa_i > \kappa_c > 1$$

Then $\kappa_i y$, $\kappa_c x$ denote the strength and the direction of these forces.

σ_i, σ_c describe the effects of the industries on one another. σ_i measures the influence of consumption goods industry on the investment goods industry. Due to the low cost of producing investment goods in the region of underproduction of consumption goods, i.e. $x < 0$, and vice versa, production of investment goods will be positively or negatively influenced, respectively. Analogously σ_c measures the influence of the investment goods industry on the consumption goods industry. Production of investment goods generates income thus fostering production of consumption goods. Thus we postulate

$$\sigma_i < 0 < \sigma_c$$

Strength and direction of these influences are measured by $\sigma_i x$ and $\sigma_c y$.

The point $x = y = 0$ is an equilibrium of the economy which means that there is no disproportion of production of consumption and investment goods. Then γ_i, γ_c denote the strength of fluctuations around this point of equilibrium and the time scale on which the decision processes take place. We postulate

$$\gamma_i, \gamma_c > 0$$

Description of the behaviour of the economy requires discussing the system of differential equations (1) with respect to the admissible parameter values discussed above. Especially, we are interested in the existence of equilibrium points, stability and closed orbits. It is not difficult to see that equilibrium points are the solutions of the system of equations

$$\begin{cases} \tanh(u(x,y)) - x = 0 \\ \tanh(v(x,y)) - y = 0 \end{cases}$$

from which we obtain

$$(2) \qquad \begin{cases} y = \dfrac{1}{\sigma_c}\left(\frac{1}{2}\ \ln\left(\dfrac{1+x}{1-x}\right) - \kappa_c x\right) = f(x) \\ x = \dfrac{1}{\sigma_i}\left(\frac{1}{2}\ \ln\left(\dfrac{1+y}{1-y}\right) - \kappa_i y\right) = g(y) \end{cases}$$

A typical diagram for admissible parameter values is shown in Figure 1.

From an inspection of (1) it turns out that all the flux lines on the boundary points of the box $[-1 \le x \le 1, -1 \le y \le 1]$ point inwards. The origin $(0,0)$ is always an equilibrium point. A sufficient condition for $(0,0)$ to be the unique equilibrium point is

$$\kappa_c \ge \frac{1}{2x^*}\ \ln\left(\frac{1+x^*}{1-x^*}\right) = \frac{\text{area tanh } x^*}{x^*}$$

$$\kappa_i \ge \frac{1}{2y^*}\ \ln\left(\frac{1+y^*}{1-y^*}\right) = \frac{\text{area tanh } y^*}{y^*}$$

where

$$x^* = \frac{1}{\sigma_i}\left(\frac{1}{2}\ \ln\left(\frac{1+\sqrt{1-\frac{1}{\kappa_i}}}{1-\sqrt{1-\frac{1}{\kappa_i}}}\right) - \kappa_i\sqrt{1-\frac{1}{\kappa_i}}\right)$$

$$y^* = \frac{1}{\sigma_c}\left(\frac{1}{2}\ \ln\left(\frac{1+\sqrt{1-\frac{1}{\kappa_c}}}{1-\sqrt{1-\frac{1}{\kappa_c}}}\right) - \kappa_c\sqrt{1-\frac{1}{\kappa_c}}\right)$$

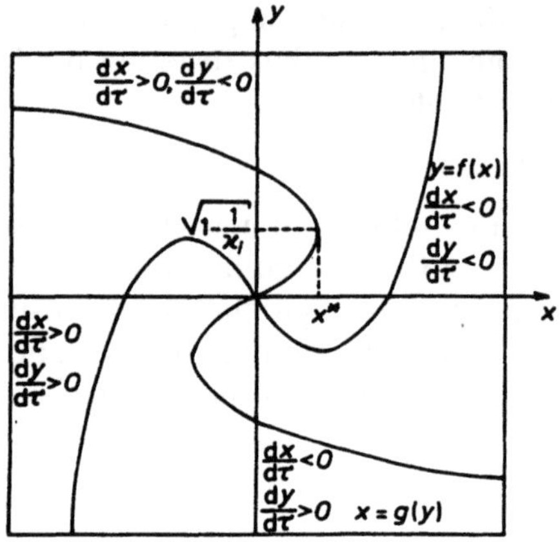

Fig. 1.

Using a linear stability analysis to investigate the behaviour of the system (1) in the vicinity of $(0,0)$ we have to examine the derivative of the r.h.s. of the system (2) at $(0,0)$ considered as a linear vector field which approximates the system (1) near the equilibrium point $(0,0)$, i.e. the linear part of (1) at $(0,0)$. We get

$$(0,0) \text{ is unstable if}$$

$$\gamma_c\kappa_c + \gamma_i\kappa_i \geq \gamma_c + \gamma_i$$

or

$$\kappa_c + \kappa_i - \kappa_c\kappa_i \geq 1 - \sigma_c\sigma_i$$

We see at once that this condition is fulfilled. Then due to a theorem by Poincaré–Bendixson there must exist a stable limit cycle. We see further that this closed orbit is structurally stable for a comparatively large domain of admissible parameter values. We have thus derived the existence of a business cycle as shown in Figure 2.

This business cycle denotes not a specific but rather the normal manner in which the economy considered above behaves. For the values of the parameters κ_i, κ_c, σ_i, σ_c $(\kappa_i, \kappa_c > 1;\ \sigma_i < 0 < \sigma_c)$ exhibit rather meaningful economic hypotheses. In most theories of the business cycle cumulative effects or self-enhancing processes are stressed. These are described by κ_i, κ_c which can be interpreted as "own multipliers" of the industries i and c. Positive effects are, *ceteris paribus*, prone to enhance themselves, and vice versa. Parameters σ_i, σ_c reflect the fact that both the industries i and c influence one another. Increasing production of investment goods always fosters production of consumption goods, and vice versa, since consumption goods are purchased by income. Investment

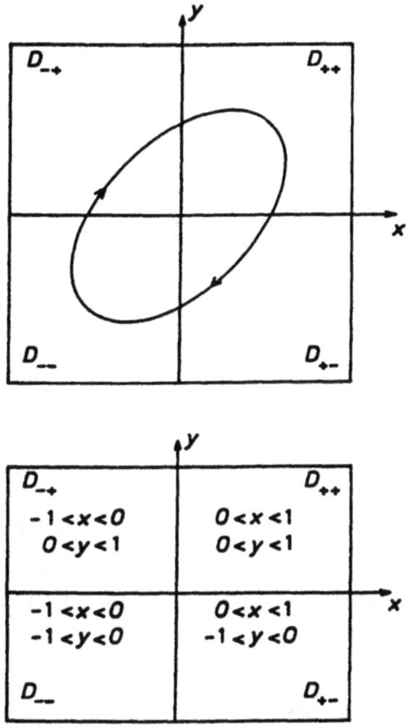

Fig. 2.

goods, however, are produced in the expectation of a future yield and are financed by means of investment funds. But the cost of producing investment goods is low in the case of underproduction and high in the case of overproduction. Thus underproduction of consumption goods fosters production of investment goods and conversely. Parameters σ_i, σ_c, therefore, may be interpreted in a similar manner as accelerator and multiplier, respectively, in some models of the business cycle.

The four parameters describe the degree and direction a business climate will evolve into that generated by the multitude of decision acts taken by individuals and, on the other hand, encouraging every producer to produce or not to produce. In the course of time this business climate gives rise to "errors of optimism and pessimism" causing over- and underproduction. In the region ($x < 0$, $y < 0$), i.e. underproduction in both the industries, $\sigma_i x > 0$, underproduction of consumption goods fosters production of investment goods. In the region ($x < 0$, $y > 0$) where $\sigma_i x$, $\kappa_i y$, and $\sigma_c y$ are positive: self-enhancing forces in industry i and positive effects on industry c cause overproduction of investment goods and increasing production of consumption goods. In region ($x > 0$, $y > 0$), i.e. overproduction in both the industries, where $\sigma_i x$ is negative and $\kappa_i y$, $\sigma_c y$, $\kappa_c x$ all are positive, overproduction of consumption goods retards production of investment goods. Finally, in the region ($x > 0$, $y < 0$), where $\sigma_i x$, $\kappa_i y$,

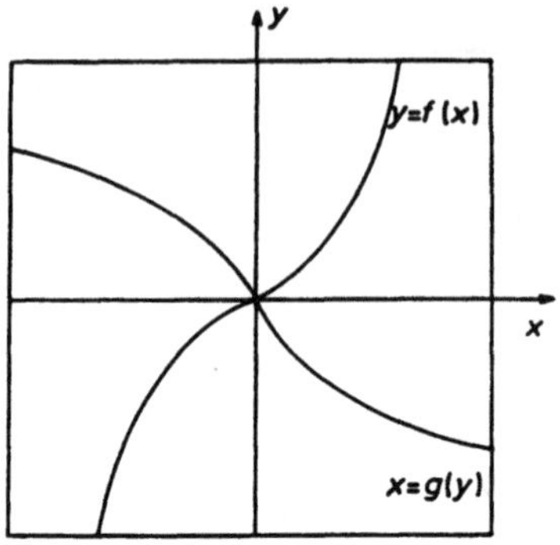

Fig. 3.

and $\sigma_c y$ are negative, self-enhancing forces in industry i in the opposite direction and negative effects on industry c bring about underproduction of investment goods and decreasing production of consumption goods. Going on to region $(x < 0,\ y < 0)$ a further business cycle is apt to start yet again.

It turns out that the business cycle contains a sequence of disproportions of the production of investment and consumption goods, a fact also heavily stressed upon in some theories of the business cycle. Here the equilibrium proportion $(x = 0,\ y = 0)$ will not be arrived at. To see this point more exactly let us consider two special cases. First, let us assume

$$0 < \kappa_i, \kappa_c < 1$$
$$\sigma_i < 0 < \sigma_c$$

A typical diagram is shown in Figure 3. Because of $g'(y) < 0$ for all y and $f'(x) > 0$ for all x, the origin $(0, 0)$ is the unique equilibrium point.

Furthermore, if κ_i, $\kappa_c < 1$ we conclude that

$$\gamma_c\kappa_c + \gamma_i\kappa_i < \gamma_c + \gamma_i$$

and

$$\kappa_i + \kappa_c - \kappa_i\kappa_c < 1 - \sigma_i\sigma_c$$

Thus $(0, 0)$ is stable and no cycle exists. Productions of investment and consumption goods are in correct proportion to one another and each perturbation (caused by fluctuations) leads to a motion back to the equilibrium point.

Second, let us assume

$$0 < \kappa_c < 1 < \kappa_i$$
$$\sigma_i < 0 < \sigma_c$$

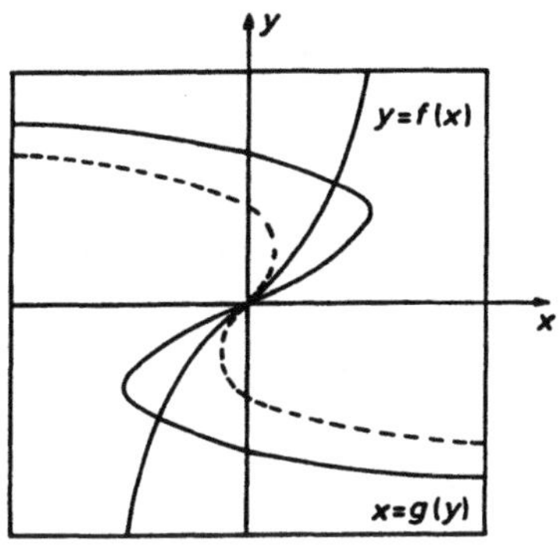

Fig. 4.

A typical diagram is shown in Figure 4. For $(0, 0)$ to be the unique equilibrium point in this case a necessary condition is

$$\kappa_i \leq \frac{1 - \sigma_c\sigma_i - \kappa_c}{1 - \kappa_c}$$

If κ_i does not satisfy this inequality two or four further equilibrium points exist in addition to $(0, 0)$ which is always an equilibrium point.

For an equilibrium point (x_e, y_e) to be stable we obtain

$$-2(\gamma_c\sigma_c\sqrt{1 - x_e^2}\, f'(x_e) + \gamma_i\sigma_i\sqrt{1 - y_e^2}\, g'(y_e)) < 0$$

and $f'(x_e)\, g'(y_e) < 1$.

We conclude that for κ_i to be sufficiently large, σ_c, $|\sigma_i|$ sufficiently small, and κ_c sufficiently large (but smaller than 1) the economy may be locked in a "semi-slump" or a "quasi-boom".[8] The driving force $\sigma_i x$ then is not strong enough to push the economy into self-enhancing processes in the upward or downward direction. Thus the system persists in one of the stable equilibria.

University of Paderborn
University of Kassel

NOTES

[1] Keynes, J.M., *The General Theory of Employment, Interest, and Money*, London, Melbourne, Toronto, 1967 (1936), pp. 313/314.

[2] Op. cit., pp. 321/322.

[3] Cf. op. cit., p. 313.

[4] Cf. Haberler, G., *Prosperity and Depression. A Theoretical Analysis of Cyclical Movements* (new edition). Cambridge, MA, 1968 (1937).

[5] The producers realize sequentially and gradually possible investment opportunities; cf. to processes of this kind: Allais, M., *The Concepts of Surplus and Loss and the Reformulation of the Theories of Stable General Economic Equilibrium and Maximum Efficiency*, in Baranzini, M. and Scazzieri, R. (eds.), *Foundations of Economics*, Oxford, 1986, pp. 135–174.

[6] Cf. Aldrich, J.H., F.D. Nelson, *Linear Probability, Logit, and Probit Models*, Beverly Hills, London, New Delhi, 1984.

[7] This is the case when the distribution of the stochastic variables $(\bar{x}(t), \bar{y}(t))$ is highly concentrated around the mean $(x(t), y(t))$ because then $(x(t), y(t))$ describes the most probable path. Cf. Haken, H., *Synergetics. An Introduction* (second enlarged edition). Berlin, Heidelberg, 1978 (1977), and Weidlich, W., and Haag, G., *Concepts and Models of a Quantitative Sociology. The Dynamics of Interacting Populations*. Berlin, Heidelberg, New York, 1983.

[8] Cf. Keynes, J.M., op. cit., p. 322.

REFERENCES

Aldrich, J.H. and F.D. Nelson (1984) *Linear Probability, Logit, and Probit Models*. Beverly Hills, London, New Delhi.

Allais, M. (1986) 'The concepts of surplus and loss and the reformulation of the theories of stable general economic equilibrium and maximum efficiency', in Baranzini, M. and Scazzieri, R. (eds.), *Foundations of Economics*, Oxford, pp. 135–174.

Haberler, G. (1968) *Prosperity and Depression. A Theoretical Analysis of Cyclical Movements* (new edition). Cambridge, MA (1937).

Haken, H. (1978) *Synergetics. An Introduction* (second enlarged edition), Berlin, Heidelberg (1977).

Keynes, H.M. (1967) *The General Theory of Employment, Interest, and Money*, London, Melbourne, Toronto (1936).

Weidlich, W. and G. Haag (1983) *Concepts and Models of a Quantitative Sociology. The Dynamics of Interacting Populations*. Berlin, Heidelberg, New York.

ROMAN KRZYSZTOFOWICZ

FILTERING RISK EFFECT IN STANDARD-GAMBLE UTILITY MEASUREMENT

ABSTRACT. Cardinal utility functions measured via the midpoint-sequence expected utility (MSEU) method have often been found incoherent because of the risk effect – that part of an individual's risk attitude which is inadmissible within the expected utility theory. In order to filter the risk effect, we propose a midpoint-sequence weighted-utility (MSWU) method. It employs a one-parameter utility model suggested by Professor Ole Hagen some two decades ago as a parsimonious descriptor of preferences for two-outcome even-chance gambles. The empirical evidence in support of the model is recounted, but a direct validation of the MSWU method awaits further research.

1. INTRODUCTION

1.1. Standard-Gamble Utility Measurement

We are concerned with measuring a cardinal utility function v of outcomes (monetary or otherwise) via methods in which the stimulus consists of two options – a sure outcome z and a two-outcome even-chance gamble (x, y) – and the subject's task is to state a preference between them. A sequence of stimuli is generated by appropriately varying one of the outcomes until the indifference is established: $z \sim (x, y)$. Such standard gamble methods have two main realizations: the midpoint sequence method wherein the variable outcome is z, and the uniform sequence method wherein the variable outcome is x. For a comprehensive review of gamble-based utility measurement methods, the reader may wish to consult Farquhar (1984).

The midpoint sequence method has been by far the most popular in applications of the expected utility theory. From an empirical standpoint, its main drawback is the chaining of responses which may induce serial positioning and recency effects. But its attractive features are numerous:

1. even probabilities preclude any bias due to the probability preference or similar phenomena;
2. the effective stimulus has only three dimensions (the outcomes) – the lowest dimensionality possible for measuring cardinal preferences;
3. the gamble lends itself easily to operational interpretations;
4. the basic judgmental task is in the form of a binary choice;
5. the choice task is simple to explain; and
6. the calculus of expected utility, pioneered by von Neumann and Morgenstern (1947), is straightforward.

M. Allais and O. Hagen (eds.), Cardinalism, 233–248.

These advantages notwithstanding, the midpoint sequence method, in conjunction with the expected utility calculus, yields biased measurements of utility. The empirical evidence to this effect is convincing, and numerous cognitive sources of biases have been hypothesized (for a review, see Farquhar, 1984). The overall conclusion is that preferences expressed by individuals in response to the standard gamble stimuli do not conform to the expected utility model. What is then desired is a more general utility model that would better describe expressed preferences and yet retain the empirical part of the midpoint sequence method with all its attractive features.

1.2. A More General Measurement Model

One such model has been proposed by Professor Ole Hagen with the intent of showing "that the shortcomings of the von Neumann–Morgenstern method of measuring utility can be overcome through a modification with the specific utility of uncertainty built in" (Hagen, 1969, p. 84). His main postulate is that an individual evaluates a gamble as if he were accounting not only for the expected utility of the gamble outcomes but also for the dispersion of the outcome utilities.

Hagen's postulate appears to dovetail with the conclusions from an empirical investigation by Krzysztofowicz and Duckstein (1980) who demonstrated the impact of the range of the gamble outcomes on the measurement of a utility function via the midpoint sequence method and expected utility calculus. The observed impact, termed for short the range effect, has been explained by hypothesizing that the range of the gamble outcomes affects the individual's risk attitude in a manner inadmissible within the expected utility theory. Hagen's model offers a parsimonious account of the range effect in terms of a preference (positive or negative) for the dispersion of the outcome utilities. Since the dispersion is a measure of risk, one could speak as well of the risk effect. This complementarity of the points of view presented in both studies gave the impetus for the present article.

In the sequel, we restate Hagen's model, offer its alternative interpretations, and hypothesize explanations of the risk effect. Next, we support the main modelling postulate by recounting the empirical evidence from four independent experiments. Finally, we explore two implications of the model for the measurement of cardinal utility. First, the model suggests a criterion for choosing a measurement method. Second, the model offers a procedure for calculating the utilities of outcomes assessed via the midpoint sequence gamble method. Relative to the expected utility calculus, the model can be viewed as a filtering procedure that eliminates the risk effect or, more specifically, that part of risk attitude which is inadmissible within the expected utility theory. The new measurement method, called for short the midpoint-sequence weighted-utility (MSWU) method, includes the traditional midpoint-sequence expected-utility (MSEU) method as a special case arising whenever the risk effect is absent.

2. HAGEN'S UTILITY MODEL

2.1. Formulation

Let $X = \{x\}$ be a set of outcomes and $v : X \rightarrow \text{Re}$ a cardinal utility function of outcomes. Any probability distribution G on X is evaluated in terms of a utility

$$u(G) = f(E(v(x)),\ S(v(x)),\ Z(v(x))) \tag{1}$$

where f is a function of three statistics of the distribution of utilities $v(x)$ induced by the distribution G of outcomes x. These statistics are: E, expectation; S, standard deviation; and Z, a measure of skewness (third central moment/variance). A particular form of f is additive:

$$u(G) = E(v(x)) + \gamma S(v(x)) + \eta Z(v(x)) \tag{2}$$

where γ and η are constants.

When the distributions under consideration are restricted to two-outcome even-chance gambles of the form $G = (x_i, x_j)$, which yield either x_i or x_j with even probabilities, then equation (2) takes the form

$$u(G) = E(v(x)) + \gamma S(v(x)) \tag{3}$$

where

$$\begin{aligned} E(v(x)) &= 0.5[v(x_i) + v(x_j)] \\ S(v(x)) &= 0.5|v(x_i) - v(x_j)| \end{aligned} \tag{4}$$

Furthermore, given a certainty equivalent $\xi(x_i, x_j)$ of the gamble (x_i, x_j), such that $\xi(x_i, x_j) \sim (x_i, x_j)$, the utility of the gamble is

$$u(G) = v(\xi(x_i, x_j)) \tag{5}$$

Together, equations (3), (4), and (5) give a parametric measurement equation:

$$v(\xi(x_i, x_j)) = 0.5[v(x_i) + v(x_j)] + 0.5\gamma|v(x_i) - v(x_j)| \tag{6}$$

For the source material on this model see Hagen (1969, 1979, 1984).

2.2. Interpretation

The parameter γ, called here the risk factor, gauges the impact of the dispersion of the outcome utilities on the utility of the gamble. Since

$v(\xi(x_i, x_j))$ must lie between the utilities of the gamble outcomes, we have the condition $-1 < \gamma < 1$.

Risk attitude, defined ordinarily in terms of a preference between the certainty equivalent $\xi(x_i, x_j)$ and the expected outcome $0.5(x_i + x_j)$, is determined jointly by v and γ. For a fixed utility function v, any of the relations

$$(7) \qquad v(\xi(x_i, x_j)) \begin{Bmatrix} < \\ > \\ = \end{Bmatrix} v(0.5(x_i + x_j))$$

is possible, depending upon the value of the risk factor γ in (6). Hence, Hagen's model allows a richer set of risk attitudes than the expected utility model, in which $\gamma = 0$ and risk attitude is implied by v.

Equation (6) admits an alternative interpretation. For the sake of simplicity, let us suppose that $v(x_i) > v(x_j)$. Then

$$(8) \qquad v(\xi(x_i, x_j)) = \omega v(x_i) + (1 - \omega)\, v(x_j)$$

where

$$\omega = 0.5(1 + \gamma) \text{ and } 1 - \omega = 0.5(1 - \gamma)$$

Thus, Hagen's model could be characterized as a skew weighted utility model: it retains the structure of the expectation, but transforms the symmetric distribution of outcomes, specified by objective probabilities $p = 1 - p = 0.5$, into a skew distribution, specified by subjective weights $\omega \neq 1 - \omega$.

The implication of the probability transformation on the inference of cardinal preferences can be seen after rewriting equation (8) in the form

$$(9) \qquad v(x_i) - v(\xi(x_i, x_j)) = \frac{1 - \gamma}{1 + \gamma} \left[v(\xi(x_i, x_j)) - v(x_j) \right]$$

It says that the individual's strength of preference for x_i over $\xi(x_i, x_j)$ is $(1 - \gamma)/(1 + \gamma)$ times as great as his strength of preference for $\xi(x_i, x_j)$ over x_j. In other words, constant $(1 - \gamma)/(1 + \gamma)$ represents the ratio of preference intensities. These interpretations are recapitulated in Table I.

2.3. *Explanation of the Risk Effect*

In summary, equation (6) offers a descriptive model of expressed preferences for two-outcome even-chance gambles. The model admits two alternative interpretations that can also be taken as operational explanations of the incoherences observed in utility functions estimated from certainty equivalents via the calculus of expected utility. These explanations are as follows:

TABLE I

Behavioural interpretation of the risk factor γ and the subjective weight ω in Hagen's model

Risk factor γ	Implied risk attitude in conjunction with linear v	Subjective weight ω	Outcome utility receiving a larger subjective weight[a]
< 0	Risk Averse	< 0.5	$v(x_j)$ – lower outcome utility
> 0	Risk Seeking	> 0.5	$v(x_i)$ – upper outcome utility
$= 0$	Risk Neutral	$= 0.5$	

[a] The assumption is that $v(x_i) > v(x_j)$.

1. The subject evaluates a gamble as if he computed the expected utility of outcomes and then adjusted it, up or down, proportionally to the dispersion of outcome utilities. (This is an explanation in terms of the range effect or the dispersion effect.)
2. The subject evaluates a gamble as if he computed the expected utility of outcomes by applying unequal subjective weights rather than equal objective probabilities. (This is an explanation in terms of the probability effect – the nonlinearity of the utility of a gamble in probability – a special case of which is known as the certainty effect.)

An experimentalist may discern subtle behavioural distinctions between the various effects (range effect, dispersion effect, probability effect, certainty effect). However, within the inference framework afforded by model (6) these effects are operationally equivalent and they will, therefore, be labelled commonly as the risk effect.

Our principal objective is to employ Hagen's model for measuring the cardinal utility function v. The premise is that the model can filter out the risk effect and thereby yield an unbiased measurement of v. The model is simple – it has only one parameter, γ, in addition to the construct being measured, v – and it seems worthwhile to investigate its potential.

3. EMPIRICAL INVESTIGATIONS

3.1. Midpoint Sequence Method

Suppose that $X = [x_0, x^*]$, the preference order increases from x_0 to x^*, and a sequence of certainty equivalents, or gamble midpoints, $\{x_1, x_2, x_3, x_{23}\}$ has been assessed such that

$$x_1 \sim (x_0, x^*)\,, \quad x_2 \sim (x_0, x_1)$$
$$x_3 \sim (x_1, x^*)\,, \quad x_{23} \sim (x_2, x_3) \tag{10}$$

This assessment scheme can be continued to find further midpoints; this is done in the Appendix.

With the utility function scaled by $v_0 = v(x_0) = 0$ and $v^* = v(x^*) = 1$, the utilities $v_i = v(x_i)$ of the midpoints computed from the expected utility model (equation (6) with $\gamma = 0$) are:

$$v_1 = 0.5\,, \quad v_2 = 0.25$$
$$v_3 = 0.75\,, \quad v_{23} = 0.5 \tag{11}$$

Since $v_1 = v_{23}$, the condition $x_1 = x_{23}$ provides a check on the consistency of the assessed midpoints with the expected utility principle.

The utilities attached to the midpoints by Hagen's model (6) are as follows:

$$\begin{aligned} v_1 &= 0.5(1+\gamma) \\ v_2 &= 0.25(1+\gamma)^2 \\ v_3 &= 0.25(3-\gamma)(1+\gamma) \\ v_{23} &= 0.5(1+\gamma) + 0.25\gamma(1-\gamma^2) \end{aligned} \tag{12}$$

The estimation of parameter γ will be addressed later.

3.2. Risk Effect Hypothesis

When $\gamma \neq 0$ measurement relations (12) imply the inequality $v_1 \neq v_{23}$. Specifically,

$$v_{23} - v_1 = \Delta = 0.25\gamma(1-\gamma^2) \tag{13}$$

The rationale that led Hagen to propose the model led him also to hypothesize that when faced with one-time (unique) gambles, people generally dislike the dispersion of the outcome utilities so that $\gamma < 0$. This in turn implies $v_{23} < v_1$, or equivalently $x_{23} < x_1$, which Hagen (1984) submitted as a behavioural hypothesis. We shall now examine the statistics of γ computed from four sets of experimental data and recorded in Table II.

3.2.1. Arizona Experiment

In an engineering context of water resource management, Krzysztofowicz and Duckstein (1980) assessed 24 utility functions, 12 for the outcome "flood level" and 12 for the outcome "storage deficit". Both outcome measures represented undesirable consequences of decisions, including monetary losses. The subjects were professional hydrologists and graduate

TABLE II

Statistics of the risk factor γ from four experiments

Experiment	Arizona	Virginia Gains	Virginia Losses	R.K.	M.A.	Overall
# of cases	24	44	44	54	4	170
% of cases with:						
$\gamma < 0$	79	41	25	39	50	35
$\gamma = 0$	4	23	34	7	0	9
Mean of γ	–0.31	0.01	0.11	0.05	–0.05	0.00
Standard Deviation of γ	0.36	0.33	0.28	0.28	0.45	0.34
Mean of $\|\gamma\|$	0.42	0.23	0.20	0.20	0.35	0.24
Standard Deviation of $\|\gamma\|$	0.23	0.23	0.23	0.20	0.28	0.23

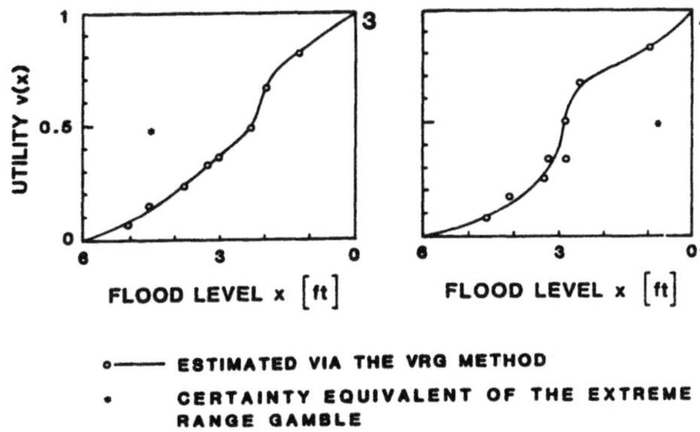

Fig. 1. Utility functions v estimated via the variable range gamble (VRG) method, and utilities of the certainty equivalent x_1 of the extreme range gamble (x_0, x^*), not used in the estimation of v, for two subjects from the Arizona Experiment. (Source: Krzysztofowicz and Duckstein, 1980.)

students of systems engineering at the University of Arizona. The utility functions were calculated by using the variable range gamble method that avoids the gamble between the extreme outcomes. We shall assume, therefore, that the functions are not distorted by the risk effect. The certainty equivalent x_1 of the extreme gamble (x_0, x^*) was, nevertheless, assessed. Figure 1 illustrates the large error that would be introduced into the measurement of v if x_1 were used as an anchor. From the estimated function v we can read $v_1 = v(x_1)$, and then via (12) compute γ. In 79% of 24 cases we find $\gamma < 0$, which concurs with Hagen's hypothesis.

3.2.2. *Virginia Experiment*

As part of a large experiment conducted at the University of Virginia in 1983/84, utility functions were assessed via the midpoint sequence gamble method according to equations (10) and (11). The subjects were 44 fourth-year students of systems engineering who had been asked to express their preferences in the context of applying for financial support to attend a graduate school. Two utility functions were assessed for each subject: one on the domain of gains $X = \$[0, 10000]$ interpreted as a stipend, and one on the domain of losses $X = \$[-10000, 0]$ interpreted as a loan that the student would have to take if no stipend were forthcoming.

The results indicate that $\gamma < 0$ in 41% of 44 cases on the domain of gains and 25% on the domain of losses. It is also interesting to note that $\gamma = 0$, implying the consistency of risk attitude with the expected utility principle, in 23% of cases on the domain of gains and 34% on the domain of losses. Estimates of γ have been obtained by linearizing v, as shown later in equations (15) and (16).

3.2.3. *R.K. Experiment*

Equation (6) applied to the gamble $G = (x_0, x)$, for any $x \in X$ and with the scaling condition $v(x_0) = 0$, gives $u(G) = 0.5(1 + \gamma)v(x)$. The multiplicative model of the generic utility theory (Krzysztofowicz, 1994) applied to the same gamble gives $u(G) = r(0.5)v(x)$, where r is a risk function. By equating the two formulas, we obtain

$$\gamma = 2r(0.5) - 1 \tag{14}$$

In general, r is a function of probability p of the preferred outcome x from a two-outcome gamble that yields either x with probability p or x_0 with probability $1 - p$.

Krzysztofowicz (1994) reports an experiment that supplied empirical measurements of the risk functions r for 54 subjects. By employing equation (14), we have been able to calculate the corresponding risk factors γ. In 39% of cases $\gamma < 0$, and in 7% of cases $\gamma = 0$.

3.2.4. *M.A. Experiment*

Recently, Allais (1986) reanalyzed the results of his celebrated experiment of 1952, and for four subjects estimated functions that appear to be compatible with the risk functions r of our generic utility theory. Hence, after reading $r(0.5)$ off the charts supplied by Allais, we have been able to apply equation (14) and get the corresponding risk factors γ.

3.2.5. *Conclusions*

The overall results, based on 170 assessments of preferences in four independent experiments, are presented in the last column of Table II and lend support to the following conclusions.

1. With $\gamma < 0$ in 35% of cases and $\gamma > 0$ in 56% of cases, the hypothesis that generally $\gamma < 0$ is not supported by the data. Inasmuch as the risk factor γ, in conjunction with the utility function v, characterizes risk attitude, the lack of a definite tendency in the sign of γ should not be surprising. Previous empirical studies (e.g. Krzysztofowicz, 1983, 1994) have shown that in a sample large enough one is most likely to encounter variability of risk attitudes, not only across individuals, but also within an individual if he is presented with different framings of an outcome (e.g. loss versus gain), or different decision contexts.

2. In 9% of cases the risk factor $\gamma = 0$. These are the cases in which the expressed preferences are not affected by the risk associated with the gamble outcomes and, consequently, the midpoint sequence assessment in conjunction with the expected utility calculus would yield an unbiased measurement of the utility function v.

3. In the majority of cases (91%) $\gamma \neq 0$, indicating thereby the presence of the risk effect. While this finding does not validate Hagen's model as the descriptor of expressed preferences, it nonetheless supports the model's merit. It also reinforces previous empirical findings that all too often methods of expected utility yield a biased measurement of v. How to overcome the bias due to the risk effect is the next topic of our inquiry.

4. IMPLICATIONS FOR MEASUREMENT

With respect to measuring the utility function v, Hagen's model has two implications: one concerns the choice of a measurement method and the other concerns a filtering procedure.

4.1. *Choice of a Measurement Method*

It is apparent from equation (6) that in order to minimize the potential impact of the risk effect on the measurement of v via a method of expected utility, the range of the gamble outcomes should be as small as possible. On the other hand, it cannot be overly small as to make the gamble insignificant. Hence, there arises the problem of establishing the outcome range that is optimal from the analytic and cognitive measurement criteria. It is a problem for further research.

At present, we recommend two measurement methods that avoid gambles over the extreme range of outcomes and allow the analyst some control over the outcome ranges. These are the uniform sequence gamble method described by Farquhar (1984) and the variable range gamble method of Krzysztofowicz and Duckstein (1980).

4.2. *Midpoint Sequence Method with Risk Effect Filter*

As noted in the introduction, the midpoint sequence gamble method offers features attractive for applications. It appears, therefore, a worthwhile proposition to retain the empirical part of the method, and to supplement the computational part with a procedure filtering the risk effect. The procedure suggested below is approximate but practical.

4.2.1. *Filtering Procedure*

Assess the certainty equivalents x_1, x_2, x_3, x_{23} according to equation (10). If $x_1 = x_{23}$, use the expected utility model (11) to compute v_1, v_2, v_3. If $x_1 \neq x_{23}$ and the subject has difficulty in reconciling the assessments, then conclude that his expressed preferences are affected by the risk associated with the gamble outcomes, and Hagen's model (12) should be employed to compute v_1, v_2, v_3. The risk factor γ can be found as a solution to reorganized equation (13),

$$\gamma(1-\gamma^2) = 4\Delta \tag{15}$$

in which Δ is substituted by an approximation $\hat{\Delta}$ obtained by linearizing the unknown utility function v, whereby

$$v_{23} - v_1 \simeq \hat{\Delta} = \frac{x_{23} - x_1}{x^* - x_0} \tag{16}$$

4.2.2. *Consistency Condition*

Equation (15) reveals interesting structural properties of Hagen's model. Within the admissible domain, $-1 < \gamma < 1$, function $\gamma(1-\gamma^2)$ attains two extrema at $\gamma_e = \pm 1/\sqrt{3} \simeq \pm 0.577$. Hence, in order to guarantee a solution, the utility difference Δ must satisfy the condition $(1-1/3)/\sqrt{3} \geq 4|\Delta|$, or equivalently

$$|\Delta| \leq \frac{1}{6\sqrt{3}} \simeq 0.096 \tag{17}$$

If this condition holds, then equation (15) has two solutions for γ, one on each side of γ_e. However, it is reasonable to suppose that γ must decrease monotonically as $|\Delta|$ decreases, and such behavior is assured only under the constraint

$$|\gamma| \leq \frac{1}{\sqrt{3}} \tag{18}$$

TABLE III

Behavioural interpretation of the filtering procedure

Relation between certainty equivalents	Risk factor γ	Relative to the prescription of the expected utility model based on v, the subject's reactions to gambles are	Relative to the expected utility measurements, the filtering procedure pulls the utility function
$x_{23} < x_1$	< 0	Overly risk averse	down
$x_{23} > x_1$	> 0	Overly risk seeking	up
$x_{23} = x_1$	$= 0$	Normatively correct	

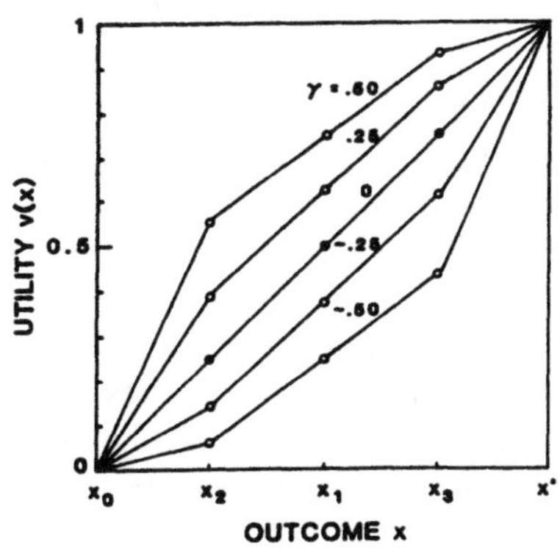

Fig. 2. Utility functions v computed from Hagen's model (equation (12)) for various values of the risk factor γ and equally spaced certainty equivalents.

which guarantees a unique solution. Interestingly, the empirical averages compiled in Table II meet this constraint.

Condition (17) states that within the framework of Hagen's model, the potential risk effect is limited. Given our linearization of v in equation (16), the practical implication is that a difference $x_{23} - x_1$ larger than 9.6% of the range $x^* - x_0$ must be considered as an inconsistency, violating Hagen's model, and therefore should be reconciled until $|\hat{\Delta}| < 0.096$. This is, undoubtedly, a less stringent measurement condition than that of the expected utility model: $|\hat{\Delta}| = 0$.

4.2.3. *Behavioural Interpretation of Filtering*

To get a feeling for the working of the filtering procedure, we have summarized its central points in Table III. The interpretation of the measurement

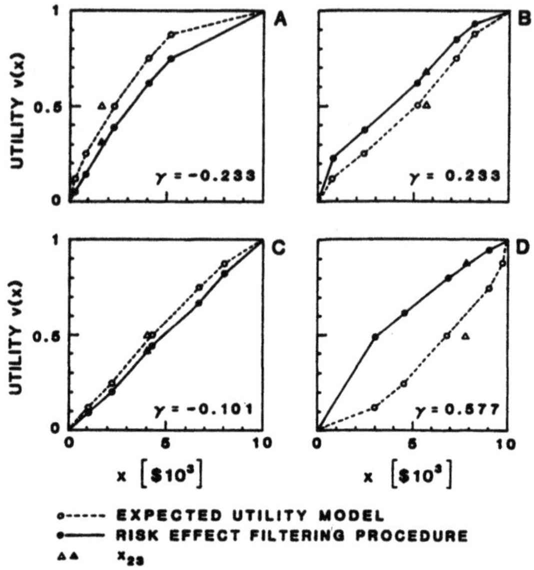

Fig. 3. Utility functions estimated through the expected utility model and the filtering procedure based on Hagen's model for four subjects from the Virginia Experiment.

bias in the third column of the table is in terms of the degree of risk attitude implied by the subject's responses in the framework of Hagen's model, relative to the degree of risk attitude that would be inferred from the subject's utility function v in the framework of the expected utility model. Figure 2 illustrates utility functions v that would have resulted from the filtering procedure for various values of γ, had the function computed from the expected utility model been linear.

As presented thus far, the filtering procedure supplies only three utility ordinates. This simplification has been maintained for the purpose of clarity of the exposition. An extension of the procedure supplying up to seven utility ordinates is presented in the Appendix.

4.2.4. An Application

An exemplary application of the filtering procedure to the data from the Virginia Experiment is shown in Figure 3. For each subject, the assessment provided five midpoints, plus x_{23}, which served to estimate two functions: one through the expected utility model and the other through the filtering procedure described above. The first observation to be made is that the filtering procedure reconciles the assessments of x_{23} and x_1, which the expected utility model shows as inconsistent. The second observation, vividly supported by the case of subject D, is that the discrepancies between the two functions can be dramatic: one may be convex and the other concave. This result does not come as a surprise; we have seen equally large discrepancies before, for instance, in the measurements from the Arizona Experiment. Such results only underscore the importance of the search for behaviourally correct utility measurement models.

5. CONCLUDING REMARKS

Starting from the premise that the empirical procedure of assessing certainty equivalents for two-outcome even-chance gambles has several plausible characteristics with respect to human judgments involved, our objective has been to supplement the popular midpoint sequence method of utility measurement with a filtering procedure; the procedure is to be used in lieu of the expected utility calculus whenever the assessed certainty equivalents indicate the presence of the risk effect. From an operational standpoint, the risk effect is synonymous with the range, dispersion, probability, and certainty effects that have been defined to explain the incoherences observed in utility functions obtained from the expected utility model. The proposed filtering procedure is an adaptation of a utility model described by Hagen some two decades ago. It is a simple, one-parameter model that purports to account for the risk effect. The new measurement method, called for short MSWU (midpoint-sequence weighted-utility), seems practical as it does not increase the experimental and computational effort significantly above that required by the traditional MSEU (midpoint-sequence expected-utility) method. The remaining question is whether or not the MSWU method yields unbiased measurements of cardinal utility functions. Toward that end further empirical research on validation of the method is called for.

ACKNOWLEDGEMENTS

This research was supported by the National Science Foundation under Grant ECE–8352536, Presidential Young Investigator Award.

APPENDIX
EXTENDED FILTERING PROCEDURE

The extended filtering procedure provides seven principal measurements of the utility function v, five equations for estimating and verifying the risk factor γ, and four consistency conditions. In total, it requires the assessment of 16 certainty equivalents, but it can be implemented in part with the number of certainty equivalents anywhere between 4 and 16.

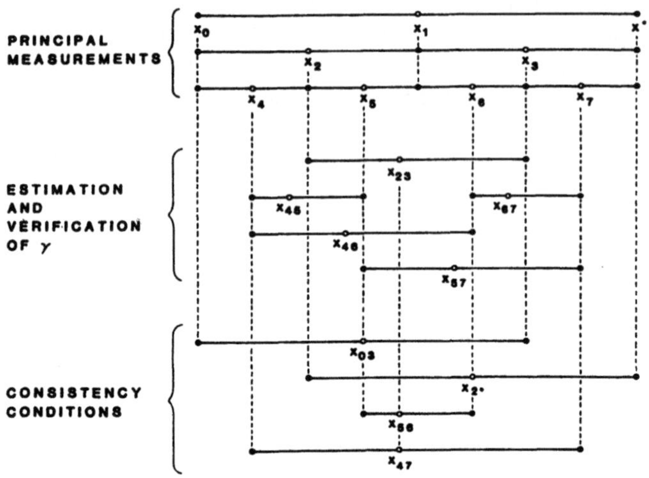

Fig. A1. Schematic illustration of assessments of the certainty equivalents for the extended filtering procedure.

TABLE A1

Principal utility measurements[a]

Utility ordinate	Expected utility model ($\gamma = 0$)	Hagen's weighted utility model ($\gamma \neq 0$)
v_1	0.5	$0.5\,(1+\gamma)$
v_2	0.25	$0.25\,(1+\gamma)^2$
v_3	0.75	$0.25\,(3-\gamma)(1+\gamma)$
v_4	0.125	$0.125\,(1+\gamma)^3$
v_5	0.375	$0.125\,(3-\gamma)(1+\gamma)^2$
v_6	0.625	$0.125\,(5-\gamma^2)(1+\gamma)$
v_7	0.875	$0.125\,(3-\gamma)(1-\gamma^2)+0.5(1+\gamma)$

[a] Equation (6).

A.1. Principal Measurements

Suppose the outcome set is $X = [x_0, x^*]$, the preference order increases from x_0 to x^*, and the utility function v on X is scaled by $v_0 = v(x_0) = 0$, and $v^* = v(x^*) = 1$. The principal measurements of v are provided by certainty equivalents $x_1, \ldots, x_7$ assessed according to the scheme shown in Figure A1, wherein $x_1 \sim (x_0, x^*)$, $x_2 \sim (x_0, x_1)$, and so on. Table A1 specifies the utility ordinates v_i assigned to x_i ($i = 1, \ldots, 7$) by the expected utility model, whenever $\gamma = 0$, and by Hagen's model, whenever $\gamma \neq 0$.

TABLE A2

Conditions for the estimation and verification of the risk factor γ

Inequality indicative of the risk effect	Utility difference equation
$x_{23} \neq x_1$	$v_{23} - v_1 = \Delta_{23} = 0.25\,\gamma(1-\gamma^2)$
$x_{45} \neq x_2$	$v_{45} - v_2 = \Delta_{45} = 0.5\,(1+\gamma)[0.25\,\gamma(1-\gamma^2)]$
$x_{67} \neq x_3$	$v_{67} - v_3 = \Delta_{67} = 0.5\,(1-\gamma)[0.25\,\gamma(1-\gamma^2)]$
$x_{46} \neq x_5$	$v_{46} - v_5 = \Delta_{46} = 0.5\,(1+\gamma)[0.25\,\gamma(1-\gamma^2)]$
$x_{57} \neq x_6$	$v_{57} - v_6 = \Delta_{57} = 0.5\,(1-\gamma)[0.25\,\gamma(1-\gamma^2)]$

A.2. *Estimation and Verification of* γ

The risk factor γ can be estimated based on one or more certainty equivalents from among $x_{23}, x_{45}, x_{67}, x_{46}, x_{57}$, assessed according to the scheme shown in Figure A1, wherein $x_{23} \sim (x_2, x_3)$, $x_{45} \sim (x_4, x_5)$, and so on. The presence of the risk effect is signaled by the inequalities listed in Table A2. Each inequality generates one equation displayed also in the table. It can be seen that the utility differences are related to one another, and thereby provide the verification conditions:

$$\text{(A1)}\qquad \begin{aligned} &\Delta_{45} = \Delta_{46} \\ &\Delta_{67} = \Delta_{57} \\ &\Delta_{23} = \Delta_{45} + \Delta_{67} = \Delta_{46} + \Delta_{57} \end{aligned}$$

In applications, utility differences Δ_{ij} can be approximated by linearizing the unknown utility function v. For instance, an approximation $\hat{\Delta}_{23}$ to Δ_{23} can be found as

$$\text{(A2)}\qquad v_{23} - v_1 \simeq \hat{\Delta}_{23} = \frac{x_{23} - x_1}{x^* - x_0}$$

Having estimated the utility differences, one can verify conditions (A1). Should they not be satisfied exactly, as one may expect in practice, the next step is to find the mean estimate of Δ_{23}, given by

$$\text{(A3)}\qquad \hat{\Delta} = \frac{1}{3}\,[\hat{\Delta}_{23} + \hat{\Delta}_{45} + \hat{\Delta}_{67} + \hat{\Delta}_{46} + \hat{\Delta}_{57}]$$

and then to insert it into the equation

$$\text{(A4)}\qquad \gamma(1-\gamma^2) = 4\Delta$$

whose solution yields the desired estimate for γ. Equation (A4) imposes certain consistency conditions which are discussed in section 4.2.2.

Having estimated γ and computed $v_1, \ldots, v_7$ by using formulas from Table A1, one can find v_{23}, v_{45}, v_{67}, v_{46}, v_{57} from the utility difference equations given in Table A2.

A.3. Consistency Conditions

The remaining four certainty equivalents x_{03}, x_{2^*}, x_{56}, x_{47}, assessed according to the scheme shown in Figure A1, provide a general check on the consistency of the assessments with Hagen's model. These consistency conditions are as follows:

$$\text{(A5)} \quad \begin{aligned} x_{03} &= x_5 \\ x_{2^*} &= x_6 \\ x_{56} &= x_{47} = x_{23} \end{aligned}$$

School of Engineering and Applied Science
University of Virginia
Thornton Hall
Charlottesville, Virginia, U.S.A.

REFERENCES

Allais, M. (1986) 'The general theory of random choices in relation to the invariant cardinal utility function and the specific probability function', presented at the *3rd International Conference on the Foundations and Applications of Utility, Risk, and Decision Theories*, Aix-en-Provence, France, June.

Farquhar, P.H. (1984) 'Utility assessment methods', *Management Science* **30** (11), 1283–1300.

Hagen, O. (1969) 'Separation of cardinal utility and specific utility of risk in theory of choices under uncertainty', *Statsøkonomisk Tidsskrift* **3**, 81–107, Bergen.

Hagen, O. (1979) 'Towards a positive theory of preferences under risk', in Allais, M. and Hagen, O. (Eds.), *Expected Utility Hypotheses and the Allais Paradox*, D. Reidel, Dordrecht, Holland, pp. 271–302.

Hagen, O. (1984) 'Neo-cardinalism', in Hagen, O. and Wenstøp, F. (Eds.), *Progress in Utility and Risk Theory*, D. Reidel, Dordrecht, Holland, pp. 145–164.

Krzysztofowicz, R. (1983) 'Strength of preference and risk attitude in utility measurement', *Organizational Behavior and Human Performance* **31**, 88–113.

Krzysztofowicz, R. (1994) 'Generic utility theory: explanatory model, behavioral hypotheses, empirical evidence', in this volume.

Krzysztofowicz, R. and Duckstein, L. (1980) 'Assessment errors in multiattribute utility functions', *Organizational Behavior and Human Performance* **26**, 326–348.

von Neumann, J. and Morgenstern, O. (1947) *Theory of Games and Economic Behavior*, Princeton University Press, Princeton, New Jersey, 2nd edn.

ROMAN KRZYSZTOFOWICZ

GENERIC UTILITY THEORY: EXPLANATORY MODEL, BEHAVIORAL HYPOTHESES, EMPIRICAL EVIDENCE

ABSTRACT. This is a fundamental, theoretical and experimental, inquiry into the nature of preferences expressed by an individual for the purpose of normative decision analysis. The generic utility theory axiomatizes choice among simple gambles and represents the strength of preference relation on the space of outcomes and probabilities $X \times P$ in terms of a cardinal utility function u. The theory enables us (i) to connect several behavioral phenomena with new necessary conditions for the multiplicative models, (ii) to obtain a general characterization of risk attitude which elucidates the restrictions within the expected utility theory, and (iii) to establish a link between the neo-cardinal and neo-Bernoullian interpretations of a cardinal utility function v on X. Furthermore, the theory provides a framework for the experimental measurement, for 54 subjects, of u on $X \times P$, and the components of its multiplicative decomposition $u(x,p) = v(x)r(p)$, the value function v and the risk function r. Their shapes confirm some of the anticipated as well as several novel behavioral hypotheses. The conclusions aim at crystallizing the empirical foundations for (i) nonlinear (in probability) utility models, and (ii) filters of probability-induced biases in the measurements of cardinal utility functions for the expected utility models.

1. INTRODUCTION

1.1. Background

1.1.1. Uniqueness of Utility Measurement

A cardinal utility function that provides a numerical representation of comparative strength (or intensity) of preference for one outcome over another is central to normative models of rational decision making under conditions of uncertainty, or with multiple objectives, or both. Yet the problem of measuring such a function reliably is unsettled. Discrepancies between empirical measurements obtained via different methods for the same individual and in seemingly identical decision situations, and alternative interpretations of the measurements themselves, have led to several schools of thought. The demarcation between them is the answer to the question of identity: Should the von Neumann–Morgenstern type utility function be identical with the Frisch–Pareto type utility function? If they need not be identical and the Frisch–Pareto type utility function gives the representation of the strength of preference, then what is being represented by the von Neumann–Morgenstern type utility function?[1]

From a cognitive standpoint, discrepancies between measurements via different methods have not been well understood, as yet. Although explanations have been offered for isolated categories of biases, we are still far away from a full-fledged error theory that would allow one to place some

M. Allais and O. Hagen (eds.), Cardinalism, 249–288.

sort of a confidence bound on the measurement of a utility function for normative applications.

1.1.2. Structure of Utility Representation

The second issue open for debate and research by results of empirical studies is the structure of representations of preferences for uncertain prospects (gambles or distribution functions over outcomes). While the dominant normative theory of expected utility orders gambles in terms of a functional that may be nonlinear in outcomes but is necessarily linear in probabilities, experimental findings have been suggesting that an individual's valuation of gambles may be nonlinear in probabilities as well. In response to this challenge, numerous new theories of decision making under uncertainty have been proposed in recent years. Most of them are descriptive and limited to offering a formal explanation of observed choices that are inconsistent with the prescription by expected utility. Some of these new theories are intended to be normative; to become operational they will have to be supplemented with empirical interpretations of their representations and suitable measurement methods. One point is clear, however. Measurement of the representation of a nonlinear theory will necessarily pose a more complex task than that present in the measurement of strength of preference over a set of outcomes – a problem which is still unresolved.

It appears, therefore, that in order to judge the empirical relevance of new utility theories and to advance our ability to apply the new and classical theories in normative decision analyses, research should proceed toward greater understanding of the fundamental measurements of expressed preferences.

1.2. Overview

This article reports the results of a fundamental inquiry into the nature of expressed preferences under conditions of uncertainty. The inquiry is both theoretical and experimental. Its objectives are (i) to add new insights and interpretations to the classical theories of utility, and (ii) to contribute empirical foundations for new developments of two kinds:

1. decision theories incorporating nonlinear (in probability) utility models – for those decision makers who accept postulates of rationality that allow such nonlinearities, and

2. filters of probability-induced biases in the measurements of cardinal utility functions that enter the expected utility models – for those decision makers who accept postulates of Bayesian rationality (Harsanyi, 1978).

1.2.1. Theoretical Inquiry

The first step of our inquiry is to formulate a generic utility theory – the minimal theory necessary for the fundamental measurement of the strength of preference on the space of outcomes and probabilities $X \times P$. A pair of points from $X \times P$ presents the individual with the simplest decision situation under uncertainty: he may take either one action that yields gain (or loss) x with probability p and the status quo otherwise, or another action that yields gain (or loss) z for sure. Since such a decision problem is, indeed, the simplest possible, the expressed preferences are assumed to be generic; that is, free of biases due to the measurement method. Any inconsistencies are attributed to random errors of perception – a result of human cognitive limitations.

Starting from the axioms of the algebraic-difference structure on the product space of simple gambles $(X \times P)^2$, a general form of the cardinal utility function u on $X \times P$ is obtained. One additional axiom, the probabilistic difference independence, leads to the two-piece multiplicative model for u and several interesting structural results. Among them is the demonstration that the behavioral phenomena observed when X is a continuum of losses and gains, such as reflection of risk attitude, and reflection duality property (quasi-reflection of utilities implies reflection of certainty equivalents, and vice versa), constitute *de facto* necessary conditions for the multiplicative, and in particular linear, utility models.

The generic utility theory offers a unifying structure for the comparison, interpretation, and measurement of constructs of the linear (expected) utility theory, the prospect theory, the CEVR model, and the anticipated utility theory. In particular, it provides a fundamental characterization of risk attitude on $X \times P$ which, in turn, enables us to elucidate the problem of inference of risk attitude within the linear utility theory; possible sources of historical controversies and confusions are highlighted and arguments are advanced in support of the viewpoint that (i) the axioms of the linear utility theory restrict the admissible risk attitude, and (ii) the relation between the Frisch–Pareto utility function and the von Neumann–Morgenstern utility function must be identity.

1.2.2. Experimental Inquiry

The generic utility theory provides a framework for the experimental part of the inquiry. Its main objective is to obtain a measurement of the cardinal utility function u on the space of outcomes and probabilities $X \times P$, a measurement that is free from assumptions about the form of u. To the best of my knowledge, this has never been accomplished before. The hypothesis that the utility of the simple gamble is a nonlinear function of the outcome and probability has been supported convincingly (e.g.

Allais, 1979; McCord and de Neufville, 1985), but indirectly, through inferences based on measurements only related to function u, not through measurements of u itself. In this inquiry, measurements of u are obtained for 54 subjects; the cross sections of u enable us not only to test hypotheses about the nonlinearity of u, but also to learn its empirical shapes.

Against the model-free surface of the utility function u, we can compare decomposable utility models, such as the multiplicative model $u(x, p) = v(x)r(p)$, a product of the value function v on X and the risk function r on P. Thus we may perform the ultimate, direct test of the validity of the decomposition and the underlying preference axiom.

The measurements of the value function v (a cardinal utility function of outcomes) are familiar, of course, but the measurements of the risk function r are unique, as are those presented recently by Allais (1986). Although several properties of r have been anticipated based on earlier, indirect empirical evidence, measurements of the entire risk functions are very significant for three reasons: (i) Within the generic utility theory, they provide a means of inferring risk attitude, and thus offer new insights into the nature of expressed preferences under conditions of uncertainty. (ii) For several nonlinear utility theories, they provide examples of the actual shapes that the theories should be able to accommodate. These shapes confirm some of the anticipated as well as several novel behavioral hypotheses. (iii) For the linear utility theory, they supply a vivid illustration of the probability effect – a cognitive noncompliance with the Bayesian rationality postulates (if one wishes to obey them) that should be filtered out during the assessment of a cardinal utility function of outcomes. A technique that can accomplish this is presented in the companion paper (Krzysztofowicz and Koch, 1989).

2. GENERIC THEORY

2.1. Preliminaries

2.1.1. Preference Relations

Let Ω be a set of objects denoted $\alpha, \beta, \gamma, \delta, \ldots$. A binary preference–indifference relation $\succsim$ is defined on Ω such that $\alpha \succsim \beta$ reads: "α is at least as preferred as β." The indifference $\alpha \sim \beta$ means $\alpha \succsim \beta$ and $\beta \succsim \alpha$. The strict preference $\alpha \succ \beta$ means $\alpha \succsim \beta$ and not $\beta \succsim \alpha$.

If the relation $\succsim$ is defined on $\Omega \times \Omega$, then the statement $\alpha \rightarrow \beta \succsim \gamma \rightarrow \delta$ means: "The strength of preference for β over α is at least as great as the strength of preference for δ over γ." A comparable difference between the strength of preference (or degrees of preference, intensities of preference) for outcomes in an ordered pair is termed, in short, a directed preference difference. The relation $\succsim$ can be operationalized in terms of a comparison between exchanges. The exchange $\alpha \to \beta$ is a situation wherein an individual having currently at hand the outcome α is given an opportunity to exchange α for β. The statement $\alpha \to \beta \succsim \gamma \to \delta$ means that the individual would view exchanging α for β (if his initial outcome were α) at least as preferred as exchanging γ for δ (if his initial outcome were γ).

2.1.2. Outcomes and Probabilities

Let $X = [x_*, x^*]$ denote a set of outcomes, a subset of the real line, bounded by the least preferred outcome x_* and the most preferred outcome x^*. It is assumed that the natural preference order on X is monotonically increasing, i.e. for any $x, y \in X$, $x \succ y \Leftrightarrow x > y$. An outcome x is interpreted as a change with respect to a status quo (a reference outcome) $x_0 = 0$. If $x_* < x_0 < x^*$, then $x \in [x_*, x_0)$ represents a loss, and $x \in (x_0, x^*]$ represents a gain.

Let $p \in P = [0, 1]$ denote a probability number. A point $(x, p) \in X \times P$ is interpreted as a simple gamble that yields outcome x with probability p and outcome x_0 (i.e. the status quo) with probability $1 - p$. Probability p is assumed to be given. We are interested in the class $\mathbf{G} = X \times P$ of all simple gambles. Throughout, the set elements will be denoted $F, G, H, K \in \mathbf{G}$, $x, y, z, w \in X$ and $p, q, s, t \in P$, when needed with primes, double primes, etc.

2.1.3. Connections Between Preference Relations

Suppose the relation $\succsim$ is defined on $\mathbf{G} \times \mathbf{G}$. It extends on $\mathbf{G}$ as follows:

$$(1) \qquad F \to G \succsim F \to H \Leftrightarrow G \succsim H$$

The relation $\succsim$ extends also on $X \times \mathbf{G}$ and $X \times X$ by including in $\mathbf{G}$ all degenerate simple gambles of the form $(x, 1)$. Then

$$(2) \qquad (x, 1) \to G \succsim (y, 1) \to H \Leftrightarrow x \to G \succsim y \to H$$

and

$$(3) \qquad (x, 1) \to (y, 1) \succsim (z, 1) \to (w, 1) \Leftrightarrow x \to y \succsim z \to w$$

The extension of $\succsim$ on X results from

$$(4) \qquad x \to y \succsim x \to w \Leftrightarrow y \succsim w$$

2.2. Generic Utility

What follows is the formal development leading to an operational representation of the strength of preference relation $\succsim$ on the space of simple gambles $X \times P$. Even though this development is straightforward, most of the details are stated for the sake of completeness as well as a background for interpretive analyses of empirical results presented in later sections.

2.2.1. *Cardinal Utility Functions on $X \times P$ and X*

Axiom 1. (Algebraic-difference structure.) The relational system $\langle \mathbf{G} \times \mathbf{G}, \succsim \rangle$, with $\mathbf{G} = X \times P$, is an algebraic-difference structure. (For the definition of such a structure see Appendix 1.)

Theorem 1. (Cardinal utility of gambles.) Suppose Axiom 1 holds. Then there exists a utility function $u : X \times P \to \mathrm{Re}$, unique up to a positive linear transformation (a cardinal scale), such that for all (x,p), (y,q), (z,s), $(w,t) \in X \times P$,

$$(x,p) \to (y,q) \succsim (z,s) \to (w,t) \Leftrightarrow u(y,q) - u(x,p) \geq u(w,t) - u(z,s) \tag{5}$$

Proof. See Krantz *et al.* (1971, p. 151).

Corollary 1. (Cardinal utility of outcomes.) Suppose Axiom 1 holds. Then there exists a utility function $v : X \to \mathrm{Re}$, unique up to a positive linear transformation (a cardinal scale), such that for all $x, y, z, w \in X$,

$$x \to y \succsim z \to w \Leftrightarrow v(y) - v(x) \geq v(w) - v(z) \tag{6}$$

Proof. In equation (5), set $p = q = s = t = 1$, then apply equation (3) on the left side, and define $v(x) = u(x,1)$ for all $x \in X$ on the right side. QED.

The last result amounts to Bernard's (1966, 1974) proposal: the cardinal utility of outcomes v can be obtained as a marginal function of the cardinal utility of simple gambles u. This relation is not useful from a measurement standpoint, however, for our problem is opposite: we know how to measure the unidimensional function v, and we would like to employ this measurement in the construction of the two-dimensional function u.[2] Our objective, therefore, is to establish an operational relation between u and v.

2.2.2. *Relation Between u and v*

With regard to measuring the strength of preference for gambles, Axiom 1 has two important implications; they are stated without a proof.

Lemma 1. (Certainty equivalent.) For every gamble $G \in \mathbf{G}$, there exists a unique outcome $x \in X$ such that $x \sim G$.

Lemma 2. (Substitutability.) If $x \sim G_x$, $y \sim G_y$, $z \sim G_z$, and $w \sim G_w$, then

$$(7) \qquad G_x \to G_y \succsim G_z \to G_w \Leftrightarrow x \to y \succsim z \to w$$

Relation (7) says that the directed preference differences between simple gambles can be substituted by the directed preference differences between certainty equivalents of these gambles.

Based on Lemma 1, we define a certainty equivalent function $\xi : X \times P \to X$ such that for every $(x,p) \in X \times P$,

$$(8) \qquad \xi(x,p) \sim (x,p)$$

Function ξ is increasing in both x and p, negative for $x < x_0$ and positive for $x > x_0$, and its boundary values are $\xi(\cdot,0) = x_0$, $\xi(x,1) = x$, and $\xi(x_0,\cdot) = x_0$.

Theorem 2. (Relation between cardinal utilities u and v.) For every $(x,p) \in X \times P$,

$$(9) \qquad u(x,p) = v(\xi(x,p))$$

Proof. Connect equations (5), (7), and (6), with appropriate substitutions of variables. QED.

The following scaling of v is assumed: $v(x_0) = 0$ and $v(x^*) = 1$. Thus $v(x) < 0$ if $x < x_0$, and $v(x) > 0$ if $x > x_0$. The scaling of v and the properties of ξ imply the following scaling of u:

$$(10) \qquad u(\cdot,0) = 0,\ u(\cdot,1) = v,\ u(x_0,\cdot) = 0$$

A general shape of u is shown in Figure 1; some of its components will be defined later. Relation (9) says that a simple gamble (x,p) has a cardinal utility $u(x,p)$ which is equal to the cardinal utility of the certainty equivalent of the gamble $v(\xi(x,p))$. Since both v and ξ can be measured, model (9) is operational.

2.2.3. Basis for Measurement

Let us first highlight implications of Axiom 1 for measurement. The first critical postulate is that an individual must accept the notion of ordering of exchanges of simple gambles, or, equivalently, the notion of comparability of the strength of preference for one gamble over another. Importantly, he has only to accept such a notion as plausible (so that u is a cardinal scale), but he has never to perform the task of ordering exchanges of gambles. It suffices that he is able to order exchanges of outcomes so that the measurement of the utility function v can take place. This is, in fact, a fundamental postulate of neo-cardinalists in economics. The second

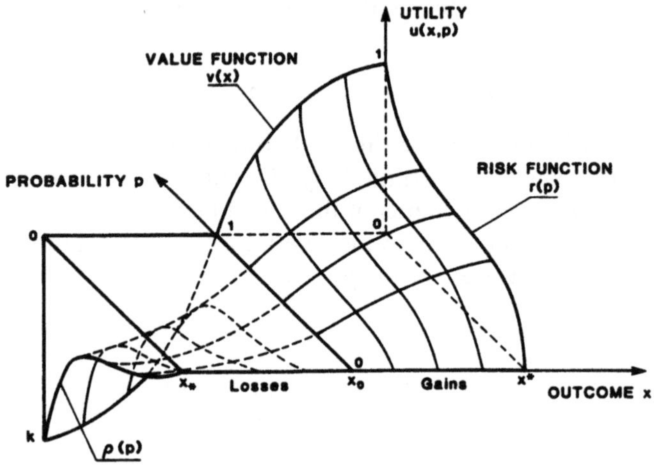

Fig. 1. General shape of the utility function u of simple gambles and components of its two-piece multiplicative decomposition.

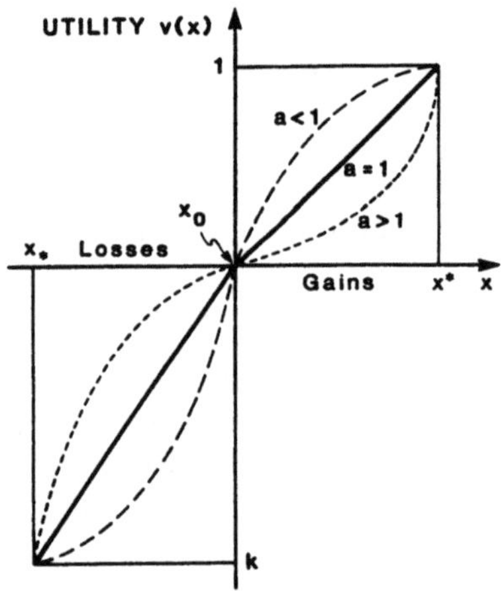

Fig. 2. Admissible shapes of the utility function v of outcomes when the utility function u of simple gambles is multiplicative and the individual is globally risk neutral.

important implication, stated as Lemma 1, is that the individual must be willing and able to specify a certainty equivalent for every simple gamble. The existence of the certainty equivalent function ξ is a basic tenet of neo-Bernoullians in decision theory.

In summary, relation (9) could be taken as a missing link between the two, often viewed as disjoint, classes of utility functions: (i) the cardinal utility functions that economists have been employing to represent strength of preference relations, as in equation (6), and (ii) the "other" cardinal utility functions that decision theorists have been using when ordering gambles in terms of utilities of their certainty equivalents, as in relation (9). We shall return to this point later on.

As a rationality postulate, Axiom 1 seems hardly disputable, amounting almost to tautology – at least with respect to its empirical testability and validity. It is also minimal, in the sense that it implies only the existence and an operational form of u but not its structure.[3] Hence relation (9) offers the most simple and general model for an empirical investigation of the structure of the utility function u on $X \times P$. Issues of particular interest are the degree of nonlinearity of u in both the outcomes x and the probabilities p, and the compatibility between u and various specialized, decomposable and parametric, models.

2.3. *Multiplicative Utility*

2.3.1. Decomposition Model

Consider three sets: $X_* = [x_*, x_0]$, the subdomain of losses; $X^* = [x_0, x^*]$, the subdomain of gains; and $X = X_* \cup X^*$, the entire domain of outcomes. For any $Z \in \{X_*, X^*, X\}$, let $\mathbf{G}(Z,p) = \{(x,p) : x \in Z\}$ be the class of all simple gambles on Z with a fixed probability $p \in P$.

Axiom 2. (Probabilistic difference independence.) The preference order on the set of all exchanges from $\mathbf{G}(Z,p) \times \mathbf{G}(Z,p)$ does not depend on $p \in P$; that is, for every $x, y, z, w, \in Z$ and some $p \in P$,

$$(x,p) \to (y,p) \succsim (z,p) \to (w,p) \Rightarrow \\ (x,q) \to (y,q) \succsim (z,q) \to (w,q)$$

for every $q \in P$.

Theorem 3. (Multiplicative utility.) Suppose the cardinal utility function u on $X \times P$ is given by relation (9). If Axiom 2 holds for $Z = X_*$, then for every $(x,p) \in X_* \times P$,

$$(11) \qquad u(x,p) = v(x)\rho(p)$$

If Axiom 2 holds for $Z = X^*$, then for every $(x,p) \in X^* \times P$,

$$(12) \qquad u(x,p) = v(x)r(p)$$

If Axiom 2 holds for $Z = X$, then equations (11) and (12) hold with $\rho = r$. Above,

$$v \text{ is scaled by } v(x_0) = 0,\ v(x^*) = 1$$

$$k = v(x_*)$$

$$\rho(p) = \frac{1}{k}\, v(\xi(x_*, p)) \tag{13}$$

$$r(p) = v(\xi(x^*, p))$$

Remark. Note that $\xi(x_*, \cdot) \leq x_0$, $\xi(x^*, \cdot) \geq x_0$; v is negative on X_* and positive on X^*; thus $k < 0$. Furthermore, r and ρ are positive everywhere, with $\rho(0) = r(0) = 0$ and $\rho(1) = r(1) = 1$. Thus u is negative on $X_* \times P$ and positive on $X^* \times P$. Its extremes are $u(x_*, 1) = k$ and $u(x^*, 1) = 1$. Function u and its components are illustrated in Figure 1.

Proof. Axiom 2 implies that for every p, $u(\cdot, p)$ on Z is a positive linear transformation of $u(\cdot, q)$ for some q, i.e.

$$u(x, p) = \rho(p) u(x, q) + s(p)\,, \quad \rho(p) > 0$$

Let $q = 1$; the scaling conditions (10) imply $u(x, 1) = v(x)$. Furthermore, $u(x_0, p) = 0 = \rho(p)v(x_0) + s(p)$, which gives $s(p) = 0$ since $v(x_0) = 0$. If $Z = X_*$, then $u(x_*, p) = v(\xi(x_*, p)) = \rho(p)v(x_*)$, so that $\rho(p) = v(\xi(x_*, p))/v(x_*)$. If $Z = X^*$, then $u(x^*, p) = v(\xi(x^*, p)) = r(p)v(x^*)$, from which $r(p) = v(\xi(x^*, p))$ since $v(x^*) = 1$. If $Z = X$, then the same positive linear transformation must hold everywhere on X; consequently $\rho = r$. QED.

2.3.2. *Interpretation and Assessment*

Theorem 3 specifies a two-piece multiplicative decomposition of the utility function u in terms of three marginal functions: a utility function v, which will also be termed a value function, and two risk functions ρ and r. The utility function v encodes strength of preference for outcomes in X. The risk functions ρ and r encode risk attitude toward gambles on the subdomains of losses X_* and gains X^*, respectively. This interpretation of ρ and r, which explains their names, is elaborated on in the next section.

To obtain u, one has to assess the utility function v on X and two certainty equivalent functions $\xi(x_*, \cdot)$ and $\xi(x^*, \cdot)$ on P. If Axiom 2 holds for the entire domain X, then the risk functions ρ and r are identical and can be obtained via either $\xi(x_*, \cdot)$ or $\xi(x^*, \cdot)$. If Axiom 2 holds for X_* and X^* but not for X, then there occur reversals between preferences on $\mathbf{G}(X, p) \times \mathbf{G}(X, p)$ and preferences on $\mathbf{G}(X, q) \times \mathbf{G}(X, q)$ for some $p, q \in P$. For instance, an individual may state that (with x in \$)

$$(-600, 0.8) \rightarrow (100, 0.8) \succ (100, 0.8) \rightarrow (1000, 0.8)$$

but that

$$(-600, 0.1) \rightarrow (100, 0.1) \prec (100, 0.1) \rightarrow (1000, 0.1)$$

In such a case, the risk function for losses ρ is distinct from that for gains r.

Each segment of the two-piece multiplicative model, (11) and (12), is structurally identical to a version of the subjectively expected utility (SEU) model, restricted to simple gambles (x, p). Edwards (1955), and later Slovic and Lichtenstein (1968), conducted extensive experiments aimed at estimating and verifying the SEU model. Both studies found that generally $\rho \neq r$.

3. RISK ATTITUDE

3.1. Basic Characterization

Types of risk attitude are defined in the usual way based on the preference between receiving the expected outcome xp for sure or having the outcome determined by the gamble (x, p).

Definition 1. At (x, p), an individual is risk averse (RA) if $xp \succ (x, p)$, risk seeking (RS) if $xp \prec (x, p)$, risk neutral (RN) if $xp \sim (x, p)$.

Since the preference order on X is assumed to be increasing, Definition 1 implies that at (x, p) an individual's attitude is

$$(14) \qquad \left.\begin{matrix} \text{RA} \\ \text{RS} \\ \text{RN} \end{matrix}\right\} \iff \xi(x,p) \left\{\begin{matrix} < \\ > \\ = \end{matrix}\right\} xp$$

The difference $\pi(x, p) = xp - \xi(x, p)$ is called the risk premium.

For further development, it is advantageous to introduce the reference utility function u_0 which the individual would have if he were RN at every (x, p):

$$(15) \qquad u_0(x,p) = v(xp)$$

Since v is increasing and one-to-one, equations (9), (14), and (15) imply that at (x, p) an individual's attitude is

$$(16) \qquad \left.\begin{matrix} \text{RA} \\ \text{RS} \\ \text{RN} \end{matrix}\right\} \iff u(x,p) \left\{\begin{matrix} < \\ > \\ = \end{matrix}\right\} u_0(x,p)$$

If risk attitude is of one type at every (x, p), then one can speak of global risk attitude.

3.2. Characterization via Risk Function

If the two-piece multiplicative model (11) and (12) holds, then equations (15) and (16) imply that risk attitude is characterized by ρ on the domain of losses, and by r on the domain of gains. For further detailed analyses, let us assume that $\rho = r$ so that the multiplicative model $u(x,p) = v(x)r(p)$ holds everywhere on $X \times P$. With the reference risk function defined as

$$(17) \qquad r_0(p) = v(x^*p)$$

the type of risk attitude at (x,p) can be inferred from the risk function r as follows:

$$(18) \qquad \begin{matrix} \text{For losses:} & \text{For gains:} \\ \text{RS} & \text{RA} \\ \text{RA} & \text{RS} \\ \text{RN} & \text{RN} \end{matrix} \left.\vphantom{\begin{matrix}a\\a\\a\\a\end{matrix}}\right\} \Longleftrightarrow r(p) \left\{ \begin{matrix} < \\ > \\ = \end{matrix} \right\} r_0(p)$$

In the multiplicative model, the two components of a preference under uncertainty are separated: strength of preference varies only with the outcome x and is encoded in the value function v; risk attitude varies only with the probability p and is encoded in the risk function r. However, it is not possible to infer the type of risk attitude from r alone. Knowledge of v is necessary in order to compute r_0. Thus r provides a relative characterization. Both the risk function r and the reference risk function r_0 are characteristics of an individual.

Perhaps the most important observation to be derived from equation (18) is that the multiplicative model contains in its structure the phenomenon of reflection of risk attitude. That is, if for some p the individual is RA for gains then he is RS for losses, and vice versa. Such risk patterns have been widely reported in the literature (Lorange and Norman, 1973; Kahneman and Tversky, 1979; Fishburn and Kochenberger, 1979; Payne *et al.*, 1980, 1981; Laughhunn *et al.*, 1980; Slovic *et al.*, 1982; Krzysztofowicz, 1983), which suggests that in some instances Axiom 2 (with $Z = X$) may be behaviorally relevant.

Risk patterns without the reflection phenomenon (RA for gains and losses, RS for gains and losses) violate the multiplicative model. Still, it is possible that preferences containing such patterns of risk attitude conform to the two-piece multiplicative model whose structure does not imply the reflection phenomenon.

3.3. Strength of Risk Attitude

Following an idea of Friedman and Savage (1948), the strength of risk attitude at (x,p) is defined by:

$$(19) \qquad s(x,p) = u_0(x,p) - u(x,p)$$

with $s(x,p) > 0$ for risk aversion, $s(x,p) < 0$ for risk seeking, and $s(x,p) = 0$ for risk neutrality. Taking the difference of utilities makes sense here because, via equations (9) and (16), $s(x,p) =$

$v(xp) - v(\xi(x,p))$, the difference of cardinal utilities. Recall that $\xi(x,p)$ is the minimum sure outcome an individual is willing to accept in lieu of the gamble with the expected outcome xp. Hence one can say that $s(x,p)$ measures the strength of preference for the expected outcome xp over the minimum acceptable sure outcome $\xi(x,p)$.

Another way of interpreting equation (19) is as follows. Suppose $x > x_0$. An individual who is just willing to accept the sure outcome $\xi(x,p)$ in lieu of the gamble (x,p) is actually trading off the desirability of x for the security of $\xi(x,p)$. Inasmuch as on the utility scale, the decrease in the degree of desirability, measured by $\sigma(x,p) = v(x) - v(\xi(x,p))$, must be equal to the increase in the degree of security, taking $\sigma(x,p)$ as a measure of the degree of preference for security (or the strength of absolute risk aversion) would seem appropriate. If the individual were RN then $\sigma_0(x,p) = v(x) - v(xp)$. If now we agree to measure the strength of one's risk aversion relative to the strength he would exhibit if he were RN, then $s(x,p) = \sigma(x,p) - \sigma_0(x,p)$, as specified in equation (19). By introducing the reference value $\sigma_0(x,p)$, we can categorize an individual as RA, or RS, or RN, and thus maintain the consistency between the ordinal measures of risk attitude, equations (14), (16), (18), and the cardinal measure, equation (19).

When v is linear, then $s(x,p)$ is proportional to the risk premium $\pi(x,p)$. Therefore, equation (19) can be viewed as a generalization of the concept of measuring the strength of risk attitude in terms of risk premium.[4]

When the multiplicative model holds, then

$$(20) \qquad s(x,p) = v(x)[r_0(p) - r(p)]$$

Note that while the type of risk attitude (RA,RS,RN) may vary only with the probability p (equation (18)), the strength of risk attitude may vary with both the probability p and the outcome x.

3.4. Monotonic Strength of Risk Attitude

From the scaling conditions (10), it follows that $s(\cdot,0) = 0$, $s(\cdot,1) = 0$, and $s(x_0,\cdot) = 0$. Thus on X_*, $s > 0$ can be monotonically decreasing, and $s < 0$ can be monotonically increasing. On X^*, $s > 0$ can be monotonically increasing, and $s < 0$ can be monotonically decreasing. On P, $s \neq 0$ cannot be monotonic. Consequently, the following types of monotonic strength of risk attitude are admissible.

On X_*, for any $p \in (0,1)$: decreasingly RA, or increasingly RS, or constantly RN.

On X^*, for any $p \in (0,1)$: increasingly RA, or decreasingly RS, or constantly RN.

On P, for any $x \in X$: constantly RN.

4. IMPLICATIONS OF MULTIPLICATIVE UTILITY

The multiplicative utility model exhibits several interesting properties. They are also important for they provide behavioral hypotheses through which the descriptive validity of the model can be tested empirically. Moreover, these properties will help us to elucidate the connections among the generic theory, the linear theory, the prospect theory, the CEVR model, and the anticipated utility theory.

4.1. Certain Properties

Recall first the two-piece multiplicative utility function u on $X \times P$ specified by Theorem 3. On the subdomain $X_* \times P$, u is constructed from two functions: v on X_* and $\xi(x_*, \cdot)$ on P; on the subdomain $X^* \times P$, u is constructed from two functions: v on X^* and $\xi(x^*, \cdot)$ on P. Each of the four functions may be assessed, or chosen, independently of the other three functions.

The multiplicative utility function u on $X \times P$ imposes a restriction: the risk functions ρ and r must be identical. Consequently, the four functions used in the construction of u must satisfy the following relation, implied by $r = \rho$ via equation (13): for every $p \in P$,

$$v(\xi(x^*, p)) = \frac{1}{k} v(\xi(x_*, p))$$

Hence, only three out of four functions may be assessed freely. For instance, given the utility function v on $X_* \cup X^*$ and the certainty equivalent function $\xi(x_*, \cdot)$ on P, one can find the other certainty equivalent function as

$$\xi(x^*, p) = v^{-1}[v(\xi(x_*, p))/k]$$

Likewise, knowing both certainty equivalent functions and the utility function v on the subdomain of losses X_*, one can find the utility function v on the subdomain of gains X^*. Specifically, let $f : X^* \to X_*$ such that $\xi(x_*, p) = f(\xi(x^*, p))$ for every $p \in P$. By inserting mapping f into the relation $r = \rho$, and denoting $z = \xi(x^*, p)$ and $X^* = \xi(x^*, P)$, one obtains, for every $z \in X^*$,

$$v(z) = \frac{1}{k} v(f(z))$$

We shall now explore several implications of these relations in conjunction with additional structural assumptions.

Theorem 4. (Quasi-reflection of utilities.) Suppose $x^* > 0, x_* = -x^*$, and the utility function u on $X \times P = [x_*, x^*] \times [0, 1]$ is multiplicative, with

$\rho = r$. If the marginal certainty equivalent functions $\xi(x_*, \cdot)$ and $\xi(x^*, \cdot)$ on P are reflections of one another, in the sense that $\xi(x^*, p) = -\xi(x_*, p)$ for every $p \in P$, then the utility function v on X is quasi-odd, i.e. for every $x \in [0, x^*]$ and some $k < 0$,

$$(21) \qquad v(x) = \frac{1}{k} v(-x)$$

Proof. The identity $r = \rho$ implies, via equation (13), $v(\xi(x^*, p)) = v(\xi(x_*, p))/k = v(-\xi(x^*, p))/k$ for every $p \in P$. With $z = \xi(x^*, p)$ and $[0, x^*] = \xi(x^*, P)$, one obtains $v(z) = v(-z)/k$ for every $z \in [0, x^*]$. QED.

Corollary 2. (Reflection of certainty equivalents.) If the utility function u on $X \times P$ is multiplicative, with $\rho = r$, and the utility function v on X is quasi-odd, then the certainty equivalent function $\xi(\cdot, p)$ on X is odd, i.e. for every $x \in X$,

$$(22) \qquad \xi(x, p) = -\xi(-x, p)$$

Proof. Suppose $x > 0$; then $v(\xi(x, p)) = v(x)r(p) = v(-x)r(p)/k = v(\xi(-x, p))/k = v(-\xi(-x, p))$; note that $\xi(-x, p) < 0$. Suppose $x < 0$; then $v(\xi(x, p)) = v(x)r(p) = kv(-x)r(p) = kv(\xi(-x, p)) = v(-\xi(-x, p))$; note that $\xi(-x, p) > 0$. QED.

[Note that equation (22) implies $\xi(x^*, p) = -\xi(x_*, p)$, an assumption of Theorem 4.] In effect, we have proven that under the multiplicative representation of the utility on the entire domain of simple gambles, encompassing losses and gains, quasi-reflection of the utilities of outcomes must be accompanied by reflection of the certainty equivalents of simple gambles, and vice versa. We shall term equations (21) and (22) the reflection duality property.

Although relations (21) and (22) must hold simultaneously, they are testable independently since v and ξ can be separately measured. This distinction between the two properties was absent in past studies of "the reflection effect". The empirical evidence cited earlier in Section 3.2 supports relation (21). On the other hand, the experimental results presented by Cohen *et al.* (1985) contradict (22); however, these experiments involved the range of outcomes $[x_*, x^*] = \$[-150, 150]$ which seems too small to uncover decisive preference patterns for money. Further experiments are in order.

Theorem 5. (Constant elasticities model.) Suppose the multiplicative model holds on $[x_*, x^*] \times [0, 1]$ with $x^* = -x_*$, and the individual is globally RN. Then there exist constants $a > 0$ and $k < 0$ such that

$$\text{(23)} \qquad u_0(x,p) = \begin{cases} k\left(\dfrac{x}{x_*}\right)^a p^a \ , & x \in [x_*, 0] \\ \left(\dfrac{x}{x^*}\right)^a p^a \ , & x \in [0, x^*] \end{cases}$$

Proof. If the individual is RN, then his utility $u_0(x,p) = v(x)r_0(p)$ can be written as $v(xp) = v(x)v(x^*p)$ which for $x \geq 0$ implies that v is a power function of x (see Roberts, 1979, p. 166, Corollary 1). This, together with our scaling conditions implies $v(x) = (x/x^*)^a$, with $a > 0$ since v must be increasing. Consequently, $r_0(p) = v(x^*p) = p^a$. Theorem 4 states that for $x \leq 0$, $v(x) = kv(-x)$, where $k < 0$; thus $v(x) = k(-x/x^*)^a = k(x/x_*)^a$. QED.

We have thus identified a condition under which the utility function v of outcomes is a two-piece power function specified by two parameters, the exponent a and the scaling constant k. As illustrated in Figure 2, this function may be linear for losses and gains ($a = 1$), convex for losses and concave for gains ($a < 1$), or concave for losses and convex for gains ($a > 1$).

Equation (23) is a special case of the CEVR model of Bernard (1966, 1974) which is discussed, along with the notion of elasticity, in Section 4.4.

4.2. Connection With Linear Utility Theory

4.2.1. Identity of Measurements

In the linear utility theory of von Neumann and Morgenstern (1947), the utility of a simple gamble $(x,p) \in \mathbf{G}$ is $u_L(x,p) = \nu(x)p$, where ν is a utility function of outcomes. The structure of u_L constitutes a special case of the generic multiplicative model with $r(p) = p$ and $u(x,p) = v(x)p$. Thus to guarantee the same order on $\mathbf{G}$ by u_L and u, the normative relation between the Frisch–Pareto utility function v and the von Neumann–Morgenstern utility function ν must be identity, as claimed by Friedman and Savage (1948), Markowitz (1952), Allais (1953), Siegel (1956), Davidson, *et al.* (1957), Halter and Dean (1971), de Finetti (1974), Harsanyi (1977), Hagen (1984), and others. This conclusion differs from many contemporary viewpoints, but concurs, it seems, with the genuine intention of von Neumann and Morgenstern (1947) who sought an operational method of measuring "utility differences", or "distances" in the sense of Pareto (1927).[5] An empirical relation between v and ν is another matter, of course, and we shall address it later.

4.2.2. Structural Properties

Inasmuch as $u_L(x,p) = \nu(x)p$ is a special case of the generic multiplicative model, the following conditions are imbedded in the structure of linear theory: risk attitude reflection phenomenon (18), and reflection duality property (quasi-reflection of utilities of outcomes (21) must be accompanied by reflection of certainty equivalents of simple gambles (22), and vice versa). These properties are proven here to be a part of the linear utility theory although they have often been hypothesized or uncovered experimentally. The key modelling postulate leading to these properties is the definition of outcome x as a change (loss or gain) with respect to a status quo, rather than as a terminal state (final asset position, or total wealth).

It was already Markowitz (1952) who argued perceptively (i) that a utility function ν of money x should be defined not for the total wealth but rather for gains and losses with respect to the present wealth x_0, (ii) that ν is quasi-reflexive, and (iii) that in the vicinity of x_0, ν is steeper for losses than for gains. Properties (ii) and (iii) have found support in experimental data compiled by Kahneman and Tversky (1979). The risk attitude reflection phenomenon has also been demonstrated conclusively; see references in Section 3.2.

4.2.3. Inference of Risk Attitude

The restriction which the linear utility theory imposes on risk attitude, by requiring $r(p) = p$, has important implications. To derive them, observe that (i) for every $p \in P$, there exists $x \in [0, x^*]$ such that $p = x/x^* = -x/x_*$, where $x_* = -x^*$, and (ii) from equations (13) and (17), $r_0(p) = v(x^*p) = v(x_*p)/k$; with the above change of variables, $r_0(p) = v(x) = v(-x)/k$. When these substitutions are introduced into relation (18), the following equivalent statement is obtained.

(24) For losses: $\left.\begin{matrix}\text{RS}\\ \text{RA}\\ \text{RN}\end{matrix}\right\} \iff \dfrac{kx}{x_*}\left\{\begin{matrix}>\\<\\=\end{matrix}\right\} v(x)$ For gains: $\left.\begin{matrix}\text{RA}\\ \text{RS}\\ \text{RN}\end{matrix}\right\} \iff \dfrac{x}{x^*}\left\{\begin{matrix}<\\>\\=\end{matrix}\right\} v(x)$

In other words, the type of risk attitude can be inferred from the shape of the utility function v relative to the linear function. In particular, the inference based on Jensen's inequality holds. Thus, contrary to some opinions, the linear theory does not contain the assumption of RN attitude, just a restriction on the admissible attitudes.

It is important to distinguish between attribution and inference. The utility function v provides a fundamental measurement of the strength of preference. Its shape can be attributed to the changes in the strength of preference for equally spaced outcomes. Thus, it is meaningful to speak of marginal utility of outcomes. Within the linear theory, function v permits one also to infer an individual's risk attitude. It is incorrect, however, to attribute the shape of v to risk attitude.[6]

By comparing relation (18) with relation (24) we may elucidate a possible source of confusion. Within the generic theory, the type of risk attitude is inferred in the domain of probabilities P by comparing the risk function r with the reference risk function r_0. The linear theory imposes a structural restriction on r such that when the inference of risk attitude is transferred from the domain of probabilities P to the domain of outcomes X, the risk function r becomes a two-piece linear function, while the reference risk function r_0 becomes the utility function v. When considering relation (24) alone, one may easily be misled to believe that the two-piece linear function is a reference, while the utility function v is the construct that measures (or is supposed to measure) risk attitude.[7]

4.2.4. Admissible Risk Attitude

The existence of an individual's cardinal utility function, being an implication of our Axiom 1, can be admitted prior to, and independently of, the acceptance of axioms of the linear theory. If subsequently the individual accepts these axioms as the rationality postulates for decision making under uncertainty, then he must conform his risk attitude to that prescribed jointly by the axioms and his utility function v. In the operational sense, his marginal certainty equivalent function $\xi(x^*, \cdot)$ must satisfy the relation $r(p) = v(\xi(x^*,p)) = p$. Inasmuch as the restriction is imposed on certainty equivalents, in terms of which risk attitude is defined, one may say that the linear theory restricts the admissible risk attitude.

For example, suppose that an individual's utility function v of outcomes x is a two-piece power function as in equation (23). Then his risk function is

$$(25) \qquad r(p) = v(\xi(x^*,p)) = \left[\frac{\xi(x^*,p)}{x^*}\right]^a$$

By equating $r(p)$ with p, we find

$$(26) \qquad \xi(x^*,p) = x^* p^{1/a}$$

In other words, once the utility function v has been assessed and parameter a estimated, the linear theory prescribes a unique marginal certainty equivalent function $\xi(x^*, \cdot)$. If a has not yet been assessed, then the linear theory itself can be employed as a measurement theory, at least in principle. More on this later.

4.2.5. Transformation Between v and ν

Recently, the concept of relative risk attitude was appended to linear utility theory (Camacho, 1979; Dyer and Sarin, 1982). It postulates that risk attitude is to be inferred from the shape of a transformation w such that

$\nu(x) = w(v(x))$. That is, risk attitude is defined relative to the utility function v. Concave $w \Leftrightarrow$ RA attitude, convex $w \Leftrightarrow$ RS attitude, linear $w \Leftrightarrow$ RN attitude. The idea of the transformation w is not new; it already appeared in the utility theory of Krelle (1968), which he recently restated (Krelle, 1984), as well as in the works of Bernard (1974), and Keeney and Raiffa (1976).

Inferring risk attitude from w is tantamount to postulating that the von Neumann–Morgenstern utility function ν encodes both the strength of preference and risk attitude, while the Frisch–Pareto utility function v encodes strength of preference only (see Camacho, 1979; Dyer and Sarin, 1982; Krzysztofowicz, 1983; Keller, 1985). This postulate does not seem to be correct. For if an individual's risk attitude is admissible within the linear theory, then $r(p) = p$, and necessarily $\nu = v$. If $r(p) \neq p$, then clearly $\nu \neq v$. In such a case, relation (18) implies that in order to infer risk attitude, we have to measure two functions: $v(\cdot)$ of x and $\xi(x^*, \cdot)$ of p. Hence, it is impossible that $\nu(\cdot)$, being a function of x alone, could properly encode risk attitude. McCord and de Neufville (1984) show several ν curves assessed for the same subject by using gambles with different probabilities. Systematic discrepancies between the resulting ν curves can be discerned, suggesting that a more general transformation, of the form $\nu_p(x) = w_p(v(x))$, is necessary to explain the data.[8]

If we accept that normatively $\nu = v$, then the transformation w must be linear. Consequently, the experimental studies of Allais (1979), Krzysztofowicz (1983), McCord and de Neufville (1984), and Keller (1985), which reveal that the transformation w is most often nonlinear, confirm the concern of many students of utility that the gamble-based methods of the linear theory provide a distorted measurement of the cardinal utility. Allais (1953), Hagen (1969), and Bernard (1974) anticipated this.

4.2.6. Conclusion

The problems raised above have no bearing on the normative plausibility of the linear utility theory.[9] But to retain it as a measurement theory as well will require intensive experimental research in order to identify those utility assessment techniques and their parameters (such as probability values and ranges of outcomes) which produce the least distortions, relative to other techniques.[10] Recent works of McCord and de Neufville (1986), McCord and Leotsarakos (1986), and de Neufville and Delquie (1986) aim in this direction. An alternative is to develop a new class of assessment techniques based on the nonlinear utility theory, as proposed by Krzysztofowicz and Koch (1989).

4.3. *Connection With Prospect Theory*

A class of descriptive preference models, which generalize the linear utility model by allowing a nonlinear transformation of probabilities, includes the subjectively expected utility (Edwards, 1955), certainty-equivalence theory (Handa, 1977), subjectively weighted utility (Karmarkar, 1978, 1979), and prospect theory (Kahneman and Tversky, 1979).

Prospect theory applied to choices from **G** states that the utility of a simple gamble $(x,p) \in \mathbf{G}$ is $u_P(x,p) = \mu(x)\pi(p)$. Structurally this model is identical with the generic multiplicative model $u(x,p) = v(x)r(p)$. The main distinction lies in the axiom systems. Prospect theory is solely descriptive, and its axioms have no operational interpretation that would allow one to directly assess the component functions μ and π. The form of these functions is neither derived nor assessed. Instead it is hypothesized so as to explain general tendencies observed in choices under uncertainty.

Because of the structural identity between the models, the following conditions proven earlier for the multiplicative model are also imbedded in prospect theory: risk attitude reflection phenomenon, relation (18), and reflection duality property (quasi-reflection of utilities of outcomes, relation (21), must be accompanied by reflection of certainty equivalents of simple gambles, relation (22), and vice versa).

Conditions (18) and (21) were observed by Kahneman and Tversky in experimental choice data and, although not proven, they were appended to prospect theory. Specifically, the value function μ was hypothesized to be commonly concave for gains, convex for losses, and steeper for losses than for gains (which in terms of our model implies $k < -1$). The weighting function π was hypothesized to be generally convex and such that $\pi(p) < p$, except for low probabilities where $\pi(p) > p$. Given these specific forms of μ and π, the inference of risk attitude within the prospect theory (Kahneman and Tversky, 1979, p. 285) is a special case of the general inference procedure described in Section 3.

4.4. *Connection With CEVR Model*

A general cardinal utility function u of simple gambles $(x,p) \in \mathbf{G}$ was suggested by Bernard (1966, 1974). Appended to his proposal was the hypothesis that in the realm of economic decisions, wherein x is money, the utility function u over the middle of the domain $X^* \times P$ could be approximated reasonably well by a multiplicative model having constant elasticities with respect to value (outcome) and risk (probability) – the CEVR model:

$$(27) \qquad u(x,p) = \left(\frac{x}{x^*}\right)^a p^c\,, \quad x \in [0, x^*]$$

where $a > 0$ and $c > 0$. The elasticities of the utility u with respect to outcome x and probability p are

$$\text{(28)} \qquad \frac{du(x,p)}{dx}\frac{x}{u(x,p)} = a \text{ and } \frac{du(x,p)}{dp}\frac{p}{u(x,p)} = c$$

Bernard suspected that as p approaches the extremes, 0 or 1, the probability elasticity c becomes variable, but, as he noted (Bernard, 1974, p. 221), "only experiments could teach us" about its real behavior. We shall return to these hypotheses in the analysis of empirical results in Section 5.2.

4.5. Connection With Anticipated Utility Theory

Quiggin (1982, 1985) formulated an axiomatic theory leading to a multiplicative utility model which is nonlinear in probabilities and, unlike the models of the prospect theory variety, it maintains the principles of transitivity and dominance and thus has a normative appeal. Specifically, the utility $u_A(\mathbf{x}, \mathbf{p})$ of a gamble $(\mathbf{x}, \mathbf{p}) = [(x_1, \ldots, x_n), (p_1, \ldots, p_n)]$, which yields outcome x_i with probability p_i, $\Sigma p_i = 1$, and whose outcomes form an increasing preference chain $x_1 \precsim x_2 \precsim \ldots \precsim x_n$, is specified by

$$\text{(29)} \qquad u_A(\mathbf{x}, \mathbf{p}) = \sum_{i=1}^{n} v(x_i)h_i(\mathbf{p})$$

where v is a cardinal utility function of outcomes, and h_i is a probability weighting function given by

$$\text{(30)} \qquad h_i(\mathbf{p}) = f(\sum_{k=1}^{i} p_k) - f(\sum_{k=1}^{i-1} p_k)$$

The cumulative probability transformation f is increasing on $[0, 1]$ and scaled by $f(0) = 0$ and $f(1) = 1$.

Applying model (29) to a simple gamble $(x, p) \in \mathbf{G}$ gives its utility $u_A(x, p) = v(x)h(p)$ with $h(p) = 1 - f(1-p)$. Thus to guarantee the same order on $\mathbf{G}$ by u_A and the generic multiplicative model $u(x, p) = v(x)r(p)$, the relation between the cumulative probability transformation and the risk function must be

$$\text{(31)} \qquad f(p) = 1 - r(1 - p)$$

It follows that the constructs of the generic utility theory, v and r, provide all information needed for an application of the anticipated utility model. However, to conform to Quiggin's (1982) axioms, the risk function must satisfy a reflexivity condition:

$$\text{(32)} \qquad r(p) = 1 - r(1 - p)$$

which also implies that $r = f$. In Section 5.2 we shall examine empirical measurements of r and determine the extent to which they satisfy condition (32).

Model (29)–(31) has also been suggested by Allais (1986), without an axiomatic foundation but with an empirical support in the form of risk functions r estimated for four subjects. None of them satisfied condition (32).

Inasmuch as the structure of $u_A(x, p)$ is multiplicative, the following conditions proven earlier for the multiplicative model are also imbedded in anticipated utility theory: risk attitude reflection phenomenon, equation (18), and reflection duality property (quasi-reflection of utilities of outcomes, equation (21), must be accompanied by reflection of certainty equivalents of simple gambles, equation (22), and vice versa).

5. EXPERIMENTAL STUDY

5.1. Experiments

Experiments were designed to obtain for each subject an independent measurement of the certainty equivalent function ξ and the utility function of outcomes v from which the utility function of simple gambles u could be constructed numerically. These empirical measurements provided the basis for testing several behavioral hypotheses.

5.1.1. Subjects

The sample includes data for 54 subjects from four experiments. The first experiment was conducted by McCord and de Neufville (1984) at the Massachusetts Institute of Technology (MIT) in 1982. Among 10 subjects were graduate students and professors of engineering. The other three experiments took place at the University of Virginia (UVA) in 1983/84. The participants were selected fourth-year students of systems engineering. They were versed in decision analysis, had experiential familiarity with preference elicitation tasks (which they acquired through earlier projects), and were taking a course on human judgment and information processing.

5.1.2. Method and Procedure

All experiments had identical basic design, though differed slightly in execution. In the MIT experiment, subjects were interviewed individually by the experimenter. In the UVA experiments, subjects were run in groups of 5 to 10. The experimenter was providing instructions and answering questions, while each subject worked individually through a questionnaire. The entire experiment (which also included tasks not reported herein) consisted

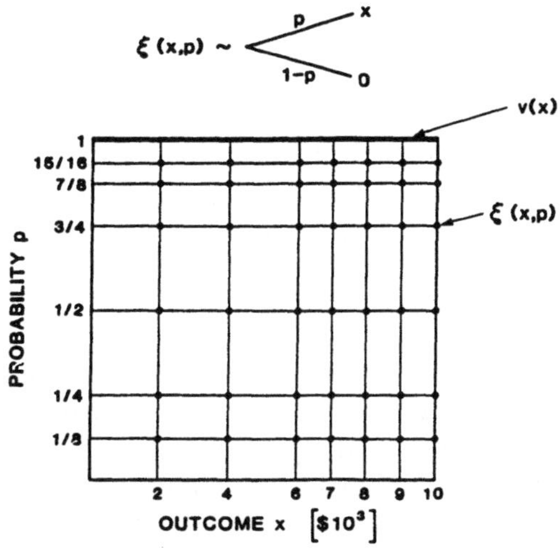

Fig. 3. Grid points (x, p) representing simple gambles whose certainty equivalents $\xi(x, p)$ are assessed. A utility function v is assessed along the heavy-shaded outcomes.

of three sessions, scheduled within one week and lasting approximately two hours each.

The description of a fairly realistic decision scenario was given to the UVA students for reading and reflecting upon prior to the first session. The students were asked to express their preferences in the context of choice between two forms of financial support, given their present financial situation. The choice was either to apply for a scholarship on the amount x, whose chance of receiving was p, or to accept a sure stipend on the amount z $(0 < z < x)$. Bounding technique (Farquhar, 1984) was used to assess the certainty equivalent $\xi(x,p) \sim (x,p)$. Forms displaying the tasks and containing response tables were designed to implement the technique and to facilitate checking the consistency and revising the responses.

The gambles (x,p) were the points of a 7×7 grid in the space $X^* \times P$ shown in Figure 3. The order of gambles in the questionnaire was random. Having assessed all certainty equivalents, the subject was asked to write them down on the grid, verify the monotonicity conditions, and reconcile any incoherences. To obtain the complete set of data required the assessment of $7 \times 6 = 42$ certainty equivalents, since $\xi(x,1) = x$. Not every subject in the MIT experiment assessed all required certainty equivalents. The missing points were estimated by Lagrange interpolating polynomials.

The utility function v of outcomes was assessed via the uniform sequence exchange method based on the relations

$$x_{i-1} \rightarrow x_i \sim x_i \rightarrow x_{i+1} ,$$

$$x_{i+1} \succ x_i \succ x_0 \,, \quad i = 1, \ldots, K$$

An arbitrary outcome $x_1 \succ x_0$ is chosen in the vicinity of x_0, and an outcome x_2 is assessed such that $x_0 \rightarrow x_1 \sim x_1 \rightarrow x_2$. The process continues as shown above, until $x_{K+1} \succsim x^*$. If $x_1, \ldots, x_{K+1}$ are assigned the utilities $1, \ldots, K+1$, and the utility I of x^* is found by interpolating between the utilities of x_K and x_{K+1}, then $v(x_i) = i/I$, $i = 1, \ldots, K$, defines the ordinates of v scaled by $v(x_0) = 0$ and $v(x^*) = 1$. In our experiments, $x_0 = 0$, $x_1 = \$1,000$, $x^* = \$10,000$, and the number of points K obtained varied between 3 and 9, with the median of 5.

The task of assessing indifference points for exchanges of outcomes is not easy because it demands deep introspection on the part of the subject. This can be facilitated, though, by introducing an auxiliary attribute and by framing questions in a decision context familiar to the subject. The context was provided by a scenario wherein x_i represented an annual stipend already awarded, and x_{i+1} represented this stipend plus a wage from a part-time job on which the subject would be spending y hours per week. The subject chose the type of job beforehand and then assessed y, the maximum number of hours he would be willing to work weekly for the annual wage of \$1,000 if no stipend were forthcoming; thus $x_0 \rightarrow x_1 \sim y$. Next, for any x_i, $i = 1, \ldots, K$, the subject assessed x_{i+1} such that $x_i \rightarrow x_{i+1} \sim y$; bounding technique was used to find x_{i+1}.

5.1.3. Reliability of Measurements

Measurement of certainty equivalents of simple gambles presents a straightforward task, from a cognitive standpoint. Since a simple gamble (x, p) is, indeed, the simplest possible uncertain prospect, and since each certainty equivalent $\xi(x, p)$ is assessed independently of other certainty equivalents, it is plausible to suppose that only random errors affect the measurement of $\xi(x, p)$. On the other hand, measurement of the utility function v of outcomes via exchange-based methods, although obtained effectively by several experimenters (e.g. Allais, 1979; Krzysztofowicz, 1983; McCord and de Neufville, 1983; Keller, 1985), is still controversial. Numerous questions are awaiting answers. For one, we are not familiar, as yet, with the kinds of random errors and biases that may be associated with such measurements. Hence, we are not in a position to affirm whether v is measured uniquely, regardless of the method. Until enough experience is accumulated and a theory of measurement errors is born, we advise qualifying any inferences as conditional on the particular utility assessment method.

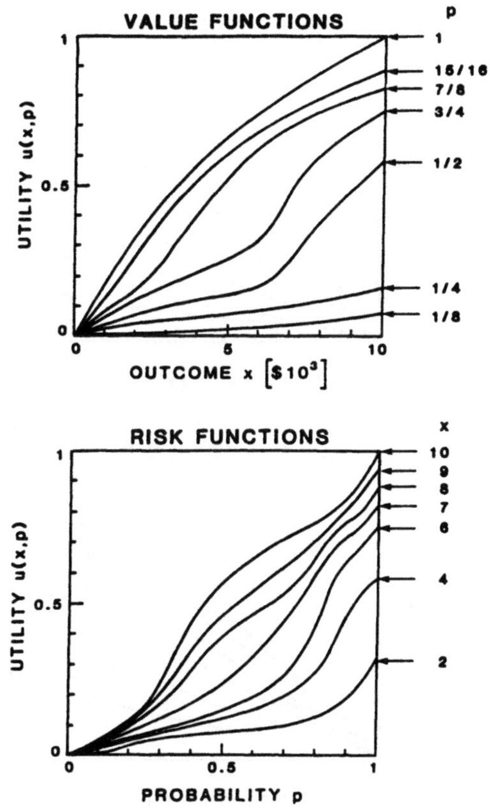

Fig. 4. Cross sections of the utility function u for subject E.

5.2. Results

5.2.1. Nonlinearity of Utility Function u

Figures 4–7 display results for four subjects which are representative of the predominant shapes of u in the sample of 54 subjects. Each figure shows two families of cross sections of the utility function u: the cross sections along the outcome axis x are termed the value functions: $\{u(\cdot, p) : p = 1/8, 1/4, 1/2, 3/4, 7/8, 15/16, 1\}$; the cross sections along the probability axis p are termed the risk functions: $\{u(x, \cdot) : x = 2, 4, 6, 7, 8, 9, 10\}$. Our observations, based on the total sample of 54 subjects, are as follows.

1. Value functions are mostly near-linear or concave.

2. Risk functions are occasionally near-linear, but most often highly nonlinear. The prevailing shape is concave for low probabilities and convex for high probabilities.

3. The nonlinearity of the risk functions usually occurs at low prob-

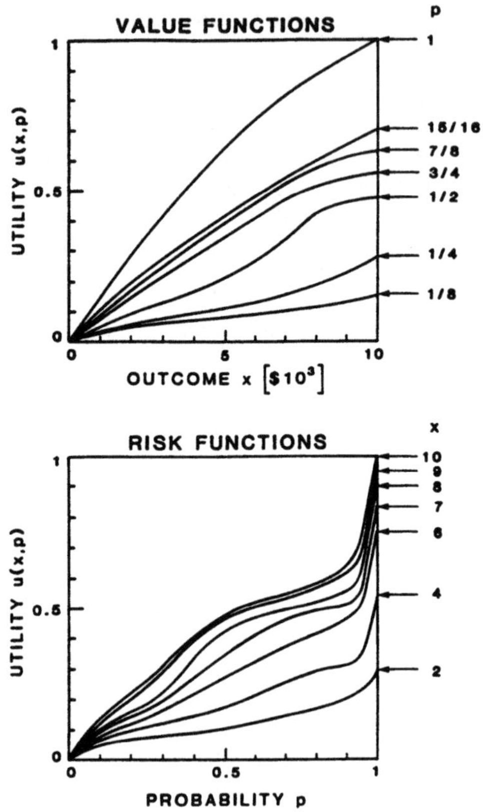

Fig. 5. Cross sections of the utility function u for subject F.

abilities ($p < 1/8$) and high probabilities ($p > 7/8$). In between ($1/8 < p < 7/8$), the risk functions are usually near-linear. This observation confirms the domain of the descriptive validity of the linear utility theory that was clearly noted by Morgenstern (1979, p. 178):

> the probabilities used must be within certain plausible ranges and not go to 0.01 or even less... Rather, one imagines that a normal individual would have some intuition of what 50:50 or 25:75 means.

On numerous occasions, models of the linear utility theory have been reported as good predictors of risky choices (e.g. Galanter, 1962; Fischer, 1976, 1977; Krzysztofowicz and Duckstein, 1979). Perhaps more often than not, the choices have been within the domain of the descriptive validity of the theory.

4. Risk functions in Figures 6 and 7 possess some of the properties hypothesized by Kahneman and Tversky (1979, pp. 280–284) as a part of their prospect theory. In particular, the risk function $r(p) = u(x^*, p)$ has

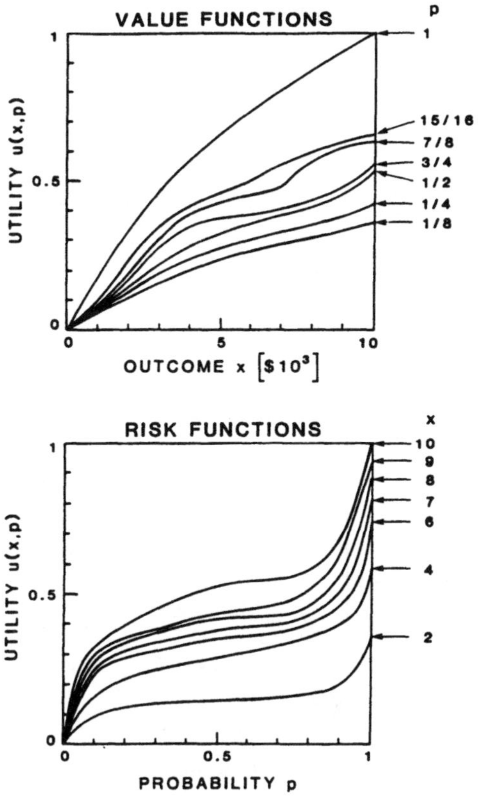

Fig. 6. Cross sections of the utility function u for subject G.

the following property: for low probabilities $r(p) > p$; for high probabilities $r(p) < p$. On the other hand, the estimated risk functions exhibit much greater departures from linearity than the function hypothesized within the prospect theory.

5. The steep parts of the risk functions near the extreme probabilities, which can be seen in Figures 5, 6, and 7, confirm Allais' (1979) observation, derived from his experiments in 1952, that the marginal utility of an outcome is much higher in the vicinity of certainty than in the middle range of probability. In Allais' (1979, p. 634) words, concluding his experiments,

> for all the subjects, there is to be seen a very strong preference for security in the neighborhood of certainty once the sums (outcomes) involved become substantial.

As to the generality of this conclusion, our results, which are based on a much larger sample, suggest two amendments. First, not everyone exhibits the "preference for security" (in our sample of 54 subjects only

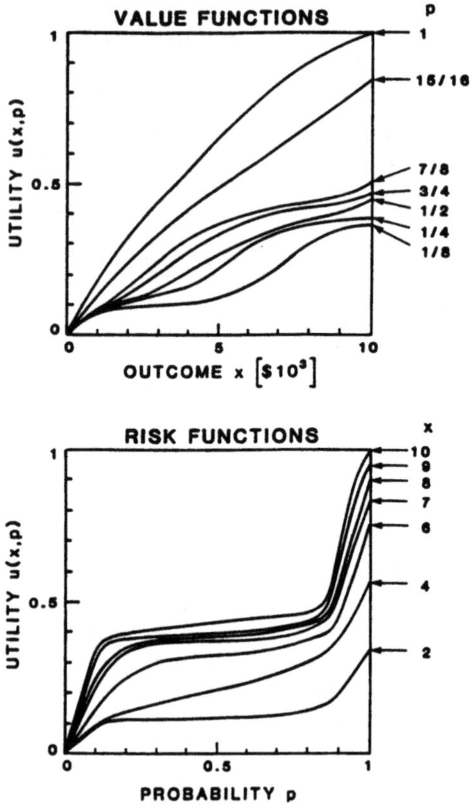

Fig. 7. Cross sections of the utility function u for subject H.

50% showed this type of preference). Second, an individual may exhibit the "preference for security" across the entire range of outcomes (from \$2,000 to \$10,000 in our case).

5.2.2. Multiplicative Utility Function u

Some risk functions form fairly regular "layers", and this suggests that they may be related to one another, at least approximately, through linear transformations. The same observation applies to some value functions. Hence, it is tempting to investigate how well the utility function $u(x,p) = v(\xi(x,p))$ is approximated by the multiplicative model $\hat{u}(x,p) = v(x)r(p)$ specified by equation (12), and how well this model performs relative to the linear multiplicative model $\hat{u}(x,p) = v(x)p$. The goodness of each approximation will be assessed via two norms: the uniform error

TABLE I

Errors of the multiplicative approximations to the utility function u on $X^* \times P$.

Statistic[a]	Nonlinear model	Linear model
Uniform Error δ		
Largest	6.94	18.14
Smallest	0.79	1.47
Mean	2.60	6.03
Std. Dev.	1.33	3.46
Maximum Error D		
Largest	36.48	57.63
Smallest	5.25	5.34
Mean	12.67	23.98
Std. Dev.	6.40	12.94

[a] Sample size = 54.
Errors have been multiplied by 100.

$$\delta = \frac{1}{x^* - x_0} \int_0^1 \int_{x_0}^{x^*} |u(x,p) - \hat{u}(x,p)| \, \mathrm{d}x \, \mathrm{d}p$$

and the maximum error

$$D = \max |u(x,p) - \hat{u}(x,p)|$$

The scaling of utilities guarantees $0 \leq \delta \leq 1$ and $0 \leq D \leq 1$.

The error statistics reported in Table I support two conclusions.

1. The nonlinear multiplicative model seems to provide, on the average, an acceptable approximation to the utility function u. In other words, preferences on $X^* \times P$ satisfy generally the condition of probabilistic difference independence although there are obvious individual exceptions such as subject E (Figure 4).

2. The nonlinear multiplicative model offers a much better approximation to the utility function u than the linear model. This result confirms what Figures 4–7 illustrate vividly: the major source of the nonlinearity of the utility function u on $X^* \times P$ is not the nonlinearity of the value function v on X^*, but the nonlinearity of the risk function r on P. In other words, the dominant descriptor of an individual's preferences among

TABLE II

Distribution of the shapes of the value functions v assessed via the uniform sequence exchange method.

	1	2	3
	Linear	Concave	Convex
Shape			
%	6	90	4

Sample size = 54.

simple gambles is not the value function but the risk function. This is merely a reiteration of the conclusion that Edwards (1955), as well as Slovic and Lichtenstein (1968), drew from their experimental tests of the subjectively expected utility model. They did not, however, estimate the entire functions v, r, and u.

5.2.3. Shapes of Value and Risk Functions

An analysis of shapes is performed for the value functions v assessed via the uniform sequence exchange method, and for the corresponding risk functions r. Table II reports the distribution of shapes of the value functions. The dominant shape is concave; other shapes found in the sample are linear and convex, but they are few.

In contrast to the value functions, risk functions take a variety of shapes. Seven general shapes have been identified (Table III). The linear shape, which implies the conformity of the subject's preferences with the linear utility theory, holds in just 4% of cases. Concave and convex shapes constitute 24% of cases, whereas shapes that contain a steep portion near one or both probability extremes are found in 72% of cases; there are more risk functions that are steep near the high extreme (50% of cases) than those that are steep near the low extreme (39% of cases).

Perhaps the most consequential observation emerging from this analysis is that there is no universal shape of the risk function, as has often been presumed, and that the interpersonal differences in preferences under uncertainty can be attributed almost entirely to the distinct shapes of the individual risk functions, for there is not much variability in the shapes of the individual value functions.

TABLE III

Distribution of the shapes of the risk functions r corresponding to the value functions v assessed via the uniform sequence exchange method.

	1	2	3	4	5	6	7
	Linear	Concave	Convex	Concave – steep	Convex – steep	Steep – convex	Steep – flat – steep
Shape							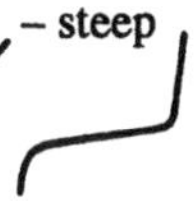
%	4	15	9	24	9	22	17

Sample size = 54.

TABLE IV

Distribution of the types of risk attitude. Inference based on the multiplicative utility model u with a value function v assessed via the uniform sequence exchange method.

	1	2	3	4
Type of risk attitude	RA	RS	RN	RS–RA
%	54	7	13	26

Sample size = 54.

5.2.4. Inference of Risk Attitude

We investigate risk attitude implied by the multiplicative utility model (12). The type of risk attitude is inferred based on relation (18), by comparing the risk function r with the reference risk function r_0. The subjects in our sample exhibit four types of risk attitude: RA globally, RS globally, RN globally, RS for low p and RA for medium and high p. The distribution of the types of risk attitude in the sample is given in Table IV. In the RS–RA type, the RA attitude is usually exhibited over a much larger subset of probabilities than the RS attitude. Thus overall, the RA attitude is dominant. Figure 8 illustrates two examples of the first type (RA), while Figure 9 shows two examples of the fourth type (RS–RA). For a fixed

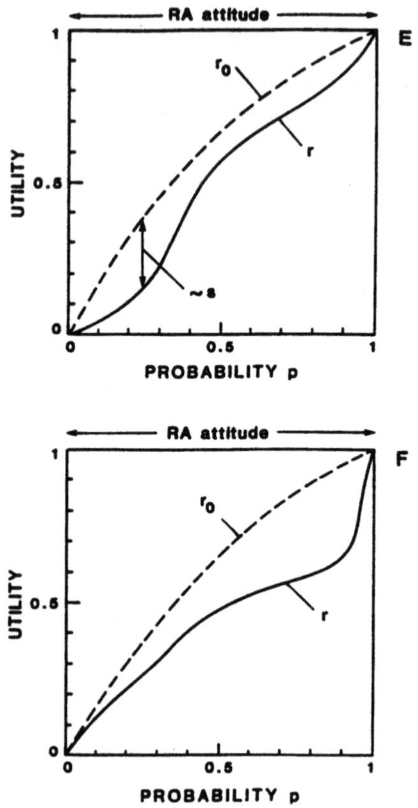

Fig. 8. Inference of risk attitude based on risk function r and reference risk function r_0 for subjects E and F.

outcome x, the difference $r_0(p) - r(p)$ is proportional to the strength of risk attitude $s(x,p)$, as defined by equation (20). In all examples, the strength of risk attitude varies (nonmonotonically) with probability p.

5.2.5. *Reflexivity of Risk Functions*

An examination of the risk functions r reveals that the reflexivity condition (32) required by the axioms of the anticipated utility theory holds for only 16.7% of subjects. In all those cases, the general shape of r is concave for $p < 1/2$ and convex for $p > 1/2$. To give an idea of the discrepancies, Table V presents the distribution of the ordinate $r(1/2)$ which satisfies (32) whenever $r(1/2) = 1/2$. Only 38.9% of cases fall within the interval $[0.45, 0.55)$; the distribution has a slight skew toward values larger than $1/2$. In conclusion, the reflexivity condition (32) is generally not satisfied by the empirical risk functions.

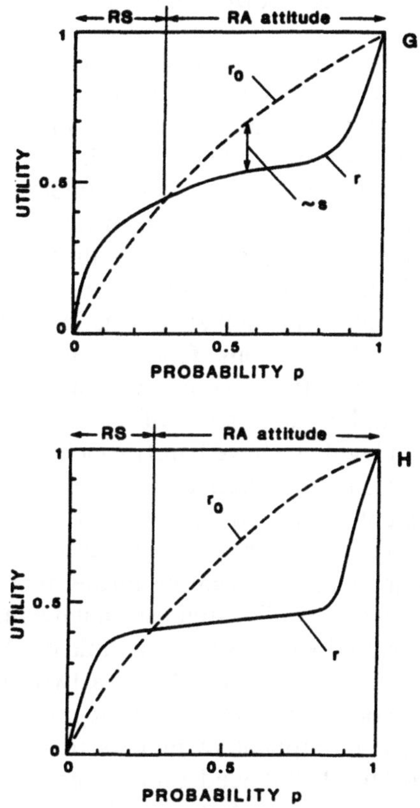

Fig. 9. Inference of risk attitude based on risk function r and reference risk function r_0 for subjects G and H.

TABLE V

Distribution of the ordinate $r(1/2)$ of the risk functions.

	1	2	3	4	5
Interval	(0,0.35)	[0.35,0.45)	[0.45,0.55)	[0.55,0.65)	[0.65,1)
%	7.4	18.5	38.9	20.4	14.8

Sample size = 54.

6. CONCLUDING REMARKS

We have endeavored to uncover the nature of preferences expressed by an individual in the simplest decision situation under uncertainty. The generic utility (GU) theory provided the framework for the fundamental measurement of the strength of preference on the two-dimensional space of outcomes and probabilities $X \times P$. The numerical representation of this measurement takes the form of a cardinal utility function u on $X \times P$.

This inquiry is far from complete. At the theoretical level, it would be worthwhile to build upon the concept of the GU theory an extension applicable to more complex decision situations involving multi-outcome gambles and continuous distributions. One possible avenue in this regard is to connect the GU theory with an axiomatization along the line suggested by Quiggin (1982), though without some of its restrictions.

At the experimental level, we have barely touched the surface of issues that perplex the fundamental preference measurement. For one, we have limited the measurement of the utility function u to the subdomain of gains $X^* \times P$. The measurement of u on the entire domain $X \times P$, encompassing losses and gains, is awaiting further research. Fragmentary empirical evidence from past studies suggests that the multiplicative utility model $u(x,p) = v(x)r(p)$ does not generally hold on $X \times P$. Should this be verified, then our Theorem 3, specifying a two-piece multiplicative decomposition of u, would have an important implication. Namely, it would indicate that the multiplicative models of the type proposed by Quiggin (1982) and Allais (1986) need a further generalization in order to accommodate two distinct risk functions, one for losses and one for gains.

At the epistemological level, there remains open the critical problem of interpretation of the measurements of expressed preferences vis-à-vis the rationality axioms one wishes to adopt as a basis for normative decision analyses. The interpretation we have attached to the constructs of the GU theory (for example, when we inferred the type of risk attitude based on the utility function u or the risk function r) is normative: that is, the expressed preferences are assumed to be also imperative for ensuing decision analyses. Because Axiom 1 does not impose any restriction on the form of u (except the monotonicity), the question of conformity of expressed preferences to the axiom is tautological. But this is precisely the virtue of the GU theory: it provides a model-free fundamental measurement of u and, therefore, it leaves room for alternative interpretations, normative or behavioral.

ACKNOWLEDGEMENTS

The experiments at UVA were executed by Jeff S. Shilling, while the numerical analyses were performed by Mark A. Reynolds and John

E. Pendleton – their skills are gratefully acknowledged. I remain indebted to Professors Mark McCord and Richard de Neufville for furnishing me with the data from their experiments and for numerous discussions on the subject. The shaping of my views benefitted also from conversations I had the privilege of having with Professors Maurice Allais, Georges Bernard, and John C. Harsanyi. Thanks are extended to Professor R. Duncan Luce for his comments on an earlier version of the manuscript.

This research was supported by the National Science Foundation under Grant ECE–8352536, Presidential Young Investigator Award.

APPENDIX
ALGEBRAIC-DIFFERENCE STRUCTURE

The following definition is adapted from Krantz *et al.* (1971, p. 151). The relational system $\langle \mathbf{G} \times \mathbf{G}, \succsim \rangle$ is called an algebraic-difference structure if it satisfies five axioms.

Axiom 1.1. (Weak order.) The relation $\succsim$ is a weak order on $\mathbf{G} \times \mathbf{G}$; that is $\succsim$ is transitive and complete.

Axiom 1.2. (Sign-reversal condition.)

$$F \to G \succsim H \to K \Longrightarrow K \to H \succsim G \to F$$

Axiom 1.3. (Weak monotonicity condition.)

$$F \to G \succsim F' \to G' \text{ and } G \to H \succsim G' \to H' \Longrightarrow F \to H \succsim F' \to H'$$

Axiom 1.4. (Solvability condition.) If $F \to G \succsim H \to K \succsim F \to F$, then there exist K' and K'' such that $F \to K' \sim H \to K \sim K'' \to G$.

Axiom 1.5. (Archimedean condition.) If $F_1, F_2, \ldots, F_i, \ldots$ is a strictly bounded standard sequence ($F_1 \to F_2 \sim F_i \to F_{i+1}$ for every F_i, F_{i+1} in the sequence; not $F_1 \to F_1 \sim F_1 \to F_2$; and there exist H and K such that $H \to K \succ F_1 \to F_i \succ K \to H$ for all F_i in the sequence), then it is finite.

School of Engineering and Applied Science
University of Virginia
Thornton Hall
Charlottesville, Virginia, U.S.A.

NOTES

* Part of this paper was presented at the 3rd International Conference on the Foundations and Applications of Utility, Risk, and Decision Theories, Aix-en-Provence, France, June 1986. The manuscript was submitted to the editors in June 1987.

[1] The von Neumann–Morgenstern utility functions are those assessed via gamble–based methods implied by the theories of linear (expected) utility (e.g. Ramsey, 1926; von Neumann and Morgenstern, 1947; Marschak, 1950; Herstein and Milnor, 1953; Savage, 1954), while the Frisch–Pareto utility functions are those assessed via exchange–based methods implied by the theories of ordered utility differences (e.g. Frisch, 1926; Pareto, 1927; Lange, 1934; Chipman, 1960).

[2] This assumption does not mirror the state of affairs but rather our optimism that reliable methods of measuring the cardinal utility function v will soon be identified. Current measurement methods are still not well understood, their error functions are virtually unknown, and, most disturbingly, they yield inconsistent measurements; see McCord and de Neufville (1983).

[3] The linear utility theory, for example, specifies the structure $u_L(x,p) = \nu(x)p$. While alternative measurements of ν suffice to test the descriptive validity of the linear theory, they by no means are sufficient to uncover the empirical structure of u, should it differ from $\nu(x)p$. Thus, many experiments have pinpointed inconsistencies in ν, but no study as yet, to the best of my knowledge, has shown an empirical estimate of u.

[4] This generalization subsumes the Pratt–Arrow (Pratt, 1964) measure of "local risk aversion" defined by $-v''(x)/v'(x)$. This measure is approximately twice the risk premium per unit of variance for all locally bounded distributions in an infinitesimal neighborhood of x. Within such a neighborhood, v is approximately linear.

[5] In the words of von Neumann and Morgenstern (1947, p. 18): "If he now prefers A to the 50–50 combination of B and C, this provides a plausible base for the numerical estimate that his preference of A over B is in excess of his preference of C over A. ... It is well known that thereby utilities – or rather differences of utilities – become numerically measurable." Later, they consider the indifference relation $A \sim (C, \alpha; B, 1-\alpha)$ and conclude: "we suggest the use of α as a numerical estimate for the ratio of the preference of A over B to that of C over B." Mathematically, this says that

$$\nu(A) = \alpha\nu(C) + (1-\alpha)\nu(B) \Longrightarrow \nu(A) - \nu(B) = \alpha[\nu(C) - \nu(B)]$$

Unequivocally, ν was intended to provide a measurement of directed preference differences; hence $\nu = v$.

[6] This is the position held by Harsanyi (1983) and seems also to have been the position of Morgenstern (1979).

[7] The confusion seems to have escalated after the Pratt–Arrow (Pratt, 1964) proposition of characterizing ν by $R(x) = -\nu''(x)/\nu'(x)$ was appended to the linear utility theory. However interesting mathematically $R(x)$ is, its interpretation as a measure of "local risk aversion" was unfortunate because it suggested that the shape of ν could be attributed to risk attitude. Moreover, restrictions imposed on $R(x)$ for the purpose of deriving functional forms of ν were interpreted as restrictions on local risk aversion, which could even be normatively desirable. Thus instead of serving solely as a means of inferring risk attitude, the utility function ν has become viewed by many as a representation of risk attitude.

[8] For earlier discussions on this subject see Allais (1984), Bernard (1984), and Krzysztofowicz (1984).

[9] For excellent expositions of this point of view, see Harsanyi (1978, 1983), Morgenstern

(1979), and Marschak (1979).

[10] This idea is not novel; it transpires from the experimental works of Davidson *et al.* (1957), Officer and Halter (1968), Krzysztofowicz and Duckstein (1980). The main reason for mastering gamble-based methods of utility assessment is that, in comparison with exchange-based methods, they are easier to operationalize and generally present simpler cognitive tasks to the subject.

REFERENCES

Allais, M. (1953) 'La psychologie de l'homme rationnel devant le risque: la théorie et l'expérience', *Journal de la Société de Statistique de Paris*, January–March, pp. 47–73.

Allais, M. (1979) 'The so-called Allais paradox and rational decisions under uncertainty', in Allais, M. and Hagen, O. (Eds.), *Expected Utility Hypotheses and the Allais Paradox*, D. Reidel, Dordrecht, Holland, pp. 437–681.

Allais, M. (1984) 'The foundations of the theory of utility and risk: some central points of the discussions at the Oslo Conference', in Hagen, O. and Wenstøp, F. (Eds.), *Progress in Utility and Risk Theory*, D. Reidel, Dordrecht, Holland, pp. 3–131.

Allais, M. (1986) 'The general theory of random choices in relation to the invariant cardinal utility function and the specific probability function', presented at the *3rd International Conference on the Foundations and Applications of Utility, Risk, and Decision Theories*, Aix-en-Provence, France, June.

Bernard, G. (1966) 'Sur les fonctions d'utilité', *Revue Française de Recherche Opérationnelle* **41**.

Bernard, G. (1974) 'On utility functions', *Theory and Decision* **5**, 205–242.

Bernard, G. (1984) 'Utility and risk preference functions', in Hagen, O. and Wenstøp, F. (Eds.), *Progress in Utility and Risk Theory*, D. Reidel, Dordrecht, Holland, pp. 135–143.

Camacho, A. (1979) 'Maximizing expected utility and the rule of long run success', in Allais, M. and Hagen, O. (Eds.), *Expected Utility Hypotheses and the Allais Paradox*, D. Reidel, Dordrecht, Holland, pp. 203–222.

Chipman, J.S. (1960) 'The foundations of utility', *Econometrica* **28** (2), 193–224.

Cohen, M., Jaffray, J.Y. and Said, T. (1985) 'Individual behavior under risk and under uncertainty: an experimental study', *Theory and Decision* **18**, 203–228.

Davidson, D., Suppes, P. and Siegel, S. (1957) *Decision Making: An Experimental Approach*, Stanford University Press, Stanford, California.

de Finetti, B. (1974) *Theory of Probability: A Critical Introductory Treatment*, vol. 1, Wiley, New York.

de Neufville, R. and Delquie, P. (1986) 'Exploration of the influence of certainty and probability "effects" on the measurement of utility', presented at the *3rd International Conference on the Foundations and Applications of Utility, Risk, and Decision Theories*, Aix-en-Provence, France, June.

Dyer, J.S. and Sarin, R.K. (1982) 'Relative risk aversion', *Management Science* **28** (8), 875–886.

Edwards, W. (1955) 'The prediction of decisions among bets', *Journal of Experimental Psychology* **50** (3), 201–214.

Farquhar, P.H. (1984) 'Utility assessment methods', *Management Science* **30** (11), 1283–1300.

Fischer, G.W. (1976) 'Multidimensional utility models for risky and riskless choice', *Organizational Behavior and Human Performance* **17**, 127–146.
Fischer, G.W. (1977) 'Convergent validation of decomposed multi-attribute assessment procedures for risky and riskless decisions', *Organizational Behavior and Human Performance* **18**, 295–315.
Fishburn, P.C. and Kochenberger, G.A. (1979) 'Two-piece von Neumann–Morgenstern utility functions', *Decision Sciences* **10** (4), 503–518.
Friedman, M. and Savage, L.J. (1948) 'The utility analysis of choices involving risk', *The Journal of Political Economy* **56** (4), 279–304.
Frisch, R. (1926) 'Sur un problème d'économie pure', *Norsk Matematisk Forenings Skrifter* **1** (16), 1–40.
Galanter, E. (1962) 'The direct measurement of utility and subjective probability', *The American Journal of Psychology* **75** (2), 208–220.
Hagen, O. (1969) 'Separation of cardinal utility and specific utility of risk in theory of choices under uncertainty', *Statsøkonomisk Tidsskrift* **3**, 81–107, Bergen.
Hagen, O. (1984) 'Neo-cardinalism', in Hagen, O. and Wenstøp, F. (Eds.), *Progress in Utility and Risk Theory*, D. Reidel, Dordrecht, Holland, pp. 145–164.
Halter, A.N. and Dean, G.W. (1971) *Decisions Under Uncertainty with Research Applications*, South-Western Publishing Co., Cincinnati, Ohio.
Handa, J. (1977) 'Risk, probabilities, and a new theory of cardinal utility', *Journal of Political Economy* **85** (1), 97–122.
Harsanyi, J.C. (1977) 'Morality and the theory of rational behavior', *Social Research* **44** (4), 623–656.
Harsanyi, J.C. (1978) 'Bayesian decision theory and utilitarian ethics', *The American Economic Review* **68** (2), 223–228.
Harsanyi, J.C. (1983) 'Use of subjective probabilities in game theory', in Stigum, B.P. and Wenstøp, F. (Eds.), *Foundations of Utility and Risk Theory with Applications*, D. Reidel, Dordrecht, Holland, pp. 297–310.
Herstein, I.N. and Milnor, J. (1953) 'An axiomatic approach to measurable utility', *Econometrica* **21** (2), 291–297.
Kahneman, D. and Tversky, A. (1979) 'Prospect theory: an analysis of decision under risk', *Econometrica* **47** (2), 263–291.
Karmarkar, U.S. (1978) 'Subjectively weighted utility: a descriptive extension of the expected utility model', *Organizational Behavior and Human Performance* **21**, 61–72.
Karmarkar, U.S. (1979) 'Subjectively weighted utility and the Allais paradox', *Organizational Behavior and Human Performance* **24**, 67–72.
Keeney, R.L. and Raiffa, H. (1976) *Decisions with Multiple Objectives: Preferences and Value Tradeoffs*, Wiley, New York.
Keller, L.R. (1985) 'An empirical investigation of relative risk aversion', *IEEE Transactions on Systems, Man, and Cybernetics* **SMC–15** (4), 475–482.
Krantz, D.H., Luce, R.D., Suppes, P. and Tversky, A. (1971) *Foundations of Measurement*, vol. 1, Academic Press, New York.
Krelle, W. (1968) *Präferenz und Entscheidungstheorie*, Mohr, Tübingen.
Krelle, W. (1984) 'Remarks to Professor Allais' contributions to the theory of expected utility and related subjects', in Hagen, O. and Wenstøp, F. (Eds.), *Progress in Utility and Risk Theory*, D. Reidel, Dordrecht, Holland, pp. 173–180.
Krzysztofowicz, R. (1983) 'Strength of preference and risk attitude in utility measurement', *Organizational Behavior and Human Performance* **31**, 88–113.

Krzysztofowicz, R. (1984) 'Prediction, measurement, and error of utility: a reply to Allais', in Hagen, O. and Wenstøp, F. (Eds.), *Progress in Utility and Risk Theory*, D. Reidel, Dordrecht, Holland, pp. 165–170.

Krzysztofowicz, R. and Duckstein, L. (1979) 'Preference criterion for flood control under uncertainty', *Water Resources Research* **15** (3), 513–520.

Krzysztofowicz, R. and Duckstein, L. (1980) 'Assessment errors in multiattribute utility functions', *Organizational Behavior and Human Performance* **26**, 326–348.

Krzysztofowicz, R. and Koch, J.B. (1989) 'Estimation of cardinal utility based on a non-linear theory', *Annals of Operations Research* **19**, 181–204.

Lange, O. (1934) 'The determinateness of the utility function', *The Review of Economic Studies* **1** (3), 218–225.

Laughhunn, D.J., Payne, J.W. and Crum, R. (1980) 'Managerial risk preferences for below-target returns', *Management Science* **26** (12), 1238–1249.

Lorange, P. and Norman, V.D. (1973) 'Risk preference in Scandinavian shipping', *Applied Economics* **5**, 49–59.

Markowitz, H. (1952) 'The utility of wealth', *The Journal of Political Economy* **60** (2), 151–158.

Marschak, J. (1950) 'Rational behavior, uncertain prospects, and measurable utility', *Econometrica* **18** (2), 111–141.

Marschak, J. (1979) 'Utilities, psychological values, and the training of decision makers', in Allais, M. and Hagen, O. (Eds.), *Expected Utility Hypotheses and the Allais Paradox*, D. Reidel, Dordrecht, Holland, pp. 163–174.

McCord, M.R. and de Neufville, R. (1983) 'Fundamental deficiency of expected utility decision analysis', in French, S., Hartley, R., Thomas, L.C. and White, D.J. (Eds.), *Multi-Objective Decision Making*, Academic Press, New York, pp. 279–305.

McCord, M.R. and de Neufville, R. (1984) 'Utility dependence on probability: an empirical demonstration', *Large Scale Systems* **6**, 91–103.

McCord, M.R. and de Neufville, R. (1985) 'Assessment response surface: investigating utility dependence on probability', *Theory and Decision* **18**, 263–285.

McCord, M.R. and de Neufville, R. (1986) '"Lottery equivalents": reduction of the certainty effect problem in utility assessment', *Management Science* **32** (1), 56–60.

McCord, M.R. and Leotsarakos, C. (1986) 'Investigating utility and value functions with an "assessment cube"', presented at the *3rd International Conference on the Foundations and Applications of Utility, Risk, and Decision Theories*, Aix-en-Provence, France, June.

Morgenstern, O. (1979) 'Some reflections on utility', in Allais, M. and Hagen, O. (Eds.), *Expected Utility Hypotheses and the Allais Paradox*, D. Reidel, Dordrecht, Holland, pp. 175–183.

Officer, R.R. and Halter, A.N. (1968) 'Utility analysis in a practical setting', *American Journal of Agricultural Economics* **50** (2), 257–277.

Pareto, V. (1927) *Manuel d'Économie Politique*, Marcel Giard, Paris, 2nd edn.

Payne, J.W., Laughhunn, D.J. and Crum, R. (1980) 'Translation of gambles and aspiration level effects in risky choice behavior', *Management Science* **26** (10), 1039–1060.

Payne, J.W., Laughhunn, D.J. and Crum, R. (1981) 'Further tests of aspiration level effects in risky choice behavior', *Management Science* **27** (8), 953–958.

Pratt, J.W. (1964) 'Risk aversion in the small and in the large', *Econometrica* **32** (1–2), 122–136.

Quiggin, J. (1982) 'A theory of anticipated utility', *Journal of Economic Behavior and Organization* **3**, 323–343.

Quiggin, J. (1985) 'Subjective utility, anticipated utility, and the Allais paradox', *Organizational Behavior and Human Decision Processes* **35**, 94–101.

Ramsey, F.P. (1926) 'Truth and probability', in *The Foundations of Mathematics and Other Logical Essays*, by Ramsey, F.P., Braithwaite, R.B. (Ed.), The Humanities Press, New York, 1950, pp. 156–198.

Roberts, F.S. (1979) *Measurement Theory with Applications to Decisionmaking, Utility, and Social Sciences*, Addison-Wesley, Reading, Massachusetts.

Savage, L.J. (1954) *The Foundations of Statistics*, Wiley, New York.

Siegel, S. (1956) 'A method for obtaining an ordered metric scale', *Psychometrika* **21** (2), 207–216.

Slovic, P. and Lichtenstein, S. (1968) 'Relative importance of probabilities and payoffs in risk taking', *Journal of Experimental Psychology* **78** (3, Pt. 2), 1–18.

Slovic, P., Fischhoff, B. and Lichtenstein, S. (1982) 'Response mode, framing, and information-processing effects in risk assessment', in Hogarth, R.M. (Ed.), *New Directions for Methodology of Social and Behavioral Science: Question Framing and Response Consistency*, no. 11, Jossey-Bass, San Francisco, California, pp. 21–36.

von Neumann, J. and Morgenstern, O. (1947) *Theory of Games and Economic Behavior*, Princeton University Press, Princeton, New Jersey, 2nd edn.

MAURICE ALLAIS

THE FUNDAMENTAL CARDINALIST APPROACH AND ITS PROSPECTS

I would like to stress two very essential points on the cardinalist approach.

1. The concept of cardinal utility, which all the founders of economic theory placed at the centre of their analyses, has almost been rejected the literature for half a century. This rejection, based on totally unjustified prejudices, deprived economic analysis of an indispensable tool.

If, as shown by Pareto, the whole theory of general economic equilibrium and maximum efficiency can indeed be worked out with the ordinal concept of preference, the theory of dynamic evolution of the economy, of fiscal policy, of income transfers, of collective preferences and political choices, of risk and the theory of insurance however cannot be appropriately developed without referring to the concept of cardinal utility and to interpersonal comparisons.

In any case, the theory of preference indices and that of demand may be considerably simplified, and become more intuitive, when using the concept of cardinal utility. In fact, if the *intensity of preferences* is not included, the theory of choices is unquestionably deprived of an essential tool.

2. Ole Hagen and I thought it useful to introduce in this volume my 1984 and 1988 papers concerning the determination of cardinal utility with extraits of *A la Recherche d'une Discipline Economique* and *Première Partie, L'Economie Pure*, published in 1943, which, together with *Economie et Intérêt*, published in 1947, won me the 1988 Nobel Prize in Economic Sciences. These extracts are essentially constituted by §§ 68, 69 and 70 of Chapter II of my 1943 work, and are reproduced in Chapter I of the present book.

They show how since the very beginning of my career as an economist in 1941 the consideration of cardinal utility has inspired a great deal of my research. It did constitute a determining factor to the criticism of Von Neumann-Morgenstern's, Marschak's, Savage's and Samuleson's theories of expected utility, which I presented in 1952, at the Paris international colloquium on risk.

MY THREE CONTRIBUTIONS OF 1943, 1984 AND 1988

3. For clarity, and to make the understanding and the linking of my 1943, 1984 and 1988 contributions easier, I think it is useful to briefly present the

M. Allais and O. Hagen (eds.), Cardinalism, 289–306.

guiding principles which framed the elaboration of my works on cardinal utility, as well as of the three contributions concerning the analysis of cardinal utility which are presented in the Chapters I, II and III of this volume, without any modification, and as they were first published.

The Absolute Satisfaction (1943)

3.1. In this book I presented a thorough analysis of the concept of absolute satisfaction (cardinal utility).[1] This analysis, published in the Chapter I of this book, is essentially based on the following principles:

(a) For each subject there exists a utility function, cardinal utility, that represents *the intensity of any preferences.*
(b) Cardinal utility *may be defined on the basis of our introspection,* either by considering the variations of ordinal utility that are deemed to be psychologically equivalent or by considering the smallest perceptible variations of that utility.
(c) Cardinal utility admits *a maximal value that corresponds to satiety.*
(d) At a first approximation, and to a large extent, cardinal utility may be considered to be a *log-linear function of the capital of the subject under consideration.*
(e) The properties of cardinal utility are *entirely analogous* to those shown by Weber, Fechner and their successors *for the case of the psychophysiology of sensations.*[2]
(f) The theory of the dynamics of disequilibrium and of general economic equilibrium, of supply and demand, and that of maximal efficiency may be elaborated only by considering ordinal utilities only, *but considering cardinal utility generally permits a simplification of the exposition and renders it more suggestive.*
(g) *Except for the case of independent goods, it is impossible to determine cardinal utility from that of observed choices.*

Publications on cardinal utility from 1943 to 1984

3.2. From 1943 to 1984 I pursued at different times my researches on cardinal utility.

In my Louvain paper, *'Notes théoriques sur l'incertitude de l'avenir et le risque'* (Theoretical notes on the uncertainty of the future and on risk), published in 1951, I based my analysis of the theory of random choices on the consideration of the concept of cardinal utility.

In Appendix I of that paper, 'Definition and properties of cardinal utility', I gave a summary of the main points of my 1943, analysis, and in 'Appendix II, Examination of the logarithmic hypothesis', I examined the log-linear hypothesis of Daniel Bernoulli, its justifications and its implications.[3]

In my paper, 'Fondements d'une théorie positive des choix comportant un risque et critique des postulats et axiomes de l'Ecole Américaine' (The foundations of a positive theory of choice involving risk and a criticism of the postulates and axioms of the American School),[4] which resulted from the 1952 Paris international colloquium on risk, I based many of my analyses upon the consideration of cardinal utility and its properties, such as I had outlined in my book (1943) and in my paper (1951).

The survey that I organized in 1952 following the Paris international colloquium was based upon a Questionnaire, published in 1953 under the title, 'La psychologie de l'homme rationnel devant le risque. La théorie et l'expérience' (The psychology of rational behavior in the presence of risk, theory and experience). Questions VI of this Questionnaire were designed to show that cardinal utility was not, as Savage had claimed, "a myth", and that it was indeed possible to determine it on the basis of appropriate questions, independently of the consideration of any random choice.[5]

The thorough analysis that was performed in 1974–1975 of the answers to Questions VI of the 1952 Questionnaire completely confirmed my previous analyses by showing that *for all the subjects analysed there does actually exist an index of psychological value* (cardinal utility) which may be determined *independently* of any consideration of random choices, and that, to a large extent, that index varies approximately as the logarithm of the argument.

The bases of my theoretical analysis were presented in my 1977 paper 'The so-called Allais' paradox and rational decisions under uncertainty',[6] and the results of the empirical analysis are indicated in Appendix C.[7]

My previous thoughts and my analysis of the empirical data have led me to put forward two axioms. According to the first, *the axiom of homogeneity*, cardinal utility is a *function of the relative variations* $\Delta C/C$ *of the capital of the subject considered*; and according to the second, *the axiom of invariance*, this function is invariant, i.e. it is *the same whatever the subject*.[8]

In October-December 1975 I proposed a method which permitted a representation of the function of cardinal utility for *positive* values of $\Delta C/C$ according to a general formula, the same for every subject, admitting a maximum corresponding to satiety.[9] However, since that analysis was relatively complex and required extensive developments, and due to lack of space I had to limit myself in my 1977 paper to the log-linear approximation.

My general formula in 1975 could only be presented nine years later, in my Venic paper (1984) 'Determination of cardinal utility according to an intrinsic invariant model', which constitutes Chapter II of this book.

However, in my 1977 paper, the log-linear approximation permitted *a satisfactory representation, as a first approximation*, of the cardinal utility of all the subjects that I had studied.[10]

My 1984 Venice and 1988 Budapest papers on *the invariant cardinal utility function*, which are published in Chapters II and III of this volume, are based on all this work on cardinal utility from 1943 to 1977.

Determination of Cardinal Utility According to an Intrinsic Invariant Model (1984)

3.3. My Venice paper (1984) outlines, on the one hand, the theoretical method that I adopted in October–December 1975, and, on the other, the empirical results I obtained. This paper is in fact only a very abridged résumé of the 200-page general paper, 'L'Utilité cardinale et sa détermination – Hypothèses, méthodes et résultats empirique', I gave in Venic which presents the complete procedure followed, the empirical results, and their interpretation.

The essential results are as follows:

- It is possible to represent the cardinal utility for *all* the individuals studied (19 in 1952, and 5 in 1975) *by the same non-loglinear formulation.*
- The formulation of the cardinal utility function was deduced *by considering only the individuals questioned in 1952.* It follows that to find this formula, also verified by the individuals questioned in 1975, is very remarkable indeed.
- The formulation obtained is approximately log-linear over a *very extended* interval of variation.[11] It is rigorously log-linear in the neighbourhood of the origin, and it admits an asymptotic value for the very high values of the argument.

  This formulation differs from *the 1977 overall log-linear approximation* in two respects: *a cash balance effect near the origin, and a satiety effect for very high values of the argument.*[12]
- The curve representing the cardinal utility *has exactly the same shape as that found by the successors of Weber and Fechner for luminous sensation.*[13]

All these results are very striking and highly suggestive.[14, 15]

Cardinal Utility – History, Empirical Findings, and Applications. Overview (1988)

3.4. In my extensive Budapest paper I deduced, on the basis of a New Questionnaire, drawn up in August 1987, the values for the function of cardinal utility, assumed to be invariant *for the negative values of the virtual variations of capital.*

Chapter III of this book was published at the same time in 1991 in the Proceedings of the 1988 Budapest Conference, *Progress in Decision, Utility and Risk Theory*, and in the same year in the Review *Theory and Decision* which is only a very abridged version (*Overview*) of my extensive 1988 paper which itself is much more developed.

The method rests on the consideration of psychologically equivalent intervals corresponding to negative and positive variations $\Delta C/C$ of capital, *so that the negative values of cardinal utility may be deduced from its positive values* corresponding to my Venice paper.

The method applied is technically far simpler than that corresponding to the method in my 1984 Venice paper, although it did turn out that the subjects involved had far greater difficulty in elaborating their responses that had been the case with Questions VI in the 1952 Questionnaire.

The essential result of this analysis is that cardinal utility declines very rapidly for the negative virtual variations of capital.[16]

This is the first time in the literature that a consistent estimate of cardinal utility could be made for all the positive and negative values of the argument independent of any consideration of random choices.

My Philosophy of Science

3.5. In all these works my conviction has been that logical deduction, if not constantly linked to the study of reality, only leads to sterility. *The only source of knowledge is, and cannot be anything but, experience.* My scientific work was thus more and more inspired by the necessity of only admitting theories to the extent to which they are capable of representing the observed facts and of being verified by empirical data.

As a matter of fact there is science only where regularities exist which can be submitted to analysis and prediction. To a very great extent, therefore, as in physical sciences, the elaboration of economic science appears to me to have to rest upon the search for relations and quantities which are *invariant in time and space.*

In this elaboration the use of mathematics, while it is indispensable in so far as it is an instrument of logical deduction, is in itself of only secondary interest. *What is really essential is the formulation of hypotheses that lend themselves to models which may be confronted with experimental facts.*

Such are the principles that have inspired all my research in cardinal utility, as indeed in all my works. All of them rest upon the conviction, confirmed by experience, that *no real progress in economic science can be derived from purely abstract reasoning, but only from the association of theoretical analysis and the econometric analysis of observed facts.*[17]

The fundamental criterion of a theory's scientific validity is its confirmation by empirical data, and *submission to the data of experience is the golden rule which dominates all scientific discipline. This rule applies just as much to economic science as to the natural sciences.*

GENERAL COMMENTS ON THE CARDINALIST APPROACH

4. I would finally like to present some general comments on the connections between my three contributions in 1943, 1984 and 1988, as well as on some developments of the literature in direct relation with these contributions.

Determination of Cardinal Utility

4.1. Two remarks seem especially essential.

• First, there is *a profound analogy* between the concept of *absolute* satisfaction (cardinal utility) and that of *absolute* temperature.

Relative to all ordinal temperature scales, absolute temperature is defined by the condition that its consideration allows the fundamental law of thermodynamics, Carnot's law, to be expressed as simply as possible.[18]

According to this, *absolute* satisfaction, $\bar{S}$, is defined by the condition that the law of minima perceptible variations may be represented *as simply as possible*, which means, in this case, by the condition that the minimum perceptible variation be a constant.[19]

• Second, and from a general point of view, absolute satisfaction cannot be determined from choices as to which subjects are observed to have been made.

However, when absolute satisfaction may be developed as follows:

$$(1) \qquad \bar{S} = \Psi_A(A) + \Psi_B(B) + \ldots + \Psi_C(C)$$

absolute satisfaction may be deduced from choices observed for variable prices.[20]

In fact, this possibility relies on two conditions. The first one is the independence of the goods; the second is that absolute satisfaction is precisely the sum of the absolute satisfactions (or cardinal utilities) corresponding to the different goods.

If the independence hypothesis of cardinal utilities is certainly unacceptable for each good considered in itself, it seems however fully justified, *at least as a first approximation*, when considering groups of goods such as food, clothing, housing, and so on...

Absolute Satisfaction and Luminous Sensation. 4.2. When luminous sensation is derived by psycho-physiologists from the consideration of the minima perceptible variations, absolute satisfaction, for its positive values, has been derived from consideration of the psychologically equivalent intervals of ordinal satisfaction.

The extraordinary similarity of the two diagrams representing absolute satisfaction and luminous sensation is thus even more striking.[21]

From this, we deduce that there is a very remarkable invariance when we proceed from the psychological value of capital (or absolute satisfaction) to the psycho-physiological sensation of a luminous excitation. This very fundamental invariance confirms strikingly our 1943 inference.[22]

The Log-linear Approximation

As pointed out in Chapter II, and as mentioned above (§ 3.3), cardinal utility is approximately log-linear in a very large variation interval of the argument.

This result confirms what I wrote in the 'Satisfaction et Capital' section of my 1943 work,[23] which was not reproduced in Chapter I.

At equilibrium, and for given prices, the absolute satisfaction $\bar{S}$ of an individual appears to be a well determined function of his capital $\bar{\Gamma}$. And thus we may write:

$$(2) \qquad S = f(\bar{\Gamma})$$

As a matter of fact, the shape of the linkage between satisfaction and owned capital may well be specified through experimental data concerning private wealth statistical distribution.

It is indeed observed that for a given economic ensemble, the representative curve of this distribution becomes Gaussian when using a simple logarithmic transformation of the abscissas. Theoretically, and according to the probability theory, this means that everything goes on as if, at any time, the effects of any element influencing the amount of wealth of an individual were proportional to this amount. This is the proportional effect law given by Robert Gibrat.

Now, causes that can influence someone's wealth are of two very different kinds. Some, such as prices variations, are external to individuals; others, such as tastes, are purely psychological. One easily realizes that the first ones operate uniformly on each unity of income, so that their effect is proportional. Such should be the case about psychological causes too; and this does mean that each individual, in his behaviour, does not integrate the $\Delta\bar{\Gamma}$ variation of his capital, but its $\Delta\bar{\Gamma}/\bar{\Gamma}$ relative variation. In other words, at every given instant, the $\Delta\bar{S}$ increase of satisfaction, derived from a $\Delta\bar{\Gamma}$ capital growth, only depends on the relative variation $\Delta\bar{\Gamma}/\bar{\Gamma}$.

We consequently may write:

$$(3) \qquad \Delta\bar{S} = K\,\frac{\Delta\bar{\Gamma}}{\bar{\Gamma}}$$

with K being a quantity which is independent of $\bar{\Gamma}$. Hence:

$$(4) \qquad \bar{S} = KL\bar{\Gamma} + B$$

where B is a constant.

When taking the satisfaction which corresponds to previously owned capital $\bar{\Gamma}_0$ for origin, we have

$$(5) \qquad \bar{S} = KL\frac{\bar{\Gamma}}{\bar{\Gamma}_0}$$

Thus we see that everything goes on as if satisfaction was a linear function of the logarithm of capital. And we find a psychological law similar to the approximate Fechner's psychological law.

However, it ought to be noticed that if such a law fits to income, it doesn't necessarily suit to each of elementary consumption in itself. If, with the founded formula, satisfaction grows indefinitely with income, such cannot be the case for any definite consumption, characterized by a satiety point.

This text, which I wrote in 1943, foreshadows my later 1984 and 1988 formulation of cardinal utility, which follows in Chapter II and III.

Frisch and Roy Formulation and Allais's Formulation of Cardinal Utility

4.4. As I have shown in my 1988 paper, 'La Théorie des Choix dans l'Oeuvre de René Roy. Une Analyse Critique', Ragnar Frisch and René Roy based their analyses of the theory of choices[24] on the assumption that ordinal satisfaction (or ordinal utility):

$$(6) \qquad S = S(A, B, \ldots, C)$$

is a function

$$(7) \qquad S = g(R/P)$$

of real income $Q = R/P$, where R, Q and P respectively represent income

$$(8) \qquad R = aA + bB + \ldots + cC$$

and appropriate indices of the $A, B, \ldots, C$ consumptions and their a, b, $\ldots$, c prices.

$$(9) \qquad \begin{cases} Q = Q(A, B, \ldots, C) \\ P = P(a, b, \ldots, c) \end{cases}$$

René Roy defined the Q and P indices of prices and real income with Divisia's chain indices:

$$(10) \qquad \frac{dQ}{Q} = \frac{\Sigma b dB}{R} \qquad \frac{dP}{P} = \frac{\Sigma B dB}{R}$$

As I have indicated in my 1988 paper, I demonstrated in February 1943 that the necessary and sufficient condition for the validity of relation (7) is that we have in any point of the field of choices:

$$(11) \qquad \Sigma B S'_B = (S)$$

where φ is a function of S, in other words that the $\Sigma B S'_B$ quantity be constant on any indifference surface.

This condition implies that all indifference surfaces are *homothetic* relatively to the origin.

It also implies that:

$$(12) \qquad \lambda_{BR} = \partial \log B / \partial \log R = 1$$

where λ_{BR} represents the elasticity coefficient of demand of (B) with respect to income. In fact, this implies *that every coefficient of elasticity of demand with respect to income be equal to unity.*

If relation (11) is verified, it is possible to demonstrate that there is an index

$$(13) \qquad J = J(A, B, \ldots, C)$$

such as

$$(14) \qquad \Sigma B J'_B = 1$$

If in addition the relations (10) are verified, one can demonstrate that

$$(15) \qquad J(A, B, \ldots, C) = \log Q$$

Thus we find the logarithmic form for cardinal utility.

If we furthermore assume that $A, B, \ldots, C$ goods are independent, which means that

$$(16) \qquad \partial^2 J / \partial B \, \partial C = 0$$

we may then demonstrate that

$$(17) \qquad J = \Sigma \beta \log B \qquad \Sigma \beta = 1$$

where the β are constants independent of $A, B, \ldots, C$, and that

$$(18) \qquad \lambda_{Bb} = \partial \log B / \partial \log b = -1$$

In fact, if the previous conditions cannot validly be accepted for each good considered in itself, empirical analyses show that they appear to be roughly confirmed, when considering groups of goods such as food, clothing, housing, and so on...

On reflection the connection between the implications of the Frishc–Roy assumption about the preference function and my own cardinal utility function, which is presented in Chapters II and III, and its log-linear approximation, appears evident.

The outcome of my formulation is indeed that cardinal utility is a function of nominal capital, but it takes place at a given instant of time when the price index is given. Thus, nothing essential changes in my formulation when substituting its real value C/P to nominal capital C.

Moreover, transition from the consideration of income R to the consideration of capital C does present any difficulty.

Thus we see that there is a *profound similarity* between the implications of Ragnar Frisch's and René Roy's assumption on the one hand, and the results of my own 1975, 1984 and 1988 analysis on the other hand. In both cases we found the same log-linearity as a first approximation.

The Preference Index as a Function of Real Income, a Consequence of Allais's Hereditary and Relativistic Theory of the Demand of Money and of the Psychological Rate of Interest, under Hypothesis of the Independence of Goods $A, B, \ldots, C$ Towards Money M.

4.5. From Allais's hereditary and relativistic theory of the demand for money and of the psychological rate of interest, (1965), (1966) and (1985)[25] we deduce that:

$$(19) \qquad iM/R = K \qquad K < 1$$

where i, M, R respectively represent the psychological rate of interest, the desired cash holding and the income, and where K is a constant below unity.

Assuming now that the expression of the ordinal preference index is:

$$(20) \qquad I = I(A, B, \ldots, C, M)$$

the conditions of maximisation of the index I under budgetary constraint

$$(21) \qquad \Sigma bB + iM = R$$

show, when referring to condition (19), that:

$$(22) \qquad I(A, B, \ldots, C, M) = \Psi(\log A + k \log M, ,$$

$$\log B + k \log M \ldots, \log C + k \log M) \quad (k > 0)$$

where Ψ is an arbitrary function and k is a constant.[26]

Moreover if we assume that the $(A), (B), \ldots, (C)$ goods are independent of money (M) and that there is a cardinal index $J = J(I)$ such that for any good (B)

$$(23) \qquad J''_{BM} = \partial^2 J/\partial B\, \partial M = 0$$

then it is possible to show that we have[27]

$$(24) \qquad J = K \log M + K' \log Q \qquad K + K' = 1$$

with

$$(25) \qquad Q = G(A, B, \ldots, C) = R/P(a, b, \ldots, c)$$

where K and K' are constants, where $G(A, B, \ldots, C)$ and $P(a, b, \ldots, c)$ are homogeneous functions of order one, respectively in $A, B, \ldots, C$ and $a, b, \ldots, c$, and where P and Q fulfil condition (10).

From all this we may also deduce that we have

$$(26) \qquad MJ'_M = K \qquad \Sigma BJ'_B = K' = 1 - K$$

Since the cardinal preference index J is defined up to a linear transformation, the second relation (26) is equivalent to condition (14). *And through this we meet with the condition of validity of Frisch's and Roy's formulation as well as with the homothetic property of the indifference surfaces and the equality to one of the elasticities with respect to income.*

This demonstration *does not assume* that couples of the goods (A), (B), ..., (C) are independent, that is to say that $J''_{BC} = 0$.

Here again, the similarity condition could not be considered as valid for all the goods considered individually, but empirical analysis shows that *it appears to be approximately satisfied when considering groups of goods.*[28]

If moreover the goods $A, B, \ldots, C$ are independent, it is then possible to demonstrate, as in § 4.4 above, that (24) and (26) imply that:

$$(27) \qquad J = K \log M + K'\Sigma\beta \log B \qquad \Sigma\beta = 1$$

Cardinal Utility and Psychological Independence of Consumptions

4.6. As a matter of fact, the different consumptions may in practice be considered as constituting independent groups, at least as a first approximation. From this we deduce that the independence hypothesis, if not being absolutely and strictly correct, is indeed a legitimate approximation which is likely to give a good idea of the general way things do shape.

Theoretical analysis ? shows that such an hypothesis is easily met with the experimental laws of supply and demand and also gives valuable indications very simply. Thus, it does constitute itself as being an indispensable starting framework for theoretical understanding of economics.[29]

Since empirical analyses show that elasticities of demand *do not vary very much* when considering groups of goods, it may be interesting to examine the consequences of a rigorous constancy of the various elasticities with respect to prices and income.

Consequently let us assume that:

$$(28)\quad \begin{array}{l} \dfrac{\partial \log A}{\partial \log a} = -\lambda_A \quad \dfrac{\partial \log B}{\partial \log b} = -\lambda_B \quad \cdots \quad \dfrac{\partial \log C}{\partial \log c} = -\lambda_C \\ \dfrac{\partial \log A}{\partial \log b} = \lambda_{Ab} \quad \dfrac{\partial \log A}{\partial \log c} = \lambda_{Ac} \quad \cdots \\ \cdots\cdots\cdots \\ \dfrac{\partial \log C}{\partial \log a} = \lambda_{Ca} \quad \dfrac{\partial \log C}{\partial \log b} = \lambda_{Cb} \quad \cdots \\ \dfrac{\partial \log A}{\partial \log R} = \lambda_{AR} \quad \dfrac{\partial \log B}{\partial \log R} = \lambda_{BR} \quad \cdots \end{array}$$

where $\lambda_A, \lambda_B, \ldots, \lambda_C, \lambda_{Ab}, \lambda_{Ac}, \ldots, \lambda_{Ca}, \lambda_{Ca}, \lambda_{Cb}, \ldots, \lambda_{AR}, \lambda_{CR}, \ldots,$ are constants which are *independent* of $A, B, \ldots, C, a, b, \ldots, c, R$.

We then may write:

$$(29)\qquad \mathrm{d}A = \frac{\partial A}{\partial a}\,\mathrm{d}a + \frac{\partial A}{\partial b}\,\mathrm{d}b + \ldots + \frac{\partial A}{\partial c}\,\mathrm{d}c + \frac{\partial A}{\partial R}\,\mathrm{d}R$$

and consequently

$$(30)\qquad \frac{\mathrm{d}A}{A} = -\lambda_A\,\frac{\mathrm{d}a}{a} + \lambda_{Ab}\,\frac{\mathrm{d}b}{b} + \ldots + \lambda_{Ac}\,\frac{\mathrm{d}c}{c} + \lambda_{AR}\,\frac{\mathrm{d}R}{R}$$

with $a, b, \ldots, c, R$ being *independent* variables. Thus we have

$$(31)\qquad A = \alpha\,\frac{b^{\lambda_{Ab}} \ldots c^{\lambda_{Ac}} R^{\lambda_{AR}}}{a^{\lambda_A}}$$

where α is a constant, and consequently

$$(32)\qquad \frac{aA}{R} = \alpha\,\frac{a^{1-\lambda_A} b^{\lambda_{Ab}} \ldots c^{\lambda_{Ac}}}{R^{1-\lambda_{AR}}}$$

and similar relations for the goods $B, \ldots, C$.

As we have

$$(33)\qquad \Sigma aA = R$$

also we have according to (32)

$$(34)\qquad \frac{\Sigma \alpha a^{1-\lambda_A} b^{\lambda_{Ab}} \ldots c^{\lambda_{Ac}}}{R^{1-\lambda_{AR}}} = 1$$

whatever the independent variables $a, b, \ldots, c, R$. This is only possible if

$$(35)\qquad \left[\begin{array}{l} \lambda_A = \lambda_B = \ldots = \lambda_C = 1 \\ \lambda_{Ab} = \ldots = \lambda_{Ac} = 0 \\ \cdots\cdots \\ \lambda_{Ca} = \lambda_{Cb} = \ldots = 0 \\ \lambda_{AR} = \lambda_{BR} = \ldots = \lambda_{CR} = 1 \end{array}\right.$$

with

$$(36)\qquad \begin{cases} \alpha + \beta + \ldots + \gamma = 1 \\ aA/R = \alpha \ldots cC/R = \gamma \end{cases}$$

As we have at equilibrium

$$(37)\qquad \frac{S'_A}{a} = \frac{S'_B}{b} = \ldots = \frac{S'_C}{c} = \frac{\Sigma B S'_B}{R}$$

we have

$$(38)\qquad \begin{cases} AS'_A/\Sigma BS'_B = aA/R = \alpha \\ \cdots\cdots\cdots \\ CS'_C/\Sigma BS'_B = cC/R = \gamma \end{cases}$$

Let us then put

$$(39)\qquad X = \alpha \log A \qquad Y = \beta \log B \;\ldots\; Z = \gamma \log C$$

where we have

$$(40)\qquad S(A, B, \ldots, C) = F(X, Y, \ldots, Z)$$

$$(41)\qquad AS'_A = \alpha F'_X \;\; BS'_B = \beta F'_Y \ldots CS'_C = \gamma F'_Z$$

where F is a function of $X, Y, \ldots, Z$, and conditions (38) may be written as:

$$(42)\qquad \begin{cases} F'_X = \alpha F'_X + \beta F'_Y + \ldots + \gamma F'_Z \\ \cdots\cdots\cdots \\ F'_Z = \alpha F'_X + \beta F'_Y + \ldots + \gamma F'_Z \end{cases}$$

One verifies at once that equations (42) are verified if

$$(43)\qquad F(X, Y, \ldots, Z) = G(X + Y + \ldots + Z)$$

where G is a function of $X + Y + \ldots + Z$.

As a matter of fact, it is the only solution of the system (42). According to (42) we indeed have

$$(44)\qquad F'_X = F'_Y = \ldots F'_Z = H(X, Y, \ldots, Z)$$

where H is a function of $X, Y, \ldots, Z$, and consequently

$$(45)\qquad \mathrm{d}F = \Sigma F'_Y \mathrm{d}Y = H(X, Y, \ldots, Z)\, \mathrm{d}(X + Y + \ldots + Z)$$

As a result F is necessarily a function G of $X + Y + \ldots + Z$.

From (39), (40) and (43) we have

$$(46)\qquad S(A, B, \ldots, C) = G(\alpha \log A + \beta \log B + \ldots + \gamma \log C)$$

We then may find an utility index J such as

$$(47) \qquad J(A, B, \ldots, C) = \alpha \log A + \beta \log B + \ldots + \gamma \log C$$
$$\Sigma\alpha = 1$$

Thus, we find again relation (17) of § 4.4, and consequently the relation

$$(48) \qquad \Sigma B J'_B = 1$$

Thus we see that when all the elasticities are constants, the Frisch–Roy hypothesis is verified, and moreover all the goods are independent.

PROSPECTS OF THE CARDINALIST APPROACH

5. The cardinalist approach, as defined *in an operational way* in my 1984 and 1988 papers, does open new prospects.

Interpersonal Comparisons

5.1. As indicated in Chapters II and III, and especially in § 2.1 of Chapter III, each cardinal utility

$$(49) \qquad u = u(1 + X/U_0) = u(1 + y)$$

is defined up to a linear transformation, Consequently, if, for each subject, cardinal utility is defined by the two conditions

$$(50) \qquad u(y = 0) = 0 \qquad u(y = +\infty) = 1$$

all cardinal utilities are comparable. It follows that all the problems about wealth transfers become solvable (see Chapter III, § 3.2), and indeed, this possibility opens up new prospects for economic analysis.

Consumption and Well-being

5.2. There is, for example, a great difference between growth as it is usually measured and well-being as we may feel it. As a matter of interest national account indicators, the evolution of which defines growth, are not really representative of the contribution of the economy to the well-being.

When it is too rapid, working of technical and economic progress may become unbearable and indeed refused. And implementing a growth policy without taking account of its direct and indirect implications on well-being may constitute a major mistake.

If the distinction between consumption and well-being is fundamental, we may deservedly wonder whether well-being may be really apprehended or whether it may really be quantified. I think that, in the present state of things, such an aim is beyond reach, and that trying, today, to quantify well-being certainly is premature. But I am also convinced that it is possible to bring corrections to the existing estimates of gross product so that they could approximate, at least partially, suitable indicators of well-being.

Such is for example the case concerning adjustments taking into account disturbances due to overpopulation in the cities, the burden, in terms of time and stress, experienced when going to work; the human cost of unemployment; the real cost of immigration, or the perverse effects of an unrestricted free trade policy, etc.

As a matter of fact, for many magnitudes in which we considered *a priori* impossible to quantity, quantification subsequently become possible. Such was especially the case of the quantification, through empirical correlations, of the hereditary transmission of intelligence, by Galton and Pearson; of the measure of social inequality in our societies through Pareto's representative law of distribution of incomes; or the many quantitative criteria defined by Sorokin's in his *Treatise of Sociology*.

I was able to give at least approximative solutions to questions which at first sight seemed beyond reach and impossible to quantify, such as the determination of the *a priori* distribution law of the value of the non-sedimentary saharian deposits,[30] the estimates of the memorization effects in monetary phenomena,[31] or the determination of psychological values, or cardinal utility, of monetary values,[32] as is shown in Chapters II and III.

There is no doubt that to work on correcting the estimates of the gross national product so that they can indeed become nearer, if not totally at least partially, as being a suitable indicator of well-being, would lead to success. And such a work would be of major interest.

In any case, if we could define, as is natural, the variation of collective well-being by adding up all the subjects of the considered society, the variations of cardinal utilities defined with comparable measuring scales, the problem of the determination of the variation of the global well-being, now being mathematically perfectly defined, all would become entirely solvable.[33]

New Prospects

5.3. On the whole, all the comments which I have presented above do show that the consideration of cardinal utilities, and the possibility to measure them, pave new exciting ways, not only for economic theory but also for its applications of any kind to sociological analyses and to economic polity.[34]

NOTES

[1] This analysis constitutes the first chapter of this book. It corresponds to §§ 68, 69 and 70 of my 1943 book, *A la Recherche d'une Discipline Economique*, see reference on page 28 of this book.

In that book I called ordinal utility and cardinal utility, respectively, "satisfaction" (satisfaction) and "satisfaction absolue" (absolute satisfaction).

In the 1952 Introduction, § 12, of the second edition of my 1943 work, I have presented new comments, in particular from an historical point of view.

In the Introduction of the third edition of 1993 I present some new comments.

[2] In my 1943 analysis I reproduced the curve of psycho-physiological sensation as a function of luminous excitation, a curve to which I referred again in my Venice paper (1984), § 4.4, and Chart XXV. In fact the cardinal utility curve of that paper is practically identical to the psycho-physiological curve (1984, p. 118–119).

[3] My 1951 Louvain analysis exists only in a mimeographed form.

[4] The English translation of this paper, 'The foundations of a positive theory of choice involving risk and a criticism of the postulates and axioms of the American School', has been published in Allais and Hagen (1979), 'Expected utility hypotheses and the Allais's paradox: Contemporary discussions and rational decisions under uncertainty with Allais's rejoinder'.

[5] The complete analysis of the answers to the 1952 Questionnaire could not be performed until 1974.

[6] *The so-called Allais's paradox and rational decisions under uncertainty*, 1977, § 23.

[7] id., § C.5 to C.9, § C.20 to C.23, and Charts I to VI.

[8] id., § 23.2.1.

[9] id., § C.21.

[10] id., § C.5 to C.10, and the associated charts.

[11] 'Determination of cardinal utility according to an intrinsic invariant model', 1984, Chart IX (Chapter II, this volume).

[12] id., 1984, Chart IX, and 'Cardinal utility – history, empirical findings, and applications. Overview', 1988, Chart I (Chapter III, this volume).

[13] id., 1984, § 4.3, and Charts III and XXV (Chapter II, this volume).

[14] In my 1984 Aix-en-Provence paper (Chapter II, this volume), I presented a table of the values of the invariant cardinal utility function as well as interpolation formulae that permit its calculation (Tables B.1 and B.2 corresponding to the maximal value $M = 1.9$ for satiety.

Table I of my 1988 paper (Chapter III, this volume) gives the values of the cardinal utility function for $M = 1$.

[15] It is appropriate to emphasize here a remarkable fact. Together with his answers ot the 1952 Questionnaire (§ 3.2 above), Marschak transmitted to me the values of his "utility function" deduced, according to his indications, from consideration of the questions of the Questionnaire. Taking into account the value of his capital, as I could estimate it on the basis of his answers, his utility index is *practically identical* with the cardinal utility function of my 1984 Venice paper (Chapter II, this volume).

On this point, see Allais, *Analyse sommaire des réponses au Questionnaire de 1952 faites par les économistes étrangers participants au Colloque de 1952: K.J. Arrow, B. de Finetti, M. Friedman, J. Marschak, L.J. Savage* (12 pp., October 1975, revised and completed text in 1988).

This is a brief analysis of the answers to the 1952 Questionnaire of the foreign economists who participated to the 1952 colloquium.

[16] Diagram VII C of my 1988 paper (Chapter III, this volume).

[17] All useful references pertaining to the works above are given in the bibliographies of my 1984 and 1988 papers (see Chapters II and II this volume).

[18] Allais, 1943, *A la Recherche d'une Discipline Economique*, (A.R.D.E.), *Première Partie, L'Economie Pure*, § 92–6.

[19] Relation (8) of the First Part of the Chapter I, this volume.

[20] Chapter I, this volume, First Part, § 2 and note 5.

[21] Chapter II, this volume, § 4.3, and Charts XXV and III.

[22] Chapter I, this volume, Second Part, § 2, and the corresponding notes, especially note 12.

[23] A.R.D.E., id., Section 99, Remark III, satisfaction and capital.

About the issues of this passage, see Chapter I below and especially § 2.2 and footnote (10) in the Second Part.

[24] On the Roy and Frisch theories see Allais, 1988, 'La théorie des choix dans l'oeuvre de René Roy. Une analyse critique' (The theory of choice in the work of René Roy. (A critical analysis), *Revue d'Economie Politique*, 1988, pp. 315–357.

[25] Allais, 'Reformulation de la théorie quantitative de la monnaie', SEDEIS Bulletin, no. 928, 10 September 1965, Supplément, p. 186; A restatement of the quantity theory of money', *American Economic Review*, December 1966, (pp. 1123–1157) (Very abridged version of 1965); 'The empirical approaches of the hereditary and relativistic theory of demand for money', *Economia delle Scelte Pubbliche (Journal of Public Finance and Public Choice)*, 1986.

[26] Allais, 1988, id., Part VII, pp. 341–344.

[27] id., pp. 342–344. See also Allais, 'Growth and Inflation', pp. 411–413, American Bankers Association, Conference of University Monetary Economists, Ditchley Park, 10–13 September 1968, *Journal of Money, Credit and Banking*, 1969, pp. 355–426 and 441–462.

[28] Allais, 1988, id., pp. 344–362.

[29] Allais, 1943, *A.R.D.E.*, id., §§ 175 and 176.

[30] Allais, 1954, 'Evaluation des perspectives economiques de la recherche minière sur de grands espaces. Application au Sahara Algérien', *Bulletin de l'Institut International de Statistique*, XXXV, 4, Rio de Janeiro, 1957, pp. 89–140. English translation: 'Method of appraising economic prospects of mining exploration over large territories – Algerian Sahara case study', *Management Science* **3** (4), July 1957.

[31] See note 20.

[32] See note 25.

[33] The global well-being could then be determined from the sum of its variations over time.

[34] All useful references are given in the Bibliographies of Chapters I, II and III, this volume.

MAURICE ALLAIS

REFERENCES

Allais, Maurice (1943) *A la Recherche d'une Discipline Economique* (To the Search for an Economic Discipline), Paris, 1943; republished as *Traité d'Economie Pure* (Treatise on Pure Economics), 1952; third edition as *Traité d'Economie Pure*. Editions Clément Juglar, Paris, 1992.

Allais, Maurice (1952a) 'Fondements d'une théorie positive des choix comportant un risque et critique des postulats et axiomes de l'Ecole Américaine' (Foundations of a positive theory of choice involving risk, and a criticism of the postulates and axioms of the American School), Econométrie, Colloques Internationaux du Centre National de la Recherche Scientifique, Vol. XL, Paris, 1953, pp. 257–332. (See also pp. 34–35, 37–39, 40, 47–48, 151–163, 194–197 and 245–247.)

This memoir was republished in Vol. 144 of the *Annales des Mines*, special issue, 1955, and again as a separate volume, under the same title by the Imprimerie Nationale 1955.

Allais, Maurice (1952b) 'Le comportement de l'homme rationnel devant le risque: Critique des postulats et axiomes de l'Ecole Américaine' (The behavior of rational man facing risk: Criticism of the postulates and axioms of the American School) in *Econometrica*, **21** (4), October 1953, pp. 503–546 (summarised version of the 1952 Memoir).

Allais, Maurice (1952c) 'La psychologie de l'homme rationnel devant le risque – La théorie et l'expérience', *Journal de la Société de Statistique de Paris*, January–March 1953, pp. 47–73.

Allais, Maurice (1976) *The Foundations of a Positive Theory of Choice Involving Risk and a Criticism of the Postulates and Axioms of the American School*, English translation of the (1952) Memoir, in Allais and Hagen, 1979, pp. 27–145.

Allais, Maurice (1977) 'The so-called Allais' paradox and rational decisions under uncertainty', in Allais and Hagen, 1979, pp. 437–699.

Allais, Maurice (1983) 'The foundations of the theory of utility and risk; some central points of the discussions at the Oslo Conference', in Hagen and Wenstop (Eds.), *Progress in Decision Theory*, Reidel, 1984, pp. 3–131.

Allais, Maurice (1984), 'The cardinal utility and its determination, hypothesis, methods and empirical results', *Theory and Decision*, forthcoming.

Allais, Maurice and Hagen, Ole (1979) *Expected Utility Hypotheses and the Allais' Paradox; Contemporary Discussions and Rational Decisions under Uncertainty with Allais' Rejoinder*, Reidel, Dordrecht, 1979, p. 715.

Pieron, Henri (1927) *Psychologie Expérimentale*, A. Colin, Paris, p. 220.

THEORY AND DECISION LIBRARY

SERIES A: PHILOSOPHY AND METHODOLOGY OF THE SOCIAL SCIENCES

Editors: W. Leinfellner (*Vienna*) and G. Eberlein (*Munich*)

1. G. Zecha and P. Weingartner (eds.): *Conscience: An Interdisciplinary View*. Salzburg Colloquium on Ethics in the Sciences and Humanities (1984). 1987 ISBN 90-277-2452-0
2. R.W. Scholz: *Cognitive Strategies in Stochastic Thinking*. 1987 ISBN 90-277-2454-7
3. H. Nurmi: *Comparing Voting Systems*. 1987 ISBN 90-277-2600-0
4. M. Schmid and F.M. Wuketits (eds.): *Evolutionary Theory in Social Science*. 1987 ISBN 90-277-2612-4
5. C.L. Sheng: *A New Approach to Utilitarianism*. A Unified Utilitarian Theory and Its Application to Distributive Justice. 1991 ISBN 0-7923-1301-1
6. F. Forman: *The Metaphysics of Liberty*. 1989 ISBN 0-7923-0080-7
7. G. Bernard: *Principia Economica*. 1989 ISBN 0-7923-0186-2
8. J.W. Sutherland: *Towards a Strategic Management and Decision Technology*. Modern Approaches to Organizational Planning and Positioning. 1989 ISBN 0-7923-0245-1
9. C. Vlek and G. Cvetkovich (eds.): *Social Decision Methodology for Technological Projects*. 1989 ISBN 0-7923-0371-7
10. P. Hoyningen-Huene and F.M. Wuketits (eds.): *Reductionism and Systems Theory in the Life Sciences*. Some Problems and Perspectives. 1989 ISBN 0-7923-0375-X
11. K.G. Grunert and F. Ölander (eds.): *Understanding Economic Behaviour*. 1989 ISBN 0-7923-0482-9
12. G. Antonides: *The Lifetime of a Durable Good*. An Economic Psychological Approach. 1990 ISBN 0-7923-0574-4
13. G.M. von Furstenberg (ed.): *Acting under Uncertainty*. Multidisciplinary Conceptions. 1990 ISBN 0-7923-9063-6
14. R.L. Dukes: *Worlds Apart*. Collective Action in Simulated Agrarian and Industrial Societies. 1990 ISBN 0-7923-0620-1
15. S.O. Funtowicz and J.R. Ravetz: *Uncertainty and Quality in Science for Policy*. 1990 ISBN 0-7923-0799-2
16. J. Götschl (ed.): *Erwin Schrödinger's World View*. The Dynamics of Knowledge and Reality. 1992 ISBN 0-7923-1694-0
17. R. von Schomberg (ed.): *Science, Politics and Morality*. Scientific Uncertainty and Decision Making. 1993 ISBN 0-7923-1997-4
18. J. Baron: *Morality and Rational Choice*. 1993 ISBN 0-7923-2276-2
19. M. Allais and O. Hagen (eds.): *Cardinalism*. A Fundamental Approach. 1994 ISBN 0-7923-2398-X

KLUWER ACADEMIC PUBLISHERS – DORDRECHT / BOSTON / LONDON

MIX
Papier aus verantwortungsvollen Quellen
Paper from responsible sources
FSC® C105338

If you have any concerns about our products,
you can contact us on
ProductSafety@springernature.com

In case Publisher is established outside the EU,
the EU authorized representative is:
Springer Nature Customer Service Center GmbH
Europaplatz 3, 69115 Heidelberg, Germany

Printed by Libri Plureos GmbH
in Hamburg, Germany